**SAP® Warehouse Management: Functionality
and Technical Configuration**

 **PRESS**

SAP PRESS is a joint initiative of SAP and Galileo Press. The know-how offered by SAP specialists combined with the expertise of the publishing house Galileo Press offers the reader expert books in the field. SAP PRESS features first-hand information and expert advice, and provides useful skills for professional decision-making.

SAP PRESS offers a variety of books on technical and business related topics for the SAP user. For further information, please visit our website: *www.sap-press.com*.

D. Rajen Iyer
Effective SAP SD
2007, 384 pp.
ISBN 978-1-59229-101-4

Martin Murray
Understanding the SAP Logistics Information System
2006, 336 pp.
ISBN 978-1-59229-108-3

Marc Hoppe
Inventory Optimization with SAP
2006, 504 pp.
ISBN 978-1-59229-097-0

Luc Galoppin and Siegfried Caems
Managing Organizational Change during SAP Implementations
2007, 384 pp.
ISBN 978-1-59229-104-5

Martin Murray

SAP® Warehouse Management: Functionality and Technical Configuration

Galileo Press

Bonn • Boston

ISBN   978-1-59229-133-5

1st edition 2007

Editor Jawahara Saidullah
Copy Editor John Parker, UCG, Inc., Boston, MA
Cover Design Silke Braun
Layout Design Vera Brauner
Production Iris Warkus
Typesetting SatzPro, Krefeld
Printed and bound in Germany

Contents at a Glance

1   Introduction to Warehouse Management 23

2   Basic Warehouse Functions 33

3   Stock Management 71

4   Warehouse Movements 113

5   Goods Receipts 163

6   Goods Issues 187

7   Stock Replenishment 227

8   Picking Strategies 257

9   Putaway Strategies 287

10   Inventory Procedures 311

11   Storage Unit Management 351

12   Hazardous Materials Management 379

13   Mobile Data Entry 399

14   Radio Frequency Identification Technology 421

15   Cross Docking 435

16   Developments in Warehouse Management 451

17   Conclusion 483

Contents

Preface 17

1 Introduction to Warehouse Management 23

1.1   Introduction to Warehousing 23
      1.1.1   Earliest Examples of Warehousing 23
      1.1.2   Tobacco Warehouses in the United States 24
      1.1.3   Bonded Warehouses 24
      1.1.4   20th Century Port Warehousing 25
      1.1.5   Warehousing as Part of Physical Distribution 26
      1.1.6   Warehousing and Distribution Centers 27
      1.1.7   Public Warehousing 28
1.2   History of Warehouse Management Systems (WMS) 29
      1.2.1   Early Warehouse Management Systems 29
      1.2.2   The Rise of Enterprise Resource Planning (ERP) 30
1.3   Summary 31

2 Basic Warehouse Functions 33

2.1   Warehouse Structure 33
      2.1.1   Configuring a Warehouse 33
      2.1.2   Assignment of the Warehouse 36
      2.1.3   Warehouse Control Parameters 37
2.2   Storage Type 41
      2.2.1   Warehouse Layout 42
      2.2.2   Configuration of a Storage Type 43
      2.2.3   Data Entry for a Storage Type 45
2.3   Storage Sections 51
2.4   Storage Bins 53
      2.4.1   Storage Bin Types 53
      2.4.2   Define Storage Bin Structure 55
      2.4.3   Creating a Storage Bin Manually 60
      2.4.4   Creating a Storage Bin Automatically 61
      2.4.5   Block Storage Bins 62
      2.4.6   Creating Blocking Reasons 64
      2.4.7   List of Empty Storage Bins 65
      2.4.8   Bin Status Report 66
2.5   Quant 68
      2.5.1   Quant Record 68

2.5.2   Display a Quant 69

2.6   Summary 70

3   Stock Management 71

3.1   Warehouse Management Data in the Material Master 71

3.1.1   Creating the Material Master 72

3.1.2   Entering Data into Warehouse Management
Screens 76

3.2   Types of Warehouse Stock 84

3.2.1   Stock Categories 84

3.2.2   Status of Warehouse Stock 88

3.2.3   Special Stock 90

3.3   Batch Management in Warehouse Management 95

3.3.1   Batch Definition 95

3.3.2   Batch Level 96

3.3.3   Batch Number Assignment 96

3.3.4   Creating a Batch Record 97

3.3.5   Batch Determination 99

3.4   Shelf-life Functionality 107

3.4.1   Shelf-Life and the Material Master 107

3.4.2   Production Date Entry 109

3.4.3   SLED Control List 109

3.5   Summary 111

4   Warehouse Movements 113

4.1   WM Movement Types 113

4.1.1   Movement Types in Inventory Management 114

4.1.2   WM Reference Movement Types 115

4.1.3   Creating Warehouse Management Movement Types ... 116

4.1.4   Assigning Warehouse Management Movement
Types 125

4.2   Transfer Requirements 129

4.2.1   Automatic Transfer Requirements 129

4.2.2   Create a Manual Transfer Requirement 130

4.2.3   Create a Transfer Requirement for Replenishment
of a Fixed Bin 132

4.2.4   Display a Transfer Requirement for a Material 137

4.2.5   Display a Transfer Requirement for a Single Item 140

4.2.6   Display a Transfer Requirement for a Storage Type 140

4.2.7   Deleting a Transfer Requirement 142

4.3   Transfer Orders 144
       4.3.1   Creating a Transfer Order with Reference to a
               Transfer Requirement 144
       4.3.2   Creating a Transfer Order without a Reference 149
       4.3.3   Cancel a Transfer Order 151
       4.3.4   Confirm a Transfer Order 153
       4.3.5   Print a Transfer Order 158
4.4   Summary 161

5   Goods Receipts 163

5.1   Goods Receipt with Inbound Delivery 163
       5.1.1   Inbound Delivery Overview 164
       5.1.2   Creating an Inbound Delivery 164
       5.1.3   Creating a Transfer Order for an Inbound Delivery 166
       5.1.4   Using the Inbound Delivery Monitor 166
5.2   Goods Receipt Without Inbound Delivery 172
       5.2.1   Goods Receipt in Inventory Management 172
       5.2.2   Review of the Material Documents 173
       5.2.3   Review of Stock Levels after Goods Receipt 174
       5.2.4   Display of the Transfer Requirement 175
       5.2.5   Display of the Transfer Order 178
5.3   Goods Receipt Without Inventory Management 180
       5.3.1   Create the Transfer Order for the Goods Receipt 180
       5.3.2   Display the Transfer Order for the Goods Receipt 182
       5.3.3   Display the Stock Levels 182
5.4   Summary 185

6   Goods Issues 187

6.1   Goods Issue with Outbound Delivery 187
       6.1.1   Display Sales Order 188
       6.1.2   Create Outbound Delivery 189
       6.1.3   Outbound Delivery Status 191
       6.1.4   Create Transfer Order 195
       6.1.5   Confirm Transfer Order 200
       6.1.6   Post Goods Issue for Outbound Delivery 202
       6.1.7   Review Material Documents 203
6.2   Goods Issue Without Outbound Delivery 204
       6.2.1   Goods Issue in Inventory Management 204
       6.2.2   Negative Balance in the Warehouse 206
       6.2.3   Creating Transfer Order 207

6.3   Multiple Processing Using Groups 210

    6.3.1   Definition of a Group 210

    6.3.2   Creating a Group for Transfer Requirements 210

    6.3.3   Creating Transfer Orders for a Group of Transfer
                Requirements. 213

    6.3.4   Definition of a Wave Pick 215

    6.3.5   Creating a Group for Outbound Deliveries 215

    6.3.6   Creating the Wave from Outbound Delivery
                Monitor 215

    6.3.7   Using the Wave Monitor 217

    6.3.8   Results of the Pick Wave Monitor 220

6.4   Picking and Packing 223

    6.4.1   Picking Schemes 224

    6.4.2   Packing 225

6.5   Summary 226

7   Stock Replenishment 227

7.1   Internal Stock Transfers 227

    7.1.1   Keeping the Warehouse Running 227

    7.1.2   Checking Empty Bins 228

    7.1.3   Moving Material Between Storage Bins 230

    7.1.4   Confirm the Stock Transfer 234

    7.1.5   Configuration of the Difference Indicator 235

7.2   Fixed Bin Replenishment 236

    7.2.1   Replenishment and the Material Master 236

    7.2.2   Configuration for Replenishment 238

    7.2.3   Creating the Replenishment 239

    7.2.4   Displaying the Transfer Requirement 240

    7.2.5   Creating the Transfer Order 242

    7.2.6   Confirming the Transfer Order 243

    7.2.7   Review the Stock Overview 244

7.3   Posting Changes 245

    7.3.1   Posting Change for a Release from Quality Inspection
                Stock 245

    7.3.2   Posting Change from Material Number to Material
                Number 250

    7.3.3   Dividing Batches Among Other Batches 254

7.4   Summary 255

8   Picking Strategies 257

8.1	Storage Type Indicator	258
8.2	Storage Type Search	260
	8.2.1 Configuring Storage Type Search	260
	8.2.2 Configuring Storage Section Search	262
8.3	FIFO (First In, First Out)	263
	8.3.1 Configuration of FIFO Picking Strategy	264
	8.3.2 Stock Removal Control Indicators	264
	8.3.3 Example of FIFO Picking Strategy	265
8.4	LIFO (Last In, First Out)	268
	8.4.1 Configuration of LIFO Picking Strategy	269
	8.4.2 Example of LIFO Picking Strategy	269
8.5	Fixed Storage Bin	271
	8.5.1 Fixed Storage Bin in Material Master	271
	8.5.2 Configuration of Fixed-Bin Picking Strategy	273
	8.5.3 Example of Fixed-Bin Picking Strategy	273
8.6	Shelf-Life Expiration	275
	8.6.1 SLED Picking and the Material Master	275
	8.6.2 Configuration of Shelf-Life Expiration Picking Strategy	275
	8.6.3 Displaying SLED Stock	278
	8.6.4 Example of Shelf-Life Expiration Picking Strategy	278
8.7	Partial Quantities	280
	8.7.1 Configuration of Partial-Quantities Picking Strategy	281
	8.7.2 Using Partial-Quantities Picking Strategy	281
8.8	Quantity Relevant Picking	282
	8.8.1 Configuration of Quantity Relevant Picking Strategy	282
	8.8.2 Quantity Relevant Picking and Material Master Record	284
8.9	Summary	285

9   Putaway Strategies 287

9.1	Fixed-Bin Storage	288
	9.1.1 Fixed Storage Bin in the Material Master	288
	9.1.2 Configuration of Fixed-Bin Storage Putaway Strategy	289
	9.1.3 Stock Placement Control Indicators	289
	9.1.4 Example of Fixed-Bin Storage Putaway Strategy	292
9.2	Open Storage	294
	9.2.1 Configuration of Open Storage Putaway Strategy	294

	9.2.2	Example of Open Storage Putaway Strategy	295
9.3		Next Empty Bin	298
	9.3.1	Configuration of Next Empty Bin Putaway Strategy	298
	9.3.2	Display of Empty Bins	299
	9.3.3	Example of Next Empty Bin Putaway Strategy	300
	9.3.4	Cross-Line Stock Putaway	302
9.4		Bulk Storage	304
9.5		Near Picking Bin	306
	9.5.1	Storage Type Control Definition	308
	9.5.2	Search Per Level Definition	309
9.6		Summary	310

10 Inventory Procedures 311

10.1		Annual Physical Inventory	311
	10.1.1	Before the Count	311
	10.1.2	Configuration for Annual Inventory	312
	10.1.3	Processing Open Transfer Orders	316
	10.1.4	Blocking the Storage Type	318
	10.1.5	Creating Annual Inventory Documents	318
	10.1.6	Displaying the Count Documents	321
	10.1.7	Entering the Inventory Count	323
	10.1.8	Count Differences	324
	10.1.9	Entering a Recount	326
	10.1.10	Clear Differences	327
10.2		Continuous Inventory	328
	10.2.1	Configuration for Continuous Inventory	328
	10.2.2	Creating a Continuous Inventory Count Document	329
	10.2.3	Printing a Continuous Inventory Count Document	331
	10.2.4	Entering the Count Results	333
10.3		Cycle Counting	334
	10.3.1	Benefits of Cycle Counting	334
	10.3.2	Materials Management Configuration Steps with Cycle Counting	334
	10.3.3	Using the ABC Analysis	335
	10.3.4	ABC Indicator and Material Master	337
	10.3.5	Cycle Counting Configuration for Storage Type	338
	10.3.6	Creating a Cycle Count Document	339
	10.3.7	Printing the Cycle Count Document	340
	10.3.8	Entering the Cycle Count	341
10.4		Zero Stock Check	342
	10.4.1	Configuration for Zero Stock Check	342

10.4.2 Performing an Automatic Zero Stock Check 343

10.4.3 Performing a Manual Zero Stock Check 346

10.5 Summary 348

11 Storage Unit Management 351

11.1 Introduction to Storage Unit Management 352

11.1.1 Activate Storage Unit Management 352

11.1.2 Define Storage Unit Number Ranges 353

11.1.3 Define Storage Type Control 354

11.1.4 Define Storage Unit Type 355

11.2 Storage Unit Record 356

11.2.1 Creating a Storage Unit Record by Transfer Order 356

11.2.2 Display a Storage Unit 358

11.3 Planning of Storage Units 359

11.3.1 Planning Storage Units by Transfer Order. 360

11.3.2 Receiving Planned Storage Units 362

11.3.3 Recording Differences in Planned Storage Units 363

11.4 Storage Unit Documentation 364

11.4.1 Transfer Order Document 364

11.4.2 Storage Unit Contents Document 366

11.4.3 Storage Unit Document 366

11.4.4 Storage Unit — Transfer Order Document 367

11.5 Putaway with Storage Unit Management 368

11.5.1 Creating a Storage Unit 368

11.5.2 Storage Unit — Single Material 369

11.5.3 Storage Unit — Multiple Materials 370

11.5.4 Storage Unit — Add to Existing Stock 372

11.6 Picking with Storage Unit Management 373

11.6.1 Complete Stock Pick 373

11.6.2 Partial Stock Pick 374

11.6.3 Complete Stock Pick with Return to Same Bin 374

11.6.4 Partial Stock Removal Using a Pick Point 375

11.7 Summary 376

12 Hazardous Materials Management 379

12.1 Introduction to Hazardous Materials 380

12.1.1 Classification of Hazardous Materials 380

12.1.2 Master Data Configuration for Hazardous Materials 381

12.1.3 Configuration for Hazardous Material Management 386

12.2 Hazardous Material Record 391
12.2.1 Create a Hazardous Material Record 391
12.2.2 Assigning the Hazardous Material to a Material
Master Record. 392
12.3 Hazardous Material Functionality 393
12.3.1 List of Hazardous Materials 393
12.3.2 Fire Department Inventory List 394
12.3.3 Check Goods Storage 395
12.3.4 Hazardous Substance List 397
12.4 Summary 398

13 Mobile Data Entry 399

13.1 Introduction to RF Devices 400
13.1.1 Graphical User Interface Devices 400
13.1.2 Character-Based Devices 400
13.1.3 SAPConsole 401
13.1.4 Functionality Available Using SAPConsole 401
13.2 Bar Code Functionality 402
13.2.1 UPC Bar Code Format 402
13.2.2 UPC and EAN 403
13.2.3 Bar Code Structure 404
13.2.4 Bar Code Readers 404
13.2.5 Bar Code Reader Technologies 405
13.2.6 Bar Code Support in SAP 407
13.2.7 Configuration for Bar Codes 407
13.3 Radio Frequency Supported Processes in SAP WM 411
13.3.1 Defining the Radio Frequency Queue 411
13.3.2 Adding a User for Mobile Data Entry 413
13.3.3 Logging on for Mobile Data Entry 414
13.3.4 RF Menus and WM Processes 414
13.4 Radio Frequency Monitor 417
13.4.1 Accessing the RF Monitor 418
13.4.2 Using the Radio Frequency Monitor 418
13.5 Summary 419

14 Radio Frequency Identification Technology 421

14.1 Introduction to Radio Frequency Identification (RFID) 422
14.1.1 The Mechanism of RFID 422
14.1.2 Electronic Product Code 422
14.1.3 The Wal-Mart RFID Mandate 423

14.1.4 RFID Benefits 423

14.1.5 RFID vs. Bar Codes 424

14.2 Types of RFID Tags 425

14.2.1 Tag Classes 426

14.2.2 Active and Passive Tags 427

14.3 Current Uses of RFID 428

14.3.1 Electronic Payments 428

14.3.2 Retail Stores 428

14.3.3 Individual Product Tagging 428

14.3.4 Parts Tracking 429

14.4 RFID and SAP 429

14.4.1 Supported Functions in SAP AII 430

14.4.2 Outbound Processing (Slap and Ship) 430

14.4.3 Flexible Delivery Processing 430

14.4.4 Generation of Pedigree Notifications 430

14.4.5 Returnable Transport Items Processing 432

14.5 Summary 432

15 Cross Docking 435

15.1 Planned Cross Docking 436

15.1.1 Types of Cross Docking 436

15.1.2 Types of Material Suitable for Cross Docking 437

15.1.3 Planned Cross Docking in SAP 437

15.1.4 Configuration for Cross Docking 438

15.1.5 Cross Docking Decisions 440

15.2 Cross Docking Movements 440

15.2.1 One-Step Cross Docking 440

15.2.2 Two-Step Cross Docking 443

15.3 Cross Docking Monitor 446

15.3.1 Accessing the Cross Docking Monitor 447

15.3.2 Cross Docking Alert Monitor 448

15.4 Summary 450

16 Developments in Warehouse Management 451

16.1 Task and Resource Management 451

16.1.1 Definitions in Task and Resource Management 452

16.1.2 Resource Management 461

16.1.3 Request Management 464

16.1.4 Task Management 465

16.1.5 Route Management 466

16.1.6 Bin Management 467
16.1.7 TRM Monitor 468
16.2 Value-Added Services 469
16.2.1 Configuration for VAS 469
16.2.2 Creating the VAS Template 473
16.2.3 Creating a VAS Order 475
16.2.4 VAS Monitor 476
16.2.5 VAS Alert Monitor 477
16.2.6 VAS and TRM 477
16.3 Extended Warehouse Management 477
16.3.1 Overview of EWM 477
16.3.2 New Functionality for EWM in SAP SCM 5.0 478
16.3.3 Increased Field Sizes 479
16.3.4 Decentralized Extended Warehouse Management 481
16.3.5 Future of Extended Warehouse Management 482
16.4 Summary 482

17 Conclusion **483**

17.1 Lessons Learned 483
17.2 Future Direction 484

Appendix **487**

A Glossary of Terms 487
B Bibliography 493
C The Author 495

Index 497

Preface

This book is a comprehensive review of SAP Warehouse Management (WM) as it functions in the latest version of SAP, which at the time of writing was SAP ERP Central Component 6.0 (SAP ECC 6.0). I also will discuss warehouse functionality outside of SAP ECC 6.0, which can be found in the SAP Supply Chain Management (SCM) business suite, currently in release SAP SCM 5.0.

Who This Book Is For

The subject matter in this book is not just of interest to those who work directly with SAP Warehouse Management, but also for those who work in related application areas such as SAP Materials Management (MM), SAP Production Planning (PP) and SAP Sales and Distribution (SD). The subject matter should also interest warehouse managers and distribution managers who wish to understand more of the functionality that they have implemented and functionality which they may be considering, such as Task and Resource Management and Storage Unit Management.

For those involved in SAP MM, this book will help them understand more of the functions that occur when material has been moved to a storage location where warehouse management is active. A general knowledge of warehouse functionality with regard to the way material is stored and moved in the warehouse is of great benefit.

Those working with SAP SD will benefit from a greater understanding of the outbound side of warehouse management, how material is picked for customer sales orders, and the movement of the material for outbound deliveries.

SAP PP staff will benefit from gaining familiarity with the way material is received from production and the picking of material for production orders.

Staff working with other SAP functionality such as Quality Management (QM) and Plant Maintenance (PM) will gain from a greater understanding of the general topics addressed in WM.

How this Book is Organized

This book is structured to serve the purposes of the various individuals that work in the SAP WM environment, be they SAP configuration experts or users who have been tasked to use SAP WM as part of their everyday work and wish to gain more understanding of the functionality.

Each chapter focuses on a specific SAP WM function, exploring the different facets of the function and providing examples related to them. The book starts examining the SAP WM functionality: from the very basic key elements through standard SAP WM functions such as stock placement and stock removal, to more advanced technology such as RFID, and the more recent developments in warehouse management, such as Value Added Services and Extended Warehouse Management. Let me briefly describe each chapter now:

▶ **Chapter 1**

Chapter 1 provides a brief history of warehousing and the development of warehouse management systems (WMS) over time. It helps to set modern warehouse management in context with its past.

▶ **Chapter 2**

Chapter 2 describes some of the basic warehouse functionality in SAP WM. These provide the basis for setting up a warehouse in SAP and are key to important to understand the makeup of a warehouse, a storage type, storage section, storage bin, and a quant. The chapter will take you though these key elements showing key configuration and examples.

▶ **Chapter 3**

Chapter 3 will be familiar to those readers who have SAP MM backgrounds. The chapter builds on the key elements described in Chapter 2 and explores the warehouse data required in the material master, batch management, and the important functionality concerning shelf-life expiration.

▶ **Chapter 4**

Chapter 4 uses the data that is part of the material master to describe the basic movements inside the warehouse using the transfer requirement and the transfer order. These drive all movements in the warehouse, and it is important to understand how these functions are processed.

▶ **Chapter 5**

Chapter 5 takes the transfer requirement and transfer order further to describe how they are used in the goods-receipt process. This chapter will be of keen interest to those involved in SAP MM, because it examines the integration of SAP WM with SAP MM for inbound deliveries.

- **Chapter 6**
Chapter 6 describes the goods issue process and the outbound delivery. Those with SAP SD backgrounds will find the examination of the integration of SAP WM and SAP SD of great benefit.

- **Chapter 7**
Chapter 7 explores the functions of the transfer requirement and transfer order and describes how these are used in replenishment of stock to areas within the warehouse, focusing on fixed bin replenishment.

- **Chapter 8**
Chapter 8 takes the elements that have been examined in previous chapters and uses them to describe the stock removal or picking function in the warehouse. The chapter describes the various picking strategies that can be adopted by the warehouse management for a variety of materials and situations. It is useful to understand why these strategies are in place and why they are used for certain materials.

- **Chapter 9**
Chapter 9 looks at the other side of the picking functionality and describes the stock placement of putaway functions in the warehouse. The development of the putaway strategies has been a key to making warehouses more efficient.

- **Chapter 10**
Chapter 10 examines the methods used to count the material in the warehouse, once it has been fully stocked. This is of particular interest to those with financial experience, as it is an important part of a company's financial health. This chapter will introduce the reader to the importance of accurate and regular counts.

The functionality examined in the first 10 chapters has involved basic warehouse management and this is implemented in almost all SAP WM implementations.

However, Chapter 11 and the subsequent chapters focus on functionality that is available for warehouse-management implementations, but is not mandatory. It is up to the individual warehouse manager or supply chain management to investigate and then make a decision on implementation. Readers can learn about the functionality and use that knowledge to advise the warehouse owner about what is available and how it can be successfully used.

▶ **Chapter 11**

Chapter 11 focuses on Storage Unit Management (SUT), which can be used in warehouses that move material in the warehouse by a container that they wish to track. SUT was originally designed for warehouse management before the idea was expanded for SAP MM, where it is called Handling Unit (HU) Management. The functionality is similar, but not identical. This chapter will highlight some of the differences.

▶ **Chapter 12**

Chapter 12 examines the warehouse functionality of hazardous materials. Every warehouse has some kind of hazardous material, and many warehouses have to use the hazardous-material functions to document and manage the dangerous materials stored. This will be of interest to anyone familiar with the SAP Environmental Health and Safety functions.

▶ **Chapter 13**

Chapter 13 examines one aspect of the technological advances that have been adopted in the warehouse. The mobile data-entry functionality in SAP WM harnesses the advantages of the bar code and the radio frequency readers to provide accurate and efficient data entry from the warehouse floor. The chapter also introduces the RF Monitor, which is the key function to managing the mobile data entry in the warehouse.

▶ **Chapter 14**

Chapter 14 moves forward with the latest technological advances in data entry in the warehouse and gives the reader an examination of the Radio Frequency Identification (RFID) functionality in the warehouse. The chapter discusses the technology of RFID and the SAP solution that integrates RFID into the standard warehouse functionality.

▶ **Chapter 15**

Chapter 15 discusses the function of cross docking. Not all industries and warehouses are suitable for cross docking, but it is a key element in making retail and grocery warehousing more efficient and cost effective. The scope of crossdocking implementation may be limited, but the functionality can be adopted by some industries to improve delivery times for certain materials. Understanding the principles and mechanism of cross docking will help readers to give knowledgeable advice to their warehouse management.

▶ **Chapter 16**

Chapter 16 briefly introduces readers to some of the new developments in warehouse management. Task and Resource Management (TRM) is a module that takes the warehouse and warehouse resources to a new level, where the efficiency of the warehouse is constantly improved by managing the resources and the tasks. The chapter is only an introduction to this powerful tool.

> **Note**
>
> Value Added Services (VAS) is a useful function for those warehouses that perform a number of tasks on the material before it is shipped to the customer. The VAS order is a method of identifying the sequence of tasks and effort involved in performing the additional services.

Extended Warehouse Management (EWM) provides warehouse functionality that is not in SAP ECC 6.0, but it is found in the SAP Supply Chain Management business suite, SAP SCM 5.0. This functionality can be operated without SAP WM, and can be used as standalone operation interfaced with SAP ECC 6.0. The discussion of the EWM is focused enough for the reader to become aware of the functionality and future path of the EWM product.

▶ **Book Conclusion**
  I conclude the book with a final chapter that briefly recaps the book, while sharing lessons learned and gives you some direction for the future. This should help you keep track of what you've discovered in this book.

Summary

Please use this preface as a guide. Now that you have an idea of what this book is about and what it covers, you can either jump ahead to specific chapters or proceed to read it chapter-by-chapter.

I hope that after reading this book, you will find that it has met its objectives of delivering a comprehensive review of SAP WM and exploring topics that will reinforce your current knowledge or help you to develop your skills in unfamiliar areas. I hope that you find yourself using this book as a key reference in your current and future SAP WM experiences. Now let us proceed to Chapter 1, in which I introduce you to SAP WM.

Warehousing has evolved from early man's need to store food in a safe environment for future use to becoming an integral part of the supply chain of almost every company on the planet.

1 Introduction to Warehouse Management

Warehouses have been around ever since humans decided to store excess food from their harvests. Today, the warehouse is a key component of the supply chain. Technological advances in computerized warehouse-management systems have meant that the warehouse can operate at maximum efficiency, thus reducing delivery times to the customer, minimizing the cost of the warehouse operation, and maximizing company profits.

1.1 Introduction to Warehousing

The history of warehouses goes back thousands of years. The earliest evidence of warehouses was found in areas where some cultures' cities used buildings to store food for their inhabitants to use.

1.1.1 Earliest Examples of Warehousing

In 1955, an archaeological study was performed in the current day Indian state of Gujarat. In that area, the study found the city of Lothal, which was part of the Indus valley civilization dating back to around 2400 BC. As part of the study, archaeologists found the earliest known example of a dock. It was discovered that the dock was used to load and unload vessels traveling from the Arabian Sea, as Lothal became a major trade center in West Asia and Africa.

The dock was connected to a warehouse by a direct ramp to facilitate loading. The warehouse was central to the prosperity of the city and was originally built on a 3.5-meter-high (11.5 ft) mud-brick podium. The pedestal was high enough to provide maximum protection from any floodwaters.

Example

We can see many other examples of early warehouses based on trade between different cultures. In the Henan Province of China many examples have been found of warehouses of the Eastern Han Dynasty (15–100 AD) where warehouses of 180 meters by 30 meters (600 ft by 100 ft) in size have been found. These are situated in areas along the "Silk Road," a route that developed from Chang'an through Xian-jiang and Central Asia to the Mediterranean. Trading between the Eastern Han Dynasty and other empires such as the Roman and the Kushan Empire in India has been documented.

1.1.2   Tobacco Warehouses in the United States

Many examples of warehouses in the United States and Europe have been found that stem from the introduction of tobacco into European society. In 1580, cultivation of tobacco started in Cuba, along with the storing of tobacco before its shipment to Spain, which led to building of the first tobacco warehouses. In 1612, John Rolfe grew the first commercial tobacco crop in Virginia that led to the trade between Virginia and England.

As the number of tobacco farmers grew in Virginia, warehouses were created where farmers could store their tobacco crop before shipment to England. In 1730, *tobacco notes* became legal tender in Virginia. Tobacco notes attested to the quality and quantity of a farmer's tobacco kept in public warehouses. Soon after, inspection warehouses were created to verify weight and kind and kind of tobacco to prevent the export of *trash tobacco:* shipments diluted with leaves and household sweepings, which were debasing the value of Virginia tobacco.

Examples of the early Virginia tobacco warehouses, such as the 1788 Mecklenburg Tobacco Warehouse in Shepherdstown, West Virginia, can still be found in much of the eastern U.S.

1.1.3   Bonded Warehouses

In 1733 in England, Sir Robert Walpole, considered the first actual prime minister of Great Britain, proposed a warehouse *excise scheme* for items that required a duty to be paid on them, such as tobacco and wine.

At the time of Walpole's suggestion, the payment of duties on imported goods had to be made at the time of their arrival at the port, or a bond with security must be issued for future payment of the duty. There were a number of issues with the duty system at that time, as it was not always possible for the importer to find the money for the duty and often needed to make an immediate sale of the goods, in order to raise the duty. Walpole saw the hindrance this was causing to commerce and proposed the bonded warehouse. Using an act of Parliament, Walpole created law that required imported goods to be placed in warehouses approved by the customs authorities, and importers were to give bonds for payment of duties when the goods were removed. This is where these warehouses received the name of bonded or bonding.

The system of bonded warehousing was of great advantage to the importers and purchasers of goods because the payment of duty was deferred until the goods were required, while the title-deeds, or warrants, were transferable by endorsement.

The bonded warehouse system is still in operation today. In many countries, companies can provide added services or operations to the material in a bonded warehouse. While the goods are in the warehouse, the owner can perform racking, vatting, mixing, and bottling of wines and spirits, the roasting of coffee, the manufacture of certain kinds of tobacco. Certain specific allowances are made for waste or byproducts resulting from such processes.

1.1.4   20th Century Port Warehousing

In the early 20th century, warehouses were often large, mostly bonded and found at big ports. In 1901 in England, the world's largest brick warehouse was built in Liverpool. The Stanley Dock Tobacco Warehouse was built to accommodate the increasing ocean traffic into Liverpool and the barges from the Leeds and Liverpool Canal.

In Los Angeles, the port's only bonded warehouse was built in 1917. It still exists today and still is used for its original function despite the revolution of cargo containerization. From the time of its completion in 1917, Warehouse No. 1 at the Port of Los Angeles was the critical site for the growth of Los Angeles as a commercial center. It allowed train access directly to the warehouse, ensuring the least possible time between ship and final destination. The warehouse is six stores high, with a capacity of a half-million square feet. In the early 20th Century, it housed the majority of non-petroleum goods shipped into and out of the Southern California markets.

The port warehouses of that time operated a break-bulk cargo system. This required a series of labor and space intensive operations.Cargo loading was labor-intensive and extremely time-consuming. Longshoremen had to load and unload the cargo, such as drums, boxes, bags, or crates, as individual pieces. This was known as break-bulk, and material was brought to the ports by train and unloaded into warehouses or buildings that lined the wharf, called transit sheds. Cargo was stored in warehouses until a ship was ready to receive it. When a ship was ready, cargo was transported to the transit sheds, where it was sorted and organized for loading. The cargo was stowed by longshoremen.

Break-bulk cargo workers operated in three areas on a ship. First, the deck men drove the winches. Hold men stowed and unstowed the cargo hold of the ship, and the front men affixed and released the sling loads on the deck. In addition to the ship gangs, dock men physically transferred the cargo to and from the ships. Warehousemen moved the cargo into and out of the warehouse building on carts known as *4-wheelers*.

For the Port of Los Angeles and many other ports with large warehouses, factors in the commerce of the early 1900s created a need for long-term warehousing. First, the shipping schedules of the day were erratic and distributors would want their goods at the port ready for shipment when a ship bound for the desired destination arrived. It was therefore more economical to store their goods at a warehouse at the port at their own site.

Second, distributors would accumulate goods at the port warehouses as they were available or produced and then arrange for shipment when enough goods had accumulated at the warehouse to make shipping economically worthwhile. This allowed for the most economical use of cargo space on the outbound ship or inbound train.

1.1.5 Warehousing as Part of Physical Distribution

Prior to World War II, commerce in the industrialized nations was primarily concerned with the production and sales of goods, with the accounting function joining the two and directing the future of the business.

However, the wartime period focused many industrialists on how goods needed to be stored and distributed to arrive at their final destination as soon as possible. Military logistics functions organized the distribution and transportation of military hardware separate from its production. This helped business to understand that physical distribution was a separate function and one that could provide significant leverage if successfully implemented.

In post-war America, the increase in consumer purchasing combined with increasingly efficient production systems and the improved advertising techniques gave companies an opportunity to serve greater geographic areas. The downside of this expansion was that the emphasis on physical distribution methods had not kept up.

U.S. businesses that wanted to become national brands had different distribution issues than did companies in Europe. For example, a business that was a national brand in England had a much smaller geographic area to distribute to than would a company in the U.S.

The idea of regional warehouse and distribution centers was one that large corporations could afford to implement. A successful local family company did not often have the funds to complete in areas outside of their hometown or state.

As companies sold their products nationally, they created regional distribution centers with large warehouses that stored the companies' products to be sold within the area serviced by that distribution center. The warehouses were sourced from the company's domestic and overseas manufacturing plants.

As national companies became international companies, the distribution centers became spread across the world to service the local markets in their respective areas.

1.1.6   Warehousing and Distribution Centers

In today's business environment, distribution centers are associated specifically with retailing.

The warehouse of a retail distribution center can contain tens of thousands of items from thousands of different vendors. Each vendor supplies the distribution center, which in turn distributes to a number of retail outlets.

In the U.S., a large retail company like Wal-Mart Stores Inc. has more than 3,800 retail operations with more than 300 regional distribution centers. In the U.S alone, Wal-Mart has 61,000 vendors.

In Oldham, England, the National Distribution Center of the Littlewoods home-shopping catalogue is Europe's largest warehouse distribution center covering 23 acres and containing 1 million sq ft of products. The one site has a workforce of close to 700. Goods are received from thousands of vendors, stored, and packed and sent to customers within the same storage facility.

These vast warehouse and distribution centers rely wholly on state-of-the-art computer warehouse management systems (WMS) in order for the warehouse to operate at maximum efficiency. Before the advent of the computer based WMS, the operation of the warehouse was a manual paper-based system that was prone to errors and relied upon the knowledge of warehouse staff in order for the warehouse to operate successfully.

1.1.7 Public Warehousing

A public warehouse is a warehouse that performs warehouse services for many companies. In a public warehouse, the company running the warehouse does not own the goods, but performs goods receiving, storing, shipping, and other warehouse functions. The company owning the warehouse charges companies a fee for using the warehouse and the facilities.

There are many reasons why a company would use a public warehouse instead of or in addition to, its own warehouse facilities. Let's take a look at these.

Cost of Warehousing

A company may decide to use a public warehouse if it does not have the space or the capital to invest in building a purpose-built warehouse and the staff to run the facility. A public warehouse has trained staff and is able to perform the warehouse functions immediately.

Seasonal Warehousing Requirements

If a company has warehousing requirements that are seasonal and would not provide the need for year-round warehousing, a public warehouse is an ideal solution.

Overflow Warehousing

Some companies may have seasonal requirements that their present warehouse facilities cannot cope with. For example, in the beverage industry, seasonal fluctuations of consumer purchasing and sales drives may require a company to use public warehousing for stock that has been produced and cannot be stored in the company's warehouse for lack of space.

1.2 History of Warehouse Management Systems (WMS)

The warehouse of today no longer runs on a paper-based system. The advances of computer based WMS, computer-enabled warehouse equipment, Radio Frequency (RF), and Radio Frequency Identification (RFID) have transformed the warehouse into a technological entity.

Not all warehouses require a WMS. As I will discuss later, there are often decisions to be made as to whether in an SAP environment, a warehouse should run SAP Warehouse Management (SAP WM) or run as a storage location in Materials Management (SAP MM). Some warehouses have operations that are simple and require limited data collection. In these cases, it would be unwise to implement a system that would hinder the operation of the warehouse.

1.2.1 Early Warehouse Management Systems

The first warehouse management systems carried out simple warehouse tasks. The systems were designed to control the movement and storage of items within the warehouse. These systems operated on algorithms that used information on the item, location, quantity, unit of measure, and order data to determine where to place and pick items, and the particular sequence required to correctly perform the operations.

In the 1960s, many of the systems implemented in company warehouses were nothing more than data-processing programs. The terminals in the warehouse were connected to card-punch machines or magnetic-tape writers. Data was entered into the terminals from paper documents relating to the inbound and outbound shipments.

The cards or tape would be run on a leased or company mainframe computer, where the data-processing systems were stored. The implemented systems in the warehouse were controlled mostly by the accounting departments and provided data on inventory levels for accounting purposes. These systems did not help the warehouse staff to run the warehouse more efficiently, and in fact these systems caused more work and increased warehouse costs. This downside was overshadowed by the accounting accuracies the systems provided.

In the 1970s, the warehouse systems were often custom-built software efforts that companies decided to develop themselves rather than implement partial-fit systems offered by large computer companies.

In the 1980s, with the advent of the IBM PC, software companies developed software packages that ran standalone from other company systems. These PC-based systems were often as simple as locator programs, but did allow more control on the warehouse floor.

1.2.2 The Rise of Enterprise Resource Planning (ERP)

In the late 1980s, when the mainframe version of SAP — SAP R/2 — was becoming popular in Europe, many companies decided to implement systems that were fully integrated; i.e., ERP systems.

For the first time, businesses had all of their main functionality on a single platform under a single suite of programs. Companies implementing SAP R/2 would implement the core functionality of their business: accounting, production, sales, and materials management. In many cases these companies would keep their existing systems for human resources, plant maintenance, and warehouse management. Often, these legacy systems would be interfaced into the R/2 system to provide batch or real-time updates.

When the client/server version of SAP — SAP R/3 — was introduced in 1992, the software became a phenomenal success in Europe and in the U.S. With the ability to use SAP on a growing number of platforms, including Microsoft NT, the number of integrated WMS offerings grew also. Even with the presence of SAP R/3 Warehouse Management (SAP WM), companies also could use external WMSs that offered more specialized functionality that the early versions of SAP WM.

Specialized WMS software companies, such as Manhattan Associates, EXE Technologies, and Catalyst International, used the 1990s to develop WMS software that contained much of the core functionality of the SAP WM software with extended transportation and distribution capabilities. Many companies bought and implemented these standalone systems prior to implementation of SAP R/3. Quite often, the WMSes remained as legacy systems until businesses decided it was economically favorable to move from the legacy WMS packages to native SAP WM.

As SAP released new versions of R/3, the functionality of SAP WM grew to become more effective than many standalone packages. By the release of SAP

R/3 4.6, many companies included the conversion to SAP WM as part of their upgrade strategies. The functionality of SAP WM has expanded further as part of the latest SAP version, ECC 6.0.

Many of the WMS software companies have diversified their portfolios to include the wider SCM functionality, SAP WM data interfacing, and SAP WM consulting and specialist functions such as RFID.

1.3   Summary

In this chapter, I have shown that warehousing is something that has been used by mankind for thousands of years. Although the primitive warehouses of the Indus Valley civilization or the tobacco warehouses of 18th Century America cannot be compared to the technological spectacles of warehouses in the 21st Century, the underlying principles remain. Goods are received, they are stored, they are picked, and they are removed from the warehouse. Today's technology allows that to occur in the most efficient and cost effective manner.

In Chapter 2, I discuss some of the basic warehouse functionality to be found in SAP WM with regard to the components that make up a warehouse.

In SAP Warehouse Management (WM), the warehouse is divided into a number of components. The storage type, storage section, and storage bin together describe a unique space where a material has been stored, and these coordinates allow that material to be located.

2   Basic Warehouse Functions

Before any implementation of SAP WM at a company, the physical warehouse layout normally exists; i.e., the warehouse is operating and contains materials. Therefore, defining the warehouse in terms of Warehouse Management components is an exercise in transposing the physical warehouse into the terms defined in SAP. In some instances, simple warehouses can be defined as storage locations within SAP Inventory Management (SAP IM). However, storage locations do not offer any of the functionality required to operate a modern warehouse.

It is important to realize that warehouse-management functionality allows us to replicate the warehouse within the SAP system and provides the necessary management of materials.

2.1   Warehouse Structure

The warehouse that we define by configuring SAP WM relates directly to storage location or storage locations in Materials Management (SAP MM). We can create a warehouse during configuration but no physical address is attached to the warehouse when configuration takes place. The warehouse only relates to a physical entity when it is assigned to a storage location.

2.1.1   Configuring a Warehouse

In the SAP Customizing Implementation Guide (IMG), the WM configuration is part of the Logistics Execution area in SAP, which incorporates other functions such as Shipping, Transportation, and Direct Store Deliveries.

The warehouse is defined in the IMG. The transaction for creating a warehouse can be found using the SAP menu navigation path: **IMG • Enterprise Structure • Definition • Logistics Execution • Define, copy, delete, check warehouse number**.

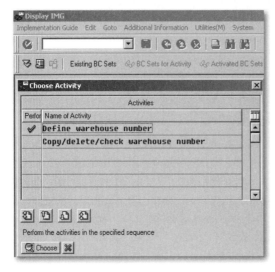

Figure 2.1 Define Warehouse Transaction: Initial Selection Screen

We can use this transaction to create a warehouse number from scratch or to create a warehouse number by copying the information from another warehouse, as shown in Figure 2.1. The option to create a warehouse by copying is particularly useful when we need to create many warehouses with the same name.

Selecting the **Define warehouse number** option, as shown in Figure 2.1, displays a list of existing warehouses, as shown in Figure 2.2.

To then enter the information to create a new warehouse, select the **New Entries** button, as shown in Figure 2.2.

The new-entry screen can be accessed in two other ways, either by using the **F5 function key** or by selecting **Edit • New Entries** from the header menu.

The warehouse number to be added can only be three characters in length, as shown in Figure 2.3. The number can be alphanumeric, and the numbering schema often will depend on existing warehouse numbering or on recommendations from a Data Governance group (DG) at your client. The DG group will administer the overall management of the availability, usability, integrity, and security of the data used in an enterprise, which would include an SAP implementation. The DG program often includes a governing body or council, an agreed-upon set of procedures, and a plan to execute those procedures.

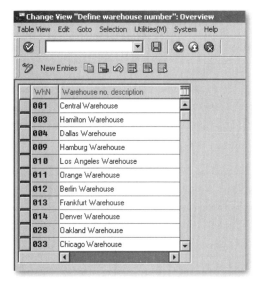

Figure 2.2 Existing Warehouses Displayed When Defining New Warehouse Number

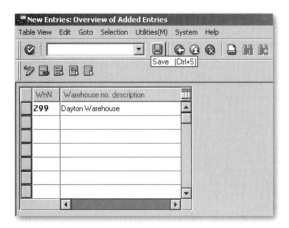

Figure 2.3 New Warehouse Details Added to New Entries Screen

The description for the new warehouse can be up to 25 characters in length. You can use a standard description template, so check the existing description, or check with the DG group.

After the warehouse number and description have been saved, the next stage is to assign the warehouse to a plant and storage location. The warehouse needs to be linked to a storage location so that the interaction between SAP IM and SAP WM can be applied. For example, when a goods receipt is posted to a storage location in SAP IM, the goods will be received at warehouse if that warehouse is assigned to the storage location.

2.1.2   Assignment of the Warehouse

A warehouse has to be assigned to a physical location in SAP MM. This would include one or more storage locations. The warehouse configuration may often refer to just one storage location, but — depending on how the storage locations have been defined in Materials Management — the warehouse may have to be assigned to more than one storage location.

You can find the transaction for assigning a warehouse to a plant/storage location combination using the SAP menu navigation path: **IMG • Enterprise Structure • Assignment • Logistics Execution • Assign warehouse number to plant/storage location**.

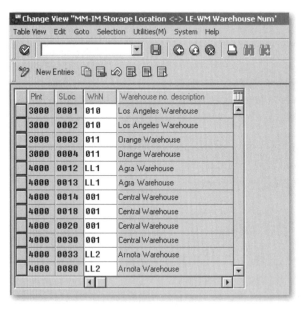

Figure 2.4 View of the Transaction Assigning Warehouse to Plant/Storage Location Combination

The warehouse can be assigned to a plant/storage location combination or to a number of plant/storage location combinations. Figure 2.4 shows a number of warehouses assigned to a more than one storage location within a plant.

To then enter the information to create a new warehouse, select the **New Entries** button, as shown in Figure 2.4. The new-entry screen can be accessed either by using the **F5** function key or by selecting **Edit · New Entries** from the header menu.

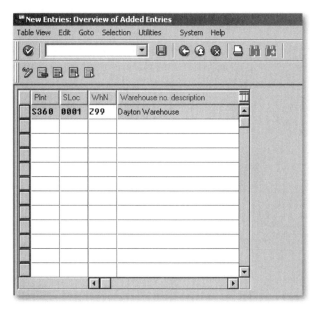

Figure 2.5 Adding Warehouse Assignment Details for Warehouse and Plant/Storage Location to the New Entries Screen

Figure 2.5 shows just one plant/storage location combination for the warehouse, but more assignments can be made on this same screen. When assignments are completed, the data can be saved.

2.1.3 Warehouse Control Parameters

After the warehouse has been defined and assigned, the control parameters can be configured. The control parameters are required for the warehouse to operate within certain constraints. If the warehouse uses only kilograms instead of pounds for the unit of measure of weight, you need to configure this parameter. The transaction for configuring the control parameters for the warehouse can be found using the SAP menu navigation path: **IMG · Logistics Execution · Warehouse Management · Master Data · define Control Parameters for Warehouse Number**.

The initial screen, displayed in Figure 2.6, shows all the warehouses that have been defined in configuration. If, as in our example above, we have created a warehouse, a blank control record is written in table T3000, and we can modify the control parameters of that record with this transaction.

To change the parameters of the warehouse, the relevant warehouse must be selected, as shown in Figure 2.6. To reach the detail screen, the details icon can be selected, or the function keys, **Ctrl + Shift + F2**, can be used. The method used in Figure 2.6 is to use header menu: **Goto • Details**.

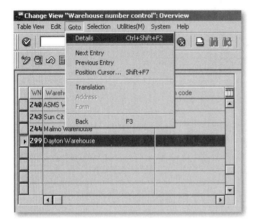

Figure 2.6 Control Parameters for Warehouse: Initial Screen

The detail screen, seen in Figure 2.7, shows the parameters relevant for the warehouse that can be entered.

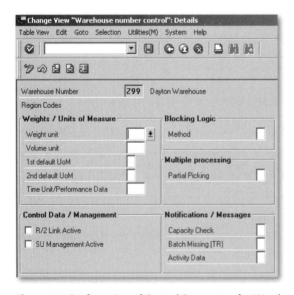

Figure 2.7 Configuration of Control Parameters for Warehouse: Detail Screen

Weight Unit

If a weight unit such as kilogram or pound is entered in this field, then all units of weight, both gross and net, will be in this defined unit. Depending on the unit of weight given, errors — including mathematical rounding errors — can occur if the unit is too small or too large. A weight unit must be entered before any storage bins can be created.

Volume Unit

Similar to the weight unit, the volume unit would define the unit of volume for the warehouse; e.g., cubic meter or cubic yards. .

First Default Unit of Measure

The material master record can contain a number of units of measures for different functions: sales, purchasing, MRP, etc. If the material master record does not contain a unit of measure for warehousing, this parameter can be used as a default. However, this default can only be used if the material is defined in the unit of measure for another function.

For example, if there was no warehouse unit of measure for material XYZ, the system would select the first default unit of measure defined. If that unit of measure was kilograms, then the system would check the material master to find if the material had been defined in any other unit of measure in kilograms. If the system found that the unit of measure for purchasing was kilograms, then the first default unit of measure would be used.

Second Default Unit of Measure

If the first default unit of measure was not one that had been defined on the material master for any other function, the system would then perform the same check for the second default unit of measure defined in the warehouse control parameter screen. If this unit of measure had been used on the material master, it would be used as a default. If the second unit of measure had not been used on the material master, then the material's unit of measure would be used as the warehouse unit of measure.

Time Unit/Performance Data

On this screen, we can define the unit of measure for time for the warehouse. This time unit, if defined, will be used in any time information and would be used for any processing time and performance data.

Blocking Logic — Method

This is a particularly important parameter because it determines the level of simultaneous access to materials in the warehouse for users. For normal warehouse operations, the blocking logic is set to ensure that when a user is creating a transfer order, the material numbers being processed are blocked for the entire warehouse and the storage bins in the transfer order are temporarily blocked. The field is left blank for this level of blocking.

For blocking that allows more than one user to access the same material, but not the same bin, the parameter should be set to **A**. Warehouses where there are few material numbers — such as a manufacturer that makes one or two products — can use this blocking logic. When the blocking logic is set to **B**, more than one user can access the same bin.

Multiple Processing — Partial Picking

In multiple processing, a number of transfer requirements (TRs) are grouped together. However, if there is a shortage of material, this parameter defines how the system deals with the shortage. The parameter selection has four options:

▶ **1**
Partial picking for multiple processing for delivery is allowed.

▶ **2**
Partial picking for multiple processing for TR is allowed.

▶ **3**
Partial picking for multiple processing for TR and delivery is allowed.

▶ **Blank**
Partial picking for multiple processing for TR and delivery is not allowed.

Notifications and Messages — Capacity Check

This field controls the type of message displayed for the warehouse when a capacity check cannot be completed because of missing data on the material master records. Warehouse management can choose no message, warning message, or error message.

Notifications and Messages — Batch Missing (Transfer Requirement)

If the material on the transfer requirement is a batch-managed material, the user creating the TR should enter a batch number. However, this parameter allows the configuration to allow an error message, warning message, or no message to be displayed when a batch number is expected but not entered.

Notifications and Messages — Activity Data

The activity data describes the planned times for activities on the transfer order. If there is an error in this data, the message display can be defined as an error message, warning message, or no message.

R/2 Link Active

This indicator is set if the warehouse in the SAP WM system is being used as a decentralized warehouse management system with SAP R/2.

Storage Unit Management Active

This indicator should be set if we are implementing Storage Unit Management at the warehouse. More information on Storage Unit Management (SUT) can be found in Chapter 11.

After the relevant parameters have been entered for the warehouse, the record can be saved by using the save icon, selecting function keys **Ctrl + S** or by using the header menu and selecting, **Table View • Save**. Now we can proceed to learning about storage types in a warehouse.

2.2 Storage Type

A number of areas can be defined within the warehouse. The defined areas of storage in SAP are called storage types. When a warehouse is initially designed, the layout of the warehouse is analyzed based on a number of objectives, including the following:

▸ To provide the most efficient handling of the stored material.

▸ To provide the maximum flexibility to meet any changes in warehousing that the company may require.

▸ To use the space inside the warehouse to a maximum.

▸ To provide the most economic warehousing procedures based on layout.

The layout of the warehouse is divided into storage types, and these defined areas relate directly to the requirements of the materials to be stored in the warehouse.

2.2.1 Warehouse Layout

Storage types need to be defined because of the nature of the material being stored or the environment a material must be stored in. Let's explore this idea further.

Fast-Moving Materials

A company will have a number of materials that are defined as fast moving; i.e., they are shipped quickly once they are received at the warehouse. Therefore, these materials need to be stored in a manner that allows for optimum handling.

In a normal warehouse, this area for the fast-moving materials should be situated along the quickest path from goods receiving to shipping. That location depends on how that material is shipped. If the material is received in large amounts, but shipped in small amounts, the fast-moving materials storage type should be placed close to the shipping area. This reduces the duration of each trip between storage type and shipping. If the material is received in small amounts and shipped in large quantities, then the storage type needs to be close to goods receiving to reduce the length of the frequent trips from goods receiving to storage type.

Rack Storage

There are a number of reasons a material should use the rack storage type. Sometimes the material is not shaped in a manner suitable for any other storage. Other materials are fragile and cannot be stacked. Some rack storage is used close to shipping to allow picking of materials that are small; a limited supply is located in the order-picking racks and replenished from bulk storage.

Bulk Pallet Storage

The majority of bulk product is stored on pallets, and the pallets are stored one upon another. This is a good use of space in the warehouse and reduces the need for and cost of racking. A number of materials can only be stacked so many pallets high.

Slow-Moving Materials

Although every company tries to reduce, if not eliminate, materials that are sold infrequently, slow-moving materials are a feature of a company's inventory. Many companies use the theory that in general, the slowest-moving 80% of materials represent only 20% of sales volume.

Slow-moving materials make up inventory that has had some movement, but less than one and a half turns a year. Slow-moving items are similar to dead stock items, but they have experienced some customer demand during the past 12 months. These items may be suitable for being discontinued.

However, if the item falls into one of the following categories it may not be suitable for being discontinued and will need to be stored in the warehouse:

▶ If it expected that demand for this material will continue or increase during the next twelve months

▶ If customers expect to always have the material available for immediate delivery

▶ If the material is inexpensive and does not require a costly investment in inventory

Slow-moving material is often stored at the furthest location from the shipping area, as it is not accessed often.

Special Storage

Some companies will have special needs as far as the storage of their materials. These will involve hazardous materials, which is discussed in Chapter 12.

Refrigeration and climate control are some other special needs for storage. Many retail companies will need to have part of the warehouse refrigerated for perishable materials. Other companies may need to define certain warm areas for chemicals that need to be stored at a certain temperature. All of these can be defined as storage types within a warehouse.

2.2.2 Configuration of a Storage Type

The transaction for creating a storage type can be found using the SAP menu navigation path: **IMG · Logistics Execution · Warehouse Management · Master Data · Define Storage Type**.

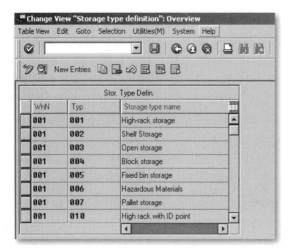

Figure 2.8 Create Storage Type, Showing Existing Storage Types

The transaction shows the storage types that have been created for warehouses previously, as shown in Figure 2.8. To create the new storage type, the **New Entries** button should be selected.

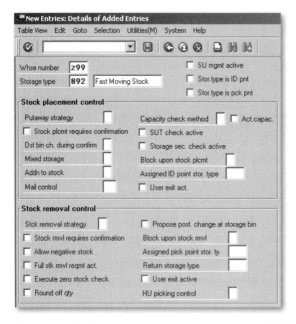

Figure 2.9 Create Storage Type Transaction: Initial Data-Entry Screen

Figure 2.9 shows the data-entry screen for the Storage Type. This screen requires decisions about the content of a number of fields. The parameters for the storage type relate to stock placement and stock removal. This content of the fields will determine how material is placed and removed from this particular storage type.

In the following subsections, I shall describe the fields on the storage type data-entry screen.

2.2.3 Data Entry for a Storage Type

Let's explore in detail the fields seen in Figure 2.9.

Storage Unit Management Active

This indicator, **SU mgmt active**, is set to active if the storage type allows the management of Storage Unit Management (SUT). A storage unit (SU) is a group of one or more amounts of material that can be managed in the warehouse as a distinct unit. If the indicator is set for the storage type, we then can assume that all material in the storage type is part of a storage unit.

Storage Type is an ID Point

If the indicator **Stor.type is ID pnt** is set, it means that the storage type is an identification point for goods movements. An identification point is a location in an <u>automated warehouse</u> where the incoming goods are identified. Identification points can be configured in the IMG. The transaction for defining ID points can be found using the SAP menu navigation path: **IMG • Logistics Execution • Warehouse Management • Storage Units • Activities • Define ID Point Transactions**.

LT⌀9
'999'

Storage Type is a Picking Point

If the indicator **Stor.type is pck pnt** is set, the storage type is a picking point for another storage type. For example, if there is a packaging storage type in the warehouse, it may be that material for the packaging storage type is picked from a storage type called Fast Moving Goods. The indicator **Stor.type is pck pnt** would be set on the Fast Moving Goods storage type.

Putaway Strategy

The stock **Putaway strategy** is a procedure that can be defined for each storage type. It operates during stock placement of material in which SAP automatically searches within a storage type for a suitable storage bin for the material to be placed into storage. This is a very brief explanation of a Putaway Strategy, which will be discussed in more detail in Chapter 9.

Stock Placement Requires Confirmation

Setting this indicator requires that all stock placements into bins within this storage type need to be confirmed. This means that the before any material is available all the relevant transfer orders must be confirmed.

Destination Storage Bin Changed During Confirmation

The field **Dst bin ch. during confirmation** can be set to allow the destination storage bin to be changed on a transfer order when the transfer order is being confirmed for this storage type. The field must be set to "1" to allow this. If the field remains blank, you will not be able to change the destination storage bin on a transfer order for this storage type.

Mixed Storage

This field determines how different materials are stored in this storage type. If the field is left blank, this means that the storage type does not allow any mixed storage. Mixed storage refers to different materials or different batches of material being located in one storage bin.

However, if the storage type does allow for mixed storage, you can set a number of parameters to reflect how mixed storage can be used, as shown in Figure 2.10.

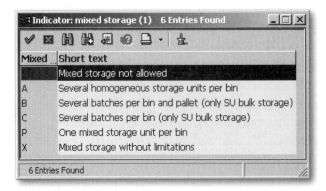

Figure 2.10 Display of Mixed Storage Parameters That Can be Selected

Addition to Stock

This field can be configured to allow a quant of a material with a certain batch number to be added to a storage bin with the same material and the same batch that exists in that bin.

> **Note**
>
> A quant is a uniquely defined object in SAP. It is a quantity of material with the same material number and the same batch number — if the material is batch managed — in a single storage bin. A quant will have a quant number to identify it.

If the field is left blank then the addition to stock is not allowed. If the field is marked with an X, then the addition to stock is allowed.

Mail Control

This field is only used for SAP Production Planning (PP) material staging. If any of the background processes for automatic creation of transfer orders for PP material staging fail, this field is used to define which user is to be informed of the error. The user for the mail notification can be found in Table T333M.

Capacity Check Method

This indicator can be configured to see if one of the six SAP WM capacity checks can be carried out for the storage bins in this storage type.

Capacity ch..	Short text
	No capacity check
1	Check according to maximum weight
2	Check based on palletization accord. to SUT 1
3	Check based on maximum quantity per bin in storage type
4	Usage check based on material
5	Usage check based on SUT
6	Usage check based on material plus SUT

Figure 2.11 WM Capacity Checks Available for Storage Type

Figure 2.11 shows the six types of capacity checks that are available to be configured for the storage type.

Active Capacity Check

If this indicator is set, an active capacity check is executed when goods are placed into stock. The check will ensure that a capacity check is made when material is moved into a storage bin. If the capacity of the bin would be exceeded, the material could not be moved into the bin.

Storage Unit Management Check Active

This indicator is set if the storage unit type check for stock placement is active. If this indicator is set, the storage unit type will need to be specified for stock placements.

Storage Section Check Active

When this indicator is set, SAP will search for storage bins in storage areas defined in the storage area check table.

Block Upon Stock Placement

With this indicator set, the quant and the storage bin can be blocked during stock placement. The following two options are available in configuration:

▶ Block the Storage Bin during Stock Placement

▶ Block only the Quant during Stock Placement

ID Point for a Storage Type

This field, **Assigned ID point stor. Type**, allows the configuration of the identification (ID) point for the storage type. Any goods movement that does not have a specific storage bin in this storage type as its destination is initially directed to the ID point.

User Exit Active

This indicator should be set if a stock placement strategy for this storage type will be accessed via a user exit. The indicator informs the system that instead of using a stock placement strategy defined in configuration, the system must use the user-defined placement strategy that has been coded outside of SAP and access it via a user exit.

Stock Removal Strategy

The stock removal or picking strategy is a procedure that can be defined for each storage type. This procedure operates during stock removal of material so that SAP automatically searches within a storage type for a suitable storage bin for the material that is to be removed.

This is a very brief explanation of a picking strategy. A more detailed discussion can be found in Chapter 8. Figure 2.12 shows the standard picking strategies that are available for assignment in the storage type configuration.

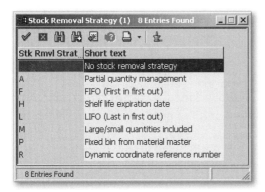

Figure 2.12 Stock Removal or Picking Strategies Defined in Standard SAP

Stock Removal Requires Confirmation

This indicator needs to be set if there is a requirement for the confirmation of a stock removal. This would require a transfer to be confirmed for every stock removal that takes place with relation to the storage type.

Allow Negative Stock

If this indicator is set, a negative figure can exist for quants in the storage type. This is not commonly configured for storage types that are not interim storage types. SAP defines interim storage types as storage types that are used for posting goods receipts, goods issues, and differences that may occur. Interim storage types are defined with numbers between 900 and 999.

Full Stock Removal Required

This indicator can be set if the warehouse needs to ensure that all quants are removed if a complete stock removal is required. A complete stock removal is a component of SUT and requires all storage units to be removed, but quants that are not part of an SU can remain. If this indicator is set, then all quants are removed.

Execute Zero Stock Check

If this indicator is set, a zero stock check must be carried out if a storage bin becomes empty after a stock removal.

Round Off Quantity

The indicator to round off requested quantity for stock removal can be set when rounding is required for transfer-order items. This indicator will set rounding for the total storage type. It may be more appropriate to set the rounding quantity in the material master record at the storage-type level.

Rounding is useful in picking when the picking is easier in certain amounts, for example in pallets or boxes. Rounding the quantity to those values can save time in filling orders.

Handling Unit Picking Control

This field is the control for the handling unit (HU), or storage unit picking. We will prove more information about storage units in Chapter 11. Figure 2.13 shows the options that are available for this field

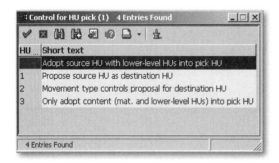

Figure 2.13 Options for Control of Handling Unit During Picking

Propose Posting Change at Storage Bin

This indicator can be set to ensure that if a posting change is made for a material the transaction is posted and the materials are left in same storage bin. If the indicator is not set, then the material can be moved to a different storage bin as part of the posting change.

Block Upon Stock Removal

This indicator can allow during stock removal that the quant and the storage bin can be blocked. The following two options are available in configuration:

▸ Block the Storage Bin during Stock Removal

▸ Block only the Quant during Stock Removal

Assigned Pick Point for Storage Type

In SUT, if complete removal of storage units is required and the **Full stk rmvl reqmt act** indicator is <u>not set</u>, the quants that are not removed should be taken to a pick point. The pick point is a storage type and is configured in this field.

Return Storage Type

Similar to the pick point, the field can be configured to set the storage type where material is returned after events such as a stock removal or overdelivery. User Exit Active is similar to the field in stock placement. If this field is set, a stock removal strategy for this storage type will be accessed via a user exit.

This section has explained the characteristics of storage type. The next section looks at the division of the storage type into storage sections.

2.3   Storage Sections

The storage type can be divided into a number of areas, which are called storage sections. A storage section contains the storage bins where the material is stored. Many storage types only have one storage section because there is no requirement to break the storage type into further distinct areas. There is a requirement that at least one storage section must be defined for each storage type. In some warehouses, storage sections are important in the stock-removal process.

Example

The storage type for high racking can be divided into several storage sections. The storage sections could refer to the levels of racks in the storage type. The first rack level could be one storage section, the second level another storage section, etc.

The transaction for creating a storage section can be found using the SAP menu navigation path: **IMG • Logistics Execution • Warehouse Management • Master Data • Define Storage Sections**.

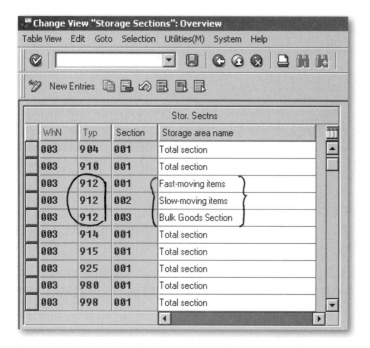

Figure 2.14 Initial Screen for Configuration of a Storage Section

The initial screen for the configuration of the storage sections shows the storage sections already created, as shown in Figure 2.14. To create a new storage section, the **New Entries** button should be selected. The configuration screen also can be reached by using the header menu and selecting **Edit • New Entries** or by using the **F5** function key.

The new storage section must be assigned to both a warehouse number and a storage type. Figure 2.15 shows the warehouse and storage type created in this chapter.Three storage sections are being assigned to the storage type 892. The storage section is a three-character field and normally is configured as 001 if only one storage section is to be used.

The storage section name field is 25 characters in length and should describe the use of the storage section. For example, if a storage section is for unboxed items on a single rack, the name may be "Level One — Unboxed." After the storage section is configured, the storage bins can be created.

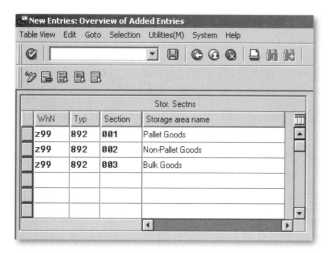

Figure 2.15 Configuration Screen for Creating New Storage Sections

2.4 Storage Bins

The storage bin is the smallest unit of storage in the warehouse. There is no set size for a storage bin, and its size can vary between companies, warehouses, and even within the same storage type.

A storage bin can be a location on a shelf, a location on a carousel, or a plastic tub in a rack. A storage bin can have many physical appearances, but as defined logically in SAP WM it is the location where a quant of material is stored.

A number of steps need to be completed in the IMG before storage bins can be created. The steps that should be configured are described in more detail in the following subsections.

2.4.1 Storage Bin Types

The storage bin type is a grouping that can be assigned to storage bins of a similar nature. For example, a storage bin type could be created called *Bin Height One Meter*. This grouping could then be assigned to bins that are one meter in height in the warehouse.

You can configure the storage bin type in the IMG. The transaction for creating a storage bin type can be found using the SAP menu navigation path: **IMG · Logistics Execution · Warehouse Management · Master Data · Storage Bins · Define Storage Bin Types**.

Figure 2.16 shows the initial screen for the configuration of storage bin types, with the existing configuration shown. Select the **New Entries** button to create a new storage bin type. The configuration screen can also be reached by using the header menu and selecting **Edit • New Entries** or by using the **F5** function key.

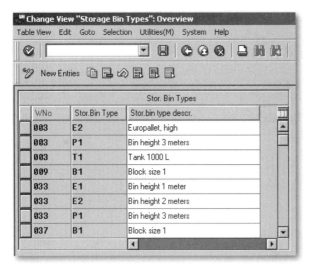

Figure 2.16 Initial Screen for Configuration of Storage Bin Types

Figure 2.17 shows the addition of a storage bin type for the warehouse in our previous examples. The storage bin type field is limited to two characters. The description for the storage bin type is 20 characters.

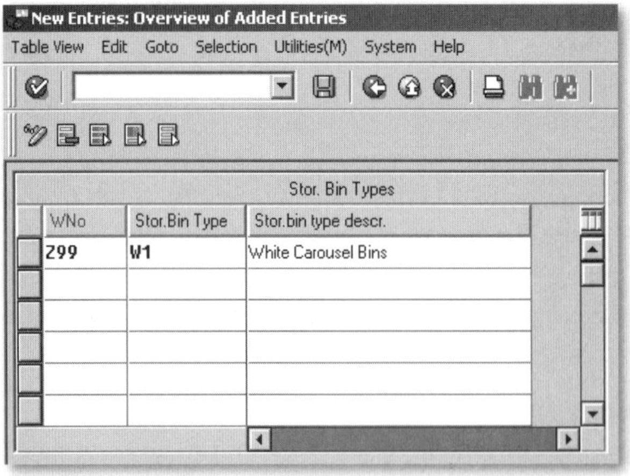

Figure 2.17 Configuration Screen for Creating New Storage Bin Types

2.4.2 Define Storage Bin Structure *LS10*

Assigning the storage bin structure is a transaction that can be configured to contain the templates and structures of the storage bin-numbering schema activated when automatic storage-bin creation is triggered.

The transaction to define the storage bin structure is Transaction LS10. This can be found in two areas. In the IMG, use the SAP menu navigation path: **IMG • Logistics Execution • Warehouse Management • Master Data • Storage Bins • Define Storage Bin Structures**.

Transaction LS10 also can be found in the application area, using the SAP menu navigation path: **SAP • Logistics • Logistics Execution • Master Data • Warehouse • Storage Bin • Create • Automatically**.

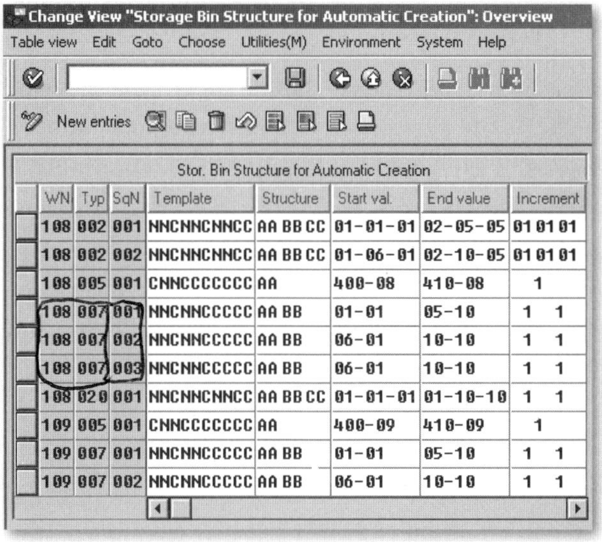

Figure 2.18 Storage Bin Structure Configuration Screen: Transaction LS10

Figure 2.18 shows the various structures for automatic creation of storage bins. The structure is defined for each warehouse/storage type combination. The third field on this screen, **SqN**, is the sequence number that will be followed in creation of storage bins for the warehouse/storage type combination.

Template

In Figure 2.18, the template is shown as a field with 10 characters. These characters represent numeric and alphabetical character ranges. This template determines the structure of the storage bin when it is created automatically.

▶ **N**

This represents a numeric character between zero and nine.

▶ **A**

This represents an alphabetical character.

▶ **C**

This represents a character that is common across the bins.

Structure

This field defines the structure of the storage bin number. Figure 2.18 shows the structure field as **AA** or **AA BB CC**. This structure defines how the number appears, as we can easily understand by using Figure 2.18 as an example.

Review the first line of the figure, Warehouse **108**, Storage Type **002**, and Sequence Number **001**. The template for this entry is Number, Number, Common Character, Number, Number, Common Character, Number, Number, Common Character, and finally another Common Character.

The structure defined for that record is **AA BB CC**. Therefore, using the structure with the template, the storage bin number could be **11-03-05**, assuming the common character between the numbers is a dash and the last two common characters are spaces. The definition of the common characters is seen in the next fields.

Start Value

This field is the storage bin starting value for the particular warehouse/storage bin/sequence number combination. This value will be the starting value for the automatic creation of storage bins. The value entered has to adhere to the template and structure defined for the combination. Taking the example above, the starting value of 03-01-01 follows both the template and structure and now includes the common characters of a dash between the numbers and spaces after the last set of numbers.

End Value

The entry for the particular warehouse/storage bin/sequence number combination is the end value for the automatic creation of storage bins for that sequence. The end value must follow the same format as the starting value.

Increment

This figure determines the addition to the numbering and is calculated during the automatic generation of storage bins. In our continuing example, the increment for the automatic generation of storage bins has been entered as 01–01–01, which implies that each set of numbers will increase by one until the end value has been reached. In this example, the start value was 03–01–01 and the end value was 03–10–10; therefore, during the automatic creation of bins, the increment will only refer to the second and third sets of numbers because the first set of numbers will always be 03 and will not change.

During the automatic storage bin creation, in this example, the starting bin location would be 03–01–01, the next bin to be automatically generated would be 03–01–02, and the next 03–01–03, etc. The last storage bin for this location is created which would be 03–10–10.

03 – 01 – 10
03 – 02 – 01
03 – 02 – 02

Enter a New Bin Structure

To enter a new storage bin structure, the **New Entries** button, shown in Figure 2.18, should be selected. The entry screen can also be reached by using the header menu and selecting **Edit • New Entries** or by using the **F5** function key.

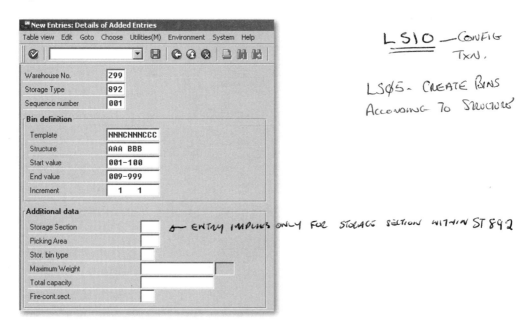

LS10 — CONFIG TXN.

LS05 – CREATE BINS ACCORDING TO STRUCTURE

← ENTRY IMPLIES ONLY FOR STORAGE SECTION WITHIN ST 892

Figure 2.19 Configuration Screen for Entering New Storage Bin Structure: Transaction LS10

The configuration screen, shown in Figure 2.19, requires the entry of the template, structure, start and end values, and the increment. Additional data fields can be entered for the storage bin structure.

Storage Section

If the bin structure is only relevant for a certain storage section, that section should be entered on this screen, shown in Figure 2.19. This may be the case if the template that is being configured is only relevant for a certain storage section; e.g., for high-racking or open storage. The start and end values for the bin number range may only relate to a single storage section.

Picking Area

A picking area is similar to a storage section in that it groups a certain number of storage bins. The difference between a storage section and a picking area is that the group of bins for a picking area relate to the picking process and removal strategies. For example, a picking area may include storage bins from several storage sections — i.e., different sizes — because they all contain material that is relevant for a certain removal strategy.

A picking area can be configured in the IMG, using the SAP menu navigation path: **IMG · Logistics Execution · Warehouse Management · Master Data · Define Picking Areas**.

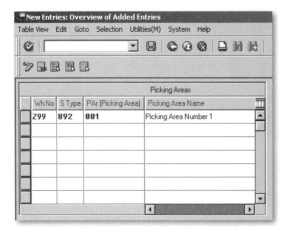

Figure 2.20 Configuration Screen for Creating a New Picking Area

Figure 2.20 shows the data entry required to configure a picking area. The picking area field allows you to fill a three-character alphanumeric field. The picking area name can be entered up to a maximum of 25 characters. Once the name is entered, the picking area can be added to the storage bin information.

Storage Bin Type

A storage bin type can be added to the entry of the bin structure that will be a default for the bins created. This is useful if the bins are all of the same kind. The storage bin type is a way to identify different types of storage bins; e.g., one type of storage bins may be one meter high, while another type represents tank containers for fluids.

Maximum Weight

This field can be entered if we know the maximum weight of the material that can be stored in the bin. This weight value is then used during any capacity check that may be activated. If the weight of the material to be added into the storage bin will cause the weight of material in that bin to exceed the maximum weight allowed, then the system would not permit the placement.

Total Capacity

This field can be entered if we know the total capacity of the storage bins to be created. This is important if the material to be stored in some bins can easily exceed the capacity of the bin. This is especially useful in warehouses with large or heavy materials.

Fire-Containment Section

This field can be entered if the fire-containment section needs to be added for the storage bins to be created. The fire-containment sections are defined as part of the hazardous-materials configuration for warehouse management. More information on hazardous materials can be found in Chapter 12.

The fire-containment section is configured in the IMG using the SAP menu navigation path: **IMG • Logistics Execution • Warehouse Management • Hazardous Materials • Master Data • Define Fire-Containment Sections**.

The new fire-containment sections can be added to a warehouse in the IMG, as shown in Figure 2.21. The fire-containment field can be two characters in length, while the name of the fire-containment section can be up to 20 characters long. Once the fire-containment section is configured, this can be entered into the storage bin structure.

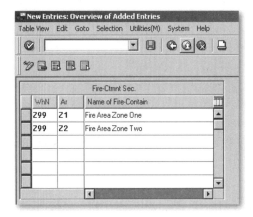

Figure 2.21 Configuration Entry Screen to Create Fire-Containment Sections in IMG Hazardous Material Area

2.4.3 Creating a Storage Bin Manually

Manual creation of a storage bin can be performed using Transaction LS01N. This can be found using the SAP menu navigation path: **SAP • Logistics • Logistics Execution • Warehouse Management • Master Data • Storage Bin • Create • Manually**.

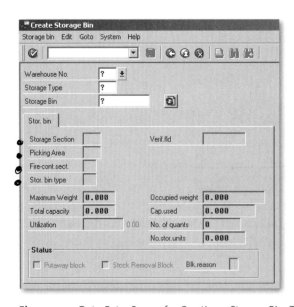

Figure 2.22 Data-Entry Screen for Creating a Storage Bin: Transaction LS01N

To create the storage bin, the warehouse number, storage type, and the storage bin number should be entered, as shown in Figure 2.22. Once these fields are entered, other fields have to be entered to create the storage bin is the storage section number. The other fields on the entry screen, such as **Picking Area** and **Fire-cont. sect** are optional.

2.4.4 Creating a Storage Bin Automatically

Storage bins can be created automatically using the storage bin structure transaction we have previously discussed: Transaction LS10. Once the template, structure, start and end values, and intervals are entered into the transaction, the storage bins can be created automatically.

Transaction LS10 can be found using the SAP menu navigation path: **SAP • Logistics • Logistics Execution • Master Data • Warehouse • Storage Bin • Create • Automatically.**

After selecting the relevant warehouse, storage type, and sequence number, the bins can be automatically created. Use the header menu and select **Environment • Create Bins**, as shown in Figure 2.23. The process will then calcu-

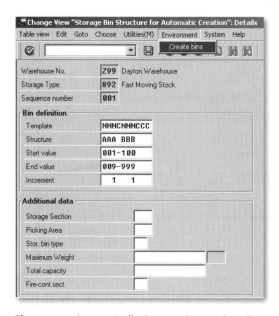

Figure 2.23 Automatically Creating Storage Bins: Transaction LS10

late the number of bins to be created and return the information to the screen, as shown in Figure 2.24.

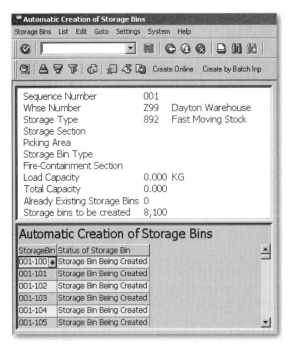

Figure 2.24 Information Screen During Automatic Creation of Storage Bins: Transaction LS10

2.4.5 Block Storage Bins   *LS Ø8*

In the course of normal warehouse operations, you may need to block storage bins or a range of storage bins. This may occur because of damage to the bins or normal warehouse maintenance, which can include cleaning of bins and racks, as well as replacing racking shelves. It is possible to block a single storage bin or a range of storage bins.

The transaction to perform this is Transaction LS08, which can be found using the SAP menu navigation path: **SAP • Logistics • Logistics Execution • Master Data • Warehouse • Storage Bin • Block • Range of Bins**.

To block a range of bins, the initial screen, shown in Figure 2.25, requires the entry of the warehouse number and the storage type. At this point, a range of storage bins can be entered, if required. If no selection is made, then all of the valid storage bins for the particular warehouse/storage type combination will be selected for blocking.

The selection screen, shown in Figure 2.26, shows the number of bins that can be selected for blocking. In this example, the bins can be blocked. However, there would be the option of unblocking them. The screen shows clearly that none of the bins are blocked for putaway and none are blocked for stock removal.

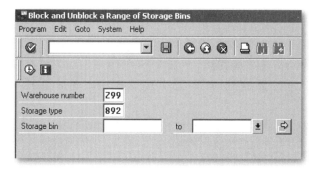

Figure 2.25 Initial Entry Screen to Block a Range of Storage Bins: Transaction LS08

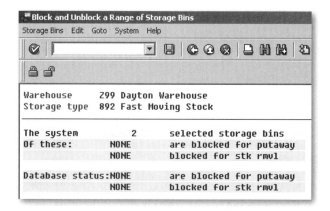

Figure 2.26 Selection of Storage Bins That Can Be Blocked: Transaction LS08

To block the bins, the locked-padlock icon should be selected. Using the **F5** function key or selecting **Edit · Block** from the header menu also can block the storage bins.

When blocking the storage bins, you need to choose the type of block assigned to the bins. Figure 2.27 shows the choices: a block to be made for putaway or for stock removal. In addition a blocking reason can be added if any have been configured. The configuration steps to create blocking reasons are shown in the next section.

When the block for putaway is selected, the bins will then be blocked for any stock placement transactions, but will still allow stock removal to take place. The resulting situation is shown in Figure 2.28.

Figure 2.27 Option to Select Type of Block Allocated to Selected Bins: Transaction LS08

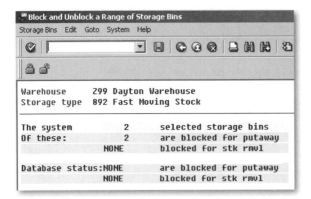

Figure 2.28 Screen Showing Number of Bins Blocked for Putaway: Transaction LS08

2.4.6 Creating Blocking Reasons

The reasons for blocking storage bins can also be applied to storage units, quants, and storage types. The blocking reasons are created at the warehouse level. Blocking reasons can be configured in the IMG using the SAP menu navigation path: **IMG • Logistics Execution • Warehouse Management • Master Data • Storage Bins • Define Blocking Reasons**.

The blocking reasons can be added at the warehouse level. In the entry screen, shown in Figure 2.29, it is possible to add a number of blocking reasons at a single time. The blocking reason is a single character, but some non-alphanumeric characters, e.g., # and @, can be selected in order to increase the number of blocking reasons for each warehouse.

A description for the blocking reason should be added. This is limited to 20 characters in length.

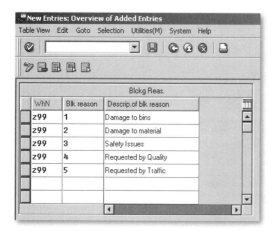

Figure 2.29 Configuration Screen for Creating Blocking Reasons at Warehouse Level

2.4.7 List of Empty Storage Bins   LXOl

This list is a key report used by warehouse managers as it is informs them immediately what empty bins are available. When the warehouse is short of space and has to unload trailers, having a list of empty bins is critical.

The transaction for this report is Transaction LX01, which can be found using the SAP menu navigation path: **SAP · Logistics · Logistics Execution · Master Data · Warehouse · Storage Bin · Evaluations · List of Empty Storage Bins**.

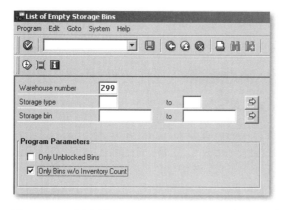

Figure 2.30 Initial Screen to Enter Parameters for List of Empty Storage Bins: Transaction LX01

You can add a number of parameters to reduce the scope of the search for empty bins. As Figure 2.30 shows, you can choose to show the empty bins at the warehouse level or by a selecting storage type or range of bins.

You also can choose to show empty bins that are unblocked and those with no inventory count. This is important, as it is often necessary to find empty bins that can be used, especially if warehouse space is short. The resulting report, shown in Figure 2.31, shows the list of empty bins for the parameters entered in Figure 2.30.

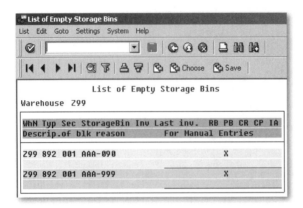

Figure 2.31 List of Empty Storage Bins Created by Transaction LX01

2.4.8 Bin Status Report

The bin status report is crucial to a successful warehouse operation. This report shows the contents of storage bins for a specified search. The transaction for this report is Transaction LX03, which can be found using the SAP menu navigation path: **SAP • Logistics • Logistics Execution • Master Data • Warehouse • Storage Bin • Evaluations • Bin Status Report.**

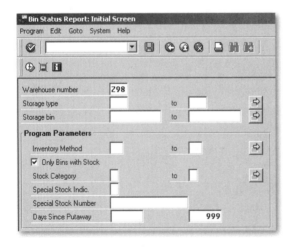

Figure 2.32 Initial Screen for Bin Status Report: Transaction LX03

The report can be made to specify a certain warehouse, range of storage types, or range of bins, as shown in Figure 2.32. In addition there are a number of parameters that can be entered to return specific bins.

Inventory Method

You can restrict the results for the bin status report to those materials that have been counted by a certain inventory method. The inventory methods can be entered into this screen.

Stock Category

The stock category can be entered to restrict the bin status. The Stock categories include the following:

- **Q**
  Stock in Quality Control
- **R**
  Return Stock
- **S**
  Blocked Stock
- **Blank**
  All available stock

Special Stock Indicator

The special stock indicator is used to identify special materials that need to be managed separately. Examples include project stock or return packaging.

Special Stock Number

This number is assigned to a quantity of material that is flagged by a special stock indicator. The special stock indicators include **Q** for project stock and **E** for sales order stock.. To identify a specific quantity of special stock, a special stock number is allocated to that unique quantity.

Days Since Putaway

You can restrict the bin status search to materials that have been in stock for a certain number of days since the putaway date.

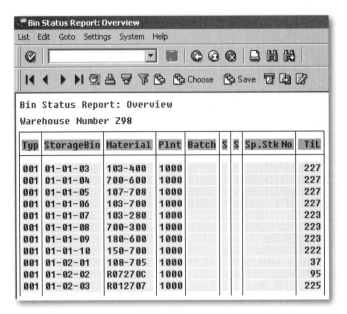

LX03

Figure 2.33 Results Screen for Bin Status Report: Transaction LX03

The results screen for the bin status report is shown in Figure 2.33. The screen shows the results for the warehouse. It identifies the storage type, storage bin, material in the bin, plant and the length of days in the bin (TiL).

The storage bin is the smallest location in the warehouse, but now we shall look at the units of material contained in the storage bin, which are the quants.

2.5 Quant

A quant is a quantity of material with the same material number and the same batch number (if the material is batch managed) in a single storage bin. The total quantity of material in a quant can be increased or decreased through the addition or removal of material for the storage bin. The quant can only change in quantity through a goods movement.

2.5.1 Quant Record

SAP automatically creates a quant when the same material, of the same batch, is placed into a storage bin that does not contain material of the same number or batch. SAP will assign a quant number to the material. When all of the quant is removed from the storage bin, the quant is automatically deleted by SAP. The record created for the quant includes the following data:

▶ Quant identification

▶ Plant

▶ Material number

▶ Batch number

▶ Stock category

▶ Special stock indicator and number   *, or VIA LXØ3 & CLICK oN BIN*

2.5.2   Display a Quant   *— LS23 .*

One method of displaying a quant is to view the details of a storage bin. One report that displays information on the contents of a storage bin is the Bin Status Report (Transaction LX03) discussed earlier in this chapter.

Figure 2.33 shows the details of material in the storage bins of a warehouse. Clicking on the line required and then selecting the magnifying glass icon can display the detail of the storage bin/material combination, which triggers Transaction LS23. The function keys — **Ctrl + Shift + F3** — can also be used to display the details. If the quant number is actually known, then the Transaction LS23 can be used directly.

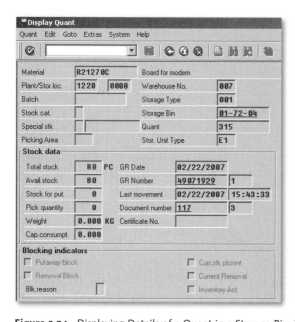

Figure 2.34 Displaying Details of a Quant in a Storage Bin: Transaction LS23

Figure 2.34 shows that the information on the quant is not just related to the quantity and location, but includes data on the goods receipt (**GR Number**), last movement date, and document number.

2.6 Summary

In this chapter, I discussed the overall warehouse structure with regard to the physical layout of the warehouse. Configuration of the warehouse its assignment to a storage location, and setting up of storage types are all parts of the initial warehouse design.

The importance of this initial design work cannot be stressed enough. The physical warehouse has to be represented in the SAP system, and it is the job of the WM consultant to understand the needs of the warehouse staff and day-to-day warehouse operations. Observation is the key to acquiring this knowledge.

Forcing the warehouse to fit into a theoretical design in SAP that does not reflect the operations of the existing warehouse can cause significant problems for shipping and receiving. If the warehouse cannot ship products, or production cannot manufacture products because stock is not available in the warehouse, the company loses money.

In Chapter 3, I will discuss the stock-management aspects of Warehouse Management and its integration with the material master.

Stock management is an important aspect of warehouse management. This chapter takes into account not just the SAP WM material master data, but also how stock is categorized in the warehouse, including batch and shelf- life expiration functionality.

3   Stock Management

In this chapter, we will discuss the stock-management aspects of material stored in warehouse management locations. Material that is stored in SAP WM-managed locations requires additional data entry to exploit the functionality of the warehouse. A material that is stored only in a storage location and not in a warehouse will not require information on the material master other than that relating to the storage location.

A material that will be stored in a warehouse will need the material master to be extended for the specific warehouses and storage types that it will be stored in. We may need to enter hazardous-material information in the warehouse section of the material master, if the material can be hazardous.

This chapter covers stock management in detail, as it relates to SAP WM.

3.1   Warehouse Management Data in the Material Master

Each material that is stored in a warehouse-managed storage location needs to have that information entered in the warehouse management area of the material master. Without that data, the material cannot be stored in a storage bin in the warehouse.

> **Note**
>
> The material master screens and fields we are about to discuss relate to SAP ECC 6.0. Please be aware that other versions of SAP may have a different number of screens for Warehouse Management and different fields may be displayed.

Let's now take an in-depth look at the material master, starting with its creation.

3.1.1 Creating the Material Master

When a material is created in SAP, the Warehouse Management transaction should be used: Transaction MM01. This can be found using the SAP menu navigation path: **SAP • Logistics • Logistics Execution • Warehouse Management • Master Data • Material • Create**.

We can create the material with SAP automatically assigning the next available material number, based on the internal number ranges configured in the IMG: Transaction MMNR. The material can also be created with the material number provided for data entry. The Data Governance (DP) team would maintain external numbering.

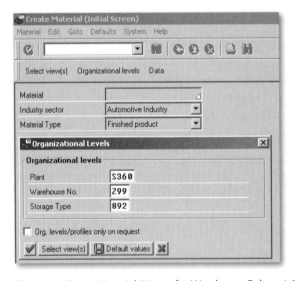

Figure 3.1 Create Material Master for Warehouse-Relevant Material: Transaction MM01

Figure 3.1 shows the initial screen for entering a material master requires the entry of an industry sector and a **Material Type**.

Industry Sector

You must assign the industry sector for each Material Master record added. In general, SAP customers use just one industry sector for all their Material Master records, but this is not mandatory.

To configure the industry sectors, use Transaction OMS3 or the menu navigation path: **IMG · Logistics — General · Material Master · Field Selection · Define Industry Sectors and Industry Sector-Specific Screen Selection**.

The ECC 6.0 SAP system has a number of pre-defined industry sectors, including:

► Pharmaceutical industry

► Chemical industry

► Mechanical engineering

► Automotive industry

Defining a new industry sector requires the choice of a single character for the industry sector and a description. The new industry sector must be linked to a field reference. This field reference is defined in Transaction OMS9 or via the navigation path: **IMG · Logistics — General · Material Master · Field Selection · Maintain Field Selection for Data Screens**

The field reference comprises a list of material master fields and determines whether the individual field is Hidden, Displayed, Optional Entry, or Required Entry. You should consider carefully when configuring a new field reference.

Note

If materials that are pharmaceuticals are entered into the material master, it may be necessary for those materials to have the EAN (European Article Numbering) category entered. In the configuration, you would need to make the field mandatory for pharmaceuticals, but not for other industries.

Material Type

A material type is defined as a group of materials with similar attributes. The material type enables management of different materials in a uniform manner. SAP is delivered with a number of standard material types, which we will describe here.

► **CONT — KANBAN Container**
This material type is delivered by SAP for creating kanban containers. These materials only have the basic data view.

► **DIEN — Services**
Services are either internally supplied or externally supplied by a vendor. Service material master records will not have storage information. The

services can involve activities such as consulting, garbage collection, or legal services.

▶ **ERSA — Spare Parts**
Spare parts are materials used for equipment maintenance in the plant. The material is purchased and stored like any other purchased item, but a spare part is not sold and therefore does not contain sales information. If a maintenance item is sold, this should use a different material type, such as a trading good.

▶ **FERT — Finished Good**
A finished good is a material that has been manufactured by some form of production from items such as raw materials. The finished good is not purchased, so it does not contain any purchasing information.

▶ **FHMI — Production Resources/Tools (PRTs)**
PRTs are purchased and used by the plant maintenance department. This material type is assigned to items used in the maintenance of plant equipment, such as test machines, drill bits, or calibrating tools. The material type for PRTs does not contain sales information, because the PRTs are not purchased to sell. In addition, PRTs are only managed on a quantity basis.

▶ **HALB — Semi-Finished Goods**
Semi-finished products are often purchased and then completed and sold as finished goods. The semi-finished products could come from another part of the company or from a vendor. The semi-finished material type allows for purchasing and work scheduling, but not for sales.

▶ **HAWA — Trading Goods**
Trading goods are generally materials purchased from vendors and sold. This type of material type only allows purchasing and sales information, as no internal operations are carried out on these materials.

▶ **HERS — Manufacturer Parts**
Manufacturer parts are materials that can be supplied by different vendors who use different part numbers to identify the material.

▶ **HIBE — Operating Supplies**
Operating supplies are vendor-purchased and used in the production process. This HIBE material type can contain purchasing data, but not sales information. This type of product includes lubricants, compressed air, or solder.

▶ **IBAU — Maintenance Assembly**
Maintenance assembly is not an individual object but a set of logical elements to separate technical objects into clearly defined units for plant

maintenance. For example, a car can be a technical object; the engine, transmission, axles, etc., are the maintenance assemblies. An IBAU material type contains basic data and classification data.

▶ **KMAT — Configurable Material**
Configurable materials form the basis for variant configuration. The KMAT material type is used for all variant-configuration materials. A material of this type can have variables that are determined by the user during the sales process. For example, automotive equipment may have variable attributes that each car manufacturer needs to be different for each car, such as length of chain, or height of belt.

▶ **LEER — Empties**
Empties are materials consisting of returnable transport packaging and can be subject to a nominal deposit fee paid to the owner of the pallet by the company renting them. Empties can be made from several materials, grouped together in a bill of material assigned to a finished material. An example of an empty can be a crate, drum, bottle, or pallet.

▶ **LEIH — Returnable Packaging**
Reusable packaging material is used to pack finished goods to send to the customer. When the finished good is unpacked, the customer is obliged to return the returnable packaging material to the vendor.

▶ **NLAG — Non-Stock Material**
The non-stock material type is used for materials that are not held in stock and not inventoried. These materials can be called consumables and include maintenance gloves, safety glasses, or grease. Items like these are purchased when needed.

▶ **PIPE — Pipeline Material**
The pipeline material type is assigned to materials that are brought into the production facility by pipeline. Materials like this are not planned for because they are always at hand. This material type is used, for example, for oil, water, electricity, or natural gas.

▶ **ROH — Raw Materials**
Raw material is purchased material that is fed into the production process and may result in a finished good. There is no sales data for a raw material, as it is not sold. If the company wanted to classify a material that would normally be treated as a raw material, then it should be classified as a trading good.

▶ **UNBW — Non-Valuated Material**
The non-valuated material type is similar to the NLAG (non-stock mate-

rial), except that the non-valuated material is held by quantity and not by value. This is often seen in plant maintenance, where there are materials that are extremely important to the plant equipment but of little or no other value. Therefore the plant-maintenance department will monitor inventory to allow for planned purchases.

▶ **VERP — Packaging Material**
Unlike LEER (empties), the packaging material type applies to materials that are packaging but that are free of charge to the customer in the delivery process. This does not mean that the packaging material has no value; often, the packaging material has a value and a physical inventory is recorded.

▶ **WETT — Competitive Products**
The sales department uses this material type to monitor competitors' goods. The material type is used to identify these types of products. Only basic data is held for these materials.

If one of the standard material types is not appropriate for the SAP client, then a new material type can be configured in the Transaction OMS2 using the navigation path: **IMG • Logistics — General • Material Master • Basic Settings • Material Types • Define Attributes for Material Type**.

We create a new material type by selecting an existing material type and copying to a new one. Copying from an existing material type reduces the amount of configuration required. The four-character material type should always start with a Z for a user-defined material type.

Organizational Levels

Any material that is to be used in the warehouse must have the correct organizational level data entered. For warehouse materials, these are Plant, Warehouse Number, and Storage Type. Once this data is entered, the material master record can be created and the correct level of data expected.

3.1.2 Entering Data into Warehouse Management Screens

In the ECC 6.0 version of SAP, there are two Warehouse Management data-entry screens for the material master. In other versions, there may only be one. Please use this section as a guide.

> **Note**
>
> You may not see all the data fields in this section in your version of SAP.

Other data would have been entered into SAP before data was entered into the WM screens. Basic data such as material description, unit of measure, purchasing information, etc., would have been entered.

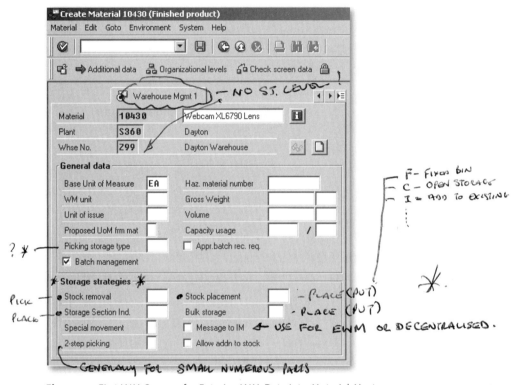

Figure 3.2 First WM Screens for Entering WM Data into Material Master: Transaction MM01

In Figure 3.2, the system has assigned the material a number, and a description and base unit of measure have been added for the new material. Other data relevant for warehouse management can be added to this screen.

Warehouse Management Unit of Measure

Like the other units of measure, this WM unit is the unit of measure defined for the material as it moves through the warehouse. For example, a material such as a can of soda may be sold in single units, but in the warehouse the material is moved in crates of 24 cans for ease of movement.

Unit of Issue

This **Unit of issue** field allows the warehouse department to define a different unit of measure for items issued from the warehouse, as an alternative to the base unit of measure.

Proposed Unit of Measure from Material

This field defines how the warehouse unit of measure was derived. The options for this field are to allow the unit of measure to be the base unit of measure from the material, where this field is left blank. The other options are as follows:

▶ **A**
   WM unit of measure to be the same as the issue unit of measure

▶ **B**
   WM unit of measure to be the same as the ordering unit of measure

WM Unit of Measure Used in the Warehouse Picking Storage Type

The **Picking storage type** is used by planning as the storage type that will contain material used in rough-cut planning. For example, in the production planning procedure, the high level of planning — called rough-cut planning — will use the material levels from this defined storage type for creating production plans.

Batch Management

The **Batch management** indicator configures the material to allow batches to be created for the material. This indicator is found in several other screens on the material master — such as purchasing, plant/storage, and MRP — and may have been activated already. If other staff members are authorized to enter material master information, the batch-management indicator may have been set and will appear on the warehouse screen as already highlighted.

Hazardous Material Number

A **Haz. material number** can be assigned to the material at the client level. This links the material number with the hazardous-material information defined for that hazardous-material number, such as water pollutant, hazardous storage class, or warnings. The hazardous material is not defined in configuration, but in the Logistics Execution functionality. A hazardous material can be created using Transaction VM01 or via the navigation path: **SAP Menu • Logistics • Logistics Execution • Master Data • Hazardous Material • Create.**

Gross Weight

The gross weight of one unit of the material should be added to this screen, with the correct unit of measure for the weight, to ensure that any limitation on bin storage is calculated correctly.

Volume

The **Volume** and volume unit of measure of the material also are key to ensuring that the material is correctly stored in the warehouse. Any incorrect data entry on the material master can cause problems during putaway.

Stock Removal Field

The **Stock removal** field enables users to enter the storage-type indicator that defines the sequence in which storage types are searched in order to pick the material in the warehouse. The storage type indicator can be defined in Transaction OMLY. The menu navigation path is: **IMG • Logistics Execution • Warehouse Management • Strategies • Activate Storage Type Search.**

Storage Section Indicator — STOCK PLACEMENT.

The storage-section search is a more specific strategy for stock placement, as it defines one level below the storage-type search for stock placement. The storage section indicator (**Storage Section ind.**) must be defined for each warehouse and storage type. The strategy allows up to 10 storage sections to be defined in sequence for the placement strategy. The configuration can be found in Transaction OMLZ or the navigation path: **IMG • Logistics Execution • Warehouse Management • Strategies • Activate Storage Section Search.**

Special Movement Indicator

The **Special movement** indicator allows the material to be identified as requiring a special goods movement. The indicator is configured in SAP WM to allow special processing for a group of materials. The configuration is found using the navigation path: **IMG • Logistics Execution • Warehouse Management • Master Data • Material • Define Special Movement Indicators.**

Once the special-movement indicator has been defined, it can be used in the LE-WM interface to inventory management, where the configuration determines the warehouse-management movement type. The special-movement indicator can allow certain materials assigned with that indicator to behave differently during goods movements. The configuration for the warehouse goods movements can be found using the navigation path: **IMG • Logistics Execution • Warehouse Management • Interfaces • Inventory Management • Define Movement Types.**

Two-Step Picking

In Warehouse Management, one can choose between one-step and two-step picking for materials. If the materials are large and bulky, one-step removal is optimal. However, if the materials to be picked are small and numerous, then one-step picking may not be an efficient use of warehouse resources.

Therefore, two-step picking is used to minimize workload. The two-step process defines an interim storage type (normally 200) to which items are picked and transferred; from there, the final pick takes place. The configuration for two-step picking is found using the navigation path: **IMG • Logistics Execution • Warehouse Management • Interfaces • Shipping • Define 2-Step Picking.**

Stock Placement Field

The **Stock placement** field acts in a manner similar to the stock removal field, except that the strategy defined in the storage type search is for a placement strategy rather than a removal strategy.

Bulk Storage Indicator

Within the placement strategies, it is possible to define how bulk materials should be placed in stock. The **Bulk storage** indicator can be used if the bulk-storage placement strategy has been activated in WM. The bulk storage indicator can indicate height or width of a particular storage type. The configuration can be found in Transaction OMM4 or via the navigation path: **IMG • Logistics Execution • Warehouse Management • Strategies • Putaway Strategies • Define Strategy for Bulk Storage.**

Message to Inventory Management

The **Message to IM** field is used if the warehouse management system is decentralized. If the indicator is set, it allows the warehouse management information for this material to be sent to inventory management immediately.

> **Tip**
>
> If Extended Warehouse Management (EWM) is used by your company on a separate server, then the communication between the regular SAP system and EWM may require that this indicator be set.

Allow Addition to Stock

Setting the **Allow addn to stock** indicator allows the sytem to add material to the existing stock of the same material in the same storage bin. This is only true if the characteristics of the two quantities of material are the same. If the storage type table does not allow additions to existing stock for this storage type, the indicator is redundant.

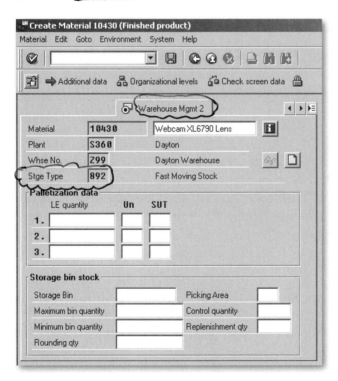

Figure 3.3 Second WM Screen for Entering WM data into Material Master: Transaction MM01

Figure 3.3 shows the second screen for WM data entry for a material. The organizational level for this screen is the storage-type level. The data on this screen relates to the storage type displayed.

Palletization Data

Palletization is used in storage-unit handling within the WM module. The palletization process uses pallets to store and move material in the warehouse. The palletization data determines how the material should be entered into stock. It may be possible to place the material into storage in different ways depending on what storage unit type is being used.

Loading Equipment Quantity

The loading equipment quantity, (**LE quantity**), entered here is the amount of material to be placed on to the storage unit type. For example, if the quantity was to be loaded on a standard pallet — which is a storage unit type — the quantity may be 24.

Unit of Measure

The field **Un** is the unit of measure for the loading equipment quantity, entered in the previous field. For example, the quantity may be 24, and the unit of measure could be EA, for each.

Storage Unit Type

The storage unit type (**SUT**) describes how the material is stored in the storage bin. For instance, some bins may not accommodate a full pallet due to height restrictions, but a half-pallet may fit. Therefore, the warehouse can define a storage unit type that defines a half pallet and the quantity of the material that can fit on that half pallet.

Suppose that 30 boxes of a material are equivalent to one half pallet. The storage unit type is configured in the IMG and has to be activated in each warehouse before it can be used. The storage unit type for each plant is defined. The configuration can be made using the navigation path: **IMG · Logistics Execution · Warehouse Management · Master Data · Material · Define Storage Unit Types.**

Storage Bin

The storage bin is the lowest level of storage defined in the warehouse. This field allows the warehouse user to enter a storage bin that this material will be added to for the plant/storage type combination. Selecting the **F4** function key makes it possible to display the empty storage bins.

Maximum Bin Quantity

This value can be entered to define the maximum quantity of a material that can be entered into any storage bin defined in the storage type. The quantity is defined in the base unit of measure, not the WM unit of measure. For example, the bin quantity may be 300 units of material, but this may be equivalent to a partial quantity in WM units — i.e., 7.45 — so the base unit of measure is used for capacity calculations.

Minimum Bin Quantity

This field allows the warehouse users to define a minimum quantity that can be stored in the bin locations for this storage type. This makes efficient use of storage bins. For example, if the material is small, the maximum bin quantity is high, and no minimum quantity is set. As a result, there could be many bins containing small amounts of stock. Entering a minimum bin quantity allows the bin to be used efficiently and minimizes picking. Like the other quantities, the minimum bin quantity is recorded in the base quantity unit.

Rounding Quantity

This quantity is used if the material is subject to the quantity-dependent picking strategy. The rounding quantity is the figure that the picking quantities are rounded down to for this material/storage type combination. This quantity is also defined in the base unit of measure.

Picking Area

A picking area is a group of warehouse management storage bins that are used for picking. The picking area is similar to the definition of storage section. The picking area can be configured using the navigation path: **IMG • Logistics Execution • Warehouse Management • Master Data • Define Picking Areas.**

Control Quantity

The control quantity can be entered to define for a particular storage type the amount of material that reaches the level where stock removal can take place. Similar to the maximum bin quantity, this control quantity is in the material base unit of measure.

Replenishment Quantity

The replenishment quantity is entered to define the quantity that should be placed in the storage bin. Similar to other quantities, the replenishment quantity is recorded in the base quantity unit of measure.

This section of Chapter 3 has discussed the warehouse-management data found in the material master record for a material. In the next section, we shall go on to discuss the types of stock that are found in the warehouse.

3.2 Types of Warehouse Stock

The warehouse contains different types of stock: available, unavailable, etc. There are also special stocks, such as Project Stock and Consignment Stock, which need to be managed separately from other stock. In this section, we shall discuss the different types of stock found in the warehouse.

3.2.1 Stock Categories

While the warehouse staff can physically see the stock in the storage bins, the WM system determines that the stock has a particular category that determines what can happen to it.

Available Stock

This is unrestricted stock. It is not subject to any restrictions on its use. The material can be picked, put away, and transferred between bins. Figure 3.4 displays a detail screen from the warehouse stock overview — Transaction LS26 — and shows the available stock for a material in a warehouse. Transaction LS26 can be found using the SAP navigation path: **SAP Menu • Logistics • Logistics Execution • Master Data • Material • Stock • Stock Overview.**

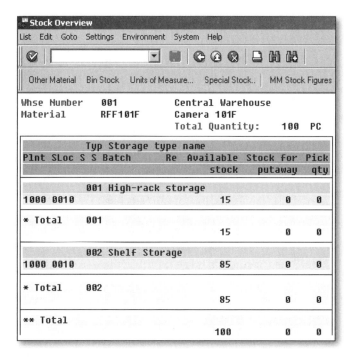

Figure 3.4 Detail Screen from the Warehouse Stock Overview: Transaction LS26

The material illustrated in Figure 3.4 is in two storage types, which are:

▶ High-rack storage

▶ Shelf storage

All the material is in available stock.

Inspection Stock

This stock carries the stock category **Q** to indicate that it is undergoing quality inspection. Stock in quality inspection has been valuated but does not count as unrestricted-use stock.

The inspection data in the Quality Management (QM) view of the material master determines whether a percentage of stock is to be designated as inspection stock when it is received in the warehouse. After the stock has been inspected and a usage decision has been made, the warehouse user can make a transfer posting in Inventory Management and subsequent Posting Change in WM to remove the category **Q** to convert it back to available stock.

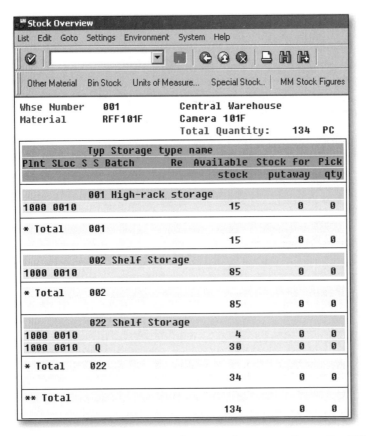

Figure 3.5 Detail Screen from Warehouse Stock Overview: Transaction LS26

In Figure 3.5, you can see there has been a goods receipt of material into the storage location and it has been moved to the shelf storage, storage type **022**. Some of the material has been put on a quality inspection hold and some has not. Figure 3.5 displays the stock overview screen of Transaction LS26, which shows that the material in quality has a **Q** indicator on the detail line. Those materials not in quality do not have this indicator

Blocked Stock

When goods arrive at the loading dock damaged or unusable, inventory management provides a function that allows the goods receipt of material to be treated as blocked stock. This stock is displayed in WM with a stock category of **S**. This stock is processed in exactly the same manner as inspection stock.

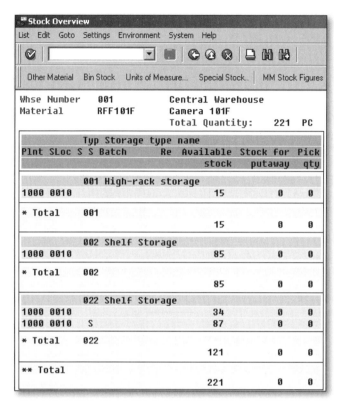

Figure 3.6 Detail Screen from Warehouse Stock Overview: Transaction LS26 (Material Designated as Blocked Stock)

The screen displayed in Figure 3.6, shows that there has been a goods receipt of material into the storage location, and it has been moved to the shelf storage, storage type **022**. This material has been into blocked stock. Figure 3.6 displays the stock overview screen of Transaction LS26, which shows that the blocked material has the **S** indicator on the detail line.

Blocked Stock Returns

When goods are returned from the customer to the warehouse, they are received using the inventory management movement type 451. In the warehouse-management stock overview report LS26, the stock is shown with a stock category of **R**. This stock is not valuated and it should not be considered to be available stock. Therefore, it is very important to ensure that this material is kept separate from the available material. Many companies maintain a special area for customer returns or ensure that returns are labeled clearly to prevent the stock from being used.

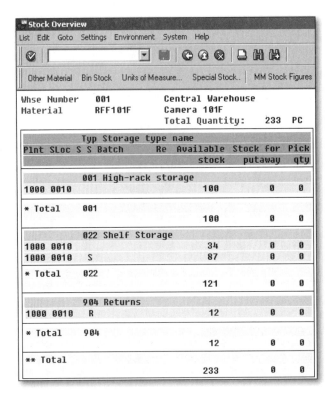

Figure 3.7 Detail Screen from Warehouse Stock Overview: Transaction LS26

In Figure 3.7, you can see that there has been a good receipt for a customer return of material into the storage location, and it has been automatically been assigned to storage type 904 for returns. Figure 3.7 displays the stock overview screen of report LS26, which shows that the material in returns has the **R** indicator on the detail line.

3.2.2 Status of Warehouse Stock

As goods arrive at the warehouse, they are moved from the arriving trailers on the loading dock or from the production area to an area where they are officially received. This is usually called the goods receipt area (GR-Area) and is either near the receiving dock or close to the end of the production line. Once the material has arrived and is received, it then is transferred using a transfer order to another storage area within the warehouse.

When the transfer orders are created, they can be confirmed or not confirmed at that time. If they are not confirmed, a period of time will elapse between the creation of transfer orders and the movement of material to the final storage bin. The stock that has not been moved thus has two availability statuses: material to be picked and material to be placed. Using the warehouse stock overview Transaction LS26, the system will display the following three headers.

Available Stock

This header defines the total quantity of material quants stored in the warehouse, not including quantities for planned putaway or picks. The display of materials in a bin also shows the total quantity in each storage bin.

Stock for Putaway

This header defines the total material intended for putaway that currently is in non-confirmed transfer orders; e.g., transfer of material from the goods receipt area to available stock. The amount can be seen in Figure 3.8 for storage type **002**.

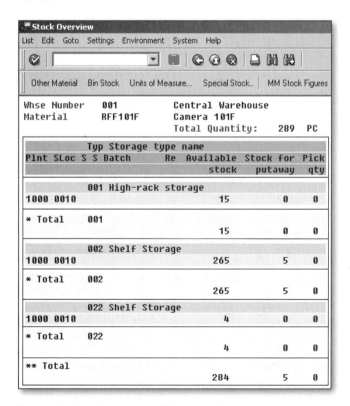

Figure 3.8 Detail Screen from Warehouse Stock Overview: Transaction, LS26 (Material in Stock for Putaway Column)

Pick Quantity

The field **Pick Qty**, defines the total material for picking that is currently in non-confirmed transfer orders; e.g., transfer of material from the available stock area to the shipping area. The pick-quantity amount can be seen in Figure 3.9 for storage type **001**.

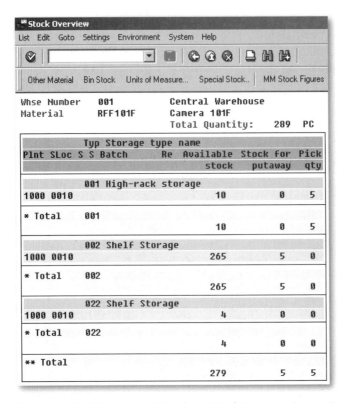

Figure 3.9 Detail Screen from Warehouse Stock Overview: Transaction LS26 (Material in Pick Quantity Column)

3.2.3 Special Stock

Special stock is material that is managed separately from regular stock. These materials are processed differently because they may be owned by a third-party or be project stock.

Each category of special stock has its own indicator, which allows it to be identified on warehouse stock reports. If the special stock is assigned during goods movement transactions, these are shown on the warehouse management stock screens — e.g., Transaction LX03 — and used in warehouse movement processing.

Sales Order Stock

Individual customer stock is managed using a special stock number and the special stock indicator **E**. The special stock number is 16 characters long and is a combination of the sales order number, which has 10 characters, and the sales order item, which has six characters.

When the system makes inventory movement to goods-receipt a material into a storage location that has a special stock indicator, **E**, the material is subsequently goods-receipted into an interim storage type in the warehouse. From there, the material is moved via a transfer order to a storage location in the warehouse. Transaction LX03 — Bin Status Report — shows the quant in a storage bin with the special stock indicator and the special stock number.

You can find Transaction LX03 using the SAP navigation path: **SAP Menu • Logistics • Logistics Execution • Master Data • Storage Bin • Evaluations • Bin Status Report**.

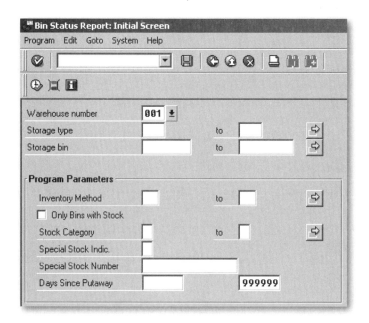

Figure 3.10 Initial Screen for Bin Status Report: Transaction LX03

Figure 3.10 shows the initial selection screen for Transaction LX03. Users can select the warehouse number, storage type, and storage-bin combination. They also can use the inventory method, special stock indicator, and other criteria to narrow the selection.

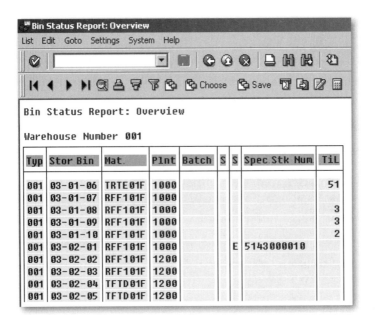

Figure 3.11 Results Screen for Bin Status Report:Transaction LX03 (Sales Order Stock with Indicator E)

Figure 3.11 shows the sales order stock with indicator **E** and the special stock number, derived from the sales-order number and the sales-order item number.

Consignment Stock

Consignment stock is material owned by a vendor but stored at a customer's premises. It is used by the customer in production orders or transferred to the customer's stock, at which time ownership of the material transfers from the vendor to the customer.

The system identifies consignment material in the customer's warehouse by using a special stock indicator, **K**. This can be seen in the Bin Status Report (Transaction LX03). The special stock number for the vendor's consignment stock is the same as the vendor number.

The vendor's consignment stock is goods-receipted into the warehouse using inventory management transactions for goods receipt; e.g., Transaction MB1C. Figure 3.12 shows the vendor consignment stock in storage bin 03–01–11. The system used vendor number **1000** for the special stock number.

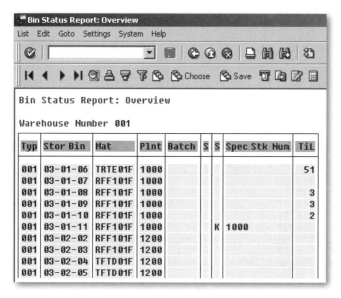

Figure 3.12 Results Screen for Bin Status Report: Transaction LX03 (Vendor Consignment Stock with Indicator K)

Project Stock

Project stock is material that is being stored in the warehouse for a project per a Work Breakdown Structure (WBS) element, defined in the Project Systems module (SAP-PS). The material is moved into a storage location by an inventory management transaction, such as MB1C. It can be seen on the Bin Status Report, identified by the special stock indicator **Q**.

The project stock is identified in the customer's warehouse by using a special stock indicator, **Q**. This can be seen in the Bin Status Report (Transaction LX03). Figure 3.13 shows the project stock in storage bin 05–02–01. The special stock number for the project stock is the same as the WBS element that was entered in the Inventory Movement transaction for the goods receipt.

Returnable Transport Packaging

With Returnable transport packaging (RTF), materials may be delivered to the warehouse on, or in, returnable transport packaging, such as pallets or containers. The delivered materials can be removed from the packaging or remain with the packaging in the warehouse. If the returnable packaging is not immediately returned to the vendor, it can be stored in the warehouse. The returnable materials are the property of the vendor and do not become part of the customer's valuated stock.

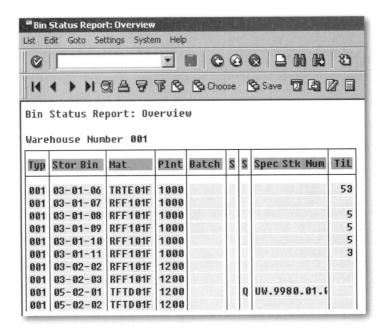

Figure 3.13 Results Screen for Bin Status Report: Transaction LX03 (Project Stock with Indicator Q)

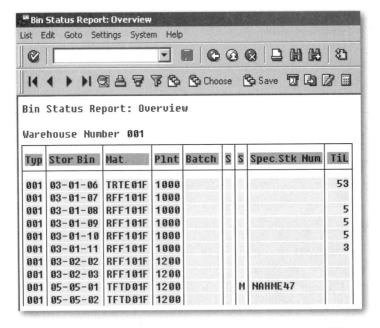

Figure 3.14 Results Screen for the Bin Status Report: Transaction LX03 (Returnable Transport Packaging with Indicator M)

The returnable transport packaging is identified in the customer's warehouse by using a special stock indicator, **M**. This can be seen in the Bin Status Report (Transaction LX03). Figure 3.14 shows the project stock in storage bin 05–05–01. The special stock number for the returnable transport packaging stock is the same as the number of the vendor that supplied the packaging material.

This section described the types of stock that can be found in the warehouse. Next, I will discuss the role of batch management in the warehouse.

3.3 Batch Management in Warehouse Management

SAP WM users can configure created materials to be batch managed. This requires that for each movement or processing of the material the quantity of material associated with that movement or process be identified by one or many unique batch numbers.

3.3.1 Batch Definition

A batch is a quantity of material grouped for various reasons. The materials often have the same characteristics and values. For instance, in the chemical industry a certain number of containers of a certain product may be considered a batch because they were produced at the same time and have the same physical and chemical characteristics. These characteristics may differ from those of another batch of material produced on the same day.

Note
The pharmaceutical industry is one sector where material batches are extremely important. Each batch of material is recorded throughout the product and distribution process. In the case of product recall, the batch number stamped on the pack or bottle of material provides the needed identification.

To understand how important batch recording has become, consider the regulations within the European Union (EU). The EU requires that each batch of pharmaceutical material imported into the EU must be accompanied with a batch certificate. This must specify the testing specifications of the product, analytical methods, and test results, statements that indicate that it conforms to current Good Manufacturing Procedures (cGMP) and signed-off by a company official.

3.3.2 Batch Level

The batch number can be determined at different levels. We need to make this determination early in any implementation project. Batches can be determined at client level, plant level, and material level.

Client Level

If the batch level is configured at the client level, the batch number can only be assigned once throughout the SAP client. One batch number will exist for one batch regardless of material or location. This poses no problem when batches are moved from plant to plant, as the batch number would not exist in the receiving plant. This is a level where, in some countries, batch numbers are unique to a company and not to a material.

Plant Level

Batch level at the plant level is the SAP default. This means that the batch is unique to a plant and material but not applicable across the company. Therefore, a batch of material at a different plant within the company could have the same batch number as another batch with different characteristics. When transferring batch material from one plant to another, the batch information is not transferred, and the batch information needs to be re-entered at the receiving plant.

Material Level

Batch level at the material level means that the batch number is unique to a material across all plants. Therefore, if a batch of material is transferred to another plant, the batch information will be adopted in the new plant without re-entering the batch information. This is because that batch number could not have been duplicated for that material in the receiving plant.

3.3.3 Batch Number Assignment

The batch-number range is predefined in SAP. The predefined range 01 is defined as 0000000001 to 9999999999. The number-range object for this is BATCH_CLT. This can be changed in configuration using Transaction OMAD or the menu navigation path: **IMG · Logistics — General · Batch Management · Batch Number Assignment · Maintain Internal Batch Number Assignment Range.**

Two configuration steps can be carried out if the customer requires batch number assignment:

1. Assign the batch number internally using the internal number range. To configure this use Transaction OMCZ or menu navigation path: **IMG • Logistics — General • Batch Management • Batch Number Assignment • Activate Internal Batch Number Assignment • Activate Batch Number Assignment.**

2. Configure the system to allow the automatic numbering of batches on a goods receipt with account assignment. Use the menu navigation path: **IMG • Logistics — General • Batch Management • Batch Number Assignment • Activate Internal Batch Number Assignment • Internal Batch Number Assignment for Assigned Goods Receipt.**

3.3.4 Creating a Batch Record

The batch record can be created manually through the SAP menu using Transaction MSC1N. The navigation path is: **SAP Menu • Logistics • Materials Management • Material Master • Batch • Create.**

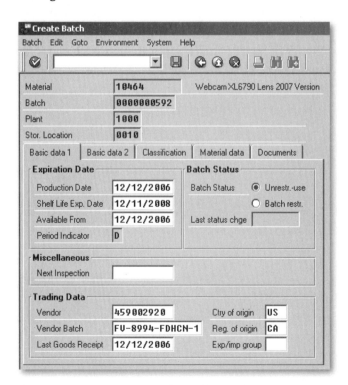

Figure 3.15 Initial Entry Screen for Batch Record Creation: Transaction MSC1N

To create a batch number for a material, a number key fields need to be entered such as material number, plant number, and storage location. Other information can be used to describe the batch, such as production date, vendor batch number, last goods receipt date, etc., as shown in Figure 3.15. The batch number assignment can be configured in the number range transactions in IMG, as described in Section 3.3.3.

Production Date

The WM user can enter the date when the batch was produced into this field. In some industries, this field is also used as the date the material was tested or re-tested. If a material is found to be still in tolerance after the shelf-life date has expired, the material can be re-tested, and the date of the re-test is entered into this field, in addition to a new shelf-life expiration date. Check with your clients to see how they need to use this field.

Shelf-Life Expiration Date

This shelf-life expiration date (SLED) is the date on which the shelf life of this batch will expire. The shelf-life of a product can vary between plants. The expiration date can be used in the sales process, when customers have set a requirement on the number of days of shelf-life remaining for a batch to be acceptable. Some companies use this field to indicate the date on which a batch needs to be re-tested.

Available From

This field indicates when the batch will be available. For example, if a material needs to remain in the quality inspection process for a certain number of days after testing, then the quality-assurance department can enter a date in order to inform other departments when to expect the batch to be available.

Batch Status

The batch-status indicator allows the batch to be classified as having restricted or unrestricted use. If the unrestricted indicator is set, then no restriction is placed on the batch's use. If the restricted indicator is set, the batch is treated like blocked stock in planning, but can be selected by batch determination if the search includes restricted-use batches.

The batch status can be set to restricted from unrestricted by changing the indicator in the batch record. The system will post a material document that will show the movement of stock between the two statuses.

Next Inspection

This date field enables the quality-assurance department to enter the date of the next quality inspection of the batch, if applicable to this material.

Vendor Batch

If the material is purchased, then we can add the batch number assigned by the vendor to the batch record. Notation of the vendor batch number is important to any product recall procedure. The vendor batch number field allows a 15-character string to be entered.

3.3.5   Batch Determination

Batch determination in SAP WM uses strategy types, search strategies, and search procedures in order for a batch to be identified in the WM transaction.

The batch-determination process uses the same type of selection protocol as found in purchasing pricing conditions; that is, it uses condition tables and access sequences.

Condition Tables

The batch determination condition table consists of fields that are selected and records that are created to assign values to those fields. The WM condition tables can be created in Transaction OMK4, which you can find using the IMG navigation path: **IMG • Logistics — General • Batch Management • Batch Determination and Batch Check • Condition Tables • Define Warehouse Management Condition Tables.**

Figure 3.16 shows the field where a new condition table can be entered. You also can create a new table by copying the conditions from an existing condition table. The search for condition tables has returned five tables that can be copied.

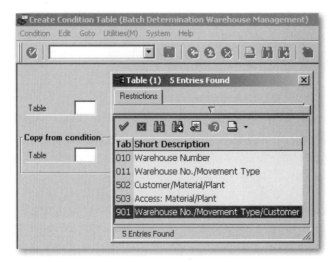

Figure 3.16 Create Warehouse Management Condition Tables for Batch Determination: Transaction OMK4

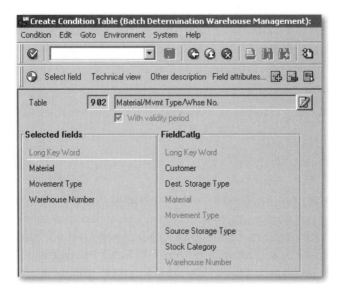

Figure 3.17 Assign Selected Fields for New Warehouse Management Condition Table: Transaction OMK4

If the condition table is not copied from an existing table, you can assign the fields to the condition table from the field catalog. Figure 3.17 shows that for the new WM condition table, three fields have been selected. Once the condition table is complete, it should then be generated, using header menu and then selecting **Condition • Generate** or by using the **Shift + F4** function key.

Access Sequence

For each batch strategy type, there is a batch determination access sequence. This allows the batch strategy type to access the condition tables in the correct sequence. The strategy type is described in the next section. Before configuring the access sequences, note carefully that these access sequences are cross-client. Any changes in one client will affect all clients.

Configuration can be completed using the IMG navigation path: **IMG • Logistics — General • Batch Management • Batch Determination and Batch Check • Access Sequences • Define Warehouse Management Access Sequences**.

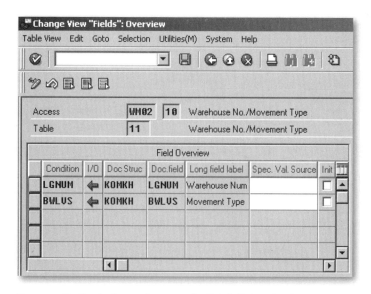

Figure 3.18 Create Access Sequence for Batch Determination

Figure 3.18 shows the access sequence WM02. The access sequence uses the condition table 11 and the sequence of the access is defined by the two condition fields. If a new access sequence needs to be created, it should begin with the character **Z** to indicate a customer-defined access sequence.

Batch Strategy Type

The batch strategy type is the specification that tells the system what type of criteria to use during the batch determination process. You can configure batch strategy type using the navigation path: **IMG • Logistics — General • Batch Management • Batch Determination and Batch Check • Strategy Types • Define Warehouse Management Strategy Types**.

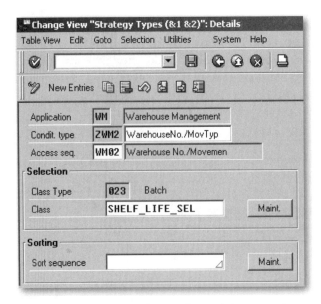

Figure 3.19 Create a Strategy Type for Batch Determination

Figure 3.19 shows the strategy type for WM02. The strategy type is defined by a class and its relevant characteristics that define how the strategy works. We define a strategy type so that different scenarios can be used when finding batches. In Figure 3.19, the strategy type is configured with a class, SHELF_LIFE_SEL, which will search for batches in the warehouse that have a certain shelf-life. Figure 3.20 shows the class and the characteristics that are defined.

Other strategy types may include a strategy to find batches in the warehouse with a certain shelf-life date, or a strategy to find batches with a certain production date. The classification data, class, and characteristics can be defined for the required strategy.

The sorting function of the strategy type let's define how batches are sorted when they are located. For example, if the strategy type was to locate certain batches by goods-receipt date, then the sort sequence could define how these are displayed. They could be shown either ascending or descending, based on the characteristic criteria based in the sort rule.

You can define the sort sequence in the IMG using Transaction CU71 or following the navigation path: **IMG • Logistics — General • Batch Management • Batch Determination and Batch Check • Batch Search Procedure Allocation and Check Activation • Define Sort Rules.**

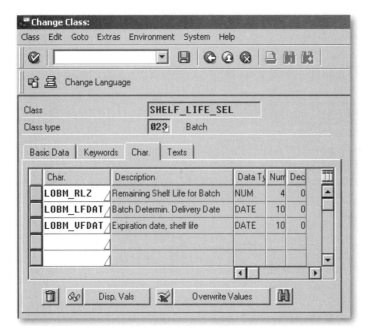

Figure 3.20 Classification Data for Strategy Type for Batch Determination

In Figure 3.20, the classification data, class, and characteristics that are defined for the batch strategy type show that there are three characteristics. Therefore the strategy for selecting batches in the warehouse can be defined accurately based on three criteria, which can be seen in Figure 3.20 and are named below:

▸ Remaining Shelf-Life for Batch

▸ Batch Determined Delivery Date

▸ Expiration Date, Shelf-life

The characteristics can be given values so that the selection of the batch will fall into the range defined by these three characteristics. Batch strategy types can have classes with more or fewer characteristics, to increase or decrease the specificity of the search for batches.

Batch Search Procedure

We define the batch search procedure to allow the combination of a single or a group of batch strategy types. The procedure is then allocated to a warehouse or material movement where it is used to determine the correct batches for the selection.

The batch search procedure can be configured using Transaction OMKV or by following the menu navigation path: **IMG • Logistics — General • Batch Management • Batch Determination and Batch Check • Batch Search Procedure Definition • Define Warehouse Management Search Procedure**.

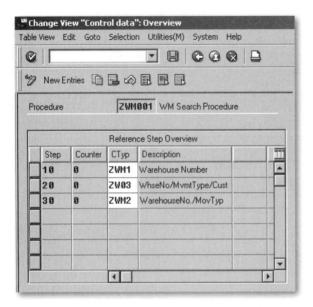

Figure 3.21 Batch Search Procedure with Associated Strategy Types: Transaction OMKV

Figure 3.21 shows the batch search procedure ZWM001, which is uses the three batch strategy types (**Ctyp**), **ZWM1**, **ZW03**, and **ZWM2** to find relevant batches based upon the criteria within those strategy types. A number of search procedures may be required, depending on the batches we need to locate within the warehouse.

Example

When material is removed from a warehouse that has racks, the search procedure may require the shelf-life to be the determining factor, while determining batches for outside warehouses may require that the batch be determined by goods-receipt date. The search procedure can be assigned to various warehouses or warehouse/movement type combination, based on the needs of the supply chain.

Batch Search Procedure Assignment

After creating the warehouse search procedures, we can assign them for batch determination based on the warehouse or the warehouse/movement type combination.

The batch search procedure assignment can be configured using Transaction OMK1 or by following the navigation path: **IMG • Logistics — General • Batch Management • Batch Determination and Batch Check • Batch Search Procedure Allocation and Check Activation • Assign WM Search Procedure**.

The transaction allows assignment of the batch search procedure to either a warehouse or a warehouse/movement type combination. Figure 3.22 shows the assignment for a warehouse.

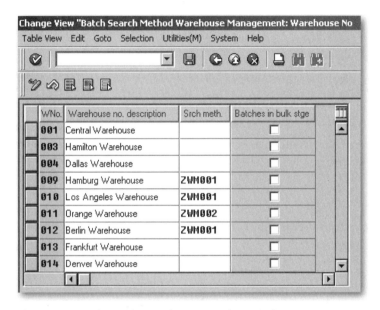

Figure 3.22 Batch Search Procedure Assigned to Warehouse: Transaction OMK1

The batch search procedure can be assigned to a warehouse, as shown in Figure 3.22. The procedure will determine how batches are determined for the warehouse.

The indicator, **Batches in bulk stge** can be set if we plan to ignore search strategy for the bulk area storage. In bulk area storage, the batches are mixed and the strategy will not pick out individual batches. By setting this indicator, we ensure that the total stock is included in the batch determination, even though it is batch-neutral.

Figure 3.23 shows the assignment of the batch search procedure to the warehouse/movement type combination. With this part of the transaction, the specific movement type that is used at the warehouse is given a batch search procedure.

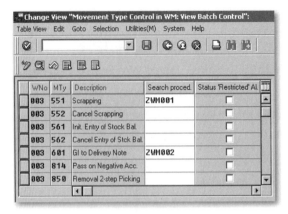

Figure 3.23 Batch Search Procedure Assigned to Warehouse/Movement Type Combination: Transaction OMK1

The indicator shown in Figure 3.23, **Status "Restricted" AI.**, can be set if the batches defined as blocked need to be included in the batch determination in the warehouse. Normally, restricted batches are not included in batch determination.

More detail on the assignment of the batch search procedure assigned to the warehouse/movement type combination can be seen in Figure 3.24. This can be found by using the header menu and selecting **Goto • Details** or by using the function keys **Ctrl + Shift+ F2**.

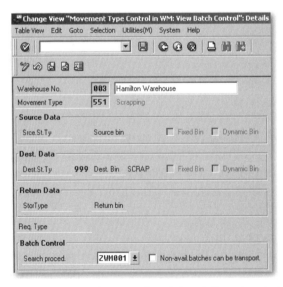

Figure 3.24 Detail Screen of Batch Search Procedure Assigned to Warehouse/Movement Type Combination: Transaction OMK1.

This section described the functionality of the batch and functionality such as batch search procedures in the warehouse. Next, we shall discuss the important topic of shelf-life functionality.

3.4   Shelf-life Functionality

In many industries, such as the grocery and pharmaceutical industries, the shelf-life of materials is a very important characteristic, both for sales and for production. It is important that the warehouse management review shelf-life expiration date (SLED) to ensure material does not expire and have to be scrapped.

3.4.1   Shelf-Life and the Material Master

When material is created using the material master record Transaction, MM01, information regarding the shelf-life characteristics can be entered on the plant storage view.

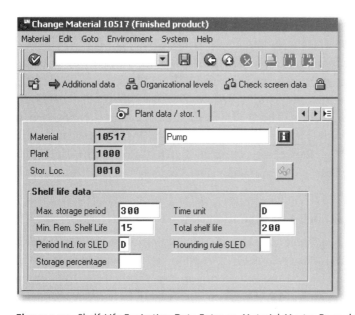

Figure 3.25 Shelf-Life Expiration Data Entry on Material Master Record Plant Data Screen

Figure 3.25 shows the shelf-life data that can be added to the material. This data is used in calculating the shelf-life expiration date in batch determination. Let's take a quick look at the fields in this figure next.

Max Storage Period

This field is for information only and does not have any functionality. Users can define the maximum storage period for a material before it expires. This field can be used for reporting.

Time Unit

This is the unit of measure of the maximum storage period in days, months, and years.

Minimum Remaining Shelf-Life

The minimum-remaining shelf-life field determines whether a material can be received via goods receipt based on the remaining shelf-life of the material. If this field has the value 100 days, and the material to be goods receipted has only 80 days of shelf-life left, then the system will not accept the goods receipt. The minimum remaining shelf-life field works at the client level and is the same for the material across all plants.

Total Shelf Life

The total-shelf-life figure is at the client level and does not vary by plant. The total shelf life is the time for which the materials will be kept, from the production date to the shelf-life expiration date. The shelf-life is only checked if the expiration date check has been activated. The activation is configured at plant level or movement type level in Transaction OMJ5 or via the menu navigation path: **IMG · Logistics — General · Batch Management · Shelf Life Expiration Date (SLED) · Set Expiration Date Check**.

Period Indicator for Shelf-Life Expiration Date

This period field is defined for the shelf-life expiration date (SLED) fields used in this Material Master screen. The period can be defined as months, days, etc. The period indicator can be configured in Transaction O02K or via the menu navigation path **IMG · Logistics — General · Batch Management · Shelf Life Expiration Date (SLED) · Maintain Period Indicator**.

Rounding Rule SLED

The rounding rule allows the SLED to be rounded up to the nearest unit of the time defined in the period indicator. For example, if the period indicator is set to months, then the rounding rule either would be the first day of the month, or the last day of the month, or no change if there were no rounding rule. The rounding rule is for calculated dates rather than dates entered into the record.

3.4.2 Production Date Entry

To ensure that the shelf-life expiration date functionality will produce the correct results, it is important that the manufacturing date for a batch is entered at the time of goods receipt.

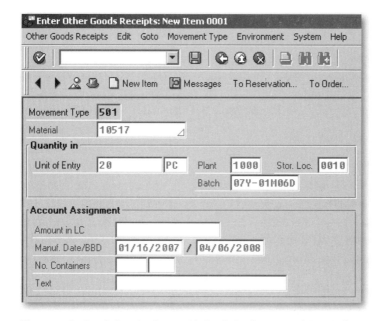

Figure 3.26 Goods Receipt Entry with Batch Production and Best-Before Dates

Figure 3.26 shows the goods receipt of a batch of material. The goods receipt requires that a manufacturing date of the batch be entered. This date is used to determine the start date for the calculation of shelf life.

3.4.3 SLED Control List

The shelf-life expiration date control list shows batches in the warehouse that are actively monitored for shelf life. The SLED control list can be run using Transaction LX27 or following the menu navigation path: **SAP • Logistics • Logistics Execution • Warehouse Management • Master Data • Material • Evaluations • SLED Control List.**

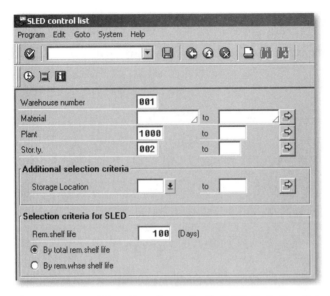

Figure 3.27 Initial Date Entry Screen for Shelf-Life Expiration Date Control List: Transaction LX27.

Remaining Shelf-Life

The remaining shelf-life field (**RemSL**) can be entered to restrict the results of the report. This field is the upper limit for the remaining shelf lives of all materials that are to be selected. It can be used in the shelf-life calculation in two ways depending on what indicator is selected. Either it can refer to the total remaining shelf-life or to the remaining shelf-life in the warehouse.

Figure 3.28 shows the shelf-life expiration date control list. The report shows the batches of product in the warehouse that is active for SLED and is within the parameters entered in Figure 3.27.

The report shows whether the batch is in exception; i.e., if the shelf-life is below the minimum stated on the material master. The remaining shelf-life is shown in column **RemSL**, as well as the expiration date, storage location, storage type, and amount of stock in the bin.

This report is provided to ensure that the warehouse management knows the stock that is soon to expire and also to inform sales management if action needs to be taken to discount the expiring stock for sale. Having expired stock in the warehouse is not a desirable situation. Because that stock takes up warehouse space with material that cannot be sold, it incurs a financial loss to the company and may create an additional cost for disposing of the expired material or reworking it.

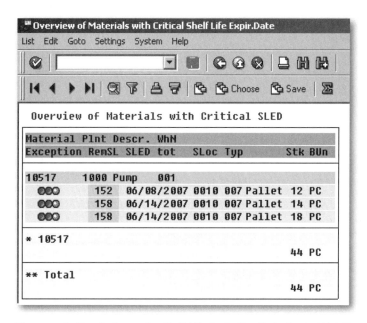

Figure 3.28 Results Screen for Shelf-Life Expiration Date Control List: Transaction LX27

3.5 Summary

In this chapter, I discussed the stock-management aspects of warehouse management. A number of subjects must be understood before entering warehouse information in the material master. It is important that the correct information be entered at the time of material creation. It is often difficult to add or change data in the material master once it released and in use. Stock categories and stock types are primarily issues for materials-management, but the warehouse consultant must understand how and why stock is categorized.

Batch management and shelf-life expiration dates (SLED) are important for the warehouse. Batch management plays an important role in many industries as does SLED. Incorrect identification of batches can be costly for the client in monetary terms and also in customer confidence. More and more products are being labeled with expiration dates so this is becoming a more important aspect of warehouse management.

In Chapter 4, I will discuss the movements that can occur in the warehouse, including transfer requirements and transfer orders.

Movements inside the warehouse determine where material goes, how it gets there, how it is stored, and how it is retrieved. The transfer requirement and the transfer order are the processes that move the material, and it is important to know how these processes work.

4   Warehouse Movements

In this chapter, I will discuss the movements that occur in the warehouse. Material moves into the warehouse, around the warehouse, and ultimately out of the warehouse. I will identify and review the mechanism of material movements and what triggers these movements. There are two different types of movements that are relevant for the warehouse. These are:

▸ Warehouse movements triggered by other SAP functionality, such as Inventory Management (IM) and shipping, that result in picking, packing, and warehouse-to-warehouse transfer.

▸ Warehouse movements internal to the warehouse, such as bin-to-bin transfers or posting changes. The goods movements inside the warehouse do not affect the total stock position, and no information is passed to the IM function.

Let us now venture deeper into this chapter, starting with movement types.

4.1   WM Movement Types

Within the WM functionality, there are goods movements that are in essence movements inside a plant that can change stock levels within the storage locations designated to that plant. The movement of stock is either inbound from a vendor, outbound to a customer, a stock transfer between plants, or an internal transfer within a plant.

4.1.1   Movement Types in Inventory Management

A movement type is a three-character field used to describe the type of material movement that needs to be performed. The movement type is used for all type of movements; receipts, issues, transfers, and reversals.

The SAP system is delivered with pre-defined movement types between 100 and 899; e.g.,movement type 201, for consuming warehouse material to a cost center. Movement types 900 and beyond can be used for customized movement types.

> **Note**
>
> You may need to change some standard movement types to accommodate warehouse processes. The standard movement type can be copied to a new movement type in the 900 range in order to be modified.

A movement type can be created with Transaction OMJJ or via the configuration navigation path: **IMG · Materials Management · Inventory Management and Physical Inventory · Movement Types · Copy, Change Movement Types.**

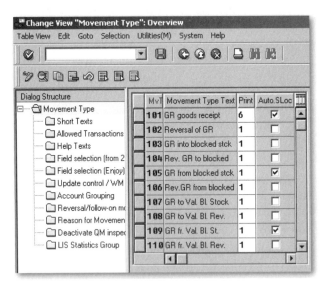

Figure 4.1 Initial screen for Configuring Inventory Management Movement Types: Transaction OMJJ

Figure 4.1 shows the initial screen of the Transaction OMJJ. The dialog structure in Figure 4.1 shows a number of configuration steps for each movement type.

The movement type is a key to the inventory-management process because it controls the updating of the quantity of the stock, determines what fields are displayed and required for entry, and also can update the account information.

When a movement type is used in IM goods movement with respect to a storage location that is warehouse-managed, a corresponding movement in the warehouse is driven by a Warehouse Management (WM) movement type. In the following subsections I will explain the connection between the IM movement types and the movement types in the warehouse.

4.1.2 WM Reference Movement Types

The IM movement type is linked to a warehouse movement type. The linkage is not direct but is made through a reference movement type, which is a key that can be assigned to an IM movement type. The same reference movement type can be associated with a number of IM movement types.

You can assign the reference movement type to the IM movement type via the configuration navigation path: **IMG • Logistics Execution • Warehouse Management • Interfaces • Inventory Management • Define Movement Types.**

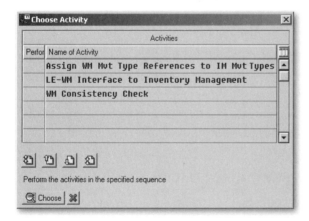

Figure 4.2 Initial Screen for Warehouse Management Movement Type Definition

Figure 4.2 shows the following three configuration steps that are defined for this transaction:

1. Add the reference movement type to the IM movement type.

2. Configure the links between warehouse management and IM.

3. Check the consistency of the configuration.

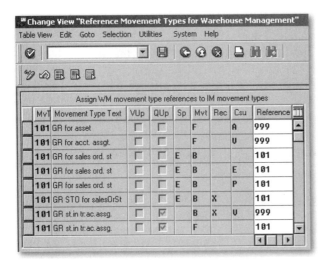

Figure 4.3 Assign Reference WM Movement Type to IM Movement Type

Figure 4.3 shows a number of IM movement types that have been assigned a reference movement type. The screen shows the IM movement type field, **Mvt**, and the WM reference movement type field, **Reference**.

Each IM movement type is unique and depends on the movement indicator, special stock indicator, and special movement indicator. Each of the combinations is assigned a reference movement type.

In Figure 4.3, only two reference movement types are noted: **101** and **999**. The reference movement type **999** indicates that for that particular IM movement type there is no corresponding WM movement type, and the IM movement has no effect on the warehouse. The reference movement type **101** is a valid reference movement type and will be linked to a WM movement type.

4.1.3 Creating Warehouse Management Movement Types

The WM movement type contains information that the system needs to determine stock placement and removal. The system is delivered with a number of predefined WM movement types. The movement type — such as 801 which represents goods receipt from production to the warehouse — contains information on what interim storage type is used, the coordinates for the interim storage bin, and control indicators for confirmations.

A WM movement type can be created via the navigation path: **IMG · Logistics Execution · Warehouse Management · Activities · Transfers · Define Movement Types**.

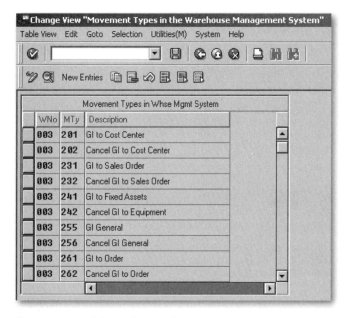

Figure 4.4 Initial Screen for Warehouse Management Movement Types

Figure 4.4 shows the initial screen for creating the WM movement types. The transaction requires that a movement type be associated with a particular warehouse. A movement type may have to function differently in different warehouses.

You can find detailed information for the warehouse/movement type combination by using the header menu and selecting **Goto • Details**. The detail screen can also be accessed using the function keys: **Ctrl + Shift + F2**.

Figure 4.5 illustrates the detailed information available concerning the WM movement type. In configurating the source, destination, and return data, you should consider a number of scenarios. I'll describe these next:

▶ If no storage type or storage bin have been specified for either the source, destination, or return fields, then the system will try to determine the storage type and bin to assist in creating a transfer order.

▶ If the storage type is defined, the system will search for a storage bin for that storage type.

▶ If the storage type and bin are entered for a movement type, then the data is transposed into the transfer order and cannot be changed in the created transfer order.

The fields shown in Figure 4.5 are described in the following subsections.

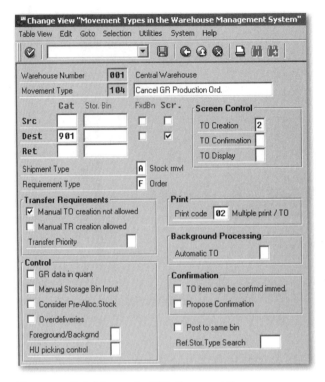

Figure 4.5 Detail Screen for WM Movement Type

Source Storage Type

This field, **Scr — Cat**, is the source storage type. This storage type is the location from which the material will be sourced for stock removal. For example, when this movement type is used for the transfer order, the transfer order processing will use this storage type as the location where the material will be sourced.

Source Storage Bin

This field, **Scr — Stor. Bin**, is the source storage bin for the source-storage type entered. So when this movement type is used, the transfer order will use this storage bin, located in the configured storage type, to indicate where the material will be sourced.

Source Fixed Bin Indicator

This indicator, **Scr — FxdBn**, identifies that a fixed storage bin is used as the interim storage bin for the relevant storage type. The fixed bin is assigned to a material for that particular storage type. It is where material is located, and is used mostly in the picking process. If this indicator is set, then the source storage bin must be left blank.

Source Dynamic Storage Bin Indicator

This field, **Scr — Scr**, is the dynamic storage-bin indicator, which when set indicates that the source storage bin is created dynamically. In a movement type where the interim bin is flagged as having a dynamic location, this signals that the bin will have the reference from the document corresponding with the movement; i.e., a cost-center or a purchase-order number.

Destination Storage Type

This field, **Dest — Cat**, is the destination storage type. This storage type is the location where the material will undergo putaway. For example, when this movement type is used for the transfer order, the transfer order processing will use this storage type as the location where the material will be moved.

Destination Storage Bin

This field, **Dest — Stor. Bn**, is the storage bin where the material will be placed for the destination storage type entered. For example, when this movement type is used for the transfer order, the transfer order processing will use this storage bin, located in the configured storage type, to indicate where the material will be moved.

Destination Fixed Bin Indicator

This field, **Dest — FxdBn**, indicates that a fixed storage bin is used as the interim storage bin for the relevant storage type. The fixed bin is assigned to a material for that particular storage type. If this indicator is set, then the destination storage bin must be left blank.

Destination Dynamic Storage Bin Indicator

If this field, **Dest-Scr**, is set then the destination storage bin will be determined dynamically. In a movement type where the interim bin is flagged as having a dynamic location, this indicates that the bin will have the reference from the document corresponding with the movement; i.e., a cost-center or a purchase-order number.

Return Storage Type

This field, **Ret-Cat**, is the return storage type used when there is a quantity left over from a complete stock removal. This is performed when the complete quantity is removed from the bin whether or not the total amount is needed. Therefore, there will be a remainder quantity that will have to be returned to stock.

Return Storage Bin

This field, **Ret — Stor. Bn**, is the return storage bin where the remaining quantity is moved if the warehouse needs a complete stock removal from the storage bin. This occurs when a quantity of material is removed from the source storage bin and sent to the destination bin, but not all the quantity is required. When this field is not configured, the remaining material will go back to the source storage bin. Where this is configured, the remainder material will go to this return storage bin. This function is used when the warhouse cannot return the material to the source storage bin because of material specifications.

Screen Control — Transfer Order Creation

This indicator can be configured to determine whether to create transfer orders using a dialog screen. There are three options:

▶ 1

Preparation screen for material putaway. This allows the amount of material to be putaway to be divided between multiple storage bins.

▶ 2

Preparation screen for material picking. This allows the total amount of the material to be picked to be searched for in the warehouse.

▶ 3

Preparation screen for each individual line item for material putaway and material picking

Screen Control — Transfer Order Confirmation

This indicator can be set either to display the amount to be confirmed for the putaway or picking or to display a screen with no input values. The options are:

▶ **1**

Produces a screen with no input values

▶ **2**

Produces a screen with putaway values for input

▶ **3**

Produces a screen with picking values for input

Screen Control — Transfer Order Display

This indicator dictates which of the standard views will be displayed in the foreground. There are three options, which I'll describe here.

▶ **1: Source Data View**

For this view, the source data, the transfer order items appear in the foreground. The source data includes the quantity to be removed from the bin and any relevant batch numbers.

▶ **2: Destination View**

For this view, the destination data is for the transfer order.

▶ **3: General View**

For this view, the system displays data about the transfer order that does not appear in other views. This includes special stock type, stock category, goods-receipt date, and confirmation date.

Shipment Type

The shipment type classifies the movement types in the warehouse, the options that can be chosen include:

▶ **A**

Stock Removal

▶ **E**

Stock Placement

▶ **U**

Posting Change

Requirement Type

The requirement type refers to the origin type; e.g., a goods receipt for a purchase order. The requirements number that also can be entered at the same time is the originating document, which can be an item such as a purchase order. Options that can be selected include:

- ▶ **A**
  Asset

- ▶ **B**
  Purchase order

- ▶ **D**
  Storage bin

- ▶ **K**
  Cost center

- ▶ **L**
  Sales document

- ▶ **V**
  Sales order

Transfer Requirements — Manual Transfer Order Creation Not Allowed

If the **Manual TO creation not allowed** indicator is set, then the transfer orders for this movement type cannot be created manually, but rather with reference to another relevant document such as a transfer requirement.

Transfer Requirements — Manual Transfer Requirement Creation Allowed

If the **Manual TR creation allowed** indicator is set, then a transfer requirement can be created manually when this movement type is used. For example, if movement type 801 — goods receipt from production — must be used, then a transfer requirement can be manually created for the movement type, providing this indicator is set.

Transfer Requirements — Transfer Priority

The **Transfer Priority** entered in the movement type determines which transfer requirements are to be processed. The smaller the transfer priority value, the higher the priority will be.

Control — Goods Receipt Data in Quant

Setting the **GR data in quant** indicator ensures that the goods-receipt date and number will be reset and automatically assigned in the quant as part of the transaction using this movement type.

Control — Manual Storage Bin Input

You need to set the **Manual Storage Bin Input** indicator if you need to manually enter the storage bins when this movement type is used. The indicator tells the system to ignore any strategy to automatically find a storage bin, so the storage bin can be entered manually.

Control — Consider Pre-Allocation Stock

If the **Consider Pre-Alloc. Stock** indicator is set, the system will check to see if the material is pre-allocated. This check will occur during the stock-putaway procedure. If the stock is pre-allocated, the system will display a message informing the user of the pre-allocation.

Control — Overdeliveries

Setting the **Overdeliveries** indicator will force the system to assign complete quants to be removed during picking. If the indicator is set and whole quants are removed, overdeliveries may occur even if the storage type does not require removal of all stock from the bin.

Control — Foreground/Background

The **Foreground/Background** indicator determines whether the system controls the transaction in the background or foreground. If the indicator is left blank, then the system will have control of the transaction. The other options include **D** for background processing and **H** for foreground processing.

Control — Handling Unit Picking Control

The **HU picking control** indicator allows definition of what happens in the system during the confirmation of a complete stock removal of handling unit. Three options can be selected, as seen here:

▶ **1**

On the confirmation screen, the issuing-handling unit is proposed as the destination storage unit during confirmation of the transfer-order item and the handling-unit copy indicator is set.

▶ **3**

On the confirmation screen, the first pick handling unit assigned to the transfer order proposed as the destination storage unit. The **HU copy** indicator is not set.

▸ **Blank**

On the confirmation screen, the first pick handling unit assigned to the transfer order is proposed as destination storage unit and the **HU copy** indicator is also set

Print Code

The **Print code** indicator entry defines the print format of the transfer order, the sort sequence, and the printer to be used. Each movement type can use a different print code.

The print code is defined in Transaction OMLV or via the navigation path: **IMG ▪ Logistics Execution ▪ Activities ▪ Define Print Control ▪ Print Code.**

Automatic Transfer Order

The **Automatic TO** indicator is used to control whether the system will automatically create a transfer order in the background for a transfer requirement or a posting change notice.

Settings for this indicator are automatically proposed when a transfer requirement or a posting change notice is created from the movement type. The transfer orders are created by batch input using the report RLAUTA10 for transfer requirements and the report RLAUTA11 for posting change notices.

This indicator can be configured using the Transaction OMKZ or via the navigation path: **IMG ▪ Logistics Execution ▪ Activities ▪ Set Up Automatic TO Creation for TRs/Posting Change Notices.**

Transfer Order Can be Confirmed Immediately

The **TO item can be confimd immed.** indicator allows the transfer order to be confirmed immediately during the transfer order creation process. The transfer order is normally confirmed when the material is moved to the destination storage bin. However, if the material is moved and the transfer order is created afterwards, this indicator allows the transfer order to be completed immediately during the creation process for this movement type.

Propose Confirmation

The **Propose Confirmation** indicator can be set when the confirmation is to be allowed during the creation of the transfer order item. For example, when a transfer order is being created, you can propose the confirmation; i.e., enter the confirmation information, but not actually confirm the transfer order.

Post to Same Bin

When the **Post to same bin** indicator is set for the movement type, the posting change does not result in a transfer; instead, the material is relabeled in the storage bin. Therefore, if the material is assigned as special stock — such as consignment stock — a posting change can convert that material to unrestricted stock. Instead of moving the material out of the bin and to a storage type for posting changes, this indicator allows the posting change to occur in the storage bin where the material is located.

Reference Storage Type Search

The **Ref. Stor. Type Search** field refers to the movement type during the storage type search. The movement type can influence the storage type search. You can set up for each movement type certain storage types to be proposed. The necessary reference movement types must be set up for the movement types concerned. You must take these reference movement types into account in the storage type search function.

4.1.4 Assigning Warehouse Management Movement Types

After each IM movement type has been assigned, you can establish a WM reference movement type, the link between the IM reference movement type and the WM movement type.

A WM reference movement type doesn't directly correlate with a WM movement type. The limiting factor is the warehouse in which the movement takes place. The combination of the warehouse number and the WM reference movement type determines what WM movement type is assigned.

Therefore a WM reference movement type 101 may refer to WM movement type 101 in warehouse 100, but refer to WM movement type 103 in warehouse 200.

Figure 4.6 shows the warehouse number and reference movement type and the corresponding warehouse movement type. For example, reference movement type **503** in warehouse **104** corresponds to WM movement type **505** in Figure 4.6. The other fields on this screen are explained next.

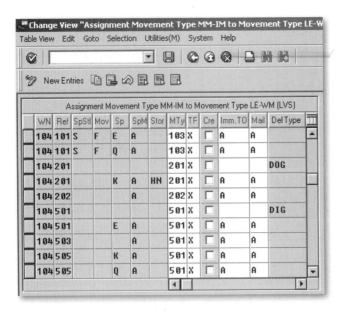

Figure 4.6 Assign WM Movement Type Based on Warehouse Number and WM Reference Movement Type

▶ **Warehouse Number**
This field, **WN**, is the warehouse number where the reference movement type is relevant. The entry of ******* in this column of the table indicates that the reference movement type is valid for all warehouses.

▶ **Reference Movement Type**
This field, **Ref,** is the reference movement type that links the IM movement type to the WM movement type.

▶ **Special Stock Indicator**
This field, **SpStl**, is the special stock indicator that allows the goods movement transaction to process differently. In this instance, it is referenced from the IM movement type to aid in the identification of the correct WM movement type.

▶ **Movement Indicator**
This field, **Mov**, is the movement indicator that specifies what type of document is the basis for the IM goods movement.

▶ **Special Stock Type Indicator**
This field, **Sp**, is the Special stock type indicator which identifies what type of stock is being moved; e.g.,project stock or consignment stock.

▶ **Special Movement Indicator**
This field, **SpM**, is the special movement indicator field. This indicator is

used to separate special posting procedures for the Materials Management (MM) documents for the standard processing method. The system uses this to determine the WM movement type. Different movement types in the warehouse can be assigned to one IM movement type.

▶ **Storage Location Reference Indicator**
This field, **Stor** is the storage-location reference indicator. Depending on the storage location, this indicator influences the storage type search within the transfer order as well as the interim storage type search in the IM posting.

The storage-location reference indicator is created in configuration via the navigation path: **IMG • Logistics Execution • Warehouse Management • Interfaces • Inventory Management • Define Storage Location Control**.

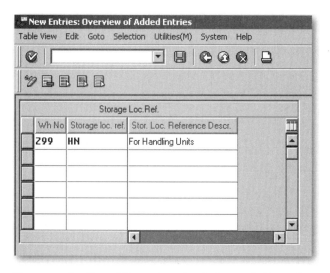

Figure 4.7 Creation of Storage Location Reference Indicator for Warehouse Z99

Figure 4.7 shows the storage-location reference indicator being created for the **Z99** warehouse. The storage-location reference field is two characters long.

Continuing with the description of the fields in Figure 4.6, the next field after **Stor** is the movement type.

▶ **Movement Type**
This field, **Mty**, is the movement type field. Each movement that occurs in the warehouse requires a WM movement type. The WM movement type affects the creation of the transfer order.

▶ **Creation and Cancellation of Transfer Requirement**
The **TF** indicator is used to create or cancellation of a transfer requirement.

▷ **X**

This entry means that a transfer requirement will be created for the material document item.

▷ **1**

With this entry, the system will try to cancel any existing transfer requirement.

▶ **Creation of Posting Change Notice**
This field, **Cre**, specifies creation of posting change notice (PCN). A PCN is created for each material document item.

▶ **Create Transfer Order Immediately**
This field, **Imm. TO**, is the create transfer order immediately indicator, creates a transfer order immediately when the IM movement is processed. Two indicators can be used.

▷ **A**

The system creates a transfer order automatically when a material document is posted in IM.

▷ **X**

The system calls up the **Create Transfer Order** transaction when you post an IM material document.

▶ **Mail Control**
This field, **Mail**, is used for mail control. When transfer orders are created in the background, this field controls who should be contacted in case of errors.

▶ **Delivery Type**
Depending on the delivery type (the **Del.Type** field), the system determines which screens to display and which data is required to be entered.

The delivery type can be configured via the navigation path: **IMG • Logistics Execution • Shipping • Deliveries • Define Delivery Types**.

This concludes our discussion of movement types used in warehouse management. Now we'll focus on transfer requirements.

4.2   Transfer Requirements

The WM movement type, described in Section 4.1, determines the movement of the material into the warehouse. Once the material is in the warehouse, it can be moved for a pick, putaway, or transfer. There are two elements to the movement, which are:

▶ Transfer requirement

▶ Transfer order

The transfer requirement is the phase of planning to move material from one warehouse location to another, while a transfer order is used to perform the move and confirm the move when it is completed.

With regards to the WM movement types, the transfer requirement is used to translate the information from the IM goods movement to a planned movement in the warehouse, based on the configuration of the WM movement type. The transfer requirement is automatically created so that the material can be moved into the warehouse.

The transfer requirement comprises header information and a number of item lines of material for the transfer requirement. The item line includes information such as:

▶ The material to be moved within the warehouse

▶ The quantity of the material to be moved

▶ The date when the material should be moved

▶ The transfer type that is the basis of the goods movement such as a putaway, pick, or transfer.

▶ A reason why the material has to be moved; e.g., it is needed to fill a production order or a purchase order

4.2.1   Automatic Transfer Requirements

An automatic transfer requirement is created when a transaction for a goods movement is executed and the warehouse movement type is configured for automatic creation of a transfer requirement.

The indicator to set for automatic creation of a transfer requirement can be configured via the navigation path: **IMG · Logistics Execution · Warehouse Management · Interfaces · Inventory Management · Define Movement Types**.

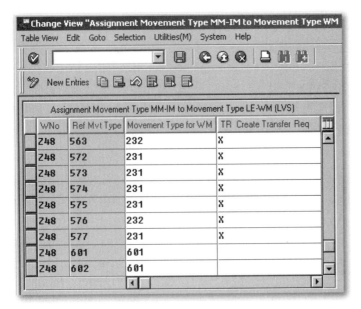

Figure 4.8 Configuration of Manual Transfer Requirements in WM Movement Type Screen

Figure 4.8 shows the configuration screen for the WM movement types. When defining the movement types, you can decide to configure the movement to automatically create a transfer requirement for the movement or to leave the creation as a manual process.

4.2.2 Create a Manual Transfer Requirement

You may need to create a transfer requirement manually for a variety of reasons. The most common include the need to perform a goods issue to a cost center — often done when issuing materials to a salesman for samples — and for replenishment of material into the fixed bins.

A manual transfer requirement can be created using Transaction LB01, which can be accessed via the navigation path: **SAP • Logistics • Logistics Execution • Warehouse Management • Transfer Requirement • Create • Without Reference**.

Figure 4.9 shows the initial data-entry screen for creating a transfer requirement. The warehouse number and the movement type must be entered. However, if the movement type does not allow the manual entry of a transfer requirement, the system will display an error message at the bottom of the screen. This will state that a manual transfer requirement is not allowed, and the creation of the transfer requirement cannot proceed.

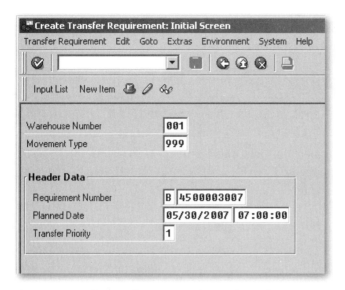

Figure 4.9 Initial Screen for Creation of Manual Transfer Requirement

You can enter the transfer requirement header data on this screen. The header data consists of the requirement type, requirement number, planned date, and transfer priority.

Figure 4.10 shows the detail screen for the creation of a transfer requirement. This screen shows the information that may have been entered on the header screen.

Let's take a closer look at what's involved in the creation of transfer requirements.

► **Automatic Transfer Order**
In addition to the header information, an **Automatic TO** indicator can be set to allow an automatic transfer order. If this is set, transfer orders are created by batch input using the report RLAUTA10.

► **Special Stock Indicator**
The **Special stock** indicator determines what type of stock is being moved; e.g.,, project stock, or consignment stock. The second of the two special-stock fields is for the special stock number. This identifies the material. If the material is a consignment stock, then the consignment vendor number is used as the special stock number. If a special stock number is entered, then a special stock indicator must be entered also.

► **Unloading Point**
The unloading point can be manually entered in the **Unload point** field.

This could be a dock or a location within the warehouse where the material is unloaded. This field can accept a value up to 25 characters long.

▶ **Stock Category**

The warehouse stock category indicator (**Stock Categ.**) can be entered if the stock is returns or blocked. The entry Q can be made if the stock is in quality control, R if the stock has been returned and S if it is blocked stock.

▶ **Ship-To Point**

A ship-to point can be entered to indicate the person or location to which the material ultimately will be shipped. The **Ship-To** Pt field can accept a value up to 12 characters long.

▶ **Items**

The line item in the transfer requirement requires the material number, the quantity, unit of measure, and the batch number if applicable. A number of lines can be added to the transfer requirement. When finished, the document can be posted, and the system will display the transfer requirement number assigned.

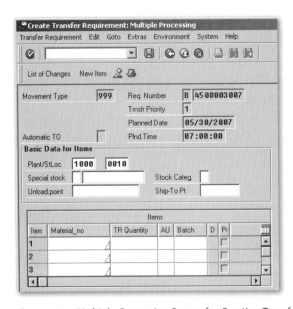

Figure 4.10 Multiple-Processing Screen for Creating Transfer Requirement

4.2.3 Create a Transfer Requirement for Replenishment of a Fixed Bin

You can use a transfer requirement to add more material to the stock in fixed storage bins. The system can automatically create transfer requirements for the required quantities. However, this process can be done manually using Transaction LP21.

Instead of the system calculating the quantity necessary for replenishment, the warehouse staff can manually determine the level required and create a transfer requirement for this amount.

To ensure that a manual transfer requirement can be created to replenish the fixed bins, the storage type must be configured with the correct movement type.

You can find the transaction in the IMG to configure the movement type for the storage type. Follow the navigation path: **IMG • Logistics Execution • Warehouse Management • Activities • Transfers • Define Stock Transfers and Replenishment Control**.

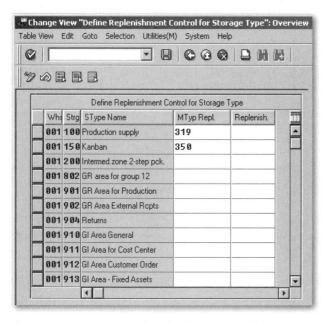

Figure 4.11 Configuration of Replenishment Control for Storage Types

Figure 4.11 shows the configuration required to allow replenishment by entering the relevant movement type against the required warehouse/storage type combination. In this case, the storage type **100** is defined as production supply bins that contain material used in production orders. The movement type **319** is defined for replenishment for production and needs to be assigned to areas. In this case, that means storage type **100**, which requires ongoing replenishment.

A manual transfer requirement can be created, using Transaction LP21, to replenish the bins in the storage type for production material. You can also use the navigation path: **SAP** • **Logistics** • **Logistics Execution** • **Warehouse Management** • **Transfer Requirement** • **Create** • **Replenishment for Fixed Bins**.

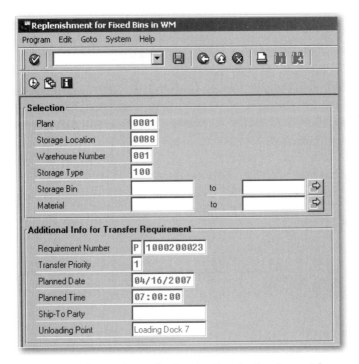

Figure 4.12 Selection Screen for Creating Transfer Requirement for Fixed Bin Replenishment: Transaction LP21

To create the transfer requirement, the warehouse user must enter the plant, storage location, warehouse number, and storage type. Figure 4.12 shows these fields entered as well as fields entered such as the requirement type and requirement number, transfer priority, and planned date and time. The planned date should always be in the future. The unloading point was added in this example, but is an optional field.

The transaction will reference the material master records of those materials in the storage type, unless specific storage bins or materials are entered. The material information for replenishment is reviewed against the stock in the storage bins of the storage type. If the stock levels are below the minimum stated in the material master, then the system will display this information in the results screen.

The material master record can contain the replenishment data for the material at the storage type level. Figure 4.13 shows the replenishment data in the material master.

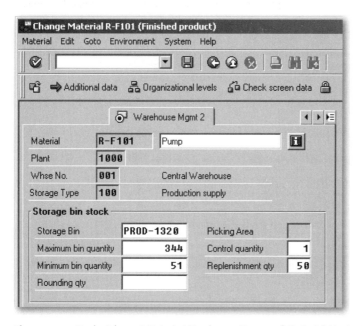

Figure 4.13 Replenishment Data in Warehouse Screen of Material Master Record

Minimum Bin Quantity

The **Minimum bin quantity** field is the minimum quantity that can be stored in the bin location of this storage type. This field is used in the calculation for the replenishment of material.

Replenishment Quantity

The **Replenishment qty** field is the quantity of material that is to be replenished in the storage bin. This replenishment quantity applies only the storage type for which it is entered. This value can be seen when the transfer requirement is created for the material.

After the selection screen for Transaction LP21 has been completed, it can be executed by using the **F8** function key.

Figure 4.14 shows the results for the fixed-bin replenishment for the storage type 100 production supply. The material shown, R-F101, shows a zero stock level and a requirement quantity of 300. The detailed information on the fixed bin can be found by selecting from the header menu **Edit • Choose Detail** or by using the **F2** function key.

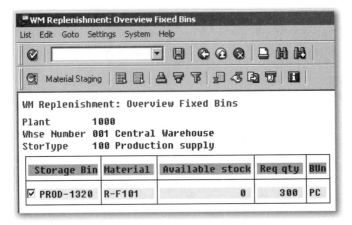

Figure 4.14 Results Screen for Fixed Bin Replenishment: Transaction LP21

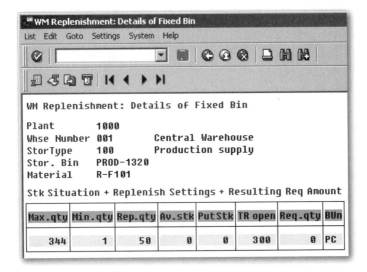

Figure 4.15 : Detailed Information on Fixed Bin Selected for Replenishment

Figure 4.15 shows details of the material in the storage bin for which the replenishment transfer requirement has been created. The detailed information shows the data from the material master record, as shown earlier in Figure 4.13. For this storage type, the maximum material in a bin is **344**, minimum quantity allowed in a storage bin is **1**, and the replenishment quantity is **50**.

4.2.4 Display a Transfer Requirement for a Material

There are a number of transactions that can be used to display a transfer requirement. The open transfer requirement shown in Figure 4.15 is for material R-F101. You can find this transfer requirement by using the system to display a transfer requirement for a material. This can be performed by using Transaction LB11 or following the navigation path: **SAP • Logistics • Logistics Execution • Warehouse Management • Transfer Requirement • Display • For Material**.

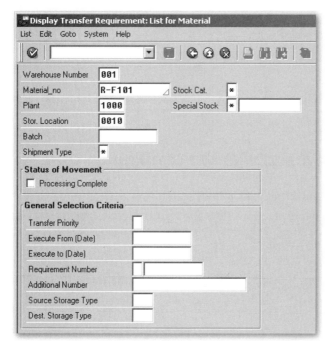

Figure 4.16 Initial Screen for Display of Transfer Requirement for Material: Transaction LB11

Figure 4.16 shows the selection screen for Transaction LB11. The material and the warehouse number are required, but the other selection fields are optional. Most of the selection options on this screen have been described previously in this chapter.

Shipment Type

The **Shipment Type** is the type of movement required in the transfer requirement. The movement can be Stock Placement, Stock Removal, Posting Change, or Warehouse Supervision.

Processing Complete

If the **Processing Complete** field is set, then the list that is produced will include transfer requirements that have been completed. If the indicator is left blank, completed transfer requirements will not be included. Choosing to see all of the transfer requirements for a material enables the system to give a complete picture of material requirements.

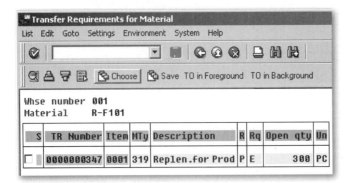

Figure 4.17 Results Screen Displaying Transfer Requirements for Material: Transaction LB11

Figure 4.17 shows that for the material and warehouse entered there is only one relevant transfer requirement. This is the transfer requirement that was created as an example earlier in this chapter for the replenishment of a fixed bin.

The transfer requirement can be viewed by double-clicking the item line you wish to review. The system will process through to Transaction LB03 to display the transfer requirement.

Figure 4.18 shows the transfer requirement for the fixed bin replenishment. The transfer requirement shows that the indicators **Processed** and **Deletion Flag** are both blank, so the transfer requirement has not been completely processed, and the line item has not been deleted.

The processing status of the transfer requirement can be displayed by selecting the **Processing Status** button, selecting the **Shift + F5** function keys, or by selecting **Goto • Processing Status** from the header menu.

Figure 4.19 shows the processing status of the transfer requirement. The processing-status screen shows that a transfer order has not been created for the transfer requirement. This is clear because the field **TO Quantity** is zero and the field **Number of TO Items** is also zero.

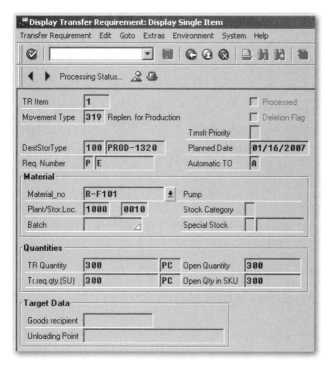

Figure 4.18 Display of Transfer Requirement for Line Item: Transaction LB03

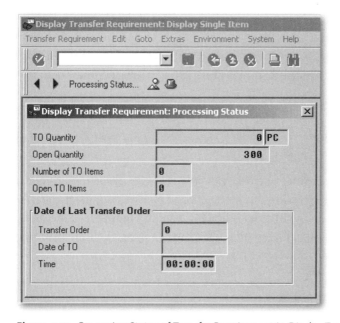

Figure 4.19 Processing Status of Transfer Requirement in Display Transfer Requirement: Transaction LB03

4.2.5 Display a Transfer Requirement for a Single Item

The Transaction LB03 can be used to display a transfer requirement for a single line item. This transaction can also be used via the navigation path: **SAP • Logistics • Logistics Execution • Warehouse Management • Transfer Requirement • Display • Single**.

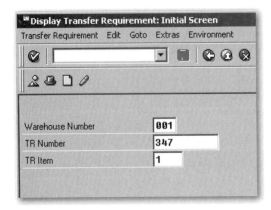

Figure 4.20 Initial Screen for Display of Transfer Requirement: Transaction LB03

Figure 4.20 shows the initial screen for Transaction LB03. The warehouse number and transfer requirement number must be entered. The system proposes the transfer-requirement number if it is not entered. The detail screen for LB03 was shown earlier, in Figure 4.18.

4.2.6 Display a Transfer Requirement for a Storage Type

Transaction LB10 can be used to display a transfer requirement for a storage type. This transaction can also be used via the navigation path: **SAP • Logistics • Logistics Execution • Warehouse Management • Transfer Requirement • Display • For Storage Type**.

Figure 4.21 shows the initial screen for the display of transfer requirements for storage types. The selection can be entered to show the transfer requirements for the source or destination storage types. In Figure 4.21, the destination storage type has been entered (**Dest. Storage Type**), and the resulting transfer requirements will only be relevant for that storage type.

The status of movement section on Figure 4.21 indicates that the selection can be made for combinations of open, partially delivered, or completed transfer requirements.

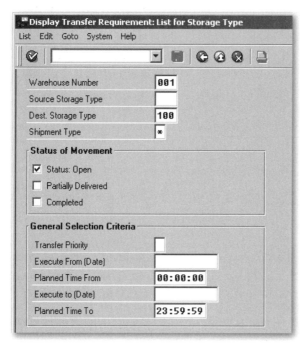

Figure 4.21 Initial Screen for Display of Transfer Requirements by Storage Type: Transaction LB10

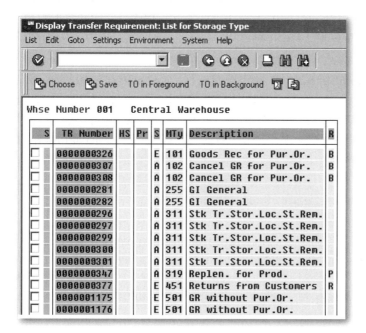

Figure 4.22 Display of Transfer Requirements for Selected Storage Type: Transaction LB10

Figure 4.22 shows the following transfer requirements that have been found for the destination storage type selected in Figure 4.21:

▶ **HS: Header Status of Transfer Requirement**
This is automatically derived from the system and refers to the amount of the transfer requirement already processed by transfer orders.

▶ **Pr: Transfer Priority**
The lower the number the higher the priority. The transfer requirements are processed by this priority list.

▶ **S: Shipment Type**
This classifies the movement types in the warehouse. The options are **A** for Stock Removal, **U** for Posting Change, and **E** for Stock Placement.

▶ **R: Requirement Type**
This refers to the origin type; e.g., a goods receipt for a purchase order. The options include **A** for an Asset, **B** for a Purchase Order, **D** for Storage Bin, **K** for a Cost center, **L** for a Sales document, and **V** for a Sales order.

From this report, a transfer requirement can be selected and processed to create a transfer order. This report can perform this process either in the background or in the foreground.

A transfer order can be created from the selected transfer requirement in the foreground by clicking the button on the screen, using the header menu, and selecting **Environment • TO in Foreground**, or by using the function keys **Ctrl + Shift + F8**.

Depending on processing time and the size of the transfer requirement, a transfer order can be created from the transfer requirement in the background by clicking the button on the screen, using the header menu, and selecting **Environment • TO in Background,** or by using the function keys **Ctrl + Shift + F9**.

4.2.7 Deleting a Transfer Requirement

You may find that the transfer requirement was created unnecessarily or with an error in the entry of the storage type. If the transfer requirement is not needed and you need to delete it, that process requires Transaction LB02. It can be found using the navigation path **SAP • Logistics • Logistics Execution • Warehouse Management • Transfer Requirement • Change.**

The data required to change a transfer requirement is the warehouse, transfer requirement number, and the item number, as shown in Figure 4.23.

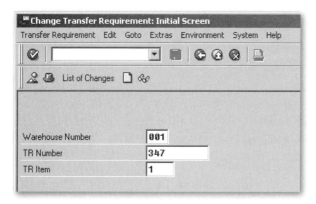

Figure 4.23 Initial Screen for Changing Transfer Requirement: Transaction LB02

Figure 4.24 Transfer Requirement Line Item with Deletion Flag Set: Transaction LB02

Figure 4.24 shows the line item for the transfer requirement with the deletion flag set. This signals that the line item will be deleted when this transfer requirement transaction has been saved.

Now that we have discussed the processes surrounding transfer requirements the next section will follow up with a discussion on transfer orders functionality.

4.3 Transfer Orders

As I mentioned in Section 4.2 when describing a transfer requirement, a transfer order is used to perform a move and confirm a move when it is completed. A transfer order can be created with reference to a source document either from warehouse management or from another SAP module, such as MM. A source document can be a transfer requirement, delivery document, material document, or a posting change notice (PCN).

The transfer order contains the information required to perform the movement of materials into the warehouse, out of the warehouse, or from one storage bin to another storage bin within the warehouse.

The transfer order can also perform logical movements in the warehouse. This includes movements from a blocked status to an unrestricted status or from quality control status to blocked.. These movements are considered to be posting changes and are executed with a transfer order.

The transfer order comprises a header and a number of item lines. The header contains the transfer-order number and the dates of creation and confirmation. If the transfer order has been created with reference to a transfer requirement, then the transfer-requirement number is shown in the header. If the transfer order is created with reference to a delivery, then the delivery number is shown on the header.

A transfer order can have a single or multiple line items. The transfer order is a document that tells where the material is coming from and where it is going. Therefore,each line item is an individual movement of a certain quantity of material from a source storage bin to a destination storage bin. The number of line items will depend on how many destination storage bins are required for the total quantity of material.

4.3.1 Creating a Transfer Order with Reference to a Transfer Requirement

A great many of the transfer orders created in the warehouse result from transfer requirements. The transfer requirement is created as a plan of what needs to be moved and when. Those transfer requirements can be converted into transfer orders in order for the movement of the material to be completed.

The transaction to create a transfer order from a transfer requirement is Transaction LT04, which can be found using the navigation path: **SAP • Logis-**

tics • **Logistics Execution** • **Warehouse Management** • **Transfer Order** • **Create** • **For Transfer Requirement**.

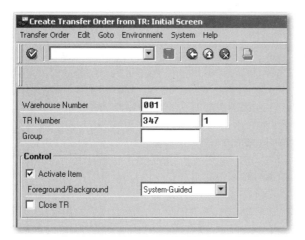

Figure 4.25 Initial Screen for Creating Transfer Order with Reference to Transfer Requirement: Transaction LT04

Figure 4.25 shows the initial screen of LT04 where the transfer-requirement number and the item number are entered as the reference document for creating a new transfer order.

The **Group** field in Figure 4.25 refers to a user-defined group number that can be used to label certain related warehouse management documents for easier retrieval at a later date. For example, if the documents all related to a certain sales order, the sales order number of customer number may be used as a group number for the warehouse documents so they are easier to retrieve.

You should set the **Activate Item** indicator should be set when it is necessary to select the line items in the transfer order and enter them into the active work list. If the indicator is not set, the items are not activated.

The **Foreground/Background** field can be used to select which type of processing is used for transfer-order creation. The process can be either in the foreground, where the processing can be seen, in the background where it processes like a batch job, or driven by the system.

The **Close TR** indicator is used to determine the processing that should occur with the transfer requirement referenced in Transaction LT04 to create the transfer order. If the indicator is set, the transfer requirement is closed when the transfer order is processed. However, if the indicator is not set, the transfer requirement is not closed if the transfer order did not totally complete the transfer specified by the transfer requirement.

Example

If the transfer requirement showed a quantity of 10, and the transfer order was processed with a quantity of eight, then the remaining quantity of two will remain open on the transfer requirement and a manual process will be required to complete the transfer requirement. This would not occur if the **Close TR** indicator had been set, because the transfer requirement would have been closed.

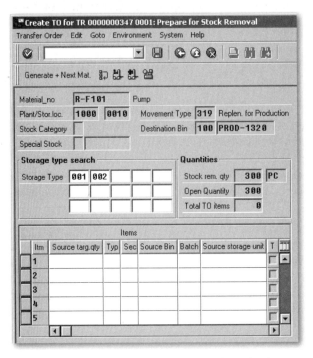

Figure 4.26 Detail Screen for Creating Transfer Order from Transfer Requirement: Transaction LT04

After the transfer requirement details are entered into the initial screen, the detail screen is displayed as shown in Figure 4.26. This screen shows the item information for the material to be moved.

You will see in Figure 4.26 the details transferred from the transfer requirement, such as the movement type, plant, storage location, and destination storage type and storage bin.

The **Storage type search** shows the storage types that will be used to find material to supply the production fixed bin, **PROD-1320**, for this transfer requirement. Initially, the items lines are blank. When the system searches the storage types listed in the storage type search, the material from the source bins will be noted on the item lines with the quantity they are supplying for the transfer requirement.

To create the item lines for the movement of quantity defined in the transfer requirement, the transaction will review the bins in the storage type search and propose a number of line items for the total quantity defined by the transfer requirement.

You can choose to have this performed either in the foreground or background. The reason to perform this in the background is that allows the user to continue with other work. If the transfer requirement has a large quantity, the process to create the number of line items on the transfer order may take some time.

If the process is to be performed in the foreground, you can choose that option from the header menu by choosing **Edit • Remove from Stock • Foreground** or by selecting the **F5** function key.

Figure 4.27 Generating Line Items for Transfer Order with Reference to Transfer Requirement: Transaction LT04

Figure 4.27 shows the first proposed movement of material from a source storage bin to the destination storage bin. This was based on the storage type search of storage types **001** and **002**, which was proposed in Figure 4.26.

In this screen the requested quantity is copied from the transfer requirement, along with the material number, plant, storage location, and the storage unit type.

The **Certificate No.** can refer to a document that relates specifically to the quant whose movement is being proposed. This document can be a certificate of origin or an identification document, for example.

The **Confirm** indicator allows the line item to be confirmed as soon as it is created. If the indicator is set then the confirmation will occur immediately. This may occur if the transfer order is being created after the movement has taken place.

The **Printer** field is used if the transfer-order line item is to be printed as used as a picking slip. The printer number should reflect the printer used for printing warehouse documents such as picking slips.

The **GR Date** is the goods-receipt date of the movement of material. This defaults to the current date, but can be amended if the movement has already occurred when the transfer order is created. The **TO Item** field is the line- item numbering for the transfer order.

The movement data section shown in Figure 4.27 shows the source and destination storage information. The data shows the storage type, storage section, storage bin, quantity of the quant, unit of measure, storage unit (if applicable), and the quant number.

In addition to entering information for the source and destination locations, you can use another section to enter information for the return of any materials. If any extra or surplus material cannot be returned to the original storage bin, then it can be returned to this storage destination, as defined in the **Backsp** indicator fields

The **Goods Recipient** field can be entered if the person or area that is receiving the material is known. The **Gross Weight** field shows the gross weight of the material for this specific line item of the transfer order. This is important for warehouse staff because the weight of the quant may require special equipment or exceed the recommended load of a forklift or storage bin.

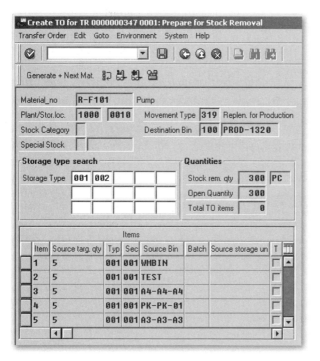

Figure 4.28 Display of Transfer Order Line Items Showing Source Storage Type and Storage Bins

Figure 4.28 shows the transfer order with five line items from the total quantity in the transfer requirement that have been proposed for movement from the source locations to the single destination fixed bin.

The total amount of source quantity from the line items will equal the required amount from the transfer requirement. After the line items have been reviewed, posting the transaction will create the transfer order. The warehouse user can achieve this by selecting the header menu and choosing **Transfer Order • Posting** or by using the **Ctrl + S** function keys. After the posting has been completed, the system will display the transfer order number on the screen.

4.3.2 Creating a Transfer Order without a Reference

The warehouse staff can create a transfer order manually, without reference to a transfer request, delivery, etc. This may be required if an error has been made or if the warehouse needs to move inventory quickly. The movement type that is used must be configured to allow a manual transfer order to be created.

The configuration to allow a manual transfer order is on the movement type configuration for a particular warehouse. Therefore, a manual transfer order for a movement type may not be allowed in other warehouses.

The configuration path is via the navigation path: **IMG • Logistics Execution • Warehouse Management • Activities • Transfers • Define Movement Types**.

Select the warehouse/movement type combination that is required, and then select **Goto • Details** from the header menu, or select **Ctrl + Shift + F2** function keys.

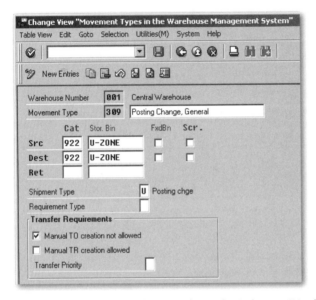

Figure 4.29 Configuration for Manual Transfer Orders per Warehouse/Movement Type Combination

In Figure 4.29, in the **Transfer Requirements** area, the configuration for **Movement Type 309** in **Warehouse 001** shows that manual transfer orders are not allowed. Transfer orders can only be created with reference if this field is not set.

If the indicator is not set and a manual transfer order can be created, you can use Transaction LT01. It can be found by following the navigation path: **SAP • Logistics • Logistics Execution • Warehouse Management • Transfer Order • Create • Without Reference**.

Figure 4.30 shows the initial screen for creating a manual transfer order. The warehouse number, movement type, material number, plant, storage location, and quantity of material to be moved should be entered.

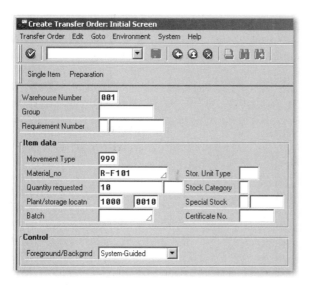

Figure 4.30 Initial Screen to Create Transfer Order Without Reference: Transaction LT01

You can include other information, such as stock category if the stock to be moved is blocked, or use a special stock indicator if the material is project stock or consignment.

You can enter a batch number for the stock to be moved if the material is batch managed and if a certain batch has been identified for movement. The control option can allow foreground, background, or system-controlled processing.

Figure 4.31 shows the entry of a source storage type, storage section, and a storage bin. When these are entered, the system will automatically assign the quant. The same is true when the destination location is entered. The system will also calculate the gross weight of the material to be moved.

When the items are complete, the transfer order can be saved. After the posting has been completed, the system will display the transfer order number on the screen.

4.3.3 Cancel a Transfer Order

After a transfer order has been created, you might need to cancel it if the material is not to be moved or is to be moved via a different movement type. A transfer order can be cancelled by using Transaction LT15 or via the navigation path: **SAP • Logistics • Logistics Execution • Warehouse Management • Transfer Order • Cancel • Transfer Order**.

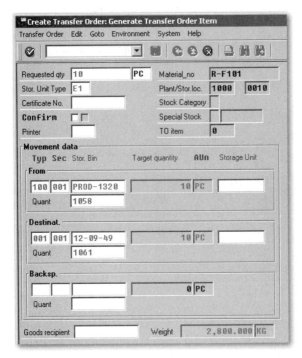

Figure 4.31 Entry Screen for Data to Create Manual Transfer Order: Transaction LT01

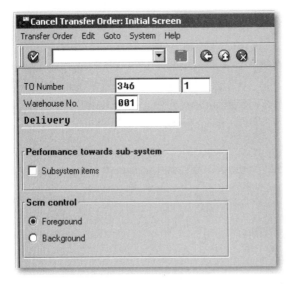

Figure 4.32 Initial Screen for Cancellation of Transfer Order: Transaction LT15

Figure 4.32 shows the initial screen for canceling a transfer order. It requires entry of the warehouse number and the transfer order number/item number. The screen also allows the entry of a delivery number if applicable.

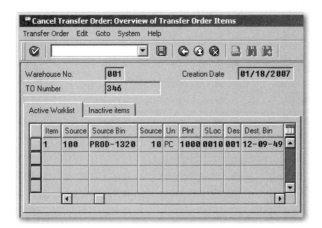

Figure 4.33 Detail Screen Showing Line Items to be Cancelled: Transaction LT15

Figure 4.33 shows the line item of the transfer order to be cancelled. The transfer order is cancelled when the transaction is posted. When the processing is complete, the system will return a message confirming cancellation.

4.3.4 Confirm a Transfer Order

When a transfer order is created, the system can confirm when the movement of the material has been completed. However a transfer order can be confirmed at any time, thus allowing the material to be picked even though the material has not been physically moved. This is useful for warehouse operations when a material has arrived from a vendor in response to a purchase order and needs to be used in production before putaway in the warehouse. A transfer order can be confirmed using these three transactions:

▸ **LT11**
Confirming a single item on a transfer order

▸ **LT12**
Confirming the transfer order

▸ **LT13**
Confirming by storage unit

Now we shall review the confirmation of the complete transfer order using Transaction LT12, which can be found using the navigation path: **SAP · Logis-**

tics • Logistics Execution • Warehouse Management • Transfer Order • Confirm • Transfer Order.

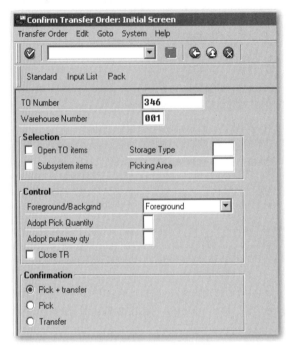

Figure 4.34 Initial Screen for Confirmation of Transfer Order: Transaction LT12

Figure 4.34 shows the selection screen for the transfer-order confirmation. The selection for the transaction can include more than the just the warehouse number and transfer order.

Open TO items

When this indicator is set it will allow only open transfer-order line items to be displayed; i.e., those line items not confirmed. This is useful when a transfer order has many line items. If all line items are to be displayed whether they are open or confirmed, then the indicator should be left blank.

Subsystem Items

This indicator refers to any external warehouse management system that is processing some element of the warehouse process. For example, the transfer order may be passed to an external system that controls a warehouse carousel system outside SAP.

If this indicator is set, then the display will show transfer orders that have been passed to the external system, and these can be re-processed. Normally, when items are passed to an external system they are not processed further in SAP. However, this will depend on the interfaces between SAP and the external system. Check with your data integrity team to confirm this.

Adopt Pick Quantity

This indicator is used to determine the link between the picked quantity and the quantity posted. Five selections can be made for this indicator:

▶ **1**

Include picking quantity in delivery

▶ **2**

Include pick quantity in delivery and post goods issue

▶ **3**

Do not include picking quantity in delivery

▶ **4**

Do not take pick quantity as delivery quantity but post goods receipt

▶ **Blank**

Allow control through the movement type

The relationship between the pick quantity and the delivery quantity is more relevant in options 1 and 2. If the pick quantity is lower than the delivery quantity, the pick quantity overwrites the delivery quantity and it is the pick quantity that gets posted.

Adopt Putaway Quantity

This indicator functions like the Adopt Pick Quantity indicator, except that this field relates to the putaway quantity and not the picked quantity. There are five options for this indicator as well:

▶ **1**

Stock placement quantity adopted into delivery as delivery quantity

▶ **2**

Copy stock placement quantity as delivery quantity and post goods issue

▶ **3**

Stock placement quantity is not adopted into delivery as delivery quantity

▶ **4**

Do not take putaway quantity as delivery quantity but post goods receipt

▶ **Blank**

Allow control through the movement type.

This indicator is used for the inbound delivery of material. Use option **1** or **2** if the delivery for transfer order is complete, even if the quantity for putaway is less than the delivery expected. If more deliveries are expected for the transfer order then the fourth option is most relevant.

Pick and Transfer Indicator

This indicator should be selected if the confirmation is required in one step for withdrawal of the material from the source storage bin and arrival of the material at the destination storage bin.

Pick Indicator

This indicator should be selected if you need only to confirm withdrawal of the material from the source storage bin for the transfer order items. When the material arrives at the destination storage bin, a second confirmation step will be required.

Transfer Indicator

This indicator should be selected if you need only to confirm the arrival of the material at the destination storage bin for the transfer-order items.

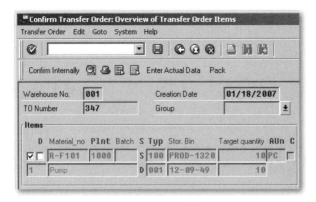

Figure 4.35 Detail Line Item Screen for Transfer-Order Confirmation: Transaction LT12

Figure 4.35 shows the line-item detail for the transfer order to be confirmed. The option to pack before confirmation is applicable when storage units are used for the material. This will be described in Chapter 11.

Enter Actual Data

Instead of accepting the values proposed by the transfer order, the actual values can be entered and a difference in quantities may arise. For example, the amount of material in the source storage bin may be less than the amount documented on the transfer order or if the amount counted into the destination bin may be more than expected.

To enter the actual quantities, select the **Input List** button shown in Figure 4.34. This allows a list to be displayed for the actual data to be entered.

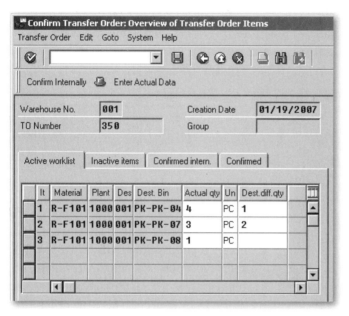

Figure 4.36 Active Worklist Allowing Actual Quantities for Transfer-Order Confirmation: Transaction LT12

Figure 4.36 shows that the quantities for line items **1** and **2** have been entered as actual quantities that have produced a difference between the actual and the quantity in the transfer order. The transfer order stated that for item 1, the quantity to be received in the destination storage bin was 3, but an actual quantity of 4 has been entered.

This has caused the destination difference quantity field (**Dest. Diff. Qty**) to show a quantity of **1**, which is the amount of the overage. Similarly, line item **2** was expected a quantity of **1** and a quantity of **3** was placed in the destination storage bin, causing a difference of **2**. Posting the confirmation of the transfer order with actual data will cause a difference to be entered.

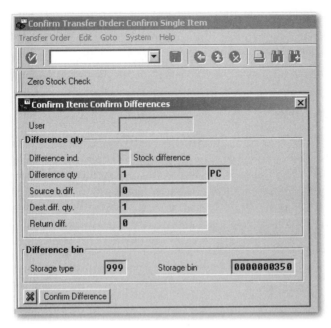

Figure 4.37 Confirmation of Quantity Differences Between Transfer Order Quantity and Actual Entered Quantity: Transaction LT12

Figure 4.37 shows every difference between the transfer order quantity and the actual quantity entered into the transfer-order confirmation screen. For each line item where there is a difference in quantities, a dialog box will be displayed so that the user confirming the transfer order can confirm each stock difference. The differences are logically stored in **Storage type 999,** and the storage bin is named the same as the transfer order where the differences occurred.

Once all the differences are confirmed, the transfer order will be completed and a message will be displayed with the information that the transfer order is confirmed.

4.3.5   Print a Transfer Order

The transfer order can be printed and used as a picking or putaway document for the warehouse staff. The transfer order is often printed so that each line item is a separate document, making it easier to manage.

The transfer order can be printed using Transaction LT31 and can be accessed using the navigation path: **SAP • Logistics • Logistics Execution • Warehouse Management • Transfer Order • Print • Transfer Order.**

Figure 4.38 shows the initial selection screen for the transfer-order print transaction. The screen allows a single line item to be entered so the document will contain just one movement.

Print Code

The print code is a two-character field that determines the printed layout of the transfer order. The print code is configured so that it is determined by warehouse. Therefore, a print code may be assigned for one warehouse only. One practical reason for this is that each warehouse needs different information printed out, such as instructions, addresses, or language.

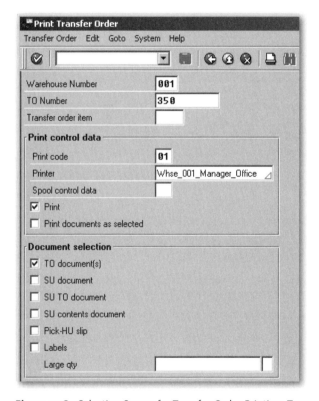

Figure 4.38 Selection Screen for Transfer-Order Printing: Transaction LT31

The print code can be configured in Transaction OMLV and accessed through the navigation path: **IMG • Logistics Execution • Warehouse Management • Activities • Define Print Control**.

Figure 4.39 shows the configuration of the print codes for the warehouse. The print code relates to a form layout that is assigned to a warehouse. If a custom layout for a form is designed, this transaction is where you would assign the form to a warehouse with a new print code. The print code can then be used in the transfer-order print transaction.

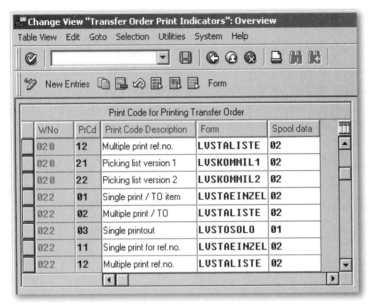

Figure 4.39 Configuration of Print Control for Transfer Order Printing: Transaction OMLV

Printer

Figure 4.38 shows the printer designation that has been entered as the location where the transfer order should be printed. The technical department should help if you have any issues with the locations of printers in the warehouse.

Spool Control Data

The spool code is defined in the same transaction as the print code, OMLV. It is a code that defines a number of parameters involved in printing documents. This print code is defined for each warehouse, and the configuration includes the number of copies, delete-after-print indicator, print-immediately indicator, new-spool-request indicator, etc.

Figure 4.40 shows the spool code configuration for each warehouse. Each spool code defines a set of parameters, and these parameters determine how the transfer order is printed along with the parameters in the print code.

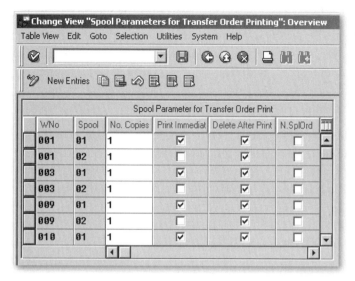

Figure 4.40 Configuration of Spool Control for Transfer-Order Printing: Transaction OMLV

Document Selection

The document to be printed can be selected from the selection on the initial screen: transfer order, storage unit documents, labels, etc. To print the document, you can use an option from the header menu **Transfer Order • Print** or use the **Ctrl + P** function key.

Now that we have examined the transfer-order functionality, we'll summarize the information contained in this chapter.

4.4   Summary

Movements of material in the warehouse are of the utmost importance in making the warehouse work efficiently. The Inventory Management (IM) module passes information to the Warehouse Management system about the movements of material in and out of the warehouse and how those movements should be addressed in WM.

Movements inside the warehouse determine where that material goes, how it gets there, how it is stored, and how it gets retrieved. The transfer requirement and the transfer order are the two documents that move material inside the warehouse. Therefore, you need to know how the processes of each work individually and in combination.

This chapter explained the basic functionality of the transfer requirement and transfer order. The best way to learn more about how these processes work and how they are used in your particular industry is to practice in your sandbox development space with test data. Develop test plans, and go through different scenarios with different materials to understand more about these important processes.

In Chapter 5, I will discuss the goods-receipt process in more detail and show you how these movements are dealt with in the warehouse.

The warehouse receives material, and most of the material is received into SAP Inventory Management (IM), which creates a transfer requirement and then a transfer order in SAP Warehouse Management (WM). It is important to ensure that the material is moved into the warehouse stock correctly.

5 Goods Receipts

In warehouse management, a goods receipt is the movement of material into the warehouse from an external source, which could be a production system, a vendor, etc. The warehouse-management system checks the goods receipt for accuracy and then processes it, moving the material into the warehouse and increasing the stock levels of the material received. A goods receipt into the warehouse is triggered by one of two documents, which can be either:

▶ A transfer requirement from inventory management or production

▶ An inbound delivery if handling-unit management or external system is used

Chapter 11 provides more information on handling-unit management and storage-unit management.

Now that we have introduced the concept of goods receipts, we can go on to discuss the goods receipt process with inbound deliveries in detail.

5.1 Goods Receipt with Inbound Delivery

The handling unit (HU) is found in functionality outside of SAP WM. It is a physical unit that combines packaging materials with the materials inside. When the HU enters the warehouse, it is stored as a storage unit.

Note
A handling unit in the beverage industry could be a plastic crate and 12 bottles of soda. The HU contains all the information from the materials in the handling unit, such as batch numbers and serial numbers.

An HU can also be nested, which means that a single unit can be made from several smaller units. For instance, in the beverage industry, a shrink-wrapped crate of soda may be one handling unit, but is made up of 24 soda bottles that are also handling units.

This section will review the goods receipt with inbound deliveries, so we will first discuss inbound deliveries.

5.1.1 Inbound Delivery Overview

An inbound delivery can be created with reference to a number of processes, which are:

▶ Purchase order

▶ Stock transport order

▶ Customer return

There are many reasons to create inbound deliveries. The most useful one is that we can perform some processes in SAP before the material arrives and a goods receipt is posted. The vendor can send information about the inbound delivery, which informs the warehouse of the HUs that are being sent, the information that they contain, and the precise date and time of delivery.

5.1.2 Creating an Inbound Delivery

We can create an inbound delivery using the information from a vendor regarding a single purchase order for which it is supplying the material. The transaction to create a manual inbound delivery is Transaction VL31N. This can be found using the navigation path: **SAP • Logistics • Logistics Execution • Inbound Delivery • Inbound Delivery • Create • Single Documents**.

Figure 5.1 shows the initial screen for the creation of a manual inbound delivery. The vendor number and the purchase order number are required fields. Let's discuss them here:

▶ **Delivery date**
The delivery date is the date the vendor has given for delivery of the material. This is not necessarily the date stipulated in the purchase order to the vendor.

▶ **External ID**
This is the identification that the vendor has assigned to this delivery. It may be the vendor's outbound delivery number or any identification that it requires. This field can be up to 35 characters long.

▶ **Means of trans.**

The means of transport is the packaging material type. It can be configured using the Transaction VHAR or by using the navigation path: **IMG** · **Logistics Execution** · **Shipping** · **Packing** · **Define Packaging Material Type**. The packaging material type defines how the materials are shipped.

▶ **Means of transport ID**

The field to the right of the **Means of trans.** field is the identification field, where a reference can be entered. For example, if the means of transport was a truck, then the means of transport ID may be the license plate of the truck, or the trailer number or the vehicle VIN number. Up to 20 characters can be entered into this field.

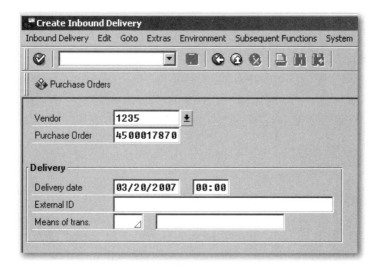

Figure 5.1 Initial Screen for Manual Creation of Inbound Delivery: Transaction VL31N

Figure 5.2 shows the item overview for the inbound delivery being created. The delivery quantity and the item number have been entered with the purchase order placed into the reference document field. The delivery item category field has been filled with **ELN**, which is used for inbound deliveries. The system proposes this value, but it can be changed. The value determines how the line item is processed.

From this screen, the inbound delivery can be processed and an inbound delivery number is returned to the screen after posting.

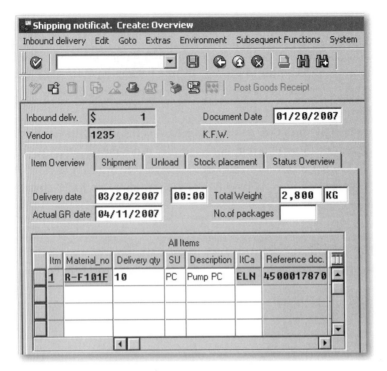

Figure 5.2 Item Overview Screen for Creating Inbound Delivery: Transaction VL31N

5.1.3 Creating a Transfer Order for an Inbound Delivery

Once the inbound delivery has been created, the transfer order is created with reference to the inbound delivery document. Use Transaction LTOF to create a transfer order for an inbound delivery. The transaction can be found using the navigation path: **SAP • Logistics • Logistics Execution • Inbound Process • Goods Receipt for Inbound Delivery • Putaway • Create Transfer Order • For Inbound Delivery**.

Figure 5.3 shows the initial screen of Transaction LTOF that shows the selections that can be made to aid the creation of a transfer order. You must have the warehouse number and the inbound delivery when creating the transfer order. The other selection fields shown in Figure 5.3 are optional.

5.1.4 Using the Inbound Delivery Monitor

If the inbound delivery is not known when using Transaction LTOF, you can use the Inbound Delivery Monitor to display open and completed deliveries. You also can use the monitor to process inbound and outbound deliveries.

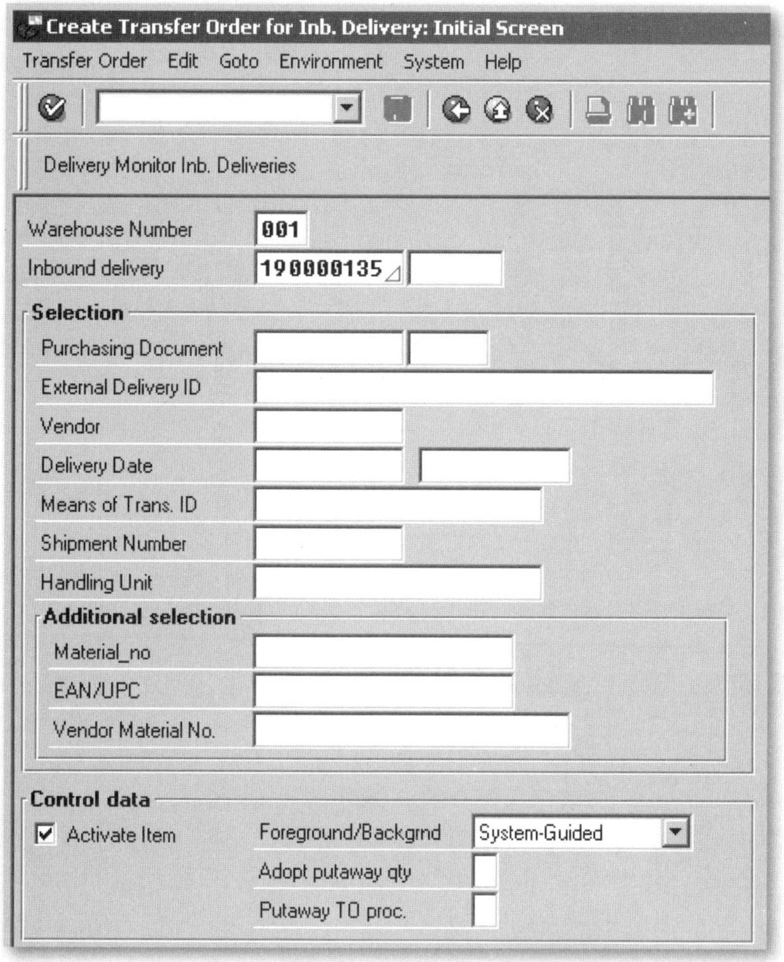

Figure 5.3 Initial Screen for Creating Transfer Order for Inbound Delivery: Transaction LTOF

Figure 5.3 also shows that the Inbound Delivery Monitor can be accessed through Transaction LTOF, by using the **Delivery Monitor Inb. Deliveries** button on the initial screen. Otherwise the Inbound Delivery Monitor can be executed by Transaction VL06I or by using the navigation path: **SAP · Logistics · Logistics Execution · Information System · Goods Receipt · Inbound Delivery Lists · Inbound Delivery Monitor**.

In Figure 5.4, the monitor allows a number of selection options. In this section, we are creating transfer orders based on goods receipts. Therefore, you should select **For Goods Receipt** on the monitor.

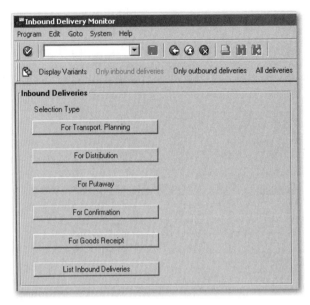

Figure 5.4 Initial Selection Screen for Inbound Delivery Monitor: Transaction VL06I

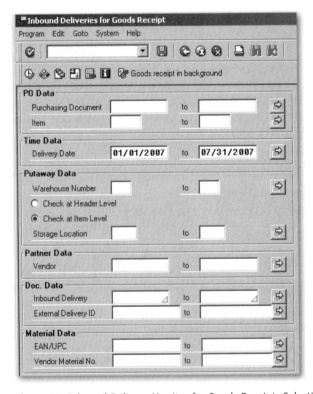

Figure 5.5 Inbound Delivery Monitor for Goods Receipts Selection Screen

Figure 5.5 shows the selection fields that can be entered to search for particular inbound deliveries based on the following search criteria. These are:

▶ **PO Data**
A range for the purchase order and purchase order item

▶ **Time Data**
The delivery date entered into the inbound delivery document

▶ **Putaway Data**
The storage location and warehouse number

The other two indicators in this area refer to warehouse checks at the header or item level.

If the **Check at Header Level** indicator is set, then the system will only find inbound deliveries that have warehouse numbers in the header that meet the selection criteria.

If the **Check at Item Level** indicator is set, then all deliveries that include at least one item that meets the warehouse number criteria are selected. Let's take a look at these:

▶ **Partner Data**
The vendor number or a range of vendor numbers of the required inbound deliveries

▶ **Doc. Data**
The inbound delivery number and the external delivery number

▶ **Material Data**
The UPC code or the vendor material number, if these are known

Once all the search criteria have been entered into the search, you can execute the transaction by choosing **Program • Execute** from the header menu or by using the **F8** function key.

After the data was entered into the selection criteria, the resulting inbound deliveries, shown in Figure 5.6, were found to have met those criteria. A transfer order can be created from a chosen inbound delivery by selecting **Subsequent Functions • Create Transfer Order** from the header menu.

In Figure 5.7 a dialog box will appear requiring an entry of parameters for creation of the transfer order from the inbound delivery. The **Adopt Putaway Qty** field can be entered with one of the options shown in Figure 5.7.

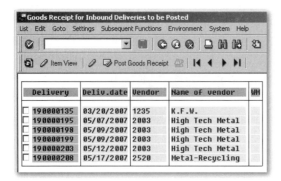

Figure 5.6 Search Results for Goods Receipt for Inbound Deliveries from Inbound Delivery Monitor

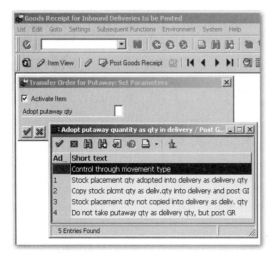

Figure 5.7 Creating Transfer Order from Inbound Delivery 190000208 — Adopting Putaway Quantity

Once you have selected a parameter, the process of creating a transfer order is performed in the background. If the transfer order is created, the system will generate a message that the transfer order has been created successfully or has not been.

If the transfer order has been created, you can see the document flow for the inbound delivery by selecting the inbound delivery from Figure 5.6 and choosing **Environment · Document Flow** from the header menu.

Figure 5.8 shows the original inbound delivery and the handling unit associated with it. The transfer order has been created for the inbound delivery and is shown as an element of document flow.

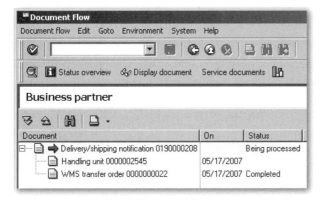

Figure 5.8 Document Flow for Inbound Delivery 190000208, Showing Created Transfer Order Number 22

Transaction LT21 enables display of the transfer order, noted in the document flow for the inbound delivery.

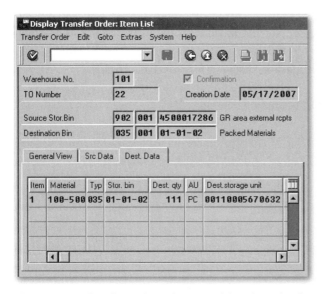

Figure 5.9 Display of Transfer Order Created for Inbound Delivery: Transaction LT21

Figure 5.9 shows the transfer order created for the inbound delivery. The system sets the confirmation flag because the transfer order was confirmed when the transfer order was created in the Inbound Delivery Monitor.

Now that we have examined the goods-receipt process with inbound deliveries, let us look at what happens when goods receipts are made without inbound deliveries.

5.2   Goods Receipt Without Inbound Delivery

A goods receipt for a delivery that is not an inbound delivery occurs when the material is not packed, as it is with an HU. This occurs when material arrives at the receiving dock from the vendor without any containers or pallets. The goods receipt occurs in the IM module, and a transfer requirement is created for the movement of the material into the warehouse.

5.2.1   Goods Receipt in Inventory Management

Goods receipts relevant to a warehouse-management system can be produced by the arrival of material at the plant from a purchase order with a vendor. A goods receipt can be defined as a company's formal acceptance that materials were received from a vendor against a purchase order. Once the material is received and the transaction completed, the value of the material is posted to the general ledger.

The goods-receipt transaction is accessed through Transaction MIGO. The transaction can be accessed via the navigation path: **SAP Menu • Logistics • Materials Management • Inventory Management • Goods Movement • Goods Receipt • For Purchase Order • GR for Purchase Order.**

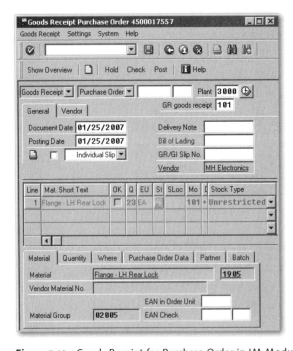

Figure 5.10   Goods Receipt for Purchase Order in IM Module: Transaction MIGO

Figure 5.10 shows the goods receipt for a purchase order of **Material 1905**. It also shows the quantity of material that will be receipted into **Plant 3000** and the **GR goods receipt** type 101, which represents a goods receipt for a purchase order.

5.2.2 Review of the Material Documents

After all the relevant details such as storage location, batch number, etc., have been added to the goods-receipt transaction, the goods receipt can be posted. If the goods receipt does not return any error messages, the transaction will post and display the number of the material document for the movement of the material.

To view the material document, use the Transaction MB03. This can be found using the navigation path **SAP Menu • Logistics • Materials Management • Inventory Management • Material Document • Display**. On the initial screen, enter the material document number displayed after the goods receipt posted and the year, as shown in Figure 5.11.

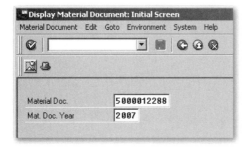

Figure 5.11 Initial Screen for Display of Material Document: Transaction MB03

After the material document number and the fiscal year have been entered, the material document can be displayed.

Figure 5.12 shows the material document that was created during the processing of the goods receipt for a purchase order. The material document shows the material, plant, storage location where the material will be stored, purchase order number, the batch number of the material being receipted, and the movement type of the goods receipt that produced the material document.

In addition the material document contains an option to show the accounting documents created because the material was received at the plant and moved into stock. The company therefore assumes financial liability for the material.

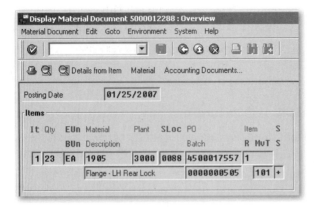

Figure 5.12 Display of Material Document Created by Goods Receipt for Purchase Order

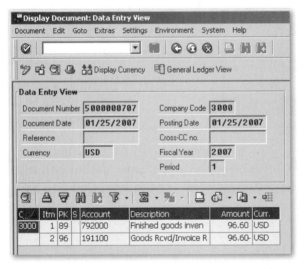

Figure 5.13 Display of Accounting Document Created as Part of Goods Receipt of Purchase Order

Figure 5.13 shows the accounting document relevant to the goods receipt of the material from the purchase order. The two lines of the accounting document show the financial liability moving from the account **191100** (goods receipt account) to the account **792000**, which is the finished goods inventory account.

5.2.3 Review of Stock Levels after Goods Receipt

Once the goods receipt of the purchase order into inventory is complete, a stock overview can be performed to show the material in stock. The stock overview can be executed using the Transaction MMBE. This can be accessed using the navigation path: **SAP Menu • Logistics • Materials Management • Inventory Management • Environment • Stock • Stock Overview**.

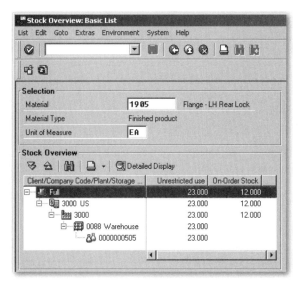

Figure 5.14 Stock Overview of Material 1905 in All Stock Locations: Transaction MMBE

The stock overview screen shows the material that has been posted as a result of the goods receipt. The information regarding the material **1905**, such as the batch number **505**, is shown on the stock overview, shown in Figure 5.14. It matches the information in the material document, shown in Figure 5.12.

5.2.4   Display of the Transfer Requirement

The goods receipt of the material from the purchase order has been receipted into stock, as shown by the material documents and the stock overview program. This information reflects the movement into the stock location relevant to IM, but not movement relevant to WM.

When the movement into the storage location was made, a transfer requirement would have been created, as the storage location is warehouse-managed. The transfer requirement can be found by using Transaction LB11 that allows for a search of the transfer requirements by material number. This transaction can be found by using the navigation path: **SAP Menu • Logistics • Logistics Execution • Internal Warehouse Processes • Transfer Requirement • Display • For Material**.

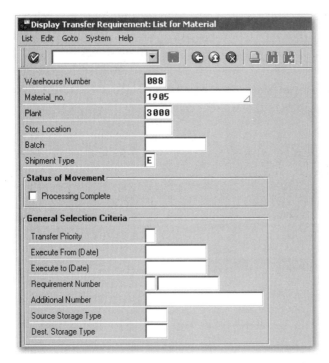

Figure 5.15 Display Transfer Requirements for Single Material: Transaction LB11

Figure 5.15 shows the initial screen of the Transaction LB11. To find all the transfer requirements for the material that has been goods-receipted, you can enter the material number, warehouse number, and plant. Other information such as shipment type can also be entered. In this example, the Shipment Type "E" has been entered, restricting the transfer-requirement search to stock placements.

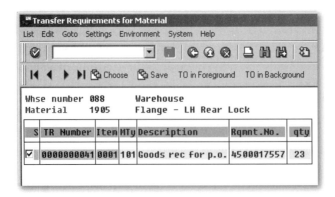

Figure 5.16 Display of Transfer Requirement Resulting From Search Criteria: Transaction LB11

Figure 5.16 shows the transfer requirement found using the search criteria entered in Figure 5.15. The transfer requirement has been created as a result of the goods receipt for the purchase order. The line item shows the transfer requirement number, movement type, and description that created the transfer requirement, the purchase order number that has been receipted into stock, and the quantity on the transfer requirement.

Now that we have identified the transfer requirement, we can convert it to a transfer order. As Figure 5.16 shows, there are two was to do this. A transfer order can be created in the foreground or the background.

To convert to a transfer order in the foreground, the **TO in Foreground** button can be selected or the **Ctrl + Shift + F8** function keys. The transfer order can also be created from the header menu and choosing **Environment • TO in Foreground.**

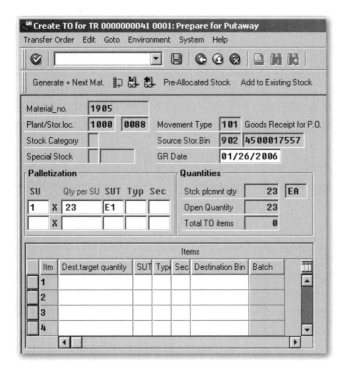

Figure 5.17 Conversion of Transfer Requirement to Transfer Order: Transaction LB11

Figure 5.17 shows the first screen displayed after the **TO in Foreground** button is selected. You can review and change the information if necessary. Once it is correct the **Generate + Next Mat** button can be selected to complete the line item.

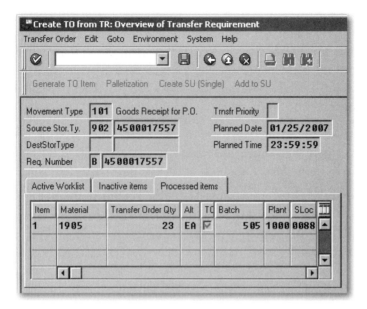

Figure 5.18 Display of Transfer Order Created From Transfer Requirement

Figure 5.18 shows the transfer order that has been created from the information that was shown in Figure 5.17. The transfer order can be posted by selecting **Transfer Order • Posting** from the header menu or the function keys **Ctrl + S**.

Once the transfer order has been posted, the system returns to the display of transfer requirements, as shown in Figure 5.16, and the transfer order number is displayed at the bottom of the screen.

5.2.5 Display of the Transfer Order

The transfer order that is created by the conversion of the transfer requirement to a transfer order can be seen using Transaction LT21 if the transfer order number is known. If just the material is known, use Transaction LT24 or follow the navigation menu path: **SAP Menu • Logistics • Logistics Execution • Internal Warehouse Processes • Stock Transfer • Display Transfer Order • For Material**.

Figure 5.19 shows the initial selection criteria screen for the display of transfer orders. All the transfer orders can be displayed for a material in a warehouse. In this example, the transfer order created for the goods receipt of material **1905** is being searched for, and the selection criteria reflect this.

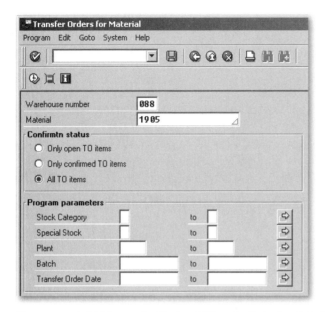

Figure 5.19 Initial Screen for Display Of Transfer Order by Material Number: Transaction LT24

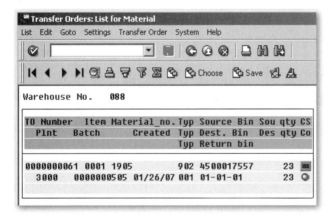

Figure 5.20 Display of Transfer Orders Available from Selection Criteria: Transaction LT24

Figure 5.20 shows the transfer order that has been created for the purchase order 4500017557 that was receipted into the plant. A transfer requirement has been created to start the putaway in the warehouse. The conversion of the transfer requirement to the transfer order and the confirmation of the transfer order have moved the 23 units of material **1905** into the warehouse storage bin **01–01–01** in storage type **001**.

In the last two sections, we described goods receipts with and without inbound deliveries. Now we shall examine goods receipts that do not involve inventory management.

5.3 Goods Receipt Without Inventory Management

At first glance, this process may appear somewhat abnormal. Normally, materials are receipted into a storage location, and that triggers a transfer requirement and a transfer order in WM. However, there are materials in the warehouse that sometimes do not require a goods receipt in IM, but are required for warehouse operations. An example of this is packaging materials, such as pallets and crates. These are used for material storage and shipment, but do not have to be goods-receipted into IM.

5.3.1 Create the Transfer Order for the Goods Receipt

The transfer order can be created without reference to a goods receipt from IM or a transfer requirement in WM. A transfer order can be created in Transaction LT01 or via the SAP navigation path: **SAP Menu • Logistics • Logistics Execution • Internal Warehouse Processes • Stock Transfer • Create Transfer Order • No Source Object**.

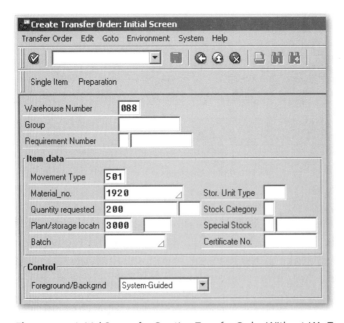

Figure 5.21 Initial Screen for Creating Transfer Order Without IM: Transaction LT01

Figure 5.21 shows the initial screen for creating the transfer order using Transaction LT01. The goods-movement number **501** used here refers to a receipt without a purchase order. In this scenario, a vendor may have dropped off a shipment of 200 pallets to be used in the shipment of parts. Many industries use pallets that are leased to them at a very small charge per day; e.g.,GKN pallets.

> **Note**
>
> A GKN pallet is a series of blue wooden strips and blocks crafted into a square shape, about 1.2 square meters. It is manufactured by CHEP, a division of GKN, and is rented to a company for a few cents per day.

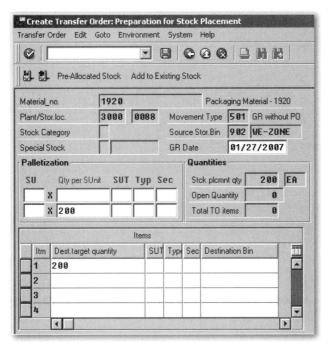

Figure 5.22 Detail Screen for Creating Transfer Order for Material Receipt Without IM: Transaction LT01

Figure 5.22 shows the detail screen for Transaction LT01. The screen shows that the material putaway will come from the source storage type 902, which is the goods-receipt area. The system will generate the destination storage type and storage bin. To create the transfer order, use the function keys **Ctrl + S** or **Transfer Order • Posting** from the header menu. Once posting is complete, the system will return to the initial screen and display the transfer order number it has created.

5.3.2 Display the Transfer Order for the Goods Receipt

The information in the transfer order can be reviewed by displaying the contents of the transfer order using Transaction LT21 or following the SAP navigation path: **SAP Menu • Logistics • Logistics Execution • Internal Warehouse Processes • Stock Transfer • Display Transfer Order • Single Document**. The transaction requires that the just the warehouse number and the transfer order number be entered to display the transfer-order details.

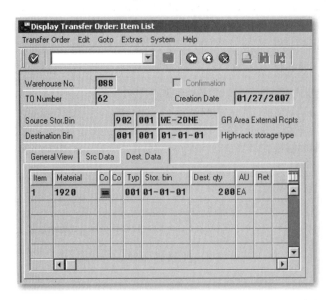

Figure 5.23 Display of Transfer Order Created for Material Goods Receipt Without IM: Transaction LT21

Figure 5.23 shows the detail of the line item in the transfer order created for the goods receipt. The material has been moved from storage type **902, storage section**001, and storage bin **WE-ZONE** to storage type **001**, storage section **001**, and storage bin **01–01–01**. Note that the quantity of **200** has not been confirmed because the confirmation indicator next to the warehouse number has not been set by the system.

5.3.3 Display the Stock Levels

Prior to the posting of the transfer order and the receipt of the material into the warehouse stock, the stock levels for the material in the warehouse can be reviewed. To do this, use Transaction LS24 or follow the SAP navigation path: **SAP Menu • Logistics • Logistics Execution • Internal Warehouse Processes • Bins and Stock • Display • Bin Stock per Material**.

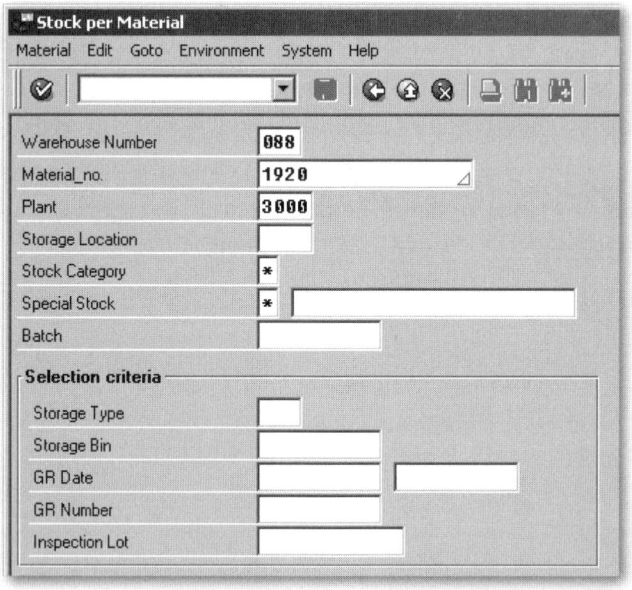

Figure 5.24 Initial Screen for Display of Transfer Order by Material: Transaction LS24

Figure 5.24 shows initial screen for Transaction **LS24** that allows selections to be made to report on the stock levels for the material required. In this example, the display for stock levels of material **1920** is limited to the warehouse number 088, but for all storage types.

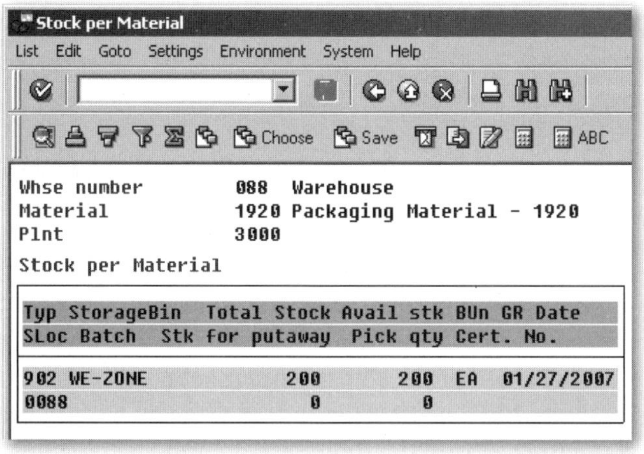

Figure 5.25 Display of Stock Levels for Material 1920 in Warehouse 088: Transaction LS24

Figure 5.25 shows the stock levels for material **1920**. It shows that the material is located in receiving area and not yet moved to storage type **001** and placed in bin **01-01-01**. Therefore, the transfer order should be confirmed using Transaction LT12 or by following the navigation menu path: **SAP Menu • Logistics • Logistics Execution • Internal Warehouse Processes • Stock Transfer • Confirm Transfer Order • Single Document • In One Step**.

Figure 5.26 Initial Screen to Confirm Transfer Order: Transaction LT12

Figure 5.26 shows the information required to confirm the transfer order and move the material from the goods receipt area to the storage bin 01–01–01 in storage type 001.

You can confirm the movement by checking the bin stock using Transaction LS24. Enter the same information in the initial screen as in Figure 5.24. The resulting screen after confirmation of the transfer order shows the material posted into the correct storage bin. The final placement of the material in the warehouse is shown in Figure 5.27.

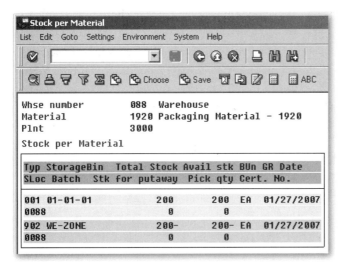

Figure 5.27 Stock per Material Report Showing Movement from WE-ZONE
to Storage Bin 01–01–01

5.4 Summary

Material is receipted into stock using purchase orders or production orders.
The material can easily be goods-receipted using inventory management, but
a number of steps are needed to move and store the material in SAP WM.
This chapter explained procedures required when material is brought into
the warehouse, either as a normal receipt or as a receipt that involves handling units.

Chapter 6 will examine the opposite of goods receipt: goods issue. Moving
the material from the warehouse involves a variety of procedures that you
should understand clearly.

The outbound delivery process can be complex and labor intensive. You should understand the goods-issue function clearly in order to use more complex strategies such as wave picking to implement a successful outbound process in the warehouse.

6   Goods Issues

In warehouse management, a goods issue is the movement of material from the warehouse to an external source, which could be a production order or a customer. The warehouse also could use goods issue as the process for consuming material and assigning the costs of the material consumed to a cost center.

A goods issue from the warehouse is triggered by one of two documents: a transfer requirement from inventory management or production, or an outbound delivery if one has been created for a customer sales order.

This chapter will examine goods-issue functionality that include outbound deliveries, groups, and wave picks. Now let's proceed to the next section, which will examine the goods-issue process with outbound deliveries.

6.1   Goods Issue with Outbound Delivery

An outbound delivery involves picking of materials in the warehouse, reducing the material level in the warehouse, and shipping the materials to the customer. The goods issue is important to the customer because it creates a link between the manufacturer and the customer. If the goods-issue process does not run at optimum efficiency, delays in delivery can cause the customer financial problems and create customer dissatisfaction.

The outbound delivery is created from a sales order that specifies an amount of material to be delivered to a customer. The sales order is usually created by the sales clerks or received in electronic format.

6.1.1 Display Sales Order

When the sales order has been created, the customer is given a delivery date by which it can expect the material to arrive at its location. The sales order contains this information as well as the material details, quantity, and pricing.

If the sales order number is known, SAP WM users can view the sales order using Transaction VA03 or by following the navigation path: **SAP • Logistics • Sales and Distribution • Sales • Order • Display**.

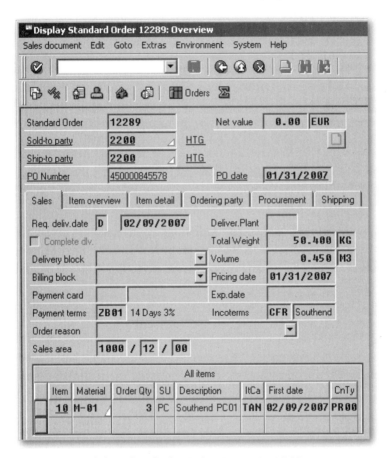

Figure 6.1 Detailed Display of Sales Order: Transaction VA03

The sales order displayed in Figure 6.1 is used to create an outbound delivery. The sales order shows that the customers purchase order was placed on **1/31/2007** and the delivery date for the material is **2/9/2007**. The sales order shows the item details, such as material number and the quantity ordered.

6.1.2 Create Outbound Delivery

When the sales order has been placed, you can create the outbound delivery, which can occur in at a specific time before the material needs to be picked. The specific procedure from which outbound deliveries are created will vary from company to company.

> Tip
>
> Ask your sales or warehouse staff when the outbound delivery needs to be done.

The outbound delivery is created by using Transaction VL01N or by following the navigation path: **SAP · Logistics · Sales and Distribution · Sales · Order · Subsequent Functions · Outbound Delivery**.

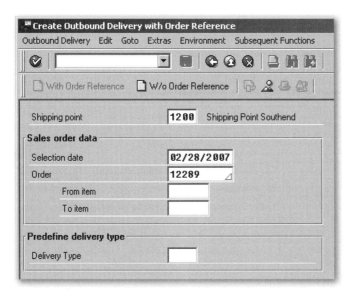

Figure 6.2 Initial Screen for Creating Outbound Delivery With Reference to Sales Order: Transaction VL01N

When creating outbound deliveries, the initial screen of Transaction VL01N (shown in Figure 6.2) requires you to enter the shipping point. The shipping point is a location from which items are shipped from and is configured in the Logistics Execution section of the IMG. The navigation path is: **IMG · Enterprise Structure · Definition · Logistics Execution · Define, Copy, Delete, Check Shipping Point**.

The shipping point can be assigned to several plants. In large distribution or retail operations, the loading area for vehicles may be a separate location that supports a number of locations on the company's campus. A shipping point can be further divided into a number of loading points.

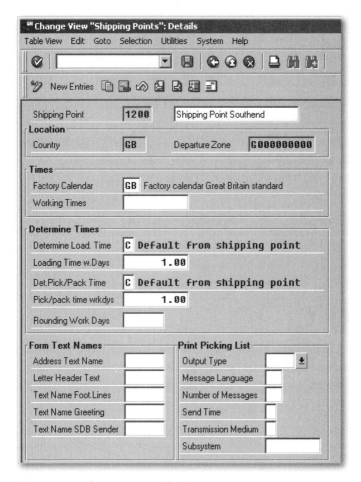

Figure 6.3 Configuration Detail for Shipping Point

Figure 6.3 shows the detail screen for a shipping point. The information required for a shipping point includes the factory calendar and country location.

After the shipping point has been entered into the initial screen of Transaction VL01N (Figure 6.2), you also can enter the sales data, which includes the delivery date and the sales order number. If no other data is required, the information, such as the delivery date and sales order document number, can be entered and the detail screen will be displayed.

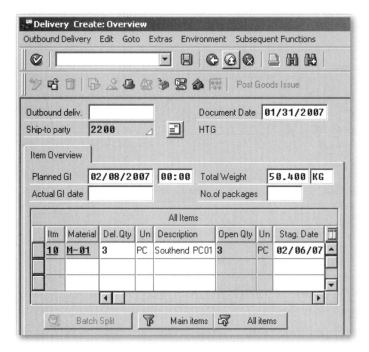

Figure 6.4 Detail Screen for Delivery Creation: Transaction VL01N

Figure 6.4 shows the detail screen for delivery creation based on a sales order. The information from the sales order has been entered, such as the material number, quantity to be delivered, date for the staging of the material for delivery, and the planned goods issue date.

If this information is correct and does not require any changes, then you can create the outbound delivery by selecting **Outbound Delivery • Save** from the header menu or by using the **Ctrl + S** function keys. Once processing is complete, the system will return you to the initial screen for outbound delivery creation and display the outbound delivery number on the screen.

6.1.3 Outbound Delivery Status

We can analyze the status of the elements of the outbound delivery by displaying the status overview. Selecting Transaction VL03N to display the outbound delivery allows display of the status overview information. The navigation path for this transaction is: **SAP • Logistics • Sales and Distribution • Shipping and Transportation • Outbound Delivery • Display**.

Figure 6.5 Status Overview Information from Outbound Delivery Display: Transaction VL03N

Figure 6.5 shows the status overview for the outbound delivery. The overview reports two elements: the delivery shown in the overall status and the material shown in the line-item status. Each element has a number of items for which a status is given.

Overall Status

This overall status line refers to the status of the delivery. A number of indicators can provide details of the status, and these are described here:

▶ **OPS**
This status field shows the overall status for the picking of the delivery. It tells whether the delivery has been completely picked (option **C**), is in the process of being picked (option B), or has not yet been processed, (option **A**).

▶ **PS**
This field contains the packing status, which indicates whether there are items that are relevant for packing. Status **A** is allocated when the packing

has not been processed, status B where the delivery is partially packed, and status **C** when it is completely packed.

▶ **WM**

This field shows the overall status of warehouse-management activities. The status shown indicates whether a transfer order for SAP WM is required, and, if required, whether it is confirmed or still open for processing.

▶ **C**

This field shows the status of pick confirmation. This confirmation status indicates whether picking must be explicitly confirmed for the delivery or whether picking already has been confirmed. The confirmation status is only relevant if transfer orders are not for picking.

▶ **GM**

This field shows the total goods-movement status. The indicator informs you whether the delivery has already left the warehouse, or is still being processed, and whether processing has begun.

▶ **BS**

This indicator shows the billing status of the sales or delivery document. The status describes if the document is completely billed, partly billed, or is not relevant for billing.

▶ **Sta**

This indicator shows the status for the inter-company billing.

▶ **TS**

This field indicates the transportation planning status. This indicator is set on the basis of the leg indicator (preliminary, subsequent, direct, return) in the headers of the shipment documents to which delivery has been assigned. Status indicators can be:

▷ **A**

Not yet planned

▷ **B**

Partially planned

▷ **C**

Completely planned

▶ **OvCS**

This indicator is relevant for the overall status of credit checks.

▶ **POD Status**

This indicator is the proof-of-delivery status (POD status) for the entire delivery. The status informs whether the customer reported a POD for this delivery. The values can be:

► **A**

Relevant for the POD process

► **B**

Differences were reported

► **C**

Quantities were verified and confirmed

Delivery Item Status

In Figure 6.5, the delivery item status line refers to item 10. A number of indicators report on the item status; these are described as follows:

► **Pick St**

The status message indicates whether the item is relevant for delivery. The status indicates whether picking has not yet processed (**A**), partially processed (**B**), or completely processed (**C**). Some items are not relevant for picking and would show no indicator. These can include text or service materials.

► **PS**

This indicator refers to the packing status for the line item.

► **WM Stat**

This indicator for the SAP WM status of the delivery item. If the delivery processing uses the WM module, then the status for each item in a delivery is updated by the system.

► **Confir.**

This indicator shows the pick-confirmation status for each delivery item. When a delivery item is subject to pick confirmation, the item is assigned the status **A** to indicate that the line is subject to confirmation but not yet confirmed. Once the pick is confirmed, the system assigns either status B for partially confirmed or status **C** if the line item is fully pick- confirmed.

► **GS**

This indicator is for goods movement status. For outbound deliveries, the status informs whether the item has already left the warehouse or company premises, or whether it is still being processed.

► **BS**

This is the billing status of delivery-related billing documents. The status line tells you if the item is not yet billed, partly billed, completely billed, or not relevant for billing.

▶ **IBS**

This indicator shows the status for the inter-company billing.

▶ **POD status**

This indicator is for the proof of delivery status of each item. The status value informs the user whether the customer reported a proof of delivery for this item. This status can have the following values:

▷ **Blank**

Not relevant for the POD process

▷ **A**

Relevant for the POD process

▷ **B**

Differences were reported

▷ **C**

Quantities were verified and confirmed

6.1.4   Create Transfer Order

The transfer order needs to be created in order for the material to be removed from its storage bin in the warehouse and moved to the area where materials are staged for delivery.

The transfer order is created with reference to the outbound delivery document that has been created. You can have more than one transfer order per delivery, but only if the configuration parameters for transfer order split have been entered for the relevant warehouse.

Transfer Order Split Configuration

Multiple transfer orders can be created for an outbound delivery to ensure that a single transfer order will not exceed certain limitations. Creating multiple transfer orders will distribute the workload more evenly. The configuration entered determines at what point multiple transfer orders are created.

The configuration for the transfer order split can be found using the navigation path: **IMG • Logistics Execution • Warehouse Management • Activities • Transfers • Processing Performance Data/TO Split • Define Profiles**.

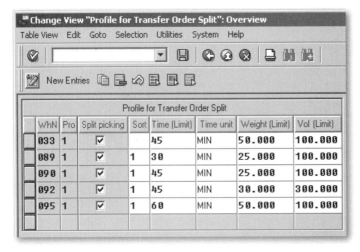

Figure 6.6 Configuration for Allowing Transfer Order Splits in Outbound Delivery

Figure 6.6 shows the configuration to create the profiles used in the relevant warehouses. Configuring the profile's parameters at certain levels cause the transfer order splits.

For each warehouse, a series of indicators can be set to define the profile for the transfer order split that occurs in that warehouse. The indicators are described as follows:

▶ **Split picking**
Various criteria can be used to control the way a transfer order is split. When this indicator is set the transfer order will be split; i.e., a new transfer order is created when the picking area is changed.

▶ **Sort**
This field determines the sort profile for the transfer order. The sort profile is used to maximize warehouse efficiency in picking transfer orders. In the sorting fields, you can enter sort criteria, such as storage bin, material weight, etc., that are saved in the sorting profile.

▶ **Time (Limit)**
You can configure this field with the value that indicates the maximum limit of processing time for a transfer order. For example, if a value of "60" is entered, this will be the total processing time for a single transfer. If the processing time exceeds this value, a new transfer order will be created. If this field is blank, there is no limit for processing time for a transfer order. A limit is used to ensure that the workload is evenly spread in the warehouse.

▶ **Weight (Limit)**

Similar to the time limit, this field allows entry of a weight limit to control transfer order splitting. If the weight of the transfer order exceeds the value in this field, this will trigger a new transfer order. For example, if a value of "200" is entered into this field and a transfer order is entered with a total weight of "670", then four transfer orders will be created. A blank field indicates that there is no weight limit to a transfer order.

▶ **Vol (Limit)**

Similar to the weight and time limit fields, this field allows you to enter a value for volume that will trigger a new transfer order when it is exceeded.

Outbound Delivery Monitor

The outbound delivery monitor is a comprehensive tool that enables the shipping department of the warehouse to view deliveries that need to be picked, based on a variety of criteria entered into the transaction. You can use the outbound delivery monitor to create the transfer order for the delivery.

You can access the Outbound Delivery Monitor using Transaction VL06P. The navigation path to this transaction is: **SAP • Logistics • Sales and Distribution • Shipping and Transportation • Picking • Create Transfer Order • Via Outbound Delivery Monitor**.

Figure 6.7 shows the selection criteria that can be entered into the Outbound Delivery Monitor to select specific deliveries. In this particular example, the criteria have been entered to select all applicable deliveries that are due to be shipped from **Shipping Point 1200** and to be picked using warehouse management between **02/01/2007** and **02/28/2007**.

To execute the transaction the **F8** function key can be used or selecting **Program • Execute** from the header menu.

Figure 6.8 shows the deliveries that fall within the criteria entered into the Outbound Delivery Monitor selection screen. These deliveries are all warehouse management relevant, to be picked between **02/01/2007** and **02/28/2007**, and all are to be shipped from shipping point **1200**.

From this screen, the SAP WM transfer order can be created. In Figure 6.8, you can see buttons for allowing a transfer order to be created either in the foreground or the background. You also can create a foreground transfer order by using the **F8** function key and a background transfer order by using the **F7** function key.

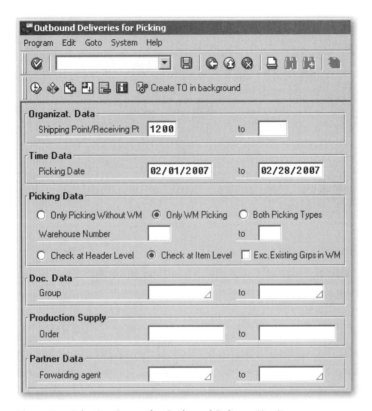

Figure 6.7 Selection Screen for Outbound Delivery Monitor

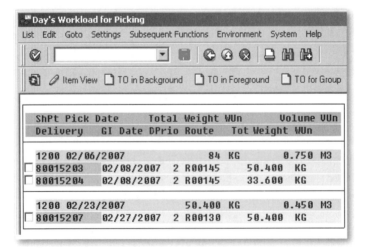

Figure 6.8 List Of Deliveries Based on Selection Criteria Entered in Outbound Delivery Monitor

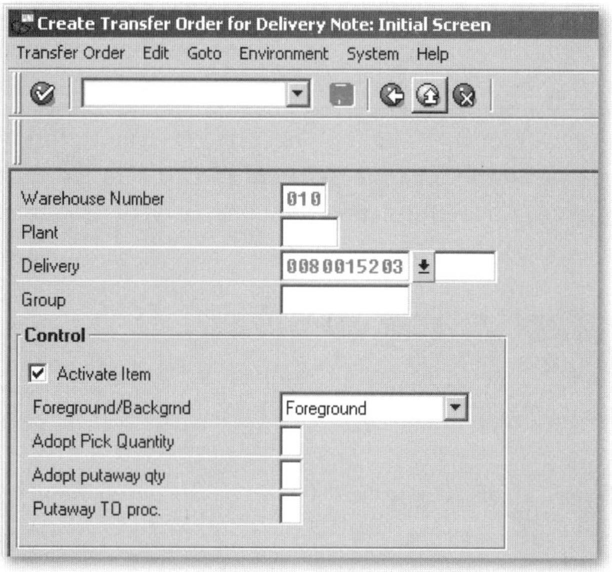

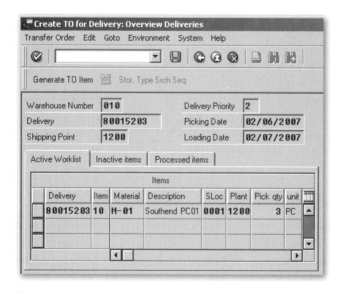

Figure 6.9 Creating Transfer Order from Outbound Delivery Monitor

After selecting a delivery and starting the process of creating a transfer order from the delivery note, the outbound delivery monitor transaction will pass the parameters to Transaction LT03. Figure 6.9 shows the initial screen of that transaction. At this point, you have the option of creating the transfer order in the foreground or in the background.

Figure 6.10 Display of Delivery Line Item Used to Create Transfer Order

Figure 6.10 shows the work list of delivery line items to be converted to a transfer order. The line item shows the outbound delivery number, material, plant, storage location, and picking quantity.

You can create the transfer order by using the **Generate TO Item** button or the from the header menu **Edit • Generate TO Item** can be selected. The transaction processes the work-list information, generates a list of processed items that can be saved, and creates a transfer order.

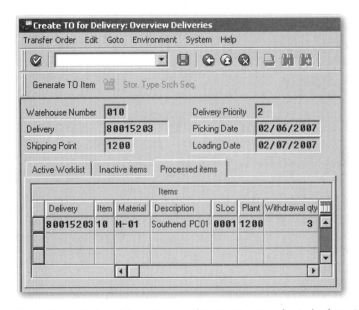

Figure 6.11 Display of Items Processed in Creating Transfer Order from Outbound Delivery

Figure 6.11 shows the item that has been processed from the work list and will be the line item in the transfer order. To complete this transaction, you must post it using the **Ctrl + S** function key or by selecting **Transfer Order • Posting** from the header menu. The transaction will return to the results for outbound delivery monitor, and the transfer order number will be displayed.

6.1.5 Confirm Transfer Order

Once the transfer order has been created, the material can be picked and moved to the packing area or loading area, depending on the processes that need to be carried out on the material before it leaves the warehouse. Many materials that are shipped on pallets are shrink-wrapped in plastic before they leave the warehouse to prevent any damage in transit.

The transfer order can be confirmed using Transaction LT12 or via the navigation path: **SAP · Logistics · Logistics Execution · Outbound Process · Goods Issue for Outbound Delivery · Picking · Confirm Transfer Order · Single Document · In One Step**.

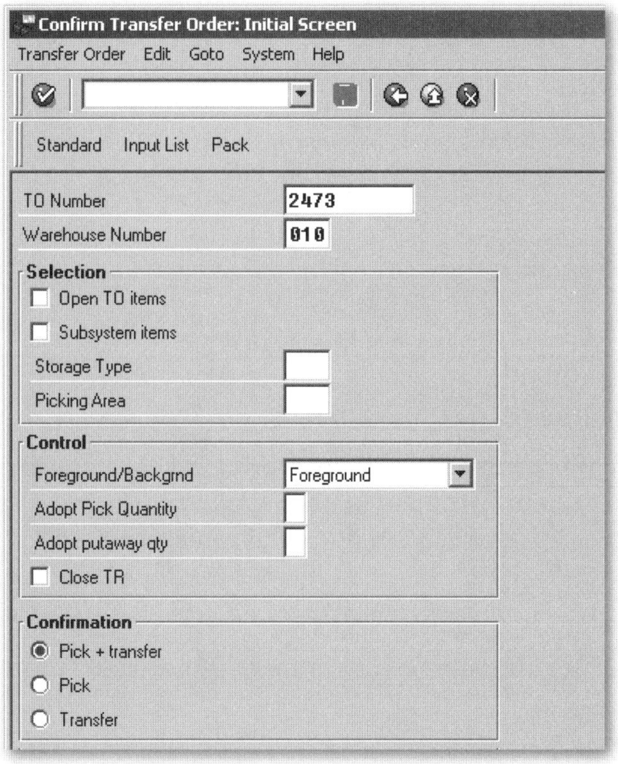

Figure 6.12 Confirmation of Transfer Order: Transaction LT12

Figure 6.12 shows the initial screen for confirmation of the transfer order for the outbound delivery. The confirmation is performed in one step that combines a pick and a transfer of the materials. If the pick and the transfer are to be separate processes, the confirmation indicator at the bottom of the screen can be changed to reflect that.

Figure 6.13 shows the material to be picked and moved is located in storage type 005 and in storage bin D-MT100. The destination storage location is 916, which is the interim storage type used as the shipping area.

The transfer order can be confirmed internally by using the button on the screen, by using the **F5** function key, or by using the header menu and selecting **Edit · Confirm Internally**.

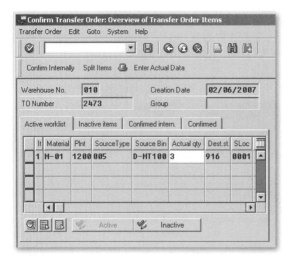

Figure 6.13 Confirmation of Transfer Order: Transaction LT12

6.1.6 Post Goods Issue for Outbound Delivery

After the transfer order has been confirmed and is completed, the material is ready for delivery. The material will be sitting in the delivery area, awaiting loading onto a delivery vehicle or delivery by a third party such as DHL or FedEx. The outbound delivery document is ready to be closed, and the movement of the material out of the warehouse is completed in the system by posting the goods issue.

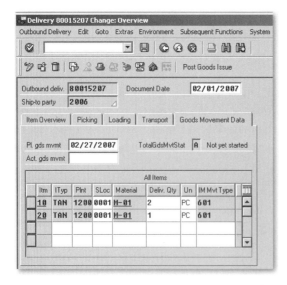

Figure 6.14 Outbound Delivery Ready for Posting of Goods Issue

Figure 6.14 shows the goods movement data for the inventory management side of the delivery. The Inventory Management movement type is **601** for a goods issue for a delivery. You can select the **Post Goods Issue** button in the toolbar to post goods issue. If for any reason the delivery cannot be posted, an error log will be displayed to identify the problems that are preventing goods issue for the line items on the document. The posting of the goods issue moves the material from the warehouse, and the inventory value is removed from the plant.

6.1.7 Review Material Documents

To review the movement of the outbound delivery, you can use two transactions for reviewing the material documents. The Transaction is MB51, which can be used to show all the movements of the material, either inbound or outbound. This transaction can also be found using the navigation menu path: **SAP • Logistics • Materials Management • Inventory Management • Environment • List Display • Material Documents**.

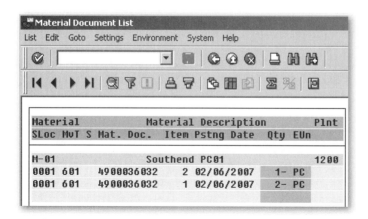

Figure 6.15 Material Documents for Single Material: Transaction MB51

Figure 6.15 shows the material documents created for the outbound delivery. The outbound delivery specified a total of three units of the material M-01, as shown with the two item lines of material document 4900036032. The single material document can be viewed in detail using Transaction MB03, which can be found using the navigation path: **SAP • Logistics • Materials Management • Inventory Management • Material Document • Display**.

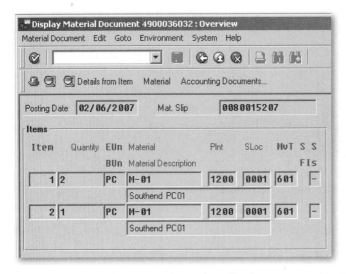

Figure 6.16 Material Document for Outbound Delivery: Transaction MB03

Figure 6.16 shows the material document that was produced by the posting of the goods issue for the outbound delivery. The outbound-delivery number is shown in the material document as the material slip number.

Now that we have examined the goods-issue process supported by outbound delivery, we'll review the goods-issue process without outbound deliveries.

6.2   Goods Issue Without Outbound Delivery

The goods issue created without an outbound delivery starts with a goods issue that is created in Inventory Management (SAP IM). This may be a goods issue to a cost center, a goods issue to a project, or a number of different scenarios.

6.2.1   Goods Issue in Inventory Management

The goods issue to a cost center does not require an outbound delivery and can be performed in inventory management. This transaction is made prior to the movement of the material in the warehouse. Therefore, the accounting movement is performed before the actual movement of the material.

The goods issue is performed using Transaction MB1A, which can be found using the navigation path: **SAP · Logistics · Logistics Execution · Outbound Process · Goods Issue for Other Transactions · Enter Goods Issue**.

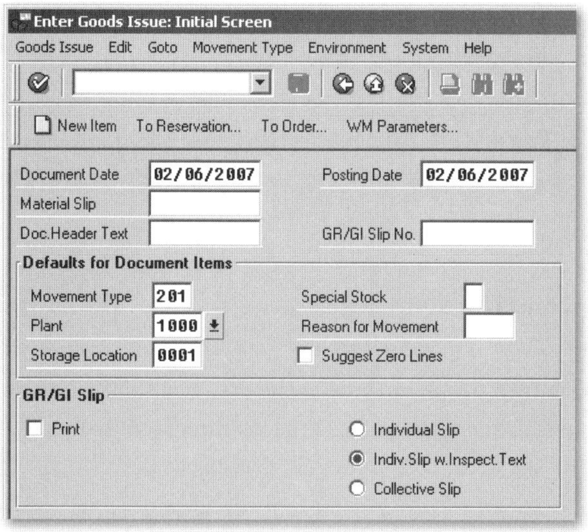

Figure 6.17 Initial Screen for Goods Issue to Cost Center: Transaction MB1A

Figure 6.17 displays the initial screen for the Transaction MB1A and shows the movement type for the goods issue as **201**, which refers to a goods issue to a cost center. There are many reasons for issuing a material to a cost center. The issue to a cost center consumes the material, and the value of the material is moved from the inventory account to the cost center. In this case, the material will be issued to the plant-maintenance cost center for use in a repair project.

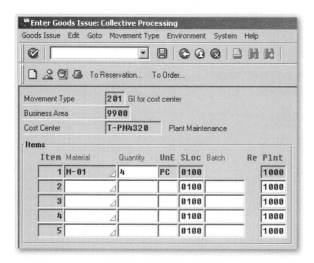

Figure 6.18 Detail Screen for Goods Issue: Transaction MB1A

Figure 6.18 shows that the cost center has been added to the detail screen. The cost center relates to plant maintenance, and the value of the material will be passed to the cost center.

The material and quantity is added to the detail screen, and the goods issue is then posted. This creates a material and accounting document for the goods issue.

6.2.2 Negative Balance in the Warehouse

Since the material in question is governed by SAP WM, the goods issue creates the need for a movement to occur in the warehouse. To initiate a transfer order to move the material, the goods issue creates a negative balance in the goods-issue interim storage area in the relevant warehouse.

To see the negative balance for the material referred to in the goods issue, you can use Transaction LS24. This transaction also can be found using the navigation path: **SAP • Logistics • Logistics Execution • Internal Warehouse Processes • Bins and Stocks • Display • Bin Stock per Material**.

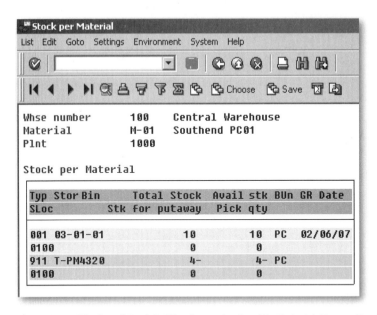

Figure 6.19 Display of Stock in Warehouse for Specific Material: Transaction LS24

Figure 6.19 shows that the goods issue created in SAP IM has created a negative balance in the interim storage type **911**. The storage bin has been named the same as the cost center where the material is to be consumed.

6.2.3   Creating Transfer Order

The transfer order is created from the material document produced from the goods issue. Normally, once the goods issue is posted the processing will automatically pass through to Transaction LT06. This transaction can be found using the navigation path: **SAP • Logistics • Logistics Execution • Outbound Process • Goods Issue for Other Transactions • Picking • Create Transfer Order • For Material Document**.

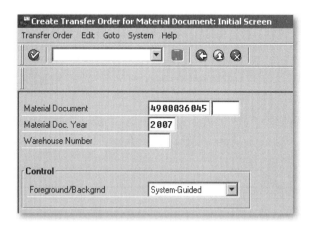

Figure 6.20   Creating Transfer Order from Goods Issue Material Document: Transaction LT06

Figure 6.20 shows the initial screen for the creation of the transfer order based on the material document for the goods issue. The system needs to create the transfer order to move the material from the warehouse to balance the negative value in the goods-issue interim storage area.

Figure 6.21 shows the requirement passed through to the transfer order from the material document. The storage type search shows that the transfer order will fulfill the requirement from either storage type **001** or **002**. The transfer order item information is generated from this screen.

Figure 6.22 shows the item detail for the transfer order. The material quantity shown is to be removed from a source storage type and transferred to the goods issue interim storage area to offset the negative value caused by the goods issue.

After the transfer order has been created in Transaction LT06, it must then be confirmed. You should do this after the material has physically been moved from the source storage bin to the goods-issue area to ensure that the correct materials are actually moved and there is no damage or loss.

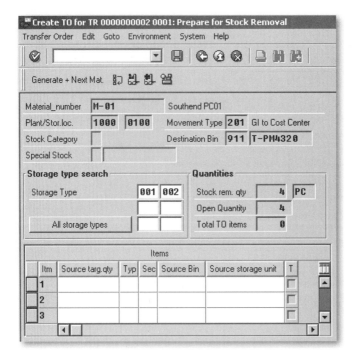

Figure 6.21 Item Information from Goods Issue Material Document: Transaction LT06

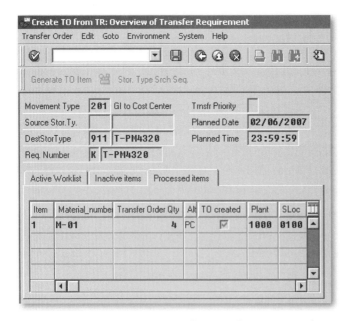

Figure 6.22 Transfer Order Creation from Goods Issue Material Document: Transaction LT06

> **Tip**
>
> In many warehouses, this situation is assumed, and the confirmation may take place as soon as the transfer order is created. Check with the warehouse staff to see how this is performed in their organization.

Complete the transfer order by using Transaction LT12, or by using the navigation path: **SAP • Logistics • Logistics Execution • Internal Warehouse Processes • Stock Transfer • Confirm Transfer Order • Single Document • In One Step**.

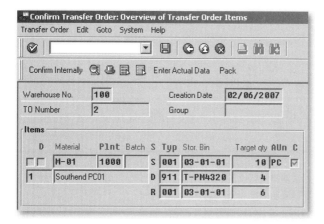

Figure 6.23 Confirmation of Transfer Order: Transaction LT12

Transaction LT12 requires that the transfer order number and the warehouse be entered for the confirmation, as shown earlier in this chapter in Figure 6.12. After the transfer order number and warehouse have been entered, the detail screen for the confirmation is displayed as shown in Figure 6.23.

The screen shows the material **M-01** has a quantity of **10** in storage bin **03–01–01** and a quantity of four is required to offset the negative quant in the goods-issue storage type. The remainder of the material, a quantity of six , is stored back in storage bin 03–01–01. The transfer order is confirmed by using the **Confirm Internally** button on the screen.

The resulting stock balance in the warehouse can be seen by again using Transaction LS24.

Figure 6.24 shows that all of the warehouse processes are now complete. The quantity of the material, **M-01**, is now six. This has been reduced because of the negative quant in storage type 911, as shown in Figure 6.19, has been offset by the quantity transferred from the storage type 001.

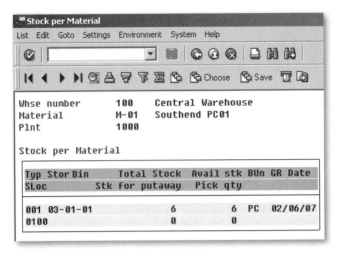

Figure 6.24 Display of Stock in Warehouse for Specific Material: Transaction LS24

In this section, we examined the goods-issue process without outbound deliveries. The next section will review multiple processing using groups.

6.3 Multiple Processing Using Groups

Multiple processing allows the SAP WM user to group transfer requirements or outbound deliveries and process the group at one time. Processing a group of requirements or deliveries, rather than converting each individual transfer requirement or each outbound delivery into a transfer order, can reduce the amount of administration time taken on these tasks.

6.3.1 Definition of a Group

A group is defined as a work package containing a number of transfer requirements or outbound deliveries. This work package is used for optimizing picking operations. Grouping together transfer requirements for the same movement type or same storage type can increase the productivity of the warehouse operation.

6.3.2 Creating a Group for Transfer Requirements

Groups are often created for transfer requirements when many material movements in the warehouse are triggered by transfer requirements. In a distribution warehouse, a great many movements are required to satisfy the deliveries to satellite warehouses or retail establishments. If these movements were based on transfer requirements, the use of a group would enable the warehouse to reduce the number of transfer order conversions to one per group.

Use Transaction LT41 to create a group for transfer requirements. The transaction can be found using the navigation path: **SAP • Logistics • Logistics Execution • Outbound Process • Goods Issue for Other Transactions • Picking • Group of Transfer Requirements • Create.**

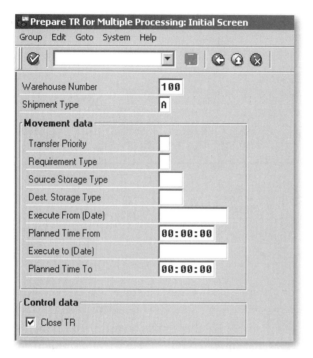

Figure 6.25 Initial Screen for Creation of Group for Transfer Requirements: Transaction LT41

Figure 6.25 shows the initial screen to search for transfer requirements that will be combined into a single group. The **Shipment Type** in the screen is "A," which indicates stock removal. Other entries can include "E" for putaway and "U" for posting change transfer requirements. The **Requirement Type** relates to the process of the transfer requirement.

Example

You can enter a "B" for a purchase order, "K" for cost centers, "V" for sales orders etc.

The **Close TR** field at the bottom of the selection screen indicates whether the transfer requirement should be closed. If this indicator is set, then once the transfer order is confirmed the transfer requirement will be considered complete and will be closed.

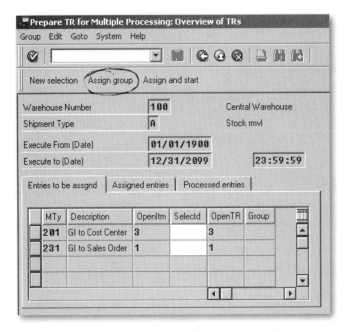

Figure 6.26 : Creating Group of Transfer Requirements for Movement Types 201 and 231

Figure 6.26 shows that for the selection criteria entered in the previous screen, four open transfer requirements for warehouse **100** refer to stock removal. Figure 6.26 shows that there are three open transfer requirements, **Open TR**, for movement type 201 and one open transfer requirement for movement type 231.

These four transfer requirements can be combined into one group for processing purposes. To create the group, start by selecting the **Assign Group** button. After you select the **Assign Group** button, a dialog box will appear, as shown in Figure 6.27. This dialog box requires entry of a description for the group and a group name.

The Two-Step Picking field for relevancy indicates whether the system will perform two-step picking. If the indicator is blank, the group records will not be subject to two-step picking. If the indicator is set to **2**, then the two step picking is relevant. The group is created once the information is entered into the dialog box screen.

Figure 6.27 Entering Group Description and Group Name: Transaction LT41

6.3.3 Creating Transfer Orders for a Group of Transfer Requirements.

After the group has been created, transfer orders for the items in the group can be created when that group of transfer requirements is ready to be converted. Use Transaction LT42 for creation of transfer orders for a group. This transaction can be found using the navigation path: **SAP • Logistics • Logistics Execution • Outbound Process • Goods Issue for Other Transactions • Picking • Create Transfer Order • for Group**.

Figure 6.28 shows the entry fields for the conversion of the transfer requirements inside the group to transfer orders. The **Reference doc cat** indicator can be set to **B** for a group of transfer requirements or **L** for a group of deliveries.

The **Foreground** control has been selected in Figure 6.28, but this is only advisable if there are a small number of transfer requirements in the group. If the group contains a vast number of transfer requirements, then the **Background** control is more appropriate.

After the necessary data has been entered, the process can be started by using the **Start multiple proc** button. When the **Foreground** control has been selected, each transfer creation will appear, and the process can be monitored.

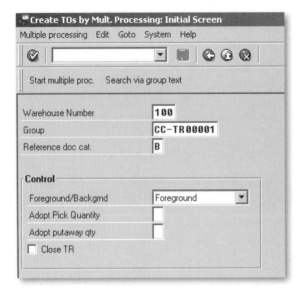

Figure 6.28 Creation of Transfer Orders from Group of Transfer Requirements: Transaction LT42

In the event that the material is missing from a storage bin or a storage bin cannot be found, changes can be made during processing to ensure that transfer orders are created. This cannot be done in background processing. Once the processing has been completed for the group, the resulting screen will displayed as shown in Figure 6.29.

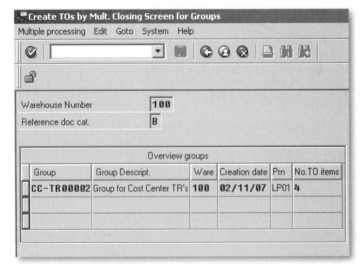

Figure 6.29 Transfer Orders Created for Group of Transfer Requirements: Transaction LT42

The closing screen for the group, shown in Figure 6.29, displays the group that was entered and the number of transfer orders and transfer order line items that were created. In addition, the screen shows the number of the printer that will output the transfer orders.

You can release and print the transfer orders by using the **F5** function key, or the padlock icon on the screen or by using the header menu and selecting **Goto • Release/print**.

6.3.4   Definition of a Wave Pick

When groups are used with outbound deliveries, we normally refer to such groups as waves. A wave pick is defined as a work package, like a group, but it contains a number of outbound deliveries. This wave pick is created using the Wave Monitor. The advantage of using a wave pick is that it is possible to select the outbound delivery according to time slots.

Example

If a warehouse has 2,000 outbound deliveries per shift, the wave pick can group these deliveries for each time slot. If the shift starts at 6 a.m. and ends at 3 p.m., a wave pick can be run for each time slot, which can be hourly, and the deliveries can be processed in that manner.

6.3.5   Creating a Group for Outbound Deliveries

A warehouse creates a wave for outbound deliveries when many transfer orders must be created for deliveries outside the warehouse. The outbound deliveries are for sales orders that have been received and need to be fulfilled by the material in the warehouse.

6.3.6   Creating the Wave from Outbound Delivery Monitor

You can create a wave pick using the Outbound Delivery Monitor, Transaction VL06P. Selection criteria can be entered to display deliveries from a specific shipping point on a certain date so that deliveries can be selected and combined in a wave-pick group.

Figure 6.30 shows the shipping point and date criteria entered to obtain all deliveries due to be shipped, so that selection can be made for a specific wave pick group.

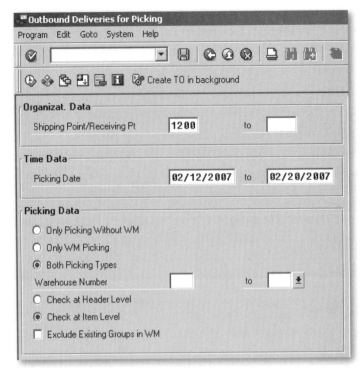

Figure 6.30 Outbound Delivery Monitor Selection Screen for Wave Creation

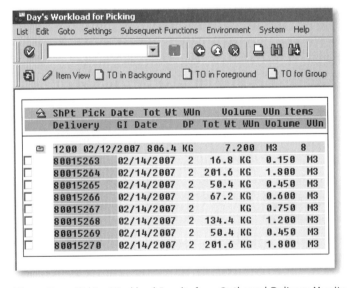

Figure 6.31 Picking Workload Results from Outbound Delivery Monitor

Figure 6.31 shows deliveries relevant for the criteria entered into the Outbound Delivery Monitor. The deliveries can be highlighted and the wave created by selecting **Subsequent Functions • Group • Wave Pick** from the header menu. The processing will return to the Outbound Delivery Monitor and the wave number will displayed at the bottom of the screen.

6.3.7 Using the Wave Monitor

The Wave Monitor allows the selection of waves for certain outbound deliveries. The Wave Monitor is executed using Transaction VL37 or by following the navigation path: **SAP • Logistics • Logistics Execution • Outbound Process • Goods Issue for Outbound Delivery • Picking • Wave Picks • Monitor**.

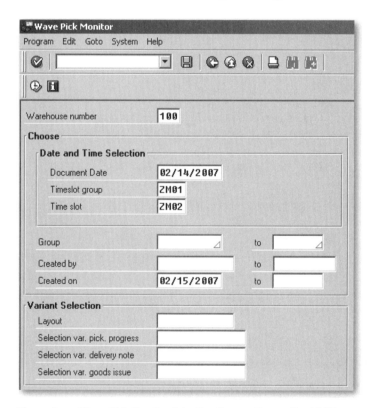

Figure 6.32 Wave Pick Monitor Selection Screen: Transaction VL37

Figure 6.32 shows the initial selection criteria screen where entries can be made to view waves from the outbound deliveries fitting the selection. The date-and-time selection allows the use of either a time slot or a time-slot group. Let's take a look at these now.

Time Slot

A time slot is defined as a period of time that can be configured in the IMG. The time slot can be defined for the warehouse where it is to be used. In many cases, a time slot can be a one hour time period in a warehouse shift or a whole shift. The time slot can be configured via the navigation path: **IMG · Logistics Execution · Shipping · Picking · Wave Picks · Maintain Time Slots**.

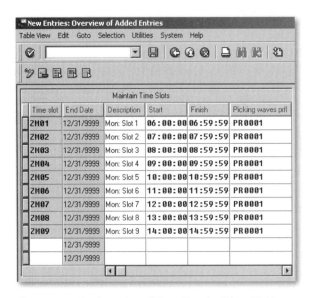

Figure 6.33 Configuration of Time Slots for Wave Picking

Figure 6.33 shows the configuration for a time slot. Each time slot is created with a description and a start and finish time. The other field you must fill to configure the time slot is the picking-wave profile. The picking wave profile is also defined in the system configuration and sets the limits for the wave.

Picking Wave Profile

The picking wave profile allows you to set limits on certain criteria when reacting to waves during wave picking.

The configuration for the picking wave profile can be made using the navigation path: **IMG · Logistics Execution · Shipping · Picking · Wave Picks · Maintain Wave Picks Profile**.

Figure 6.34 shows the configuration for the picking wave profile used in time-slot configuration. The picking wave profile is defined for each warehouse, and capacity limits can be configured for each time slot.

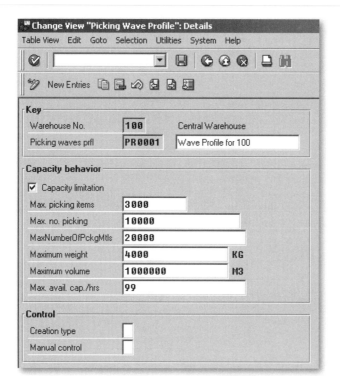

Figure 6.34 Configuration for Picking Wave Profile

You can limit the number of items to be picked, the number of picking activities, maximum number of packaging materials, maximum weight and volume, and maximum number of available hours for the pick wave.

Time Slot Group

In Figure 6.32, the other date-and-time selection field is the **Timeslot group.** The time-slot group is configured from a number of time slots. For example a time-slot group can contain all the time slots for a particular shift or a particular working day.

The time-slot group can be configured in the IMG using the navigation path: **IMG • Logistics Execution • Shipping • Picking • Wave Picks • Maintain Time-slot Group for Wave Pick**.

Figure 6.35 shows the time-slot group ZM01 created from the nine individual time slots, which reflect each hour for the first warehouse shift on a Monday. Each time slot is assigned a sequence number for the time-slot group. The start and finish times of the time slots cannot overlap.

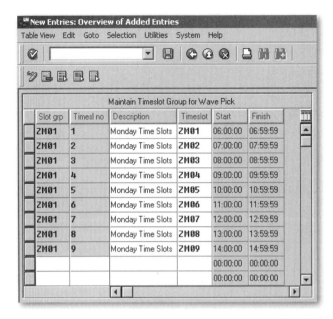

Figure 6.35 Creating Time-Slot Groups from Individual Time Slots

6.3.8 Results of the Pick Wave Monitor

After you have entered the selection criteria, execute the transaction by using the **F8** function key. The Wave Monitor displays all waves for the relevant time slot that was entered for the specific warehouse.

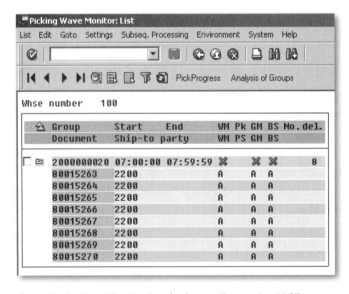

Figure 6.36 Wave Monitor Results Screen: Transaction VL37

Figure 6.36 shows the wave and the deliveries within that wave for the time slot that was selected. The wave shown here can be highlighted and the transfer orders created for the deliveries that make up the wave pick.

Create the transfer order by using the header menu and selecting the options **Subsequent Processing • Transfer Order** or by using the function key **Shift + F4**.

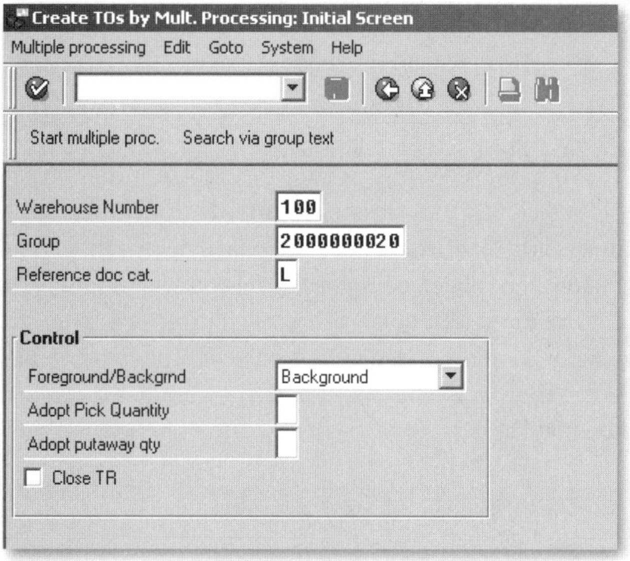

Figure 6.37 Creating Transfer Orders for Deliveries in Wave Pick

Figure 6.37 shows the transfer order creation screen for the wave pick group, **2000000020**. The reference document category is defaulted to **L**, which indicates outbound deliveries.

The transfer orders can be created using the **Start multiple proc** button or the **F5** function key. Once the transfer orders have been created, they need to be released and printed for the material to be pulled. Release and print the wave by selecting **Subsequent Processing • Release/Print** or by using the function key **Shift + F5** from the header menu.

Figure 6.38 shows that the wave group has been released and printed. The transfer orders are printed at the printer on the warehouse and are given to the staff so they can pick the materials. Once the materials are picked, the transfer orders can be confirmed for the wave. You can confirm the transfer order by using the Wave Monitor and selecting **Subsequent Processing • Confirm** or by using the function key **Shift + F7** from the header menu.

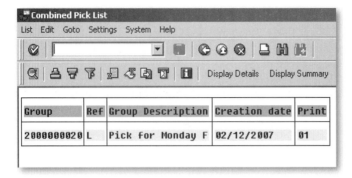

Figure 6.38 Pick List for Wave Group 2000000020

The transaction will display the selection screen for the transfer order confirmation, as shown in Figure 6.39. The transfer orders that have been produced for the wave pick can be confirmed after they have been printed and the movement of the material has been completed. The confirmation screen, as shown in Figure 6.39, allows selection of certain transfer orders in the wave by storage type or picking area, depending on what movements had been completed in the warehouse. If all transfer orders are ready for completion, these fields will be blank.

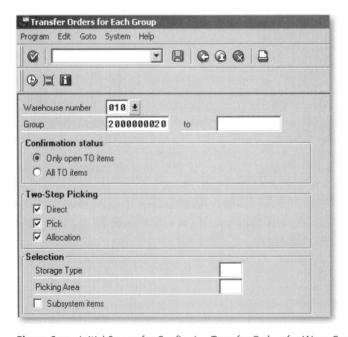

Figure 6.39 Initial Screen for Confirming Transfer Orders for Wave Group

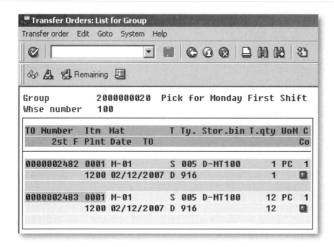

Figure 6.40 Transfer Orders Selected for Confirmation from Wave Group

From the selection used in Figure 6.39, the relevant transfer orders are displayed and ready for confirmation, as shown in Figure 6.40. The confirmations can be made by selecting **Transfer Order** · **Confirm in Foreground** or by using the **F5** function key.

This section has examined the multiple processing using groups. Now we'll discuss the processes of picking and packing in goods issue.

6.4 Picking and Packing

The picking process has been touched on in Sections 6.1.3 and 6.1.5. The transfer orders created to remove material from the warehouse can be used as the picking instructions. As a part of the picking process, a number of optional steps can be carried out with the material.

These steps can include pricing of the material with price stickers. This may involve re-pricing, if the material was priced at the end of the manufacturing process or inbound delivery process and the price has since changed. In addition to the pricing process, a packing process can occur after picking and before the materials leave the warehouse.

Picking within the warehouse can be the most costly part of the warehouse operation. Order picking is the most labor-intensive operation within the warehouse and usually employs the majority of the staff. Furthermore, picking errors, and therefore delivery errors, are a major source of customer dissatisfaction.

Warehouse designers try to reduce or combine a number of human functions in the picking process, including:

▶ Removing items from the storage bin
▶ Traveling between the storage bins and the picking station
▶ Searching for the storage bins
▶ Sorting items for transfer orders
▶ Confirming the line-item picking, using SAP or noting in paperwork

6.4.1 Picking Schemes

Warehouses can adopt a number of picking schemes to reduce the time and effort spent by the warehouse staff picking material. Not all of these schemes are relevant for all companies. In the following subsection, I will briefly describe some of those that are currently found in warehouse operations.

Single-Order Picking

In this picking scheme, the picking staff completes one order at a time. This takes a great deal of time and effort but does give the most accurate picking. This method is used in the majority of warehouses.

Batch Picking

The batchpicking method is similar to the single-order method, except that the picker picks a batch of orders at one time, rather than a single order. Picking errors do creep in when line items are missed, and additional time is required to sort the items for each order when the items are returned to the picking station. The efficiencies of this type of picking are limited and are negligible for more than five orders in a batch pick.

Zone Picking

In this scheme, a picking operator is assigned to one zone, which can be an aisle, a partial aisle, a carousel, etc. For this scheme, the picker is only responsible for picking items in their zone and not responsible for all the items in the transfer order. The advantages of this method are that the picker's travel time is reduced because of the smaller area of his or her operation. The also become familiar with the items they pick every day and errors are reduced. The disadvantage found with this method is that it can cause bottlenecks if the pickers work at different speeds; slower zone operators can minimize the benefits of this method.

Progressive Assembly

In the progressive assembly method, the contents of the transfer order to be picked is moved from one zone to the next. This is also called the pick-and-pass system. The line items of the transfer order can be moved from zone to zone in a tote container on a conveyor belt or some other transport method.

Downstream Sortation

This method uses some aspects of the progressive assembly but is used for wave picking. In a wave, many transfer orders will be grouped. Downstream sortation allows the picker to deposit all the materials listed on all transfer orders of the wave into the tote on the conveyor. This means that a significant level of sorting will take place after the material leaves the picking zone. This method can only be used where downstream sorting has been perfected; otherwise, shipping delays will most likely occur.

6.4.2 Packing

We will discuss Storage Unit Management and the way packing is performed with storage units in Chapter 11. In the warehouse, the material that has been picked is usually packed before it is loaded on to vehicles or sent via a shipping company, such as UPS or FedEx.

The packing area contains the packaging material used for packing the materials to be shipped. These packaging materials can be as simple as cardboard boxes, shipping pallets, and tape. However, there may be specialized packaging materials that are used only for a specific item. For example, a fragile item may be stored in one container while it was in the warehouse, but for shipping it may require custom polystyrene packaging for a specific size of container.

Whichever materials are needed in the packaging area, they must be available to the packing staff. In the same way that a production line comes to a halt if material is missing for the production order, the packaging of materials will stop if the packaging material is missing in the packing area.

> **Note**
>
> Some companies spent some of their labor resources in pre-assembling packaging items. If the same person has to locate a flat cardboard box, assemble it, pack it with pellets, place the item inside, seal it, label it, and move it to the next location, this can be time consuming and not the best use of labor. Pre-assembling boxes and filling them with pellets can make the packing area more efficient.

Another labor-saving method used in warehouses is to standardize the packing materials and packing process. Reducing the number of sizes of the materials and formalizing a packing process that all employees follow are important ways to save time getting product from the packing area into shipment.

This section has examined the aspects of picking and packing in the goods issue process. Now we'll summarize what has been discussed in this chapter.

6.5   Summary

Goods-issue is a labor-intensive process that has been refined to minimize waste in picking and maximize the output of the warehouse. A company has to ship product to make a profit, and the outbound process of the warehouse is key to successful shipping. In this chapter, we have discussed how goods issues can be created with outbound deliveries and without them.

We have also discussed some of the more complex scenarios for outbound shipping; e.g., the use of wave picks in a busy warehouse. It is important to realize that the outbound delivery process is twofold. First, the configuration and the processes used by the warehouse must be suited to the warehouse operations, because an overly complex solution will stop products from being shipped. Second, because the outbound process is labor intensive, training staff on the warehouse solution is very important. Once these two factors have been balanced, significant productivity should flow from the SAP WM outbound process.

In Chapter 7, I'll discuss the stock replenishment that takes place in the warehouse. Keep in mind that a warehouse is not just a place where material is stored. Material constantly moves in the warehouse, and replenishment of fixed bins for picking and for production supports some of this movement.

Stock replenishment and internal movements are daily activities that support efficient warehouse operations. Posting changes occur less frequently but must be carefully processed to ensure synergy between the warehouse and Inventory Management (SAP IM) stock balances.

7 Stock Replenishment

Material is moved from one location to another as a part of everyday warehouse operations. Some movements are initiated within the inventory management process; e.g., plant to plant or storage location to storage location. If the storage location is warehouse-managed, then this will trigger the movement of the material in the warehouse.

Replenishment of storage bins in the warehouse requires moving material from one location to another location. With this overview of stock replenishment in mind, we'll now discuss internal stock transfers.

7.1 Internal Stock Transfers

The internal stock transfer can only be triggered by a requirement to move a material from one part of the warehouse to another, storage bin to storage bin.

There are many reasons for moving material in the warehouse, but every time a quant is moved a cost is incurred. Sometimes the labor cost of moving material outweighs the need to move the material.

7.1.1 Keeping the Warehouse Running

Many warehouses have come to a complete standstill when there was no more space in the warehouse to unload trailers at the goods-receiving dock. In the worst situation, warehouses have become grid-locked because material that needs to be shipped instead sits in trailers outside the warehouse, unable to be unloaded into the warehouse.

Warehouses need a certain amount of empty space where material can be unloaded and stored. Without a working reserve of empty bins, the warehouse can become congested and customer orders won't be fulfilled on time.

To keep a reserve of empty bins, a warehouse needs regular analysis of the material in the storage bins to see where combining quants can free up a bin, or ensure that the picking areas are fully supplied. The optimum amount of empty bin space in the warehouse depends on the materials and industry involved but is usually somewhere between 10 % and 20 %.

To move this material in the warehouse, a requirement must be created in SAP WM to move the stock.

7.1.2 Checking Empty Bins

You can analyze the empty-bin situation by using Transaction LS04, which displays the empty bins for a specific warehouse and storage type.

The transaction can also be found using the navigation path: **SAP • Logistics • Logistics Execution • Internal Whse Processes • Bins and Stock • Display • Empty Storage Bins**.

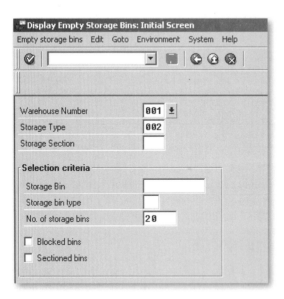

Figure 7.1 Initial Selection Screen for List of Empty Bins: Transaction LS04

Figure 7.1 shows the initial screen for the list of empty bins. The warehouse number and storage type fields must be filled, but use of the storage section is optional. Additional selection criteria can be entered, such as the storage bin — if only one storage bin has to be reviewed — or the storage bin type, tank, bin height, etc. The number of storage bins reflects the number of bins required on the report.

Note

If the warehouse staff only wants to see if there are a few empty bins in a specific storage type, they may only want to see the first 10 and not all of the empty bins. By entering a figure in this field, the report stops after the specific number of bins are retrieved.

You can set the blocked bins and sectioned bins indicators if the report should only show empty storage bins that are blocked or sectioned, rather than all empty bins.

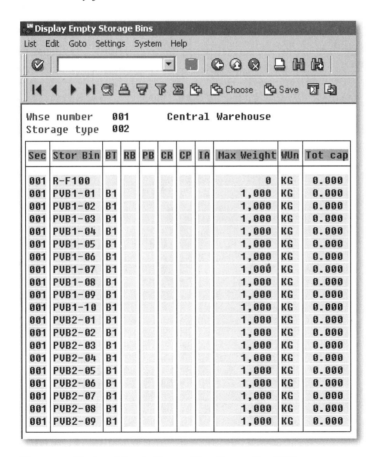

Figure 7.2 Display of Empty Storage Bins: Transaction LS04.

Figure 7.2 shows the 20 empty storage bins that were requested by the selection criteria in Figure 7.1. The display shows the storage bin, bin type, blocking indicator for stock removal, blocking indicator for putaway, current block for removal, current block for putaway, current block due to physical inventory count, maximum weight, and total capacity.

The display is useful to the warehouse staff because they can see at a glance where the empty bins are for stock putaway.

7.1.3 Moving Material Between Storage Bins

Movement of material between storage bins is triggered by creation of a transfer order. If material needs to be moved from one storage bin to another storage bin, a transfer order is required.

Transaction LT10 can produce a transfer order for a stock transfer. This transaction can be found using the navigation path: **SAP • Logistics • Logistics Execution • Internal Whse Processes • Stock Transfer • Create Transfer Order • From Stock List**.

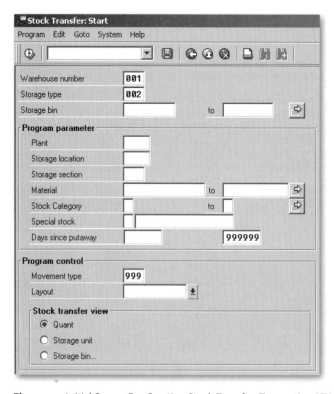

Figure 7.3 Initial Screen For Creating Stock Transfer: Transaction LT10

Figure 7.3 shows the selection screen for Transaction LT10. The **Warehouse number** and **Storage type** fields must be filled, as must the **Movement type** field in the **Program control** section.

The user must enter a warehouse management movement type in the **Movement type** field. This entry controls the type of internal stock transfer that will take place.

The **Stock transfer view** section allows the resulting data to be shown in either a quant format, by storage unit, or by storage bin. The default is for the results to be shown by quant. Execute the transaction by using the **F8** function key.

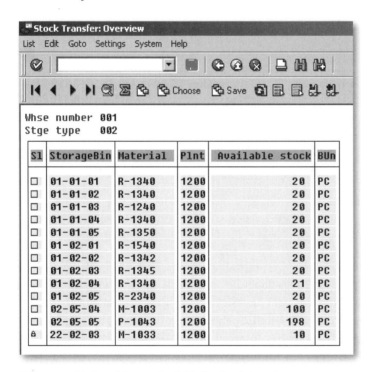

Figure 7.4 Display of Quants Available for Stock Transfer

Figure 7.4 shows the material that is available for stock transfer. The available quants are identified with a blank box in the **Sl** (Selection) field. If the quant is not available, then the field will contain a lock.

To select a line item for a stock transfer, highlight the selection box with an X. The line item is then available for a stock transfer. The stock transfer can be created in the foreground by selecting the **Ctrl + Shift + F12** function keys.

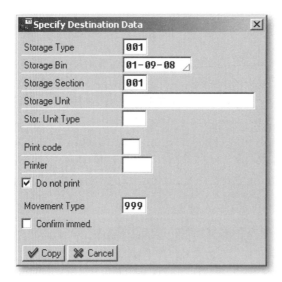

Figure 7.5 Destination Data-Entry Dialog Box for Stock Transfer

Figure 7.5 shows the dialog box that is displayed when the stock transfer is created in the foreground. You must enter destination data for the stock transfer. You can enter a print code and printer number or set the **Do not print** indicator so that the stock transfer is not printed.

After the required data is entered, the transaction uses the information to create a transfer order. Once the transfer order is created by the transaction, the results screen is re-displayed.

Use Transaction LT21 to view the transfer order that has been created by Transaction LT10. If the transfer order number is not known, use Transaction LT24 to find the relevant transfer order using the material number matchcode. Transaction LT24 is also found using the navigation path: **SAP • Logistics • Logistics Execution • Internal Whse Processes • Stock Transfer • Display Transfer Order • For Material**.

Figure 7.6 shows the information that should be selected to find the transfer order via the material involved in the stock transfer. The warehouse and material entries are mandatory. This selection has also included the date of transfer-order creation in order to narrow down the potential list.

Execute the transaction by selecting the **F8** function key or by using the header menu and selecting **Program • Execute**. The display of the resulting transfer order (see Figure 7.7) shows the information that was entered in Transaction LT10.

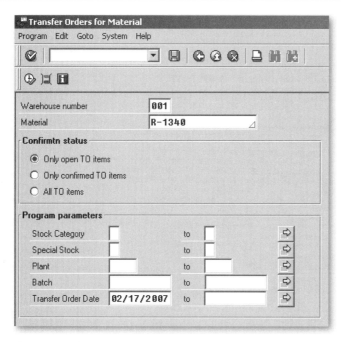

Figure 7.6 Selection Screen to Display Transfer Orders by Material: Transaction LT24

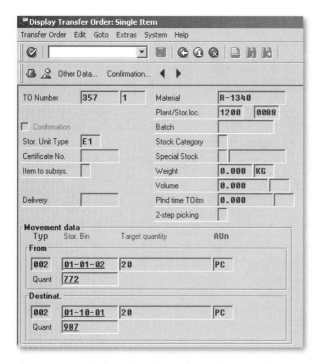

Figure 7.7 Detailed Display of Transfer Order Created by Stock Transfer

7.1.4 Confirm the Stock Transfer

The movement information shows the material that needs to be moved from storage bin **01–01–02** to **01–10–01** within the storage type 002. The stock transfer can be confirmed in this screen using the header menu and selecting **Transfer Order • Confirm in Foreground** or by using the **F8** function key.

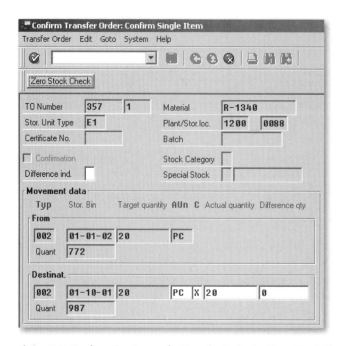

Figure 7.8 Confirmation Screen for Transfer Order to Move Stock Storage Bin to Storage Bin

Figure 7.8 shows the confirmation screen for the transfer order created for the stock transfer. In the **Movement data** section of this screen, the destination information in the **Destinat.** area must be entered for the quantity of the material to be transferred.

Often, material is transferred and the quantity of material received into the destination storage bin is not equal to the quantity removed from the storage bin. In these instances, it is important to enter the correct quantity in the receiving storage bin as well as a reason for this discrepancy. Four options are available for the confirmation indicator:

▶ X

Target quantity is equal to the actual quantity

▶ U

Actual quantity is the balance between the target and difference quantity

▶ **S**

Difference quantity is the difference between actual and target quantity

▶ **Blank**

Allows the actual and difference quantities to be entered manually

In this case, Figure 7.8 shows that an "X" has been entered for the confirmation indicator, so that target and actual quantities are equal and there are no differences.

7.1.5 Configuration of the Difference Indicator

The other field on this screen you should pay attention to is **Difference ind.** This indicator can be used to control how the difference is managed. The field is configured using Transaction OMLX in the IMG. The transaction can be found using the navigation path: **IMG · Logistics Execution · Warehouse Management · Activities · Confirmation**.

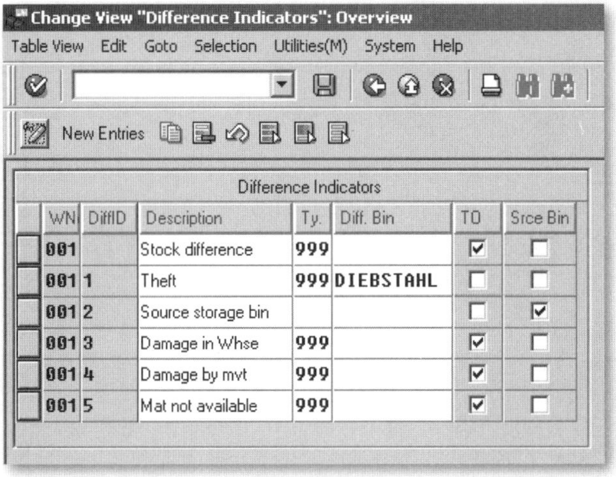

Figure 7.9 Configuration of Difference Indicator: Transaction OMLX

The configuration-of-confirmation screen, shown in Figure 7.9, defines how the confirmation transaction deals with the difference between the source and destination storage bins. Let's look closely at the fields seen in Figure 7.9:

▶ **Ty**

This field is the storage type to which any differences in the source and target quantities are posted.

- ▶ **Diff Bin**

  This should be configured if a specific storage bin must contain the stock differences.

- ▶ **TO**

  If this indicator is set, the system creates a dynamic storage location, which is named the same as the transfer order number, and the difference is posted to this bin.

- ▶ **Srce Bin**

  If this indicator is set, the quantity difference is posted to the source storage bin.

This section has described the functionality of internal stock transfers. Now we'll examine the process of fixed bin replenishment.

7.2   Fixed Bin Replenishment

A fixed storage bin is a storage bin where a specific material is stored. This material is always stored in this bin. This may be because it is a bin that has been specifically created for the material. In many cases, it is a storage bin in the picking area, where storage bins do not need different material constantly moved in and out.

In fixed storage bin replenishment, the storage bin in the picking area needs to be replenished so that the outbound deliveries remain at maximum efficiency.

> **Example**
>
> In a warehouse that ships vacuum cleaners, each vacuum may have to be packed with the attachments. The attachments should be stored in the picking area and in sufficient quantity that the shipping process does not slow down due to lack of attachments. Fixed bin replenishment is a process that will help keep this from happening

7.2.1   Replenishment and the Material Master

The basis for the replenishment process is defined in the material master record for the items that need to be replenished. Replenishment details for a material in a specific fixed bin can be entered using the material master change Transaction MM02, if the material has already been created. This transaction can be found using the navigation path: **SAP • Logistics • Materials Management • Material Master • Material • Change • Immediately**.

You should select the WM views, although this may vary depending on the version of SAP.

The information that must be entered can be found in the **Warehouse Management 2** screen seen in Figure 7.10. To access this screen, the plant, warehouse number and storage type for the fixed bin location must be entered.

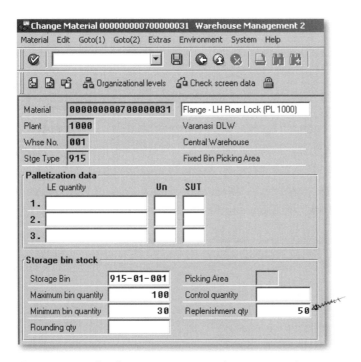

Figure 7.10 Replenishment Data in Material Master Record

The information stored in the material master record for the storage bin defines how replenishment is processed. Figure 7.10 shows the data in the storage bin stock section in the second WM screen.

I'll now describe the fields displayed in the **Storage bin stock** section, shown in Figure 7.10:

▶ **Storage Bin**
The specific bin of storage type 915 where the material is stored

▶ **Maximum bin quantity**
The largest quantity that can be stored in this storage bin, and used for checking the capacity of the storage bin

▶ **Minimum bin quantity**
The minimum quantity that can be stored in the storage bin. This figure is used in the calculation for the bin replenishment

▶ **Replenishment quantity**
The quantity of material to be replenished in the storage bin

In addition to the information found in the material master file, you need to complete a number of configuration steps. I'll describe these in the next section.

7.2.2   Configuration for Replenishment

You need to complete the warehouse management movement type configuration for replenishment before transfer orders can be created for replenishment of fixed bins. A replenishment movement type needs to be assigned to the storage type so that any transfer orders are created correctly.

The transaction for this configuration can be found using the navigation path: **IMG · Logistics Execution · Warehouse Management · Activities · Transfers · Define Stock Transfers and Replenishment Control**.

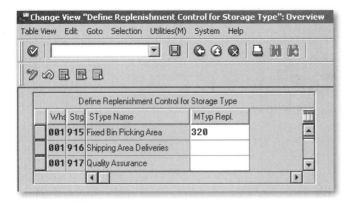

Figure 7.11 Configuration for Fixed Storage Bin Replenishment

Figure 7.11 shows the configuration for the replenishment control for storage type 915, the fixed bin picking area. A movement type is entered that is appropriate for fixed bin replenishment. This is normally movement type 320, but it can be copied to a user-defined movement type that can be used for the configuration. Replenishment of the production supply bins uses movement type 319.

7.2.3 Creating the Replenishment

To create the transfer orders for the replenishment of the fixed bins, use the Transaction LP21. The transaction can also be found using the navigation path: **SAP • Logistics • Logistics Execution • Internal Whse Processes • Stock Transfer • Planning for Replenishments • According to Bin Situation**.

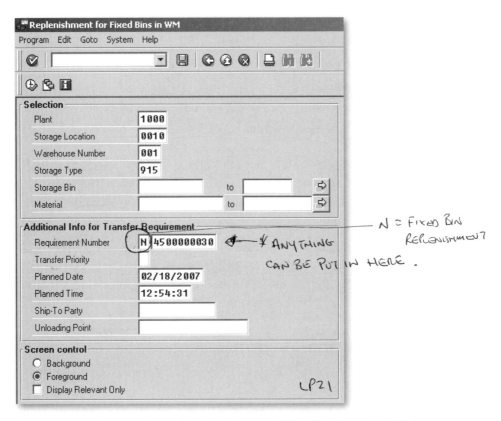

Figure 7.12 Initial Selection Screen for Replenishment of Fixed Bins: Transaction LP21

Figure 7.12 shows the selection screen for stock replenishment. The plant, storage location, warehouse number, and storage type are entered. Because the movement type is set for the replenishment of fixed bins, the requirement number is needed.

The requirement number is prefixed by a one-character requirement type that is set to **N**, representing the replenishment for fixed bins. The requirement number entered is usually the purchase-order number or sales-order number. The selection screen is executed by using the F8 function key or by selecting **Program • Execute** from the header menu.

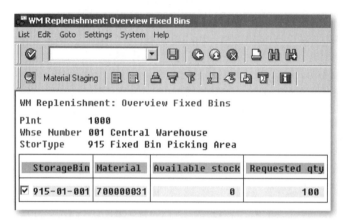

Figure 7.13 Overview of Fixed Bins Subject to Replenishment

Figure 7.13 shows the storage bin selected for replenishment based on the selection criteria entered. The storage bin 915–01–001 is the storage bin entered into the material master record for material 700000031, as shown in Figure 7.10.

To produce the picking documents for the highlighted line on the report, the transaction must be saved. This can be performed by using the **Ctrl + S** function key. When the transaction has been executed, the processing will return to the initial screen of LP21 as shown in Figure 7.12.

7.2.4   Displaying the Transfer Requirement

The replenishment Transaction LP21 created a transfer requirement which can be displayed using Transaction LB11, or by following the navigation path: **SAP • Logistics • Logistics Execution • Internal Whse Processes • Transfer Requirement • Display • For Material**.

Figure 7.14 shows the selection screen for the display of transfer requirements for a specific material. The warehouse number and the material number fields must be filled. If there are many transfer requirements for the material, other selection criteria should be entered to filter the results.

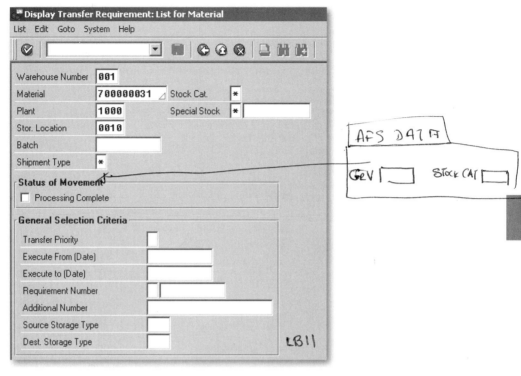

Figure 7.14 Selection Screen to Display Transfer Requirement

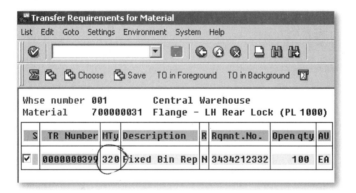

Figure 7.15 Display of Transfer Requirements for Criteria Entered in Selection Screen

Figure 7.15 shows the transfer requirements that match the criteria entered. The transfer requirement, shown by the field **TR Number** in Figure 7.15, is the result of the fixed bin replenishment. To complete the replenishment, you must convert and then confirm the transfer requirement into a transfer order.

241

7.2.5 Creating the Transfer Order

To convert the transfer requirement to a transfer order, select the correct transfer requirement and select the button from the application toolbar to either convert in the background or foreground, as shown in Figure 7.15.

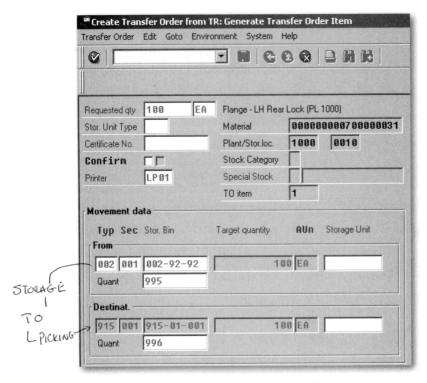

STORAGE
|
TO
└ PICKING

Figure 7.16 Creation of Transfer Order from Transfer Requirement

Figure 7.16 shows creation of a transfer order from the information entered in the transfer requirement. The movement data shows the source storage bin and the destination storage bin in the fixed bin storage type, **915**. The transfer order has a quantity of **100**, which is the maximum bin location, and a multiple of the replenishment quantity for this material in storage type **915**. This information is shown in Figure 7.10.

Once the data in the transfer order has been checked, the transfer order can be completed. The system will return processing to the transfer requirement display, as shown in Figure 7.15, and the transfer order number is shown at the bottom of the screen.

7.2.6 Confirming the Transfer Order

The transfer order is the document that directs the warehouse staff to move the material from the source to the destination storage bins. In the case of the replenishment of fixed bins, the material is moved from the source bin in the main warehouse to the picking area.

The confirmation of the transfer order is Transaction LT12. This can also be found using the navigation path: **SAP • Logistics • Logistics Execution • Internal Whse Processes • Stock Transfer • Confirm Transfer Order • Single Document • In One Step**.

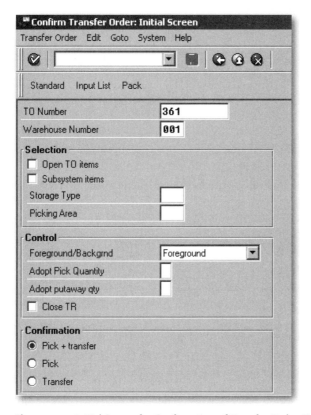

Figure 7.17 Initial Screen for Confirmation of Transfer Order: Transaction LT12

Figure 7.17 shows the initial screen for confirming the transfer order. The transfer order number and warehouse number are required. You have the option to confirm the transfer order in the foreground or background and to confirm **Pick**, **Transfer**, or **Pick + Transfer**.

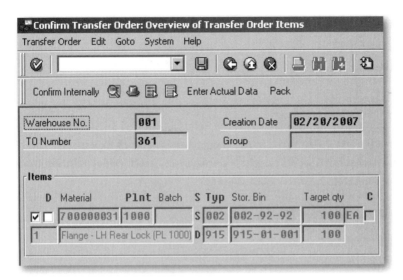

Figure 7.18 Overview of Transfer Order Items for Confirmation

Figure 7.18 shows the line item of the transfer order that describes the movement of material **700000031** from the source bin **002–92–92** to the fixed bin 915–01–001 in the picking area. You can process the confirmation by selecting the **Confirm Internally** button on the application toolbar and then saving the transaction.

7.2.7 Review the Stock Overview

After confirmation of the transfer order, a review of the stock in the warehouse shows that the material is stored in the fixed storage bin in the picking area.

The transaction to view the bin stock for a material is LS24. This can be found using the navigation path: **SAP • Logistics • Logistics Execution • Internal Whse Processes • Bins and Stock • Display • Bin Stock per Material**.

Figure 7.19 shows that the confirmed transfer order moved a quantity of **100** to the fixed storage bin **915–01–001**.

This section has discussed the replenishment of fixed bins; the next section will examine the process of posting changes.

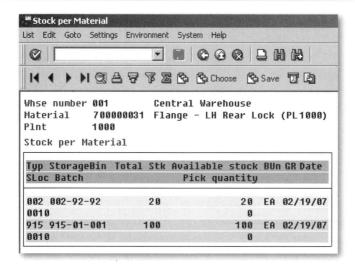

Figure 7.19 Bin Stock Display for Material 70000003: Transaction LS24.

7.3   Posting Changes

A posting change is a change to the stock level of a material. This can result from a change in the status of a material in a storage bin. The material does not physically move, but the status changes. A number of posting changes can be made to material in the warehouse, including:

▶ Release from quality inspection stock

▶ Posting change from material number to material number

▶ Dividing batches among other batches

Let's examine these in detail now.

7.3.1   Posting Change for a Release from Quality Inspection Stock

Release of quality inspection stock occurs in both in inventory management and warehouse management, if applicable.

The change in status from quality inspection to unrestricted occurs in the SAP IM module using a goods movement. In SAP WM, a movement type is also used in conjunction with a posting change notice. The posting change notice is created automatically in WM as a result of the posting of the transaction in IM.

To view the posting change notice for the IM movement, you must know the material document number from the IM posting. The transaction to view the posting change notice is LB12 and can be found using the navigation path: **SAP • Logistics • Logistics Execution • Internal Whse Processes • Posting Change • Via Inventory Management • Posting Change Notice • Display • For Material Document**.

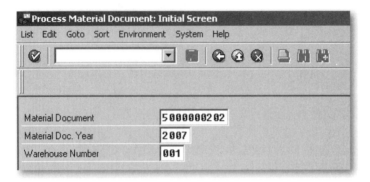

Figure 7.20 Viewing Posting Change Notice for Specific Material Document

Figure 7.20 shows that in order view the posting change notice created by the inventory movement, the material document from that material posting should be entered with the relevant year and warehouse number.

The posting change notice shows the information needed by to change the status of the material in a storage bin from quality inspection (**Q**) to unrestricted stock.

Figure 7.21 shows the details for the posting change notice. The stock details show that the material is being moved from stock category **Q** to blank, which represents a status change from quality inspection to unrestricted. These item details are used to create the transfer order that will process the status change.

To create a transfer order from the posting change notice that references a material document, use Transaction LT06. The transaction can be found using the navigation path: **SAP • Logistics • Logistics Execution • Internal Whse Processes • Posting Change • Via Inventory Management • Transfer Order • Create • For Material Document**. The initial screen requires the material document number, year, and warehouse to be entered.

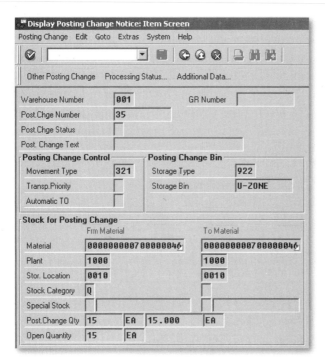

Figure 7.21 Display of Posting Change Notice Details

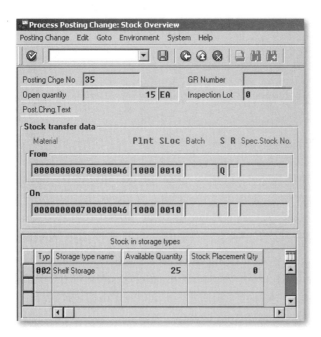

Figure 7.22 Stock Overview for Posting Change Notice Relevant to Material Document

Figure 7.22 shows the stock that is available to have its status moved from quality to unrestricted. The overview shows that there is a quantity of 25 in storage type **002**. This quantity is greater than the quantity to be changed in status. As a result processing will require manual input to determine the specific material and in what storage bins this material is currently stored. By selecting the line item and posting the transaction, using the function keys **Ctrl + S**, you can stop the processing and require the manual input shown in Figure 7.23.

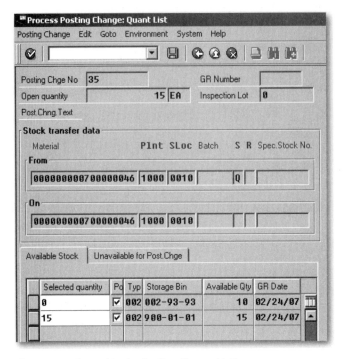

Figure 7.23 Quant List for Posting Change Notice

Manual input is required in this example because the quantity to be moved to unrestricted could have been split over two bins or stored in one bin. In this example, shown in Figure 7.23, the quantity to be moved to unrestricted is all stored in storage bin **900–01–01**.

The transaction can now be posted using the **Ctrl + S** function key and the transfer order will be created. If you review the material stock in the warehouse, using Transaction LS24, you will see the material that was entered into the transfer order using the posting change notice.

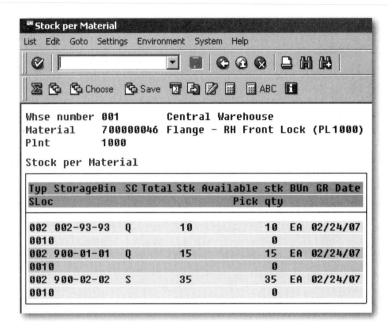

Figure 7.24 Stock Overview of Material in Warehouse: Transaction LS24

Figure 7.24 shows the storage bin **900–01–01** containing the quantity of 15, which has a status of quality inspection. The transfer order created from the posting change notice, as shown in Figure 7.23, will change the status of this material in storage bin **900–01–01** to unrestricted.

You can confirm the transfer order by using Transaction LT12 or by following the navigation path: **SAP • Logistics • Logistics Execution • Internal Whse Processes • Posting Change • Via Inventory Management • Transfer Order • Confirm • In One Step**.

Figure 7.25 shows the transfer order item details for the posting change. The material does not physically move from the storage bin, but moves it in the system using interim storage type **922**. The interim storage type is a logical location that allows changes to be made to the material, even though the material does not necessarily move from the bin it is stored in. To check that the material has changed status, use the material overview in the warehouse: Transaction LS24.

Figure 7.26 shows the material in storage bin **900–01–01** does not have a stock category of **Q** but is blank, showing that it is unrestricted stock.

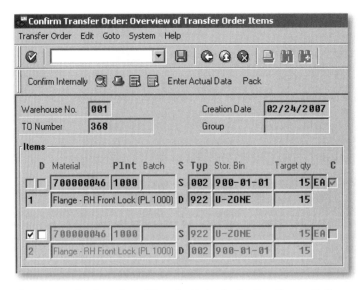

Figure 7.25 Confirmation of Transfer Order for Posting Change Notice

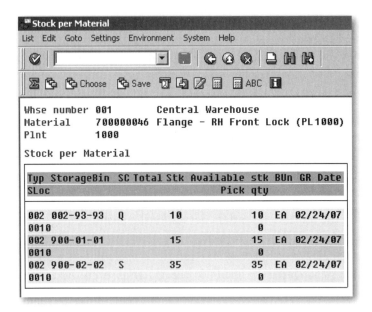

Figure 7.26 Stock Overview of Material in the Warehouse: Transaction LS24

7.3.2 Posting Change from Material Number to Material Number

A material number may be changed while there is still material in stock. This may result from a duplicate part number or a business requirement.

The material number will change change when a transfer posting occurs in inventory management that will move the material stock from the old material number to the new material number.

The corresponding movement in the WM module occurs when a posting change notice has been created via an IM material document, as shown in Figure 7.20 and Figure 7.21 in Section 7.3.1.

To view the posting change notice for the IM movement, you must know the material document number from the IM posting. The transaction to view the posting change notice is LB12 and can be found via the navigation path: **SAP • Logistics • Logistics Execution • Internal Whse Processes • Posting Change • Via Inventory Management • Posting Change Notice • Display • For Material Document**.

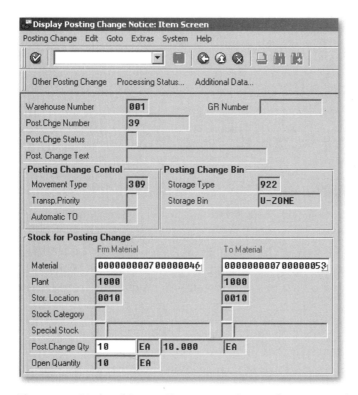

Figure 7.27 Display of Posting Change Notice for Transferring Material Number to Material Number

Figure 7.27 shows the two material numbers for the transfer posting. The movement type for this transfer posting is **309**, which is used for material-to-material postings.

To create a transfer order from the posting change notice, which references the material document for the material-to-material transfer, use Transaction LT06. The transaction can be found using the navigation path: **SAP • Logistics • Logistics Execution • Internal Whse Processes • Posting Change • Via Inventory Management • Transfer Order • Create • For Material Document**.

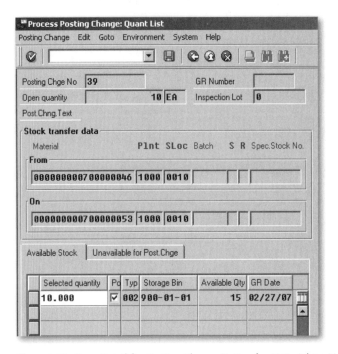

Figure 7.28 Item Detail for Posting Change Notice for Material-to-Material Transfer Posting

Figure 7.28 shows the detail of the posting change notice where a quantity of material **700000046**, ignoring the leading zeros, is transferred to material **700000053**. The selection has been made to transfer a quantity from storage bin **900–01–01**.

The transfer order for the material posting can be confirmed by using Transaction LT12 or via the navigation path: **SAP • Logistics • Logistics Execution • Internal Whse Processes • Posting Change • Via Inventory Management • Transfer Order • Confirm • In One Step**.

Figure 7.29 shows the detail of the transfer order where the two materials are shown. The new material does not remain in the same storage bin as the old material number, and the transfer order has proposed an empty storage bin in the same storage type in which to place the stock with the new material number.

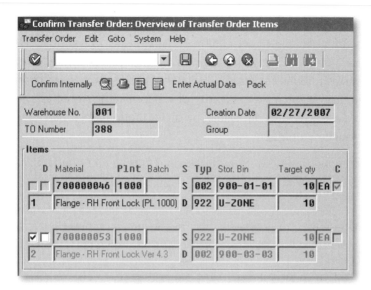

Figure 7.29 Confirmation of Transfer Order for Posting Change Notice for Material-to-Material Posting

To check whether the material has been transferred to the new material number, use the material overview in the warehouse: Transaction LS24.

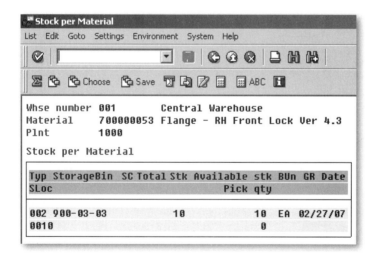

Figure 7.30 Stock Overview of Material in the Warehouse: Transaction LS24

Figure 7.30 shows the stock with the new material number in storage bin **900–03–03**, transferred from the material **700000046**.

7.3.3 Dividing Batches Among Other Batches

This process is similar to the material-to-material transfer except that the material batch numbers are changed, not the material number, which stays the same. The batch-number change can occur if material batches are combined or divided. For example, if a quantity of sheet metal is stored as one batch number in a storage location, it may be divided into two storage bins ,each with its own batch number.

The transfer posting occurs in IM with the movement type 309, the same as material-to-material, but the batch number is changed rather than the material number.

The posting change notice created by the material document shows the batch numbers that were entered into the inventory posting, as shown in Figure 7.31.

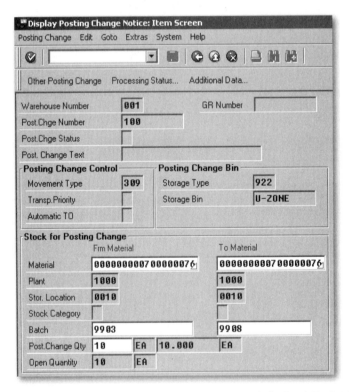

Figure 7.31 Display of Posting Change Notice Details for Batch-To-Batch Transfer

The posting of the posting change notice produces the transfer order, which when confirmed will move a quantity of the material from one batch number to another.

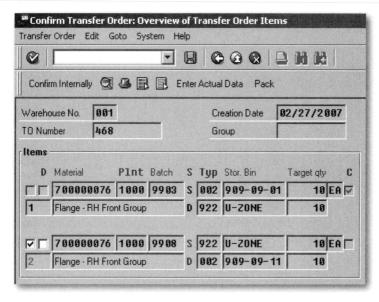

Figure 7.32 Transfer Order Confirmation for Posting Change Notice for Batch-to-Batch Posting

Figure 7.32 shows details of the transfer order with the two batches for the same material shown. The new batch does not remain in the same storage bin with the old batch number. The transfer order has proposed an empty storage bin in the same storage type in which to place the stock with the new batch number.

This section has examined the aspects of the posting changes process; now we shall summarize what has been discussed in this chapter.

7.4 Summary

In this chapter, we discussed internal transfers and stock replenishment using internal transfers and posting changes. Material is moved around the warehouse every day. Therefore, it is important that the system transactions are kept up to date to ensure that the warehouse stock is in the right bin with the right quantity and the right status.

In Chapter 8, I will discuss the different picking strategies that can be assigned, how these are configured, and how they are used.

Picking strategies are important to the outbound process of the warehouse. Implementing the correct strategy can vastly improve efficiency in this critical area. Choosing a picking strategy that makes processing more complex can severely increase picking time and hinder deliveries.

8 Picking Strategies

A picking strategy is a method that determines the way a material is chosen to be picked.

Example

A material may be selected because of a strategy to pick materials by their remaining shelf-life or by the sequence in which they are added to stock.

When picking strategies are discussed, there is often confusion between the method of picking the material and the strategy for which material is to be removed. The method of picking involves how a company physically removes the stock; e.g., batch picking or wave picking.

The strategy of picking involves deciding what material is to be picked. A number of picking strategies can be used, including:

▶ First in, first out (FIFO)
▶ Last in, first out (LIFO)
▶ Fixed storage bin
▶ Shelf-life expiration
▶ Partial quantities
▶ Quantity relevant

The warehouse operation doesn't need to introduce picking strategies into the material removal process, but how material is removed from the warehouse should be discussed and effective strategies adopted.

Once the picking strategy has been adopted, the warehouse-management system uses the picking strategy to assign the appropriate picking location.

There is a chance to manually intervene for certain stock movements, where it is possible to change the source and destination storage bins that the system already proposed.

Accepting the system-generated picking location removes a responsibility from the warehouse staff and effectively reduces picking time. Manual changes should be kept to a minimum and reviewed periodically to ensure that the picking strategies still follow the most effective configuration.

You need to complete a number of steps to configure the picking strategies before the strategy can be applied to materials. These steps begin with the storage type indicator.

8.1 Storage Type Indicator

The storage type indicator in SAP WM allows only certain materials to be picked from storage types, and the order of picking can be defined by the storage type search for each storage type indicator. It is not necessary to configure the storage type indicator if all materials are picked the same way within the same storage type.

If the storage type indicator is to be used, it needs to be configured using the Transaction OMLY or following the SAP navigation path: **IMG • Logistics Execution • Warehouse Management • Strategies • Activate Storage Type Search**.

Figure 8.1 shows the selection available for the storage type search transaction. To configure the storage type indicator, select the **Define** button. If you need to configure a storage type indicator to create a separate search for a group of materials, you can make the entry in the screen shown in Figure 8.2.

The entry for a storage type indicator is simply the warehouse number, the storage type indicator that has been chosen, and a relevant description. Some storage type indicators and descriptions are shown in Figure 8.2.

Figure 8.3 shows the warehouse information entered into the material master record for item **700000031**. The material has been configured with the storage type indicator **FIX** for picking. This means that the storage type search that contains the storage type indictor **FIX** will be the only storage type search applicable for this material.

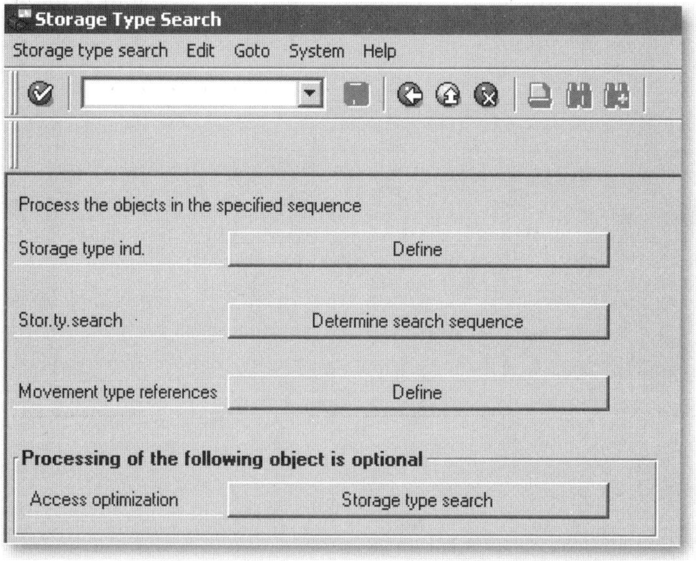

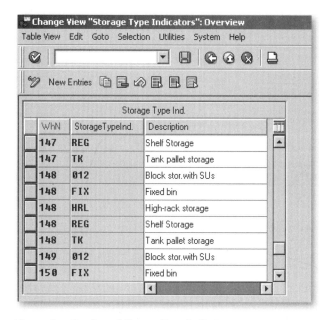

Figure 8.1 Storage Type Search Selection Screen: Transaction OMLY

Figure 8.2 Creation of Storage Type Indicator

Now that we have discussed the storage type indicator, we'll examine the storage type search functionality.

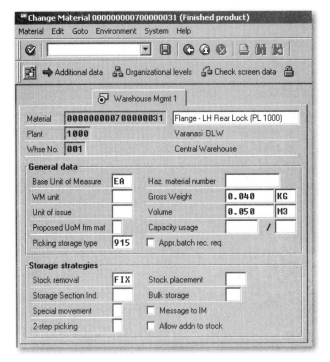

Figure 8.3 Storage Type Indicator Entered into Material Master Record

8.2 Storage Type Search

Once you have configured the storage type indicator, you can configure the storage type search. You don't have to configure a single storage type indicator, but you can confer with the warehouse staff to decide if the storage type search differs for certain materials or groups of materials.

8.2.1 Configuring Storage Type Search

Creation of a storage type search begins in the selection menu in Transaction OMLY, as shown in Figure 8.1. The storage type search is the starting point for the picking of a material from the warehouse. The search defines what storage type is to be used for the picking strategy.

Before entering the storage type search, choose the search in consultation with the warehouse-management staff who plan the layout of the material in the warehouse. How they have stored certain material and how the storage types are positioned will determine the configuration of the sequence of storage types that are searched.

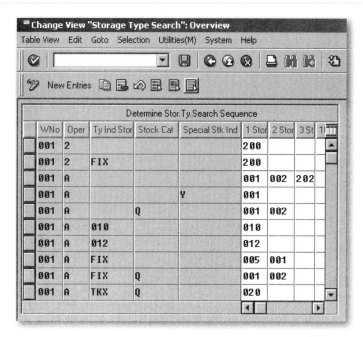

Figure 8.4 Detail Screen for Storage Type Search

Figure 8.4 shows the information entered for each storage type search. Each line entry is relevant for a particular warehouse. The unique keys for each entry are as follows:

▶ Warehouse

▶ Warehouse operation

▶ Storage type indicator

▶ Stock category

▶ Special stock indicator

For the warehouse indicator enter a "2" for two-step picking, "A" for stock picking, and "E" for stock putaway. The stock category and special stock indicators are used when a different storage type search is required for materials with these special statuses.

Using the example in Figure 8.4 where the warehouse operation is "A" for picking and the stock category "Q" for quality inspection (QI) stock, the picking strategy will search storage type 001 and if no appropriate material has been located then the search will be processed in storage type **002**. If no material is found in storage type **002**, the process will require manual intervention.

A maximum of 30 storage types can be configured for each search. Depending on the complexity of the warehouse and the location of the material, the number of storage types entered per search will vary.

8.2.2 Configuring Storage Section Search

In addition to the storage type indicator and storage type search, there is similar configuration and functionality for the storage section. In complex warehouses, storage section functionality is frequently used and searching by storage section is a way to increase warehouse-picking efficiency.

The storage section indicator is configured using Transaction OMLZ, or can be found using the navigation path: **IMG • Logistics Execution • Warehouse Management • Strategies • Activate Storage Section Search**.

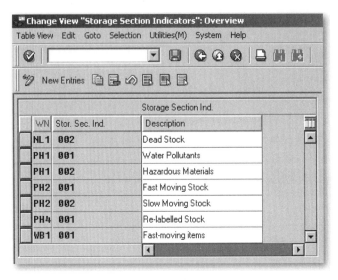

Figure 8.5 Configuration of Storage Section Indicator

Figure 8.5 shows the configuration of the storage section indicator. The indicator is configured specifically for each warehouse. The indicator enables the definition of a group of materials that all can be allocated to one storage section search.

Figure 8.6 shows the configuration for storage section search if it is required. The storage section indicator is part of the unique key along with the warehouse, storage type, hazardous material storage class, and the water pollution class. It is possible to configure up to 10 storage sections for each unique search.

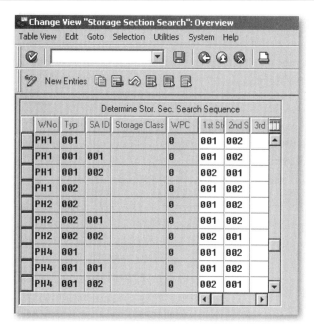

Figure 8.6 Configuration for Storage Section Search

This section examined the storage type search. We'll now discuss the first-in, first-out picking strategy.

8.3 FIFO (First In, First Out)

The picking strategy for first in, first out — or FIFO, as it is more commonly known — removes the oldest quant from the storage type defined in the storage type search. This is found in most manufacturing industries where the material companies wish to sell first is that which has been stored in the warehouse the longest.

FIFO is a very common picking strategy. It ensures that the oldest material is removed from the warehouse for production or sales orders. In many instances, the warehouse layout is configured to optimize FIFO picking.

Warehouses that have deep racks make it difficult for warehouse staff to get to the correct material. One method of ensuring the oldest material is picked is to use gravity flow racks for materials that are picked individually and not in boxes. The boxes are placed at the back of the rack, and the flow racks filled so that the picking at the front moves material forward from the back. This is important in picking areas.

8.3.1   Configuration of FIFO Picking Strategy

The FIFO picking strategy can be defined using the navigation path: **IMG** • **Logistics Execution** • **Warehouse Management** • **Strategies** • **Stock Removal Strategies** • **Define FIFO Strategy**.

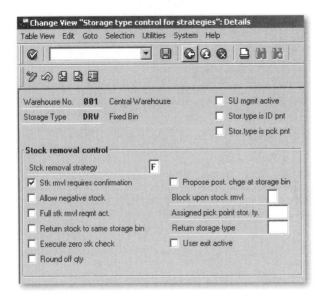

Figure 8.7 Defining Stock Removal Strategy as FIFO

Figure 8.7 shows the configuration of the stock-removal strategy for warehouse 001 and storage type **DRW**. The stock-removal strategy is entered as an **F** for FIFO.

8.3.2   Stock Removal Control Indicators

Figure 8.7 shows that, apart from the stock removal strategy, a number of other control indicators that can be configured for the strategy. These are described next:

▸ **Stk rmvl requires confirmation**
   If this indicator is set, the picking of the entire item must be confirmed in the destination storage type or return storage type before the quantity is made available.

▸ **Allow negative stock**
   Allowing negative stock is done for the interim storage areas. When this indicator is set, the system allows the posting of negative quants in the storage type.

► **Full stk rmvl Reqmt act**

This indicator is set when the entire quant must be picked, regardless of the quantity required for the pick.

► **Return Stock to same storage bin**

This indicator is set when it is required that the remainder of the picked stock that was not needed will be returned to the same bin it was picked from.

► **Execute zero stk check**

If the warehouse needs a zero-stock check when a storage bin is emptied after a stock pick, then this indicator should be set. When the zero-stock check is made, the storage bin can only be used for putaways when the zero-stock check is completed and confirmed.

► **Round off qty**

This field is for rounding off the requested quantity for picking. When this indicator is set, then the processing will use the rounding-off quantity in the warehouse screen for the storage type in the material master record.

► **Propose post chge at storage bin**

This indicator is set when the warehouse needs to post and leave materials in same storage bin, a key procedure in re-labeling. This signals that no transfer is to take place for a posting change.

► **Block upon stock rmvl**

This field can be entered when the blocking indicator is required to be set when the material is picked. The values that can be used are **1** for blocking a storage bin and **2** for blocking the quant only.

► **Assigned pick point stor. Ty.**

This field can be entered with the assigned pick point for the storage type.

► **Return storage type**

This field contains the storage type into which any remaining quantity of the picked material to be stored.

After reviewing this list of indicators, you can move on to an example of a FIFO picking strategy.

8.3.3 Example of FIFO Picking Strategy

The following example will show you how the FIFO configuration for a storage type affects how the material is picked in the warehouse.

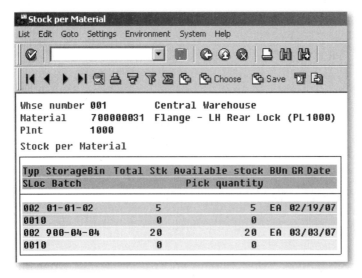

Figure 8.8 Stock Overview for Material in Warehouse

Transaction LS24 can be used to show the material stock. Figure 8.8 shows the warehouse stock for material 700000031. The material is stored in two bins, but the material in storage bin 01–01–02 was received into stock before the material in storage bin **900-04-04**. Therefore, in any FIFO picking strategy the material in storage bin **01–01–02** should be selected first.

The picking strategy configuration for a storage type is displayed using the navigation path: **IMG · Logistics Execution · Warehouse Management · Strategies · Stock Removal Strategies · Define FIFO Strategy**.

Figure 8.9 shows that for the storage type 002, the picking strategy is FIFO, option **F**, and this will be used when material is withdrawn from any storage bin in the storage type. Transaction LT01 can be used to create a transfer order that will pick material from the storage type **002**.

Figure 8.10 shows the initial screen for the creation of a transfer order to pick material from storage type 002. The **Movement Type 201**, is used because it will remove the material and consume it at a cost center.

Figure 8.11 shows the system-generated transfer order item information for the material **700000031**. Based on the configuration for the storage type **002**, the material that has been selected is from the storage bin **01–01–02,** which is the material that was receipted into stock first.

Now that we've discussed the FIFO picking strategy, let us consider the opposite picking strategy, which is last in, first out, or LIFO.

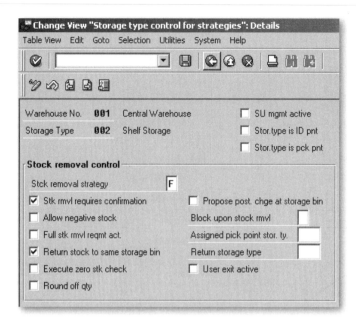

Figure 8.9 FIFO Picking Strategy for Storage Type 002

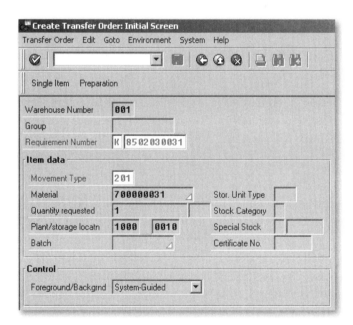

Figure 8.10 Creating Transfer Order: Transaction LT01

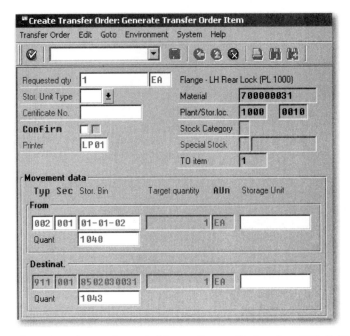

Figure 8.11 System-Generated Source Storage Bin Based on FIFO Picking Strategy

8.4 LIFO (Last In, First Out)

Last in, first out — or LIFO — is based on the principle that the last delivery of material to be received is the first to be used. LIFO is used by a number of companies for inventory cost accounting. The value of warehouse stock impacts reported gross profit margins. Investors tend to carefully review gross profit margins, which are often considered a measure of the value provided to consumers. LIFO can give a more accurate valuation of warehouse stock.

Retailers such as Walgreens and Kohl's use LIFO picking. When LIFO picking occurs, no value change occurs for older material when new materials are received. Because the LIFO method is in effect, the older material is not affected by the potentially higher prices of the new deliveries of material. If the older material is not affected, that means it is not valuated at the new material price. If the older material value is not increased, this prevents false valuation of current inventory.

Picking with the LIFO method is not as common as FIFO picking. It may be used for if the financial department wishes to report inventory using LIFO because it gives a more conservative view of the cost of inventory and therefore will be seen in a positive light by some financial analysts. Check with the warehouse staff and accounting department to determine whether any storage types need to be configured for LIFO picking.

8.4.1 Configuration of LIFO Picking Strategy

The LIFO picking strategy can be defined using the navigation path: **IMG • Logistics Execution • Warehouse Management • Strategies • Stock Removal Strategies • Define LIFO Strategy**. For this configuration, we are changing the picking strategy of storage type 002 from FIFO to LIFO.

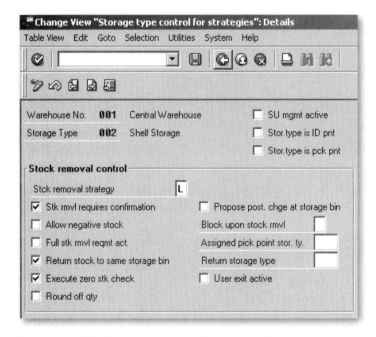

Figure 8.12 LIFO Picking Strategy for Storage Type 002

Figure 8.12 shows that for the storage type **002**, the picking strategy has been changed to LIFO, option **L**, and this will be used when material is withdrawn from any storage bin in the storage type.

8.4.2 Example of LIFO Picking Strategy

The following example will show how the LIFO configuration for a storage type affects the way the material is picked in the warehouse. The warehouse stock for material **700000031** is displayed by using Transaction LS24.

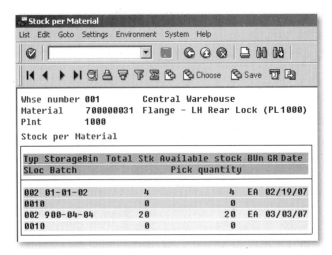

Figure 8.13 Stock Overview for Material in Warehouse

Figure 8.13 shows the stock position for material **700000031** in storage type **002**. By creating a transfer order for this material, the LIFO picking strategy now configured for storage type **002** should select the material in storage bin **900-04-04**, because it is the last material to be goods-receipted.

Transaction LT01 can be used to create a transfer order that will pick material from the storage type **002**. Figure 8.14 shows the initial screen for creation of

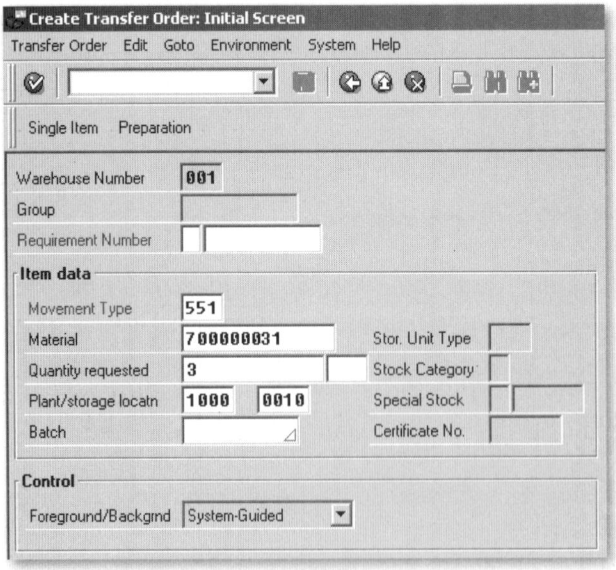

Figure 8.14 Creating Transfer Order: Transaction LT01

a transfer order to pick material from storage type **002**. The movement type, **551**, is used for scrapping materials. This will remove the material from the warehouse for disposal. This is similar to consuming the material at a cost center.

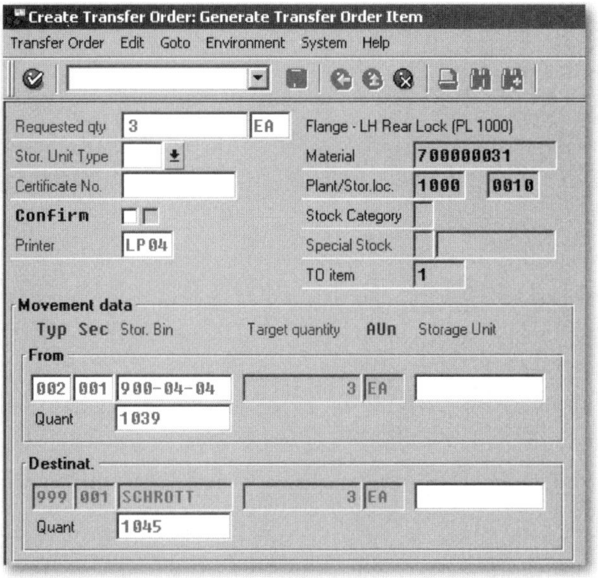

Figure 8.15 System-Generated Source Storage Bin Based on LIFO Picking Strategy

Figure 8.15 shows the system-generated transfer order based on the LIFO picking strategy. In this case, the material has been removed from the storage bin where the material has a goods-receipt date later than material in the other storage bins.

Having explored the functionality of the LIFO picking strategy, we will continue by discussing the fixed storage bin picking strategy.

8.5   Fixed Storage Bin

The picking strategy for fixed storage bins relies on the data that has been entered into the material master record for the material to be picked.

8.5.1   Fixed Storage Bin in Material Master

The fixed storage bin is entered into the material master record in the SAP WM screen.

> **Note**
>
> In SAP version ECC 6.0, this is the second WM screen, but for you this may vary depending on the version you are using.

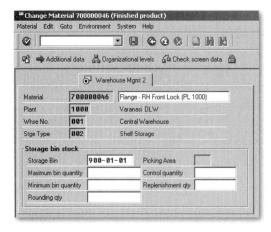

Figure 8.16 Fixed Storage Bin Information in Material Master Record: Transaction MM02

Figure 8.16 shows the WM screen for the material **700000046**. In the storage bin stock section of the screen, the storage bin has the entry **900-01-01**. This is the storage bin fixed for this material in this specific storage type, **002**. This information is then used for the fixed-bin picking strategy.

The material in storage type **002** should be stored in storage bin **900-01-01**; however, it may have been manually moved to other bin locations if there is an overflow of material. Transaction LS24 enables you to see the stock situation for the material.

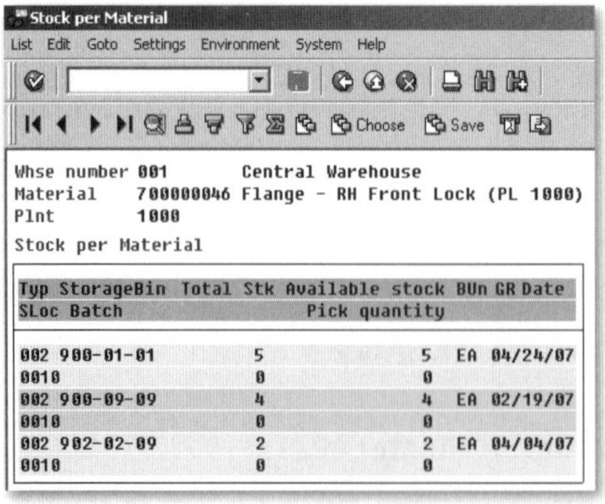

Figure 8.17 Stock Overview for Material in Warehouse

Figure 8.17 shows that material **700000046** is in fact located in three storage bins in storage type **002**. The fixed-bin picking strategy will generate a transfer order that picks material from the fixed storage bin as noted in the material master record.

8.5.2   Configuration of Fixed-Bin Picking Strategy

The fixed-bin picking strategy can be defined using the navigation path: **IMG • Logistics Execution • Warehouse Management • Strategies • Stock Removal Strategies • Define Fixed Bin Strategy**

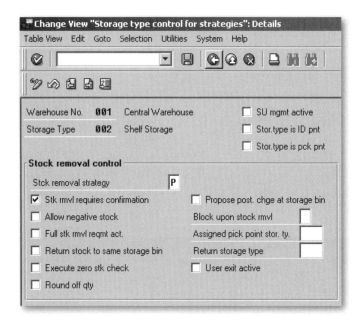

Figure 8.18   Fixed-Bin Picking Strategy for Storage Type 002

Figure 8.18 shows that for the storage type **002**, the picking strategy has been configured to option **P**, which represents fixed bin, and this strategy will be used when material is withdrawn from any storage bin in the selected storage type.

8.5.3   Example of Fixed-Bin Picking Strategy

In this section, I will show you how the fixed-bin picking strategy configuration for a storage type affects how the material is picked in the warehouse. Transaction LT01 can be used to create a transfer order that will pick material from the fixed bin defined in the material master for the storage type **002**.

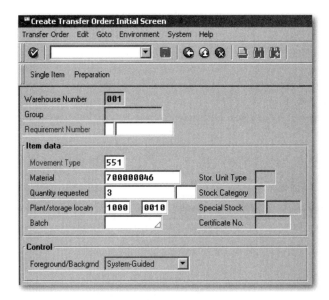

Figure 8.19 Creating Transfer Order: Transaction LT01

Figure 8.19 shows the initial screen for creating a transfer order to pick material from the fixed bin in storage type **002**. The **Movement Type**, **551**, is used for scrapping materials. This will remove the material from the warehouse for disposal.

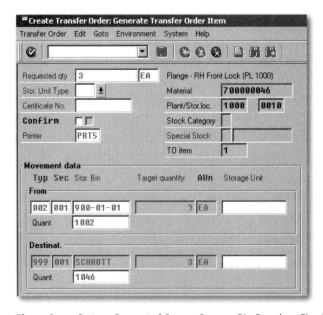

Figure 8.20 System-Generated Source Storage Bin Based on Fixed-bin Picking Strategy

Figure 8.20 shows the system-generated transfer order based on the fixed-bin picking strategy. In this case, the material has been removed from the storage bin, **900–01–01** that is defined in the material master for storage type **002**.

This section has described the fixed-bin picking strategy. Let's now focus on the picking strategy using shelf-life expiration.

8.6 Shelf-Life Expiration

In many industries, especially retail and grocery, the shelf-life of materials is a very important characteristic. This can be a sale-focused shelf-life, where the material can only sit on a store shelf until its sell-by date. Alternatively, it can be production focused, as when chemicals and raw materials can be kept only for so long and still meet tolerance limits for use in the production process. It is important that the warehouse managers review the shelf-life expiration date (SLED) to ensure that out-of-date material does not have to be scrapped.

Under the shelf-life expiration picking strategy, the material is picked based on the shelf-life of the quants of material in the warehouse. To ensure that this picking strategy will produce the correct results, WM users must perform a number of configuration steps or check them for accuracy.

8.6.1 SLED Picking and the Material Master

Before using the shelf-life picking strategy, check that the material to be picked has the correct information regarding the shelf-life characteristics entered on the plant storage view. Use Transaction MM03 to display the material or MM02 to change the material.

Figure 8.21 shows the shelf-life data that has been entered for the material **700000046**. This data is used in calculating the shelf-life expiration date in batch determination and is used in the picking strategy.

8.6.2 Configuration of Shelf-Life Expiration Picking Strategy

The fixed-bin picking strategy can be defined using the navigation path: **IMG • Logistics Execution • Warehouse Management • Strategies • Stock Removal Strategies • Define Strategy for Expiration Date**.

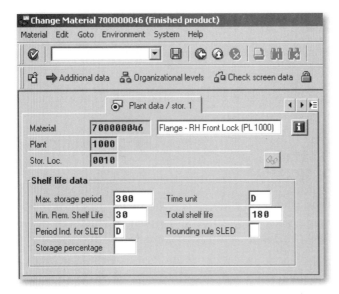

Figure 8.21 Shelf-Life Expiration Data Entry on Plant-Data Screen of Material Master Record

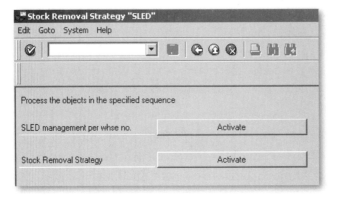

Figure 8.22 Two-Part Configuration for SLED Picking Strategy

Unlike some other picking strategies, this configuration has two parts, as shown in Figure 8.22. The first part of the configuration is to activate the shelf-life expiration date management for the warehouse where the picking will take place. The second part is to activate the stock removal strategy for shelf-life expiration for the warehouses that require it.

The SLED management can be activated for the warehouse by setting the indicator, as shown in Figure 8.23 (**001**; **Central Warehouse**). After this configuration has been made, you can configure the picking strategy for the storage type, using the second option shown in Figure 8.22.

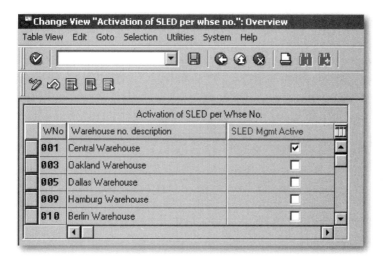

Figure 8.23 Configuration to Active SLED for Warehouse

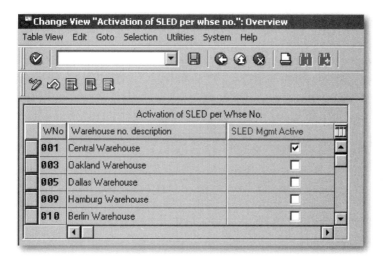

Figure 8.24 Shelf-Life Expiration Picking Strategy for Storage Type 002

Figure 8.24 shows that for the storage type **002**, the picking strategy has been configured to be shelf-life expiration, which is represented by option **H**. This will be used when material is withdrawn from any storage bin in the storage type.

8.6.3 Displaying SLED Stock

The shelf-life expiration date control list shows stock in the warehouse that has an expiration date. The SLED control list can be run using Transaction LX27 or through the navigation path: **SAP · Logistics · Logistics Execution · Warehouse Management · Master Data · Material · Evaluations · SLED Control List.**

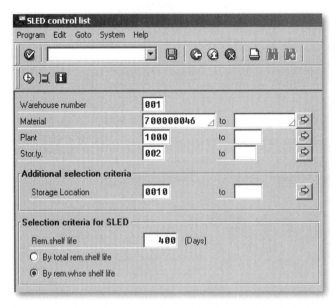

Figure 8.25 Initial Screen for Shelf-Life Expiration Date Control List: Transaction LX27

Figure 8.25 shows the entry of the material, warehouse number, plant, and storage type along with the remaining shelf-life in days for the maximum storage time allowed for a material in the warehouse.

The program reviews the SLED date entered when the transfer order was created against the current date in order to calculate the remaining shelf-life.

Figure 8.26 shows the shelf-life expiration date control list. The report shows the quants of material **700000046** in the warehouse that is active for SLED and is within the parameters entered in Figure 8.25.

8.6.4 Example of Shelf-Life Expiration Picking Strategy

In this section, we'll explain the shelf-life expiration picking strategy configuration for a storage type affects the way material is picked in the warehouse.

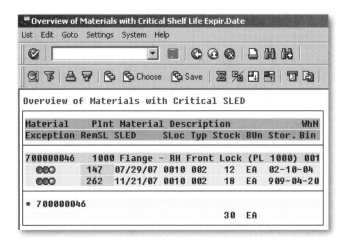

Figure 8.26 Results Screen for Shelf-Life Expiration Date Control List: Transaction LX27

Transaction LT01 can be used to create a transfer order that will pick material with the shortest shelf-life defined in the material master for the storage type 002.

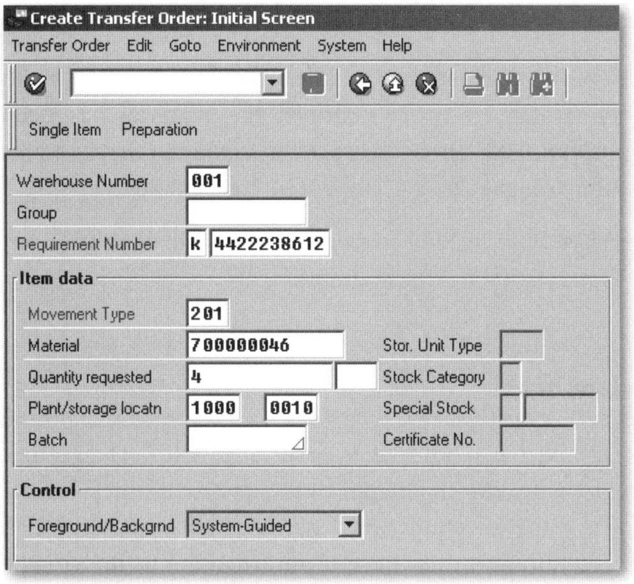

Figure 8.27 Creating Transfer Order: Transaction LT01

Figure 8.27 shows the initial screen for the creation of a transfer order to pick material from storage type **002**. The movement type, **201**, is used because it will remove the material and consume it at a cost center.

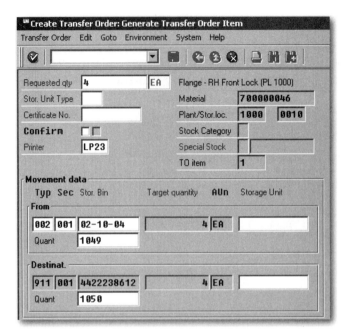

Figure 8.28 System-Generated Source Storage Bin Based on Shelf-Life Expiration Picking Strategy

Figure 8.28 shows the system-generated transfer order based on the shelf-life expiration picking strategy. In this example, the material has been removed from the storage bin, **02–10–04** because this is the bin that contains the material with the shortest shelf-life, as shown in Figure 8.26.

Now that we have reviewed the picking strategy for shelf-life expiration, let us examine the partial-quantities picking strategy.

8.7   Partial Quantities

The picking strategy for partial quantities is associated with storage unit management, which we'll discuss in Chapter 11. The partial pick can be required by a warehouse if the warehouse manager does not want to pick all the contents of a storage unit and then have to return some to the storage bin. A partial quantity allows the staff to remove some of the contents of a storage unit.

Warehouse staff will often try to reduce the number of storage units with partial quantities, and the partial-quantities picking strategy can be an appropriate way to accomplish this.

8.7.1 Configuration of Partial-Quantities Picking Strategy

The partial-quantities picking strategy can be defined using the navigation path: **IMG · Logistics Execution · Warehouse Management · Strategies · Stock Removal Strategies · Define Strategy for Partial Pallet Quantity**.

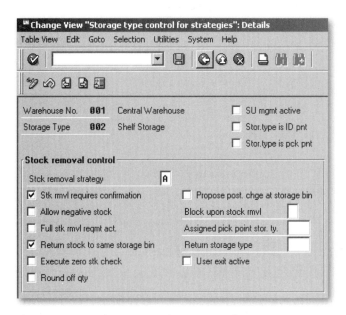

Figure 8.29 Partial-Quantity Picking Strategy for Storage Type 002

Figure 8.29 shows that for the storage type **002** the picking strategy has been configured for partial pallet quantity, which is represented by option **A**. This will be used when material is withdrawn from any storage bin in the storage type.

8.7.2 Using Partial-Quantities Picking Strategy

When a transfer order is created for a material with the storage type configured for partial-quantities picking, transaction processing searches for a relevant quant of material. The logic behind the picking strategy is defined as follows:

▸ Initially the system will determine whether the quantity in the transfer order equals or is greater than the quantity of a standard storage unit. If this is the case, then a standard storage unit can be picked from stock. However, if no standard storage units are available, the partial storage-unit quantities in the warehouse are used.

▶ If the system determines that the quantity in the transfer order is less than the quantity of the standard storage unit, then the system will initially proceed to remove partial storage unit quantities from the warehouse. However, if no partial storage unit quantities are available, the sytem will need to break down full storage units to obtain the correct quantity for the transfer order.

I'll provide further information regarding storage units in Chapter 11. After this discussion of partial-quantities picking, we'll turn our attention to the quantity relevant picking strategy.

8.8   Quantity Relevant Picking

The quantity relevant picking strategy is less frequently used but is useful for companies whose warehouses store the same material in varying sizes of bins and storage types. We find this scenario often in older warehouse buildings.

The quantity relevant picking strategy is based on the quantity required in the transfer order and whether that quantity is defined as *large* or *small*. Warehouses may have storage types where small quantities of material are stored and also have storage types where large quantities are stored.

8.8.1   Configuration of Quantity Relevant Picking Strategy

The quantity relevant picking strategy can be defined using the navigation path: **IMG • Logistics Execution • Warehouse Management • Strategies • Stock Removal Strategies • Define Strategy for Large/Small Quantities**.

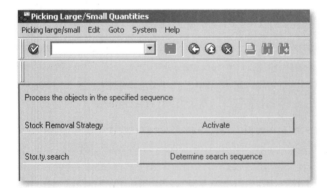

Figure 8.30 Two-Part Configuration for Quantity Relevant Picking Strategy

Unlike some other picking strategies, this configuration has two parts, as shown in Figure 8.30. The first part of the configuration is to activate the quantity relevant strategy for the warehouse where the picking will take place. The second part of the configuration is to determine the sequence in which the storage types are searched so that the relevant material to be picked is found.

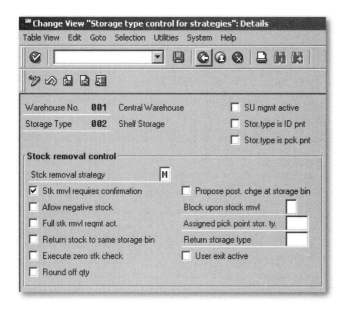

Figure 8.31 Quantity Relevant Picking Strategy for Storage Type 002

Figure 8.31 shows that for the storage type 002, the picking strategy has been changed to quantity relevant, option **M**, and this will be used when material is withdrawn from any storage bin in the storage type. The second part of the configuration is to define the search sequence for the storage type.

When the entries in the storage type search sequence are made, it is necessary to enter the first storage type for the smallest quantity. The second in the sequence should be larger than the first, and subsequent storage types should get larger in the search sequence, as shown in Figure 8.32.

Figure 8.32 shows the storage types that have been entered in the storage type search sequence. The picking functionality will search these storage types in sequence.

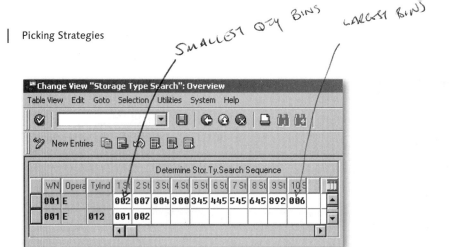

SMALLEST QTY BINS   *LARGEST BINS*

Figure 8.32 Storage Type Search Sequence for Quantity Relevant Picking

In Figure 8.32, two sequences of storage types can be used to find the relevant material for picking. In the first line, this is the sequence used for warehouse **001** and the operation is **E**, for picking. For a transfer order that uses quantity relevant picking to pick material in warehouse **001**, the function will review the material in the first storage type **002**. If the material cannot be found in this storage type, the system then will review the material in the second storage type **007** and so forth until the material is found.

If the material cannot be found, then warehouse staff would have to process the transfer order manually and enter a storage type and storage bin into the transfer order.

8.8.2   Quantity Relevant Picking and Material Master Record

When a transfer order is being processed, the transaction determines whether the transfer order line item quantity is *small* or *large*. The source storage bin that is proposed in the transfer order will either be from a small-quantity storage type or large-quantity storage type.

The check for this definition of *large* versus *small* quantity is performed for this picking strategy based on the control quantity field of the WM screen in the material master record. The control quantity that is entered for this material and storage type combination is the threshold that divides large from small.

In this case, as shown in Figure 8.33, the dividing threshold is a quantity of 20. This means a transfer-order line item with a quantity of 18 is deemed a small quantity, while a line item quantity of 21 is deemed large. This threshold will vary from material to material and storage type to storage type.

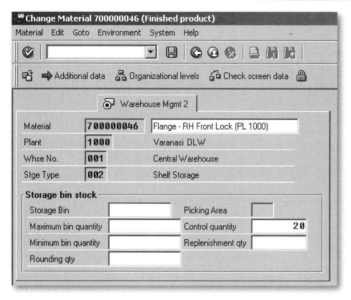

Figure 8.33 Control Quantity Field in Material Master Record

For the quantity relevant picking strategy, the system uses <u>movement type</u> ✗.
603 to determine which storage type is to be used in the transfer order for
picking.

(handwritten annotations)
(603– GI DLN - FIXED BIN)→ 915 FIX BIN PICK AREA
(601 – GI DLN ── 916 DYNAMIC.
↳ SHIPPING AREA DELIVERIES.

8.9 Summary

This chapter discussed picking strategies used in the warehouse. All of the
strategies we have discussed here may be used at any site. Although FIFO
and fixed-bin picking strategies are very common, do not discount other
picking strategies that may improve the efficiency of a particular warehouse.

Some companies, such as Walgreens and Kohl's, use picking strategies that
are not FIFO, so be prepared to ask companies' financial departments how
they value their stock and whether FIFO is the strategy they wish to use.
Consult with the warehouse staff to see if the picking strategies in SAP reflect
they way they need to work. Be prepared to demonstrate how each of the
different strategies work and how material is assigned to the transfer order.
Meeting the needs of warehouse management may require changes to the
configuration for the picking strategies.

In Chapter 9, I will discuss the different putaway strategies that can be
assigned, how these are configured, and how they are used.

Putaway strategies are important in locating material quickly and logically and thus helping to improve warehouse efficiency. Material for which putaway is performed without protocol is often difficult to locate, and costs extra time and money to move and ship.

9 Putaway Strategies

The putaway strategies discussed in this chapter will help you to decide where to store material received into the warehouse. A number of putaway strategies can be used, including:

- Fixed bin storage
- Open storage section
- Next empty storage bin
- Bulk storage
- Near picking bin

You do not have to define a putaway strategy for placement of material into the warehouse; indeed, many warehouses manually determine the putaway storage bin during the transfer-order process. However, in your efforts to produce warehouse efficiency using SAP WM, it is important to discuss the process of material putaway in the warehouse and to adopt putaway strategies if necessary.

Once the putaway strategy has been adopted, the system uses the putaway strategy to assign the appropriate storage bin to store the material. A putaway strategy may not be necessary, but accepting the system-generated putaway location relieves the warehouse staff of one more responsibility and effectively speeds up material putaway.

Having introduced the concept of putaway strategies, let's look at the first of these, the fixed-bin storage putaway strategy.

9.1 Fixed-Bin Storage

The putaway strategy for fixed-bin storage takes into account the data that has been entered into the material master record for the material to be placed in stock. The material is stored in a single bin; i.e., a fixed bin. The data regarding this bin and the parameters of the bin are found in the material master record of the material. For example, the storage bin is entered into the material master record and does not change unless the material master record is changed.

9.1.1 Fixed Storage Bin in the Material Master

The fixed storage bin is entered into the material master record in the warehouse-management screen.

> **Note**
>
> In SAP version ECC 6.0, this is the second warehouse-management screen, but it may vary for you depending on the version you are using. This storage bin is used for the fixed-bin picking and fixed-bin putaway.

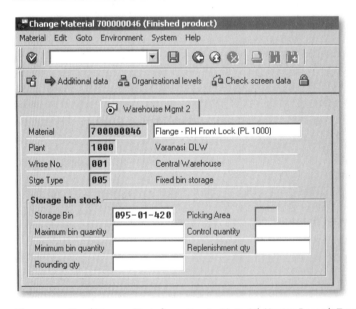

Figure 9.1 Fixed Storage Bin Information in Material Master Record: Transaction MM02

Figure 9.1 shows the warehouse management screen for the material 700000046. In the **Storage bin stock** section of the screen, the **Storage Bin** field has the entry **095–01–420**. This is the storage bin fixed for this material in this fixed-bin storage type: **005**. This information is then used for the fixed-bin putaway strategy.

9.1.2 Configuration of Fixed-Bin Storage Putaway Strategy

The fixed-bin storage putaway strategy can be defined following the navigation path: **IMG · Logistics Execution · Warehouse Management · Strategies · Putaway Strategies · Define Strategy for Fixed Bins**.

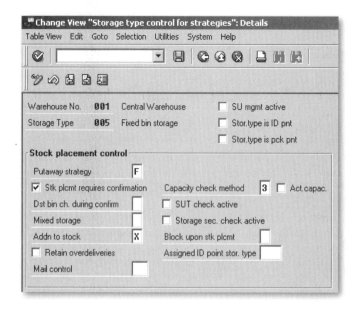

Figure 9.2 Configuration for Fixed-Bin Storage Putaway Strategy

Figure 9.2 shows the putaway strategy for storage type **005**. Fixed-bin storage strategy is entered as an **F** for fixed-bin storage putaway. You can set a number of other stock placement configuration fields as well.

9.1.3 Stock Placement Control Indicators

Figure 9.2 shows that, apart from the stock putaway strategy, a number of other control indicators that can be configured. These are described here:

▶ **Stk plcmt requires confirmation**
This indicator is set when putaway must be confirmed, including confirmation of the removal from the source storage bin, the placement in the destination bin, and the placement in the return bin, if relevant.

▶ **Dst bin ch. during confirm**
This indicator controls whether the transaction allows a change to the destination storage bin during confirmation of the transfer order. If this indicator is set, it will be possible to change the destination storage bin during confirmation of the transfer order. If the indicator is not set, then it is not possible to change the destination storage bin.

▶ **Mixed Storage**
This indicator can be set to allow different quants to be stored in a storage bin in this storage type. There are a number of options for this field, as seen here:

▷ **Blank**
Mixed storage is not allowed.

▷ **A**
A number of storage units with the same material can be stored in a single bin.

▷ **B**
This allows one material, but in different batches per bin and storage unit. Each storage unit can contain more than one batch of the same material.

▷ **C**
This option allows a number of batches in one storage bin, but only one material. However, it is not possible different batches in a single storage unit.

▷ **X**
This option allows any mixed storage without restrictions. Different material numbers and different batches can co-exist in the storage bin and in individual storage units.

▶ **Addn to Stock**
This indicator allows a quant of a material and a batch number to be stored in a storage bin with the same material and the same batch as an addition to existing stock.

▶ **Retain Overdeliveries**
This indicator can be set if the storage type into which the material is being placed can accommodate the over-delivery.

▶ **Mail Control**
This field is the mail control for the replenishment storage type. If an error occurs during automatic creation of transfer orders in production planning, this field is used to define which user is to be informed.

▶ **Capacity Check Method**

Setting this indicator means that a capacity check will be carried out for the storage bins in this storage type. This indicator is required if there is a possibility that the capacity can be exceeded. There are a number of options for the capacity check method, as seen here:

  ▶ **Blank**

  No check of capacity

  ▶ **1**

  Check of the maximum weight

  ▶ **2**

  Check based on palletization of storage unit type

  ▶ **3**

  Check of maximum quantity per storage bin in a storage type

  ▶ **4**

  Capacity usage check based on material

  ▶ **5**

  Capacity usage check based on storage unit type (SUT)

  ▶ **6**

  Capacity usage check based on the sum of the material and the storage unit (SU)

▶ **Act. Capac**

This is the active capacity check. Setting this indicator ensures that an active capacity check is executed when goods are placed into stock. This is not needed for strategies B, F, and I.

▶ **SUT Check Active**

Setting this indicator activates the storage unit type check for the putaway. The storage unit type must be entered for transfer orders using this putaway strategy. The storage unit type refers to the type of storage unit, such as a pallet or wire container.

▶ **Storage sec. check active**

This indicator is set when a storage section check is required for stock putaway. When the indicator is set, the transfer order will search the storage bins in the storage sections that have been identified in the configuration of the storage section search.

▶ **Block upon stk plcmt**

Setting this indicator will execute a blocking indicator at time of storage putaway. Two blocks can be activated: one for the storage bin and one for the quant. If the storage bin block is set, this indicates that the storage bin is blocked from any activity when the material is placed into it. This may be done to make sure the material is not moved or sold until a check or inspection is made on the contents of the bin. If a block is activated only on the quant, then this block applies only to that quant that has undergone putaway and not to any other quants in the storage bin.

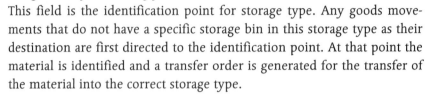

▶ **Assigned ID point stor type**
This field is the identification point for storage type. Any goods movements that do not have a specific storage bin in this storage type as their destination are first directed to the identification point. At that point the material is identified and a transfer order is generated for the transfer of the material into the correct storage type.

Now that you have a good idea of these indicators we can move on to an example of the putaway strategy for fixed bin storage.

9.1.4 Example of Fixed-Bin Storage Putaway Strategy

In this section, I will show you how the fixed-bin strategy configuration for a storage type affects material putaway in the warehouse. The putaway strategy has been configured for storage type **005** as fixed bin, as shown in Figure 9.2.

A stock placement is initiated by creation of a transfer order that will move the material from a location, Normally, this means movement from a goods-receipt interim storage type to the fixed-bin storage bin of the storage type defined in the material master.

Transaction LT01 can be used to create a transfer order that will move the material into the fixed-bin storage type 005. The material assigned for putaway has been goods-receipted into storage type 902 and the storage bin for receiving: WE-ZONE.

Figure 9.3 shows the initial screen for the creation of a transfer order for putaway of the material from a goods receipt. The movement type **501** is used as it will remove the material from the goods receiving interim storage type **902** and place it in the appropriate storage bin for the fixed-bin storage strategy.

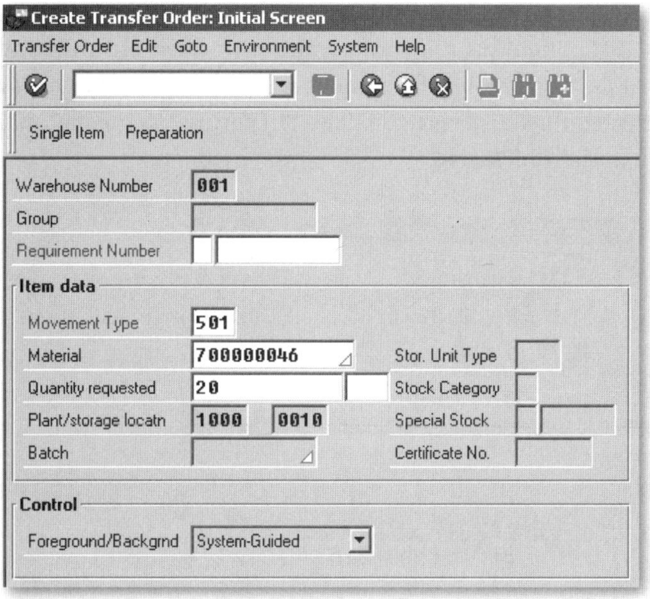

Figure 9.3 Creating a Transfer Order: Transaction LT01

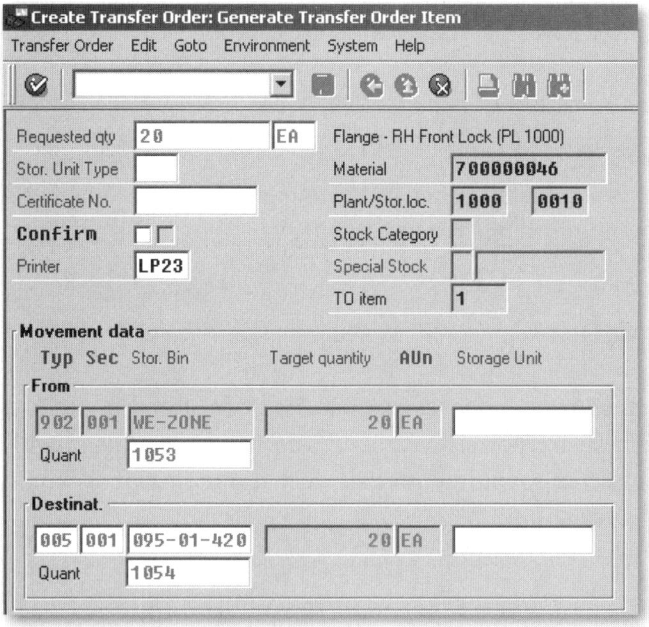

Figure 9.4 System-Generated Destination Storage Bin Based on Fixed-Bin Storage Putaway Strategy

Figure 9.4 shows the system-generated transfer order item information for the material **700000046**. Based on the configuration for fixed-bin putaway strategy, the material has been moved from the interim storage for the goods receipt and been selected for transfer to the fixed bin defined in the material master record for material **700000046**.

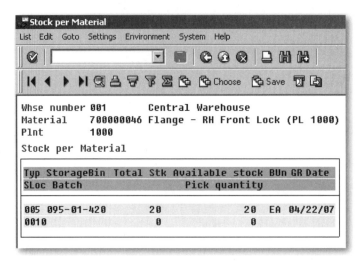

Figure 9.5 Stock Overview for Material 700000046 in Warehouse 001

Figure 9.5 shows that quantity of material **700000046** has now been placed in the fixed-bin location **095–01–420** in storage type **005**.

After reviewing the functionality of putaway strategies for fixed bins, we'll turn our attention to open storage putaway strategy.

9.2 Open Storage

The concept of open storage applies when materials are stored in areas of open floor, where there are no racks or lines. The storage type is roughly divided into storage sections, and the protocol is that one storage section is represented by one storage bin.

9.2.1 Configuration of Open Storage Putaway Strategy

The open storage putaway strategy can be defined following the navigation path: **IMG · Logistics Execution · Warehouse Management · Strategies · Putaway Strategies · Define Strategy for Open Storage**.

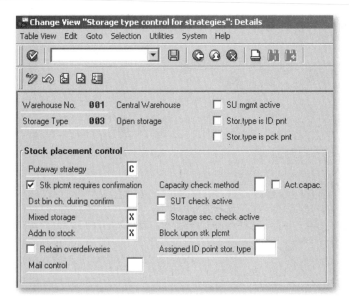

Figure 9.6 Configuration for Open Storage Putaway Strategy

Figure 9.6 shows the putaway strategy for storage type **003**. Open storage strategy is entered as a **C** for fixed-bin storage putaway. Because the storage is open and not as restrictive as rack storage, you must set the **Mixed Storage** and the **Addition to Stock** indicators so that multiple materials can be entered into the one storage bin.

9.2.2 Example of Open Storage Putaway Strategy

Now let's see how the open strategy configuration for a storage type affects material putaway in the warehouse.

The open storage allows the storage of different materials in the same storage bin. The current stock in one open storage bin shows that two materials are stored in one bin. This can be seen by using Transaction LS02N, or by following the navigation path: **SAP • Logistics • Logistics Execution • Internal Whse Processes • Bins and Stock • Single Displays • Storage Bin**.

Figure 9.7 shows that in one storage bin — **003–03–001** — there are two materials. The configuration for the open storage putaway allows for mixed storage and an addition to existing storage. This is how open storage works.

Transaction LT01 can be used to create a transfer order for material putaway into the open storage type 002. The material for putaway has been goods-receipted into storage type 902 and the storage bin for receiving: WE-ZONE.

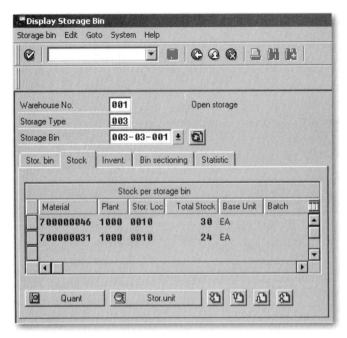

Figure 9.7 Materials Stored in Open Storage Type 003: Transaction LS02N

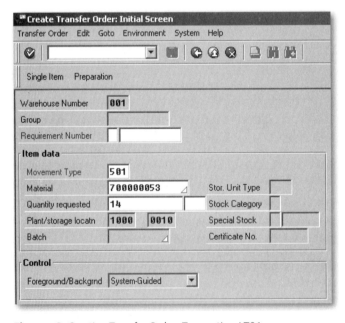

Figure 9.8 Creating Transfer Order: Transaction LT01

Figure 9.8 shows the initial screen for the creation of a transfer order for putaway of the material from a goods receipt. The movement type **501** is used because it will remove the material from the goods-receiving interim storage type 902 and place it in the appropriate storage bin for the open storage strategy.

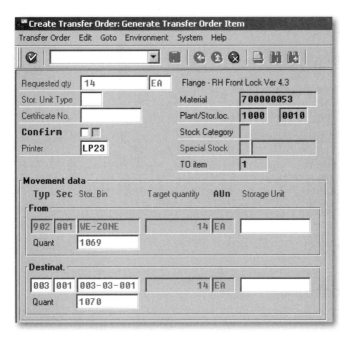

Figure 9.9 System-Generated Destination Storage Bin Based on Open Storage Putaway Strategy

Figure 9.9 shows the system-generated transfer order item information for the material **700000053**. Based on the configuration for open storage putaway strategy, the material has been moved from the interim storage for the goods receipt and selected to be transferred to the open storage bin: **003–03–001**.

Figure 9.10 shows information about the open storage bin **003–03–001** for open storage. It now shows that the bin has three materials stored in it and this can continue if material needs to be stored in the open storage type of the warehouse.

Now that we've reviewed the open storage putaway strategy, we'll examine the next empty bin putaway strategy.

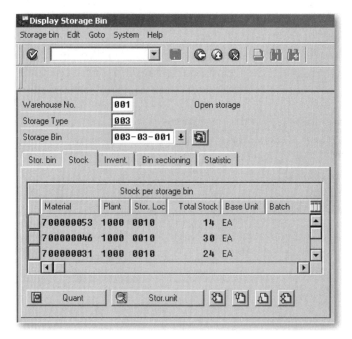

Figure 9.10 Materials Stored in Open Storage Type 003: Transaction LS02N

9.3   Next Empty Bin

Some warehouses are structured so that material can be stored in any bin within the storage type. This structure can result from the nature of the material stored in the warehouse; e.g., it may be different materials all stored in the same size container. If this is the case, the putaway strategy can be configured so that the system will select the next empty bin.

In manufacturing industries that produce electronic components, the parts are often small, delicate, and liable to damage by static. These components are stored in containers in the warehouse that are safe for all products. Many warehouses that store these products use carousel storage where the parts are stored in identical containers in a carousel system that places new items in the next empty bin available.

9.3.1   Configuration of Next Empty Bin Putaway Strategy

The next empty bin putaway strategy can be defined following the navigation path: **IMG • Logistics Execution • Warehouse Management • Strategies • Putaway Strategies • Define Strategy for Empty Storage Bin**.

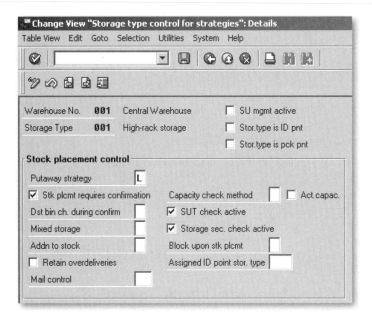

Figure 9.11 Configuration for Next Empty Bin Putaway Strategy

Figure 9.11 shows the putaway strategy for storage type **001**. The next empty bin putaway strategy is entered as an **L** for next empty bin. Note that other indicators are switched on for this strategy. The most significant is the storage section check indicator: **Storage sec check active**. Because the strategy is to find the next empty bin, further strategies can be used at the storage section and storage bin. Defining a storage section search gives the warehouse staff a better idea of where the next empty bin will be located. This is not necessary, but is often used with the next empty bin strategy.

9.3.2 Display of Empty Bins

You can view the empty bins for a warehouse and storage type by using the Transaction LS04 or by following the navigation path: **SAP • Logistics • Logistics Execution • Internal Whse Processes • Bins and Stock • Display • Empty Storage Bins**.

Figure 9.12 shows the empty bins that could be used for a stock putaway. However the bins with an indicator set in the **IA** field means are unavailable because of an inventory count. These bins need to be counted and therefore cannot be used in stock putaway. The only bins in **Storage type 001**, **Storage Section 001** that can be used in the next empty bin strategy are **07–08–01**, **07–08–02** and **07–08–03**.

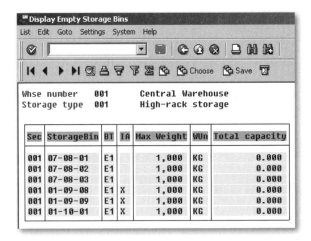

Figure 9.12 Display of Empty Bins in Storage Type 001:Transaction LS04

9.3.3 Example of Next Empty Bin Putaway Strategy

Let's now examine how the next empty bin strategy configuration for a storage type affects the material putaway in the warehouse.

Transaction LT01 is used to create a transfer order for material putaway into the storage type 001. In this case the material has only been created for storage type 001 and no other. The material to be putaway has been goods-receipted into storage type 902 and the storage bin for receiving: WE-ZONE.

Figure 9.13 shows the initial screen for the creation of a transfer order to putaway the material from a goods receipt. The movement type **501** is used because it will remove the material from the goods-receiving interim storage type **902** and place it in the appropriate storage bin for the next empty bin putaway strategy.

Figure 9.14 shows the system-generated transfer order item information for the material **700000031**. Based on the configuration for next empty bin putaway strategy, the material has been moved from the interim storage for the goods receipt and selected to be transferred to the next empty bin in storage type **001**, which was **07–08–01**, as we saw previously in Figure 9.12.

After the material has been stored in the empty storage bin 07–08–01, the Transaction LS04 should now only show two valid empty storage bins: 07–08–02 and 07–08–03. These lack the indicator in the IA column to show that they are blocked for an inventory count, while three storage bins do have **X** in the **IA** column to indicate they are blocked for the inventory count, as shown in Figure 9.15.

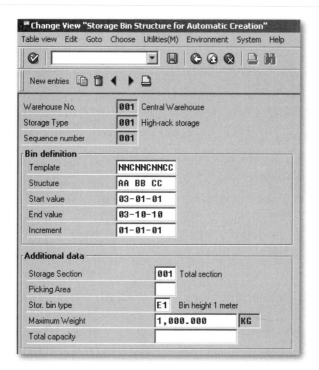

Figure 9.16 Configuration of Storage Bin Structure for Storage Type 001: Transaction LS10

Once you have reviewed the bin structure for storage type **001**, you can configure the cross-line stock putaway using a sort sequence based on the bin structure.

Cross-Line Stock Putaway Configuration

The cross-line stock putaway can be configured using the Transaction OMLM or by following the navigation path: **IMG • Logistics Execution • Warehouse Management • Strategies • Define Sort Sequence for Putaways**.

Figure 9.17 shows how the sort configuration can select any of the 10 characters that can make up the storage bin. In our example for storage type **001**, the storage bin uses only eight characters. Positions **3** and **6** are non-numeric and therefore cannot be used in the sort sequence.

In this example, the structure of the storage bin is based on a row, stack, level scenario, which is very common. The configuration in Figure 9.17 shows that the numeric characters in positions **7** and **8** are the first part of the sort. Therefore, the level is the primary sort characteristic, and the empty bins on a level will be filled first.

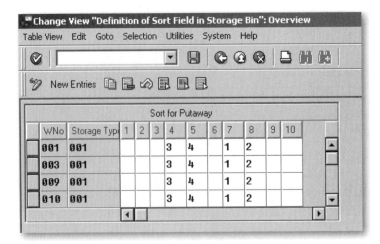

Figure 9.17 Configuration of Cross-Line Stock Putaway Strategy: Transaction OMLM

The next part of the sort is configured for the numeric characteristics in positions **4** and **5**, which represent the stack. Therefore, the level will be filled first, and the next empty bin will be found on the next stack. The row is not part of the sort sequence and has no role in selecting the next empty bin.

That concludes our discussion of the next empty bin putaway strategy. Now we shall examine the bulk storage putaway strategy,

9.4 Bulk Storage

Bulk storage is for material that is stored in large quantities. This is not to be confused with material that can be stored in bulk containers, such as grain, sand, cement, fertilizer, etc.

> **Example**
>
> In the beverage industry, a production run of beer may produce several thousand cans of product. Once this is placed in packs and then stored on pallets, it will be stored in the bulk storage type.

The options for the bulk storage putaway strategy can be defined using the Transaction OMM4 or through the navigation path: **IMG · Logistics Execution · Warehouse Management · Strategies · Putaway Strategies · Define Strategy for Bulk Storage**.

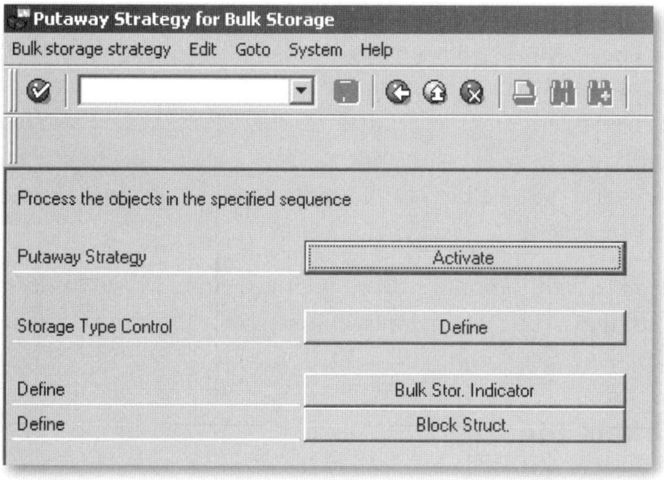

Figure 9.18 Configuration Options for Bulk Storage Putaway Strategy

Figure 9.18 shows that a number of options that can be configured for bulk storage putaway. The first option is for activation of the bulk storage putaway strategy for the storage type. The other three options seen in Figure 9.18 all relate to bulk storage putaway scenarios that involve storage units. Storage unit management will be discussed in Chapter 11.

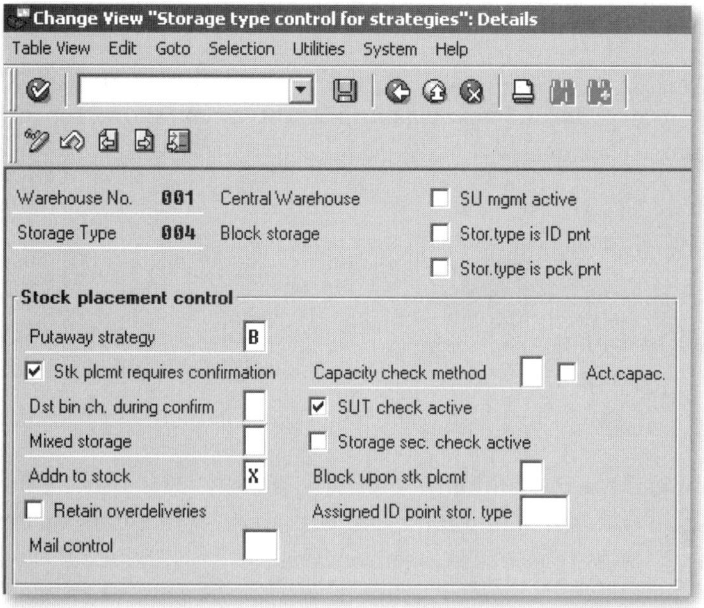

Figure 9.19 Configuration of Bulk Storage Putaway for Storage Type 004

Figure 9.19 shows the bulk storage putaway strategy for storage type **004**. The strategy is entered as a **B** for bulk storage. Note that other indicators are switched on for this strategy. The storage unit check (**SUT check active**) indicator has been set to be active because much of bulk storage used storage units. The other indicator to be set is the addition to stock (**Addn to stock**). This allows more material to be added to the same material currently in the bulk storage type.

Now that we have reviewed the bulk storage putaway strategy, we can discuss the putaway strategy. This is called near picking bin.

9.5   Near Picking Bin

This strategy is used for material that is being frequently picked, because it is appropriate to store the material close to the picking area. The warehouse can use this strategy to see of the material can be placed in the fixed bin. If not, the system will try a reserve area, and finally try to find a bin that is closest, using a configured search.

The options for the next picking bin putaway strategy can be defined using the Transaction OMLA or through the navigation path: **IMG • Logistics Execution • Warehouse Management • Strategies • Putaway Strategies • Define Strategy for Near Picking Bin.**

The options in Figure 9.20 show the configuration that can be carried out to fully define the strategy for the near picking bin. This screen shows six possible configuration selections, which are:

- ▶ Putaway strategy activation
- ▶ Storage type control definition
- ▶ Search per level definition
- ▶ Row and shelf assignment
- ▶ Storage bin generation
- ▶ Consistency check

The first option is the activation of the putaway strategy. This may be the only configuration that is required for a simple strategy, if that is all that is recommended by the warehouse management.

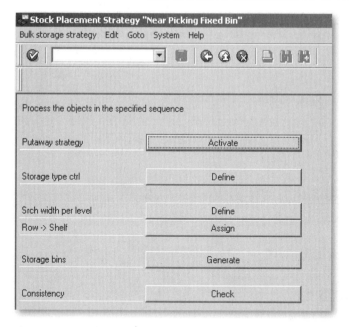

Figure 9.20 Configuration Options for Near Picking Bin Putaway Strategy

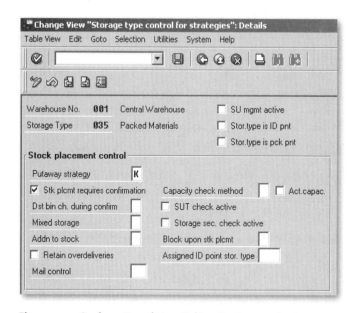

Figure 9.21 Configuration of Near Picking Bin Putaway for Storage Type 035

Figure 9.21 shows the near-picking-bin putaway strategy for storage type **035**. The strategy is entered as a **K** for near picking bin. It is perfectly correct to leave the configuration with just this one setting. This will perform putaway in the reserve storage bin, without searching for the fixed bin or carrying out a search for a relevant bin.

9.5.1 Storage Type Control Definition

If the storage type control is configured, this can be used when the fixed-bin storage is full. The control enables configuration of a reserve storage type for a fixed-bin area and how that area is to be filled.

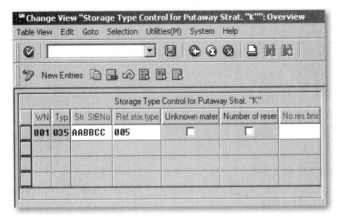

Figure 9.22 Storage Type Control Function Configuration for Storage Type 035

Figure 9.22 shows that storage **Type 035** has been configured as the reserve area for fixed-bin storage type **005**. When the fixed-bin area is checked for open bins, using putaway strategy **F**, the system will look at storage type **035**, which is used for putaway strategy **K**, to find an empty storage bin.

The structure of the storage bin name is configured in the field **Str.StBNo**. The **A** co-ordinate represents the shelf, the **B** co-ordinate represents the stack, and **C** represents the level.

You can set the **Unknown Material** indicator if storage of a material is allowed in the reserve area even if it is not assigned to the reference storage type, in this case 005. This allows warehouse staff to add material to the reserve area even if that reserve area is not meant for the material assigned for putaway.

The **Number of Reserve Bins Limited** indicator allows the number of bins set aside as reserve bins to a set to a limited number. The actual number of reserve bins can be set in the last field.

9.5.2 Search Per Level Definition

This configuration allows the search for a bin to be confined, initially, to a limited area. For example, materials of a specific height may be stored on only one level, and the search should only take into account that one level, given that the material would not be stored elsewhere. The first part of the configuration is the search on each level.

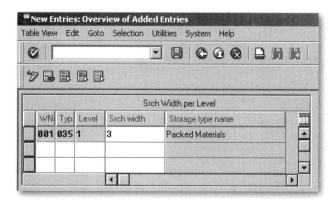

Figure 9.23 Configuration for Search for a Bin on a Certain Level

Figure 9.23 shows the configuration needed to search for an empty storage bin within the reserve storage type. If a fixed bin is selected, but is occupied, this configuration initially determines how many stacks to either side of the fixed bin — in this case a fixed bin on level one — should be checked for an empty bin. The value in the field **Srch width** is the number of stacks that are searched on either side of the fixed bin. If there is no configuration in this transaction for a level, then the search for a empty bin will occur across the whole level.

Figure 9.24 should be configured only if the storage type is not numbered by aisles. Check with the warehouse staff before setting this configuration. If a storage type is numbered by aisles, then the shelves on either side of the aisle will be numbered the same. If they are not numbered by aisle then they will be different.

> **Example**
>
> If you are standing in an aisle between two racking systems, there will be shelves on either side at the same level. If the physical entity of the storage type is made up of the aisle and the shelves on each side of the aisle, then the shelves will have the same number. However, some storage types are physically divided by the aisle so the shelves on either side will be numbered differently.

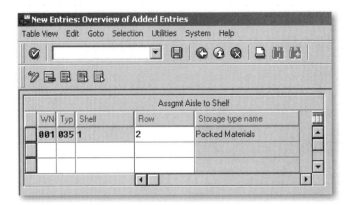

Figure 9.24 Assignment Aisle to Shelf Configuration

9.6 Summary

Putaway strategies often are considered less than the picking strategies that define warehousing-management decisions. While considerable time and effort are spent tweaking the efficiency of the outbound picking procedures, management often forgets the time and effort involved in locating material for which putaway has been illogical.

If putaway is not performed sensibly, all the effort involved in efficient shipping will not bear fruit, because the material for picking will not be moved to the picking area in a timely manner. The strategies for putaway are important to the efficient flow within the warehouse and should be carefully examined to determine which configuration is best for the warehouse.

In Chapter 10, I will discuss inventory procedures such as cycle counting and physical inventory.

Inventory procedures are important because they ensure that system information about the material in the warehouse is correct. Materials can be counted by annual inventory or by frequent cycle counting, which is more popular and can yield more accurate results.

10 Inventory Procedures

Inventory counting happens in every warehouse, but the method of counting inventory varies between companies and often between locations within companies. The annual inventory counts often start with a group of trained and untrained counting staff and end up with a large pile of discrepancies that need to be investigated rather than adjusted immediately.

Other procedures have been adopted, such as continuous and cycle counting, which reduce the emphasis on the annual count. In this chapter, we'll discuss the inventory procedures that clients use and how these are performed within the system.

Now that I have outlined the contents of this chapter, let us examine the first topic: the annual physical inventory.

10.1 Annual Physical Inventory

The annual physical inventory occurs in many places other than the warehouse. At the end of the fiscal year, company finance departments require the counting of assets and stock in order to start the fiscal year with an accurate financial picture. In order for an annual count to be as painless as possible, the organization needs formal procedures and documents, as well as fully trained counters.

10.1.1 Before the Count

The count will often take place on a weekend or on a day when vendors have been told that deliveries will not be received while the physical inventory is in progress. Making sure all physical purchase orders have a *non-delivery* notice stamped on them for the day of the inventory effectively reinforces this. Accounting staff should be available for any financial issues that occur or decisions that need to be made. Because stock movement in the warehouse will be impossible, the sales force and customers need to be informed about the non-shipment period.

The organization should use the experience of previous inventory counts to calculate the staff required for a successful count and fully train the employees designated as counters. Training of the counters should take place just before the count, with an emphasis on accuracy.

If the annual inventory is the first in a location or has not been successful in the past, it may be prudent to perform a test count of a small storage type, noting the number of storage bins counted and the time required. This is a good way to determine how many counters and how much time are needed for the physical inventory.

To make sure the process is as easy as possible for the counters, it is best to send out the warehouse a team to make sure materials are contained within their assigned locations and that all materials and storage bins are clearly identified. Often, a lot of time is wasted when the material cannot be identified or counters cannot find a specific location. That warehouse team also can count in advance the bulk storage types and dead stock. This will reduce the shutdown time caused by the inventory count.

> **Tip**
>
> Counted material and material not to be counted, such as warehouse equipment and packaging, should be clearly labeled to prevent confusion. It's also a good idea to label damaged material and material that has been written off and is awaiting disposal.

10.1.2 Configuration for Annual Inventory

You need to address a number of configuration steps before any count can be performed. Let's review these now:

1. Set the default values for each storage type in the warehouse via the navigation path: **IMG • Logistics Execution • Warehouse Management • Activities • Physical Inventory • Define Default Values.**

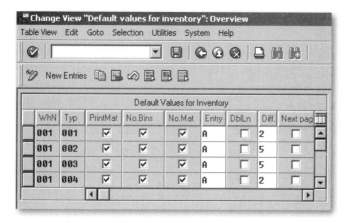

Figure 10.1 Physical Inventory Configuration Values for Storage Types

These default values for each storage type, shown in Figure 10.1, need to be configured before the physical inventory. A number of variables need to be addressed, and we'll describe these now:

▸ **PrintMat**

This indicator should be set if you have to have the material information printed on the count document. The material information is quite extensive and includes the material number, material description, plant number, batch number (if defined), special stock indicator, special stock number, stock category, and the quant number.

▸ **No.Bins**

This indicator should be set if the storage bin must be displayed during the entry of the inventory. If manual entry is required, the indicator should not be set.

▸ **No.Mat**

This indicator should be set if you need the material number to be displayed during the entry of the inventory. If manual entry of the material is required, then the indicator should not be set.

▸ **Entry**

This field defines the input method for the inventory count. There are three possible entries: **P** for via a list of items, **S** for page by page, and **A** for sequential.

▸ **DblLn**

If set, this indicator allows the inventory to be counted on two lines rather than one.

▶ **Diff.**

This field allows configuration of a percentage value for deviation between book and actual stock. If the material counted is entered and is greater than the percentage configured in this field, a warning message will be displayed and a decision made to allow the difference or reject it. For example, if percentage of 5 is entered and the counted material is 10 % greater than the book stock, then a warning will be issued. Normally, this deviation value is very low or is zero because most deviations will require investigation.

▶ **Next Page**

This indicator allows quants in the same bin to be printed on different pages. This need arises when mixed storage occurs, such as in open storage bin locations.

2. Set the inventory type for each storage type via the navigation path: **IMG • Logistics Execution • Warehouse Management • Activities • Physical Inventory • Define Types per Storage Type**.

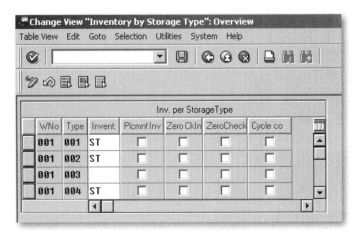

Figure 10.2 Inventory Configuration for Storage Types

This transaction, shown in Figure 10.2, allows configuration of the storage type for annual, continuous, or cycle counting. The fields that can be configured in this screen are described here:

▶ **Invent.**

This field defines the inventory procedure for the storage type. These can be **ST** for annual inventory, **PZ** for continuous inventory, or blank for no specific inventory method.

▶ **Plcmnt Inv**

This indicator is set when you must make an inventory each time material is moved into an empty bin. The indicator is often set when a company is using continuous inventory procedures.

▶ **Zero Ckln**

This indicator is used for continuous inventory based on zero stock checks. When this indicator is set, a count should be taken for all storage bins in this storage type when the remaining material is removed from a bin.

▶ **ZeroCheck**

This indicator is set to trigger a zero stock check, but not just for continuous inventory. If this indicator is set, a zero stock check is required when a storage bin becomes empty.

▶ **Cycle Co**

Setting this indicator sets the storage type for the cycle counting procedure that is discussed later in this chapter.

3. Set the procedure for inventory differences and the movement types to deal with these. This can be found using the navigation path: **IMG • Logistics Execution • Warehouse Management • Activities • Physical Inventory • Define Differences and Document Limits**.

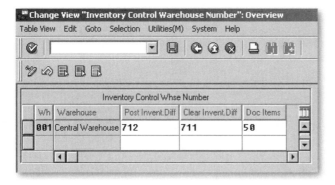

Figure 10.3 Configuration for Differences and Document Limits for Each Warehouse

Figure 10.3 shows the movement types and document limits that have been configured for warehouse 001.

The movement types are configured for posting of any inventory differences or clearing any differences that may occur when the count document is entered. The document that has been used by the counter may have a quantity different from the book stock, and after investigation and more checks a difference is agreed upon. The difference is posted, and the internal movement type defined in this configuration is used to post the difference to an interim record.

The **Doc Items** field refers to the number of items that are allowed for each record. This can be changed to a larger or smaller amount as required.

10.1.3 Processing Open Transfer Orders

When the physical inventory count begins, the storage types to be counted must be clear of open transfer orders. Check for open transfer orders by using Transaction LT22 or following the navigation path: **SAP · Logistics · Logistics Execution · Internal Whse Processes · Stock Transfer · Display Transfer Order · For Storage Type**.

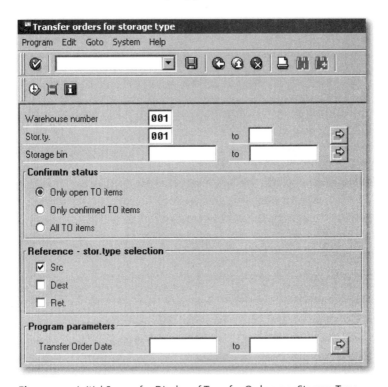

Figure 10.4 Initial Screen for Display of Transfer Orders per Storage Type

Figure 10.4 shows the selection screen for Transaction LT22. In this instance, you must view all open transfer orders for the storage type that is ready to be counted. You need to ensure that the open transfer orders are displayed, because it will be necessary to confirm or close these open transfer orders.

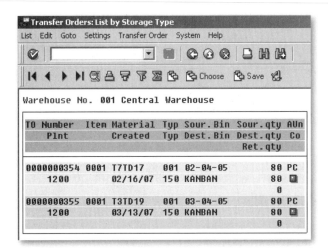

Figure 10.5 Display of Open Transfer Orders for Storage Type 001

Figure 10.5 shows that there are two open transfer orders for the storage type 001. You can see that the transfer orders are still open because the confirmation indicator **Co** is still red, which indicates not confirmed. The open transfer orders need to be confirmed or closed, depending on whether the material can be transferred, has been transferred, or cannot be transferred before the count starts.

Each transfer order can be confirmed using Transaction LT12 or the navigation path: **SAP · Logistics · Logistics Execution · Internal Whse Processes · Stock Transfer · Confirm Transfer Order · Single Document · In One Step**.

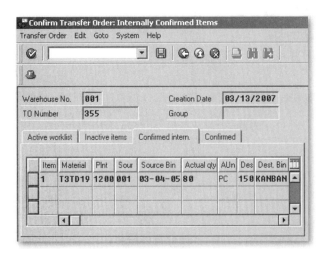

Figure 10.6 Confirmation of Transfer Orders Prior to Inventory Count

Figure 10.6 shows confirmation of an open transfer order for the storage type to be counted. Once all the transfer orders are closed for the storage type that will be counted, it can then be blocked so that no other inbound or outbound movements can take place.

10.1.4 Blocking the Storage Type

The storage type can be blocked for stock placement and stock removal by using Transaction LI06 or via the navigation path: **SAP • Logistics • Logistics Execution • Internal Whse Processes • Physical Inventory • In Warehouse Management • Block Storage Type.**

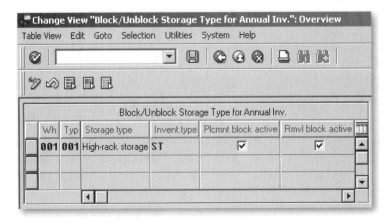

Figure 10.7 Blocking Stock Placement and Removal for Storage Type 001

Figure 10.7 shows the block on storage type 001 for both stock placement and stock removal. The block should remain in place until all the inventory documents have been processed for the storage type.

10.1.5 Creating Annual Inventory Documents

Once the storage types to be counted have been decided upon, checked for activity, and blocked for movements, the count documents can be printed and given to the counters.

The transaction to produce the count documents is Transaction LX15, which can be found using the navigation path: **SAP • Logistics • Logistics Execution • Internal Whse Processes • Physical Inventory • In Warehouse Management • Physical Inventory Document • Create • Annual Inventory.**

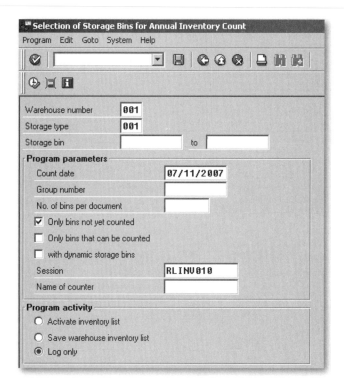

Figure 10.8 Selection of Storage Types for Annual Inventory Count

The initial selection screen, shown in Figure 10.8, allows entry of specific storage bins if not all the bins in the storage type are to be counted.

The session name is used to create the documents in a batch job. This can be run in the background or in the foreground. After entering the data that may be required, the transaction can be executed, and the process will display a summary of the counting that can begin.

Figure 10.9 shows the bins that can be counted, in this case **300**, with **306** quants. All of the bins in storage type **001** can be counted as well.

To process the documents, you can activate the transaction by using the header menu and selecting **Physical Inventory Document** • **Activate** or by using the **Shift + F4** function keys. The transaction will create a background job so that the documents can be printed.

The background session called **RLINV010** has been created, as shown in Figure 10.10. It can be processed to create the six new count documents based on the information that was entered in Figure 10.8. To execute this transaction, use the **Process** button or the header menu: **Session** • **Process Session**.

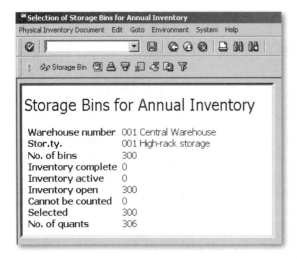

Figure 10.9 Summary of Physical Inventory Count that Can be Processed

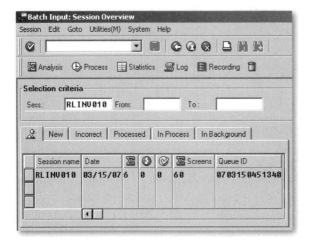

Figure 10.10 Batch Input Session for Processing Inventory Count Documents

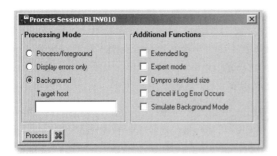

Figure 10.11 Dialog box During Processing Session for Count Documents

The dialog box, shown in Figure 10.11, is displayed after the session has begun processing. You can enable processing in the background or foreground and choose additional functions such as the ability to cancel if an error log is triggered.

10.1.6 Displaying the Count Documents

After the count documents have been processed they can be viewed by using the Transaction LX22 or the navigation path: **SAP • Logistics • Logistics Execution • Internal Whse Processes • Physical Inventory • In Warehouse Management • Physical Inventory Document • Overview**.

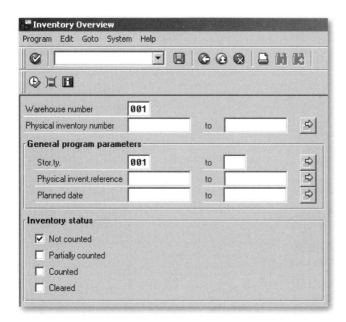

Figure 10.12 Initial Selection Screen for Displaying Count Documents: Transaction LX22

Figure 10.12 shows the initial data entered to select the count documents created by the batch processing. The warehouse number and storage type has been entered, along with the criteria to show only documents that have not been counted. Once the data has been entered, you can use the **F8** function key or the **Execute** button to process the transaction.

Figure 10.13 shows the six inventory count documents created by Transaction LX15. You can activate these documents by selecting the **Activate** button and then print them by using the **Print** button on the application toolbar or by using the header menu and selecting **List • Print**.

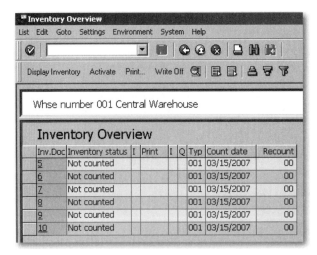

Figure 10.13 Overview of Six New Inventory Count Documents

```
      Warehouse inventory list for annual inventory
      ======================================================

Wareh.number: 001 Central Warehouse   Inventory no.: 5
Storage type: 001 High-rack storage   Page.........: 1/4
Date........: 03/15/2007              Main count

It.   Stor.bin Plnt Material number.... Qty....... UoM
      Quant no. SLoc Material short text

0001 01-01-02 1000 103-200            _____  PC
      272          0088 Fly wheel W-103

0002 01-01-03 1000 103-400            _____  PC
      275          0088 Pressure cover

0003 01-01-04 1000 100-600            _____  PC
      278          0088 Support base

0004 01-01-05 1000 100-700            _____  M2
      281          0088 Sheet metal ST37

0005 01-01-06 1000 103-100            _____  PC
      284          0088 Casing 103

0006 01-01-07 1000 103-200            _____  PC
      287          0088 Fly wheel W-103
```

Figure 10.14 First Page Of Printed Inventory Count Document For Storage Type 001

Figure 10.14 shows the first page of the count document that has been printed for the storage type **001**. The count document is handed to the counter, who then will manually enter the count figure into the document. Once finished, the count document will be returned for data entry.

10.1.7 Entering the Inventory Count

After the counter has returned the count document to the data entry area, the count document can be entered into SAP. The transaction to enter count documents is Transaction LI11N and can be reached through the navigation path: **SAP • Logistics • Logistics Execution • Internal Whse Processes • Physical Inventory • In Warehouse Management • Count Results • Enter**.

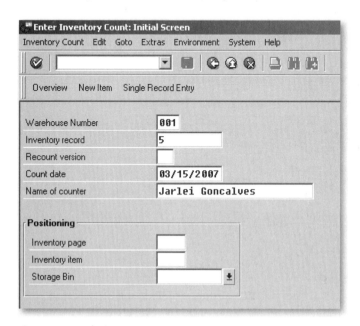

Figure 10.15 Initial Entry Screen to Enter a Count Document: Transaction LI11N

Figure 10.15 shows the initial screen for entering the count document. The count document number, the warehouse and count date can be entered. The name of the counter can be entered if there are many counters and recounts may require different counters.

Figure 10.16 shows the detail screen, which reflects the information on the count document. The data-entry clerk will enter the amount from the count document into the appropriate line in this transaction. If the counter found additional material, and there was not a line on the count document to reflect this, the data-entry clerk can add this by using the **New Item** button on the application toolbar.

After the total count for the document has been entered, the document can be posted by using the **Ctrl + S** function key or by selecting **Inventory Count • Posting** from the header menu.

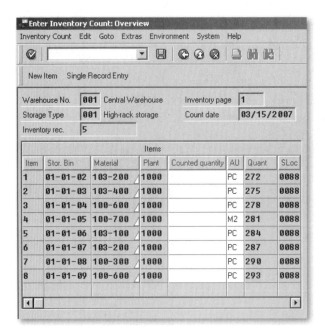

Figure 10.16 Detail Screen for Entering Data from Inventory Count Document

10.1.8 Count Differences

After the count has been entered, the count can be accepted or recounted if the variance is too great. The variance can be seen by using Transaction LI14, which can be found by using the navigation path: **SAP • Logistics • Logistics Execution • Internal Whse Processes • Physical Inventory • In Warehouse Management • Count Results • Recount**.

Figure 10.17 shows the initial screen for Transaction LI14, to initiate a recount. You can choose to allow a certain percentage deviation in book inventory against the count or to allow a value deviation.

> **Note**
>
> A large deviation in the count may only account for a few dollars in value, which the accounting department will allow. When a small deviation in the count causes a large difference in value, the accounting department may require a special investigation of the deviation.

Figure 10.18 shows some of the count for the document entered. There is a count for storage bin **01–01–03** that has only a **1.11** % count variance, but a value variance of **$3,171.78**. The other variance in storage bin **01–01–05** shows a **3.91** % count variance, but a dollar value of just **$70.76**.

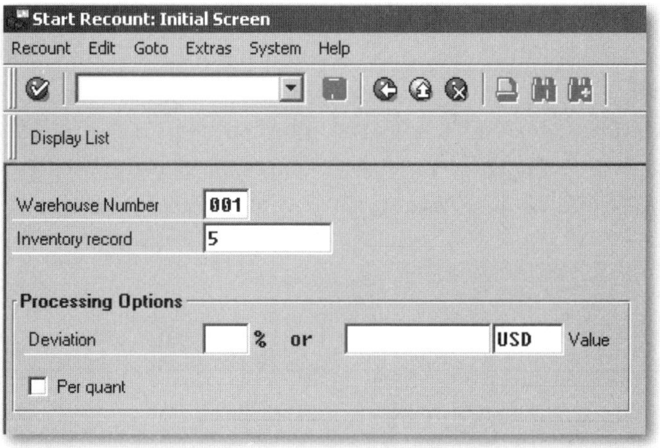

Figure 10.17 Initial Screen for Recount Of Inventory Count Document

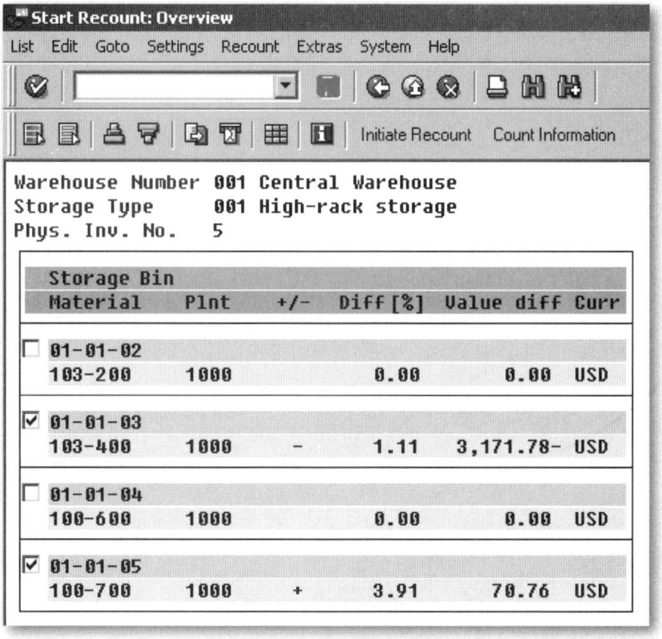

Figure 10.18 Count Document and Deviations in Value and Count

Depending on the accounting departments procedures on variance, a recount may be required on certain storage bins in this count document. To create a recount document, click on the **Initiate Recount** button or use the function keys **Shift + F4**. The processing will return to the initial screen and a message will be displayed that shows the recount number.

10.1.9 Entering a Recount

After the recount has been initiated and the recount number is known, the recount can be entered. The count can be entered into the transaction used for the initial count, Transaction LI11N. This can be reached via the navigation path: **SAP • Logistics • Logistics Execution • Internal Whse Processes • Physical Inventory • In Warehouse Management • Count Results • Enter**.

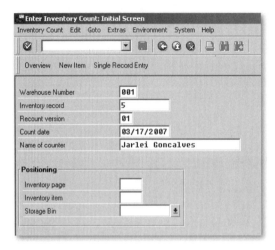

Figure 10.19 Initial Screen for Recount Document Entry

The recount is entered into Transaction LI11N with the same information as the original count — as shown in Figure 10.19 — but with the recount number that was provided. In this case, the recount number is **01**.

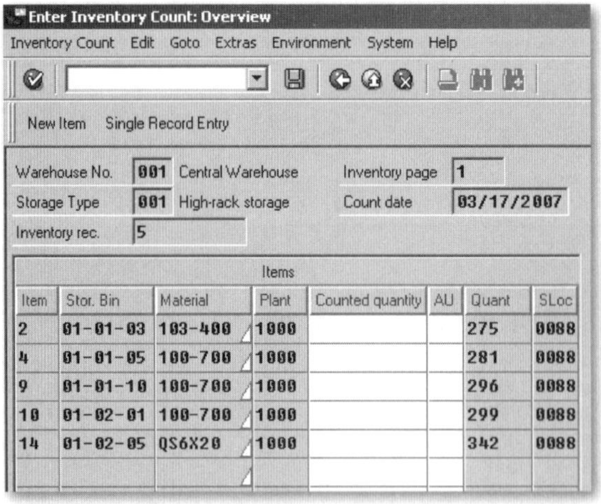

Item	Stor. Bin	Material	Plant	Counted quantity	AU	Quant	SLoc
2	01-01-03	103-400	1000			275	0088
4	01-01-05	100-700	1000			281	0088
9	01-01-10	100-700	1000			296	0088
10	01-02-01	100-700	1000			299	0088
14	01-02-05	QS6X20	1000			342	0088

Figure 10.20 Line Items from Count Document that Are Part of Recount

The recount document, shown in Figure 10.20, can be printed and given to a counter to perform the recount. Once the line items have been recounted, the document can be returned to the data entry clerk for re-entry. If the accounting department wants to ensure the most accurate count, the organization can perform a further recount using Transaction LI14.

10.1.10 Clear Differences

If no more recounts have been deemed necessary, the count differences can be cleared and a final posting made to the warehouse inventory.

The differences between the book inventory and the count information can be written *off* or *on*, by using Transaction LI20 or following the navigation path: **SAP • Logistics • Logistics Execution • Internal Whse Processes • Physical Inventory • In Warehouse Management • Clear Differences • Warehouse Management**.

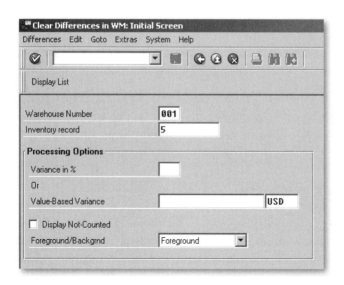

Figure 10.21 Initial Screen for Transaction to Clear Inventory Count Differences

Figure 10.21 shows the initial screen for allowing differences between the book stock and the count to be made. There is an allowance to enter a variance in percentage or in value to restrict the write-off. In the example shown in Figure 10.21, no variance has been entered.

Figure 10.22 shows the storage bins that have a material variance between the inventory count and the book stock. The details show the percentage difference and the difference in value.

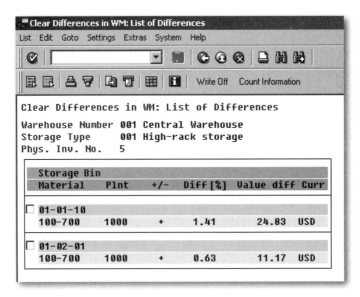

Figure 10.22 Materials with Variance Between Book Stock and Inventory Count

The difference between the book value and count value can then be written off by selecting the **Write Off** button on the application toolbar or using the function keys **Shift + F5**.

Now that we've examined the processes involved in the annual physical inventory, we'll move on to a process called continuous inventory.

10.2   Continuous Inventory

The principle behind continuous inventory is that dividing the annual physical inventory count into a number of smaller inventory counts performed over the year ensures that all material is counted. Many companies prefer this method because it reduces the effort required and the stress involved in conducting a single count.

The key to performing a successful continuous inventory is to ensure that all storage bins are counted in a systematic manner and the counts are successfully documented.

10.2.1   Configuration for Continuous Inventory

The configuration for continuous inventory is to set the inventory type for each storage type. This can be found using the navigation path: **IMG • Logis-**

tics Execution • **Warehouse Management** • **Activities** • **Physical Inventory** • **Define Types per Storage Type**.

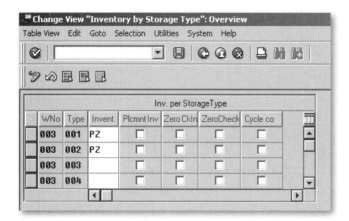

Figure 10.23 Configuration for Continuous Inventory for Storage Types

Figure 10.23 shows the configuration that has been entered for storage types 001 and 002 as **PZ**, which indicates continuous inventory.

10.2.2 Creating a Continuous Inventory Count Document

The transaction to produce the count documents for continuous inventory is Transaction LX16, which can be found using the navigation path: **SAP • Logistics** • **Logistics Execution** • **Internal Whse Processes** • **Physical Inventory** • **In Warehouse Management** • **Physical Inventory Document** • **Create** • **Continuous Inventory**.

Figure 10.24 shows the initial screen for creating a continuous inventory count document. The warehouse number and storage type are entered, and a range of storage bins can be selected. The following parameters can be selected:

▸ **Group Number**
This is a user-assigned number for grouping together certain counts. This can be as simple as the number of the week if you are combining counts that take place in the same week.

▸ **Bins with qty less than**
The bins will be selected if they contain a quantity of material that is less than the figure entered in this field.

▶ **No activity since (no. of days)**
This bin will be selected if there has been no activity in the bin in more than the number of days entered in this field.

▶ **Max no. of quants per bin**
The bin will be selected if the number of quants in the bin is less than the number entered into this field.

▶ **Only empty bins**
This indicator should be set if only bins are to be selected.

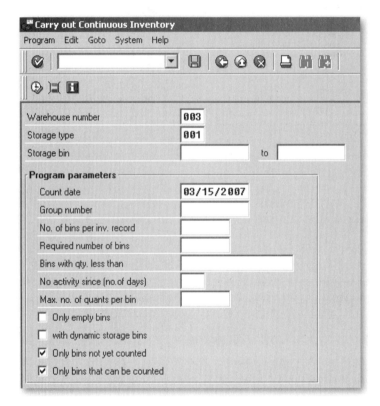

Figure 10.24 Initial Data-Entry Screen to Create Continuous Inventory Count Document: Transaction LX16

After all the parameters that have been required have been entered, you can execute the transaction by using the **F8** function key.

Figure 10.25 shows that there are three storage bins with material that can be counted in warehouse **003**, storage type **001**. These can be highlighted and activated for counting by using the **Shift + F4** function keys or selecting **Physical Inventory Document • Activate** from the header menu.

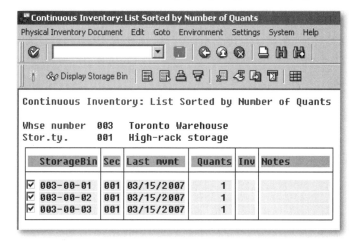

Figure 10.25 List of Quants that Can Be Counted as Continuous Inventory

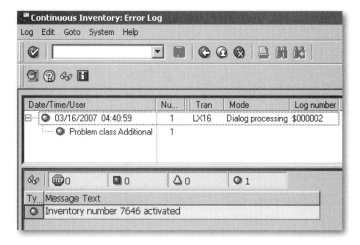

Figure 10.26 Continuous Inventory Document 7646

Figure 10.26 shows that after the three storage bins were activated, a continuous count document **7646** was created by Transaction LX16. This document can then be printed.

10.2.3 Printing a Continuous Inventory Count Document

The continuous count document can be printed using the Transaction LI04 or by following the navigation path: **SAP • Logistics • Logistics Execution • Internal Whse Processes • Physical Inventory • In Warehouse Management • Physical Inventory Document • Print Warehouse Inventory List**.

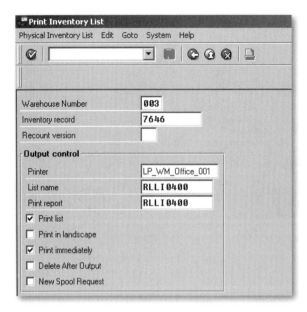

Figure 10.27 Initial Entry Screen for Printing of Continuous Count Document 7646

Figure 10.27 shows the initial screen for the printing of the continuous count document. The warehouse and document number are entered as well as the recount number, if appropriate. The printer is selected, and other options can be included such as print in landscape, print immediately, etc.

```
    WAREHOUSE INVENTORY LIST FOR CONTINUOUS INVENT.
    =====================================================
Wareh.number:003 Toronto Warehouse  Inventory no.: 7646
Storage type:001 High-rack storage  Page.........: 1/1
Date........:03/16/2007              Main count

It.   Stor.bin   Plnt Material number....   Qty.   UoM
      Quant no.  SLoc Material short text

0001 003-00-01  1000 700000031          _____  EA
      64             0010 Flange - LH Rear Lock

0002 003-00-02  1000 700000031          _____  EA
      65             0010 Flange - LH Rear Lock

0003 003-00-03  1000 700000031          _____  EA
      66             0010 Flange - LH Rear Lock
```

Figure 10.28 Printout of Continuous Inventory Count Document

Figure 10.28 shows the count document that is printed via Transaction LI04. The document shows the storage bins to be counted, the material expected in those storage bins, and a space where the counter can write the quantity that he or she counted in the storage bin.

The completed count document should be returned to the warehouse staff member responsible for entering continuous inventory counts.

10.2.4 Entering the Count Results

Once the items on the continuous count document have been counted, the count figures can be entered into Transaction LI11N. This transaction can be found via the navigation path: **SAP • Logistics • Logistics Execution • Internal Whse Processes • Physical Inventory • In Warehouse Management • Count Results • Enter**.

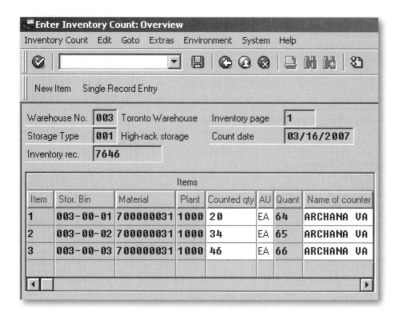

Figure 10.29 Count Entered for Continuous Inventory Count Documents

Figure 10.29 shows the count that has been entered for the continuous inventory count document. Once all the figures are entered, the count can be saved.

Now that the three storage bins have been counted, they do not need to be counted again until the next fiscal year. If you tried to include these storage bins in a count document, the bins would not appear. A manual check on the materials might be made for some outbound orders, although this would take place outside of normal cycle-counting procedures.

After the fiscal year is complete and all the bins have been counted, the storage bins should then become available for counting. To ensure that the storage bin table — LAGP — is clear of the count date and time of the previous fiscal year, a report called **RLREOLPQ** should be run using Transaction SE38 or included as part of an end-of-year batch job. Make sure the Basis team knows that this needs to be performed. I suggest that you ask if this job can be placed in any end-of-year batch runs that may occur for the finance or production department.

Now, after examining the processes of continuous inventory, we can focus on the popular method used in counting inventory, known as cycle counting.

10.3 Cycle Counting

Cycle counting is basically the process of continually validating the accuracy of the inventory in the warehouse by regularly counting a portion of the inventory, on a daily or weekly basis. In this way, every item in the warehouse is counted at least several times a year.

10.3.1 Benefits of Cycle Counting

Many companies choose the cycle-counting method because they cannot afford to pay the costs involved in large annual inventory events. Frequent cycle counting shortens the time between physical counts of any material and, as a result, any discrepancies that turn up during a cycle count will have occurred recently. This gives the warehouse management the opportunity to understand the cause of the discrepancy and perform any remedial action. Inventory write-offs, as a percentage of inventory investment, are much lower with regular cycle counting.

10.3.2 Materials Management Configuration Steps with Cycle Counting

The cycle counting indicators, **A**, **B**, **C**, etc., are configured using Transaction OMCO that is found in the configuration of the Materials Management module (SAP MM). The navigation path is: **IMG • Materials Management • Inventory Management and Physical Inventory • Physical Inventory • Cycle Counting**.

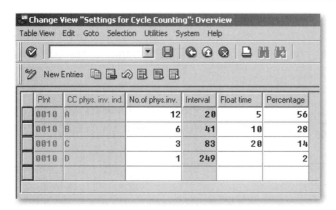

Figure 10.30 Configuration for Cycle Counting: Transaction OMCO

Figure 10.30 shows the configuration for the four cycle-counting indicators, **A**, **B**, **C**, and **D**. The configuration fields contain the following information.

▶ **No.of phys.inv**
This field defines the number of times a material must be counted per year. For example, materials that are assigned an **A** indicator will be counted 12 times.

▶ **Interval**
The interval is the maximum number of work days, as defined by the factory calendar, which can pass before the material has to be counted again.

▶ **Float time**
The float time is defined as the number of days after the planned count date that the material can be still be counted.

▶ **Percentage**
This field is the percentage of materials assigned an indicator. Therefore, in the example shown in Figure 10.30, 56 % can be allocated **A** materials, 28 % are **B** materials, 14 % are **C** materials, and only 2 % are **D** materials. The total percentage must add up to 100 %. These percentages are used in defining the indicators for the materials in the plant.

To automatically determine the indicators for materials in a plant, you must execute the ABC analysis.

10.3.3 Using the ABC Analysis

If the ABC indicators are configured for a plant, an ABC analysis can be performed in order to assign the correct indicator to each material. The ABC analysis can be run for cycle counting by using Transaction MIBC, which can be found via the navigation path: **SAP • Logistics • Materials Management • Physical Inventory • Special Procedures • Cycle Counting • Set Cycle Counting Indicator**.

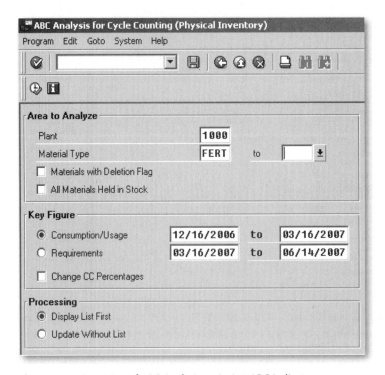

Figure 10.31 Execution of ABC Analysis to Assign ABC Indicators

Figure 10.31 shows the Transaction MIBC that allows the entry of the plant and a material type. In this case, the ABC analysis will be performed on material type **FERT**: finished goods.

The transaction proposes a range of dates for either consumption or requirements. The user then decides whether to use the material consumption data or material requirement data as the basis for defining the ABC indicator. You also have the option of altering the percentages already configured for the plant.

Figure 10.32 shows the results of the ABC analysis that was performed on the finished goods in plant 1000. The results show that a number of materials have changed ABC indicator. This will result in the number of cycle counts needing to be performed to change.

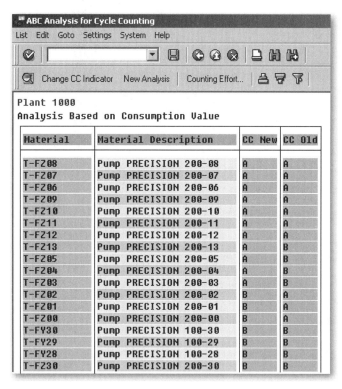

Figure 10.32 Results of ABC Analysis Performed on Finished Goods in Plant 1000

10.3.4 ABC Indicator and Material Master

After the ABC analysis has been performed and the ABC indicator has been assigned to the material, the indicator is written into the material master record. You can see the ABC indicator by viewing the plant data screen in the material master, using Transaction MM03.

Figure 10.33 shows the plant data screen for the material master record of material **T-FZ08**. In Figure 10.32, this material is the first material in the list and is assigned an **A** indicator. In the plant-data screen, this indicator is seen as the cycle count physical inventory indicator: **CC phys. inv. id.** .

There is also a field next to that indicator labeled **CC fixed**. This indicator can be set manually on the material master. Setting this indicator prevents the ABC indicator from being changed by the ABC analysis process. This guarantees that no matter how much the consumption or requirements of this material change, it would always remain the same ABC indicator unless it was manually changed on the material master record. Check with the warehouse staff to ensure that this indicator is set correctly.

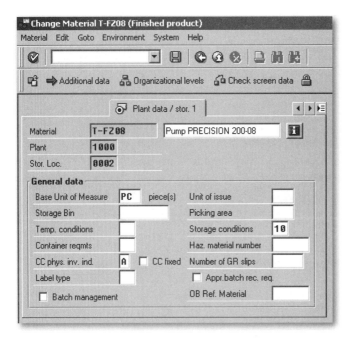

Figure 10.33 ABC Indicator Shown on Material Master Record as Cycle Count Physical Indicator

10.3.5 Cycle Counting Configuration for Storage Type

The configuration for cycle counting can be set to the inventory type for each storage type. This can be found using the navigation path: **IMG • Logistics Execution • Warehouse Management • Activities • Physical Inventory • Define Types per Storage Type**.

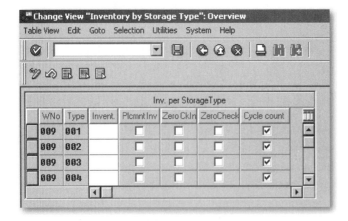

Figure 10.34 Cycle Counting Configuration for Storage Types

Figure 10.34 shows the configuration for warehouse **009**, storage types **001** through **004**. No inventory method is defined — neither continuous nor annual — but the cycle-counting indicator is set for these four storage types. Therefore, the storage types will use the cycle counting indicators set in the material master records to define how the material is counted.

10.3.6 Creating a Cycle Count Document

Transaction LX26 is used to produce the count documents for cycle counting. It can be found using the navigation path: **SAP • Logistics • Logistics Execution • Internal Whse Processes • Physical Inventory • In Warehouse Management • Physical Inventory Document • Create • Cycle Counting**.

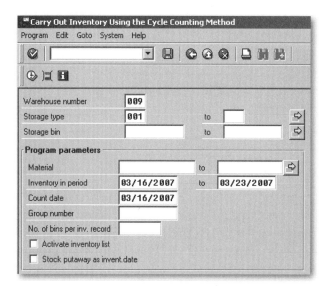

Figure 10.35 Creating a Cycle Count Document: Transaction LX26

Figure 10.35 shows the selection entered into Transaction LX26 for warehouse **009** and storage type **001**. When this transaction is executed, the system will review all the material in the storage bins to ascertain whether a cycle count is required, based on the cycle count indicator on the material master and the last time the material was counted.

Figure 10.36 shows an overview of the count documents that can be created for the warehouse number and storage type entered in the initial selection screen. In this example, two storage bins that have been selected: **07–08–01** where the cycle count is overdue, and **04–10–10** where a cycle count is scheduled.

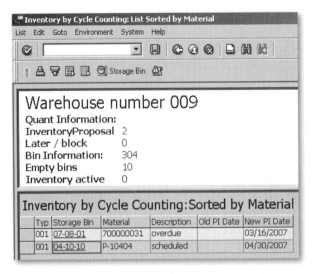

Figure 10.36 Review of Storage Bins that Require Cycle Counting

To activate a count document, highlight the line item and select the activate icon. The transaction will return the inventory count document number for the cycle count selected.

10.3.7 Printing the Cycle Count Document

After the cycle count document has been created, it can be printed for warehouse staff to perform the count. The document is printed using the Transaction LI04 or via the navigation path: **SAP • Logistics • Logistics Execution • Internal Whse Processes • Physical Inventory • In Warehouse Management • Physical Inventory Document • Print Warehouse Inventory List**.

```
    WAREHOUSE INVENTORY LIST via CYCLE COUNTNG
    ================================================

Wareh.number: 009 Warehouse           Inventory no.: 12
Storage type: 001 High-rack storage  Page.........: 1/1
Date........: 03/16/2007              Main count

  It.  Stor.bin   Plnt Material number....   Qty.  UoM
       Quant no.  SLoc Material short text

  0001 07-08-01   1000 700000031             _____ EA
       313             0088 Flange - LH Rear Lock
```

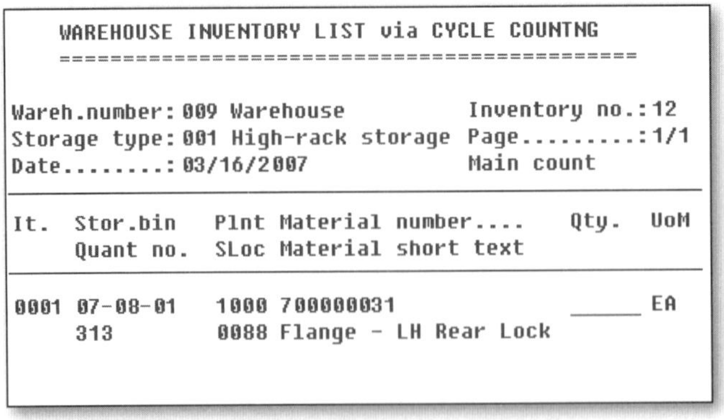

Figure 10.37 Printout of Cycle Count Document Created by Transaction LI04

The cycle count document can be given to a member of the warehouse staff to perform the count as part of his or her daily warehouse routine. Figure 10.37 shows the printout of the count document that the warehouse operator will use to record the count of the storage bin.

10.3.8 Entering the Cycle Count

After the item on the cycle count document has been counted, the result can be entered into Transaction LI11N. This transaction can be found using the navigation path: **SAP • Logistics • Logistics Execution • Internal Whse Processes • Physical Inventory • In Warehouse Management • Count Results • Enter.**

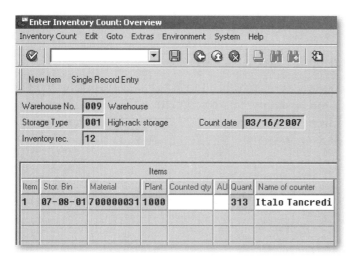

Figure 10.38 Entering Count from Cycle Count Document

Figure 10.38 shows the information for the storage bin that has been counted. Once all the figures are entered, the count can be saved.

Now that the count has been entered for this storage bin, the material does not need to be counted again until the date that is determined by the configuration of the ABC indicators for this plant. In this case, the material will have an **A** indicator, and the configuration for the plant will be set for the material to be counted six times a year.

Now we have examined the functionality of cycle counting we shall examine the zero stock check.

10.4 Zero Stock Check

A zero stock check is essentially the process of performing a stock check on a storage bin after the material has been removed, in order to ensure that the storage bin is empty. You cannot do this in storage types such as open storage where there is mixed storage, or for storage-unit-managed bulk storage.

However, in warehouses with very few open storage bins, the zero stock check is a valuable tool to ensure the next transfer order to use the storage bin will not fail. The zero stock check is a good step to take where the warehouse has not been good at maintaining inventory accuracy. If the warehouse is new to SAP and in the past has not been accurate regarding bin contents, a zero stock check can provide a level of comfort to ensure that the inventory accuracy is improving.

10.4.1 Configuration for Zero Stock Check

The zero stock check indicator can be set for each storage type. The configuration can be set in the inventory type configuration for each storage type. This can be found using the navigation path: **IMG • Logistics Execution • Warehouse Management • Activities • Physical Inventory • Define Types per Storage Type**.

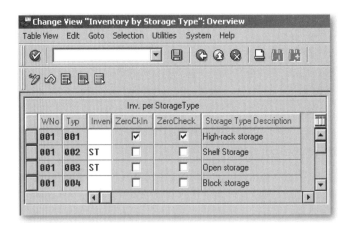

Figure 10.39 Zero Stock Check Configuration for Storage Type 001

This transaction, shown in Figure 10.39, enables configuration of the storage type for annual, continuous or cycle counting. The other fields allow for configuration of zero stock check with and without continuous inventory and are described here:

▶ **ZeroCkln**

This indicator is used for continuous inventory based on zero stock checks. When this indicator is set, a count should be taken for all storage bins in this storage type when the remaining material is removed from a bin.

▶ **ZeroCheck**

This indicator is set to trigger a zero stock check, but not just for continuous inventory. If this indicator is set, a zero stock check is required when a storage bin becomes empty.

10.4.2 Performing an Automatic Zero Stock Check

If the configuration for a storage type is set to require a zero stock check on the removal of all materials from a storage bin, the check will be triggered from the transfer order.

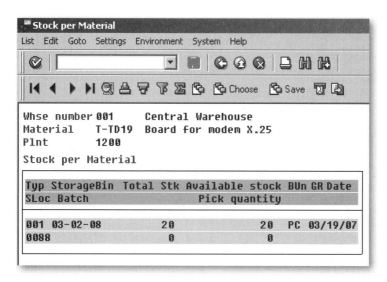

Figure 10.40 Warehouse Stock Overview for Material T-TD19

The stock overview for material T-TD19, seen in Figure 10.40, shows that there is a quant of 20 pieces in storage bin **03–02–08** in storage type **001**. From the configuration shown in Figure 10.39, we know that the zero stock check is required when a storage bin has been emptied. Therefore, a transfer order from this bin to the KANBAN area in the warehouse will empty the bin in and create the requirement for a zero stock check.

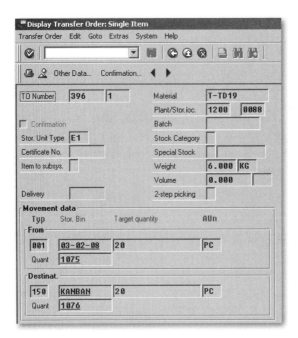

Figure 10.41 Transfer Order to Trigger a Zero Stock Check

Figure 10.41 shows a transfer order created by Transaction LT10 that is moving the total material from storage bin **03–02–08** to the KANBAN storage bin in the production supply area. The zero stock check indicator is set for this storage type, so it is possible to view this inside the transfer order. You can do this by selecting **Extras • Other Data** from the header menu or by using the **F7** function key.

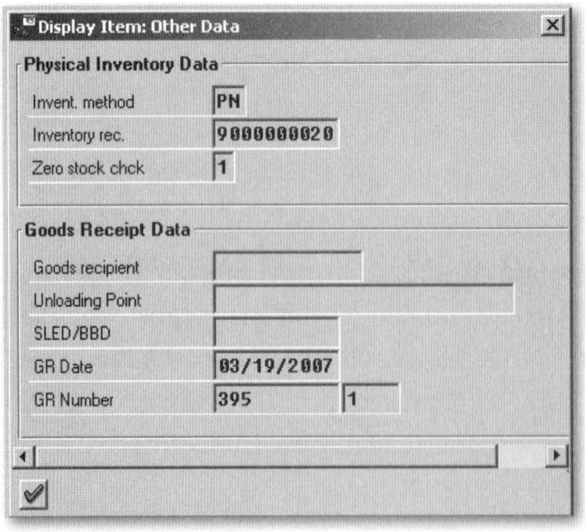

Figure 10.42 Physical Inventory Data of Transfer Order

Figure 10.42 shows the physical inventory information based on the item in the transfer order. In this case there are three fields, which are relevant for the zero stock check. These are described next:

▶ **Invent. method**
This inventory method is designated via the configuration. In this case, the **PN** represents continuous inventory based on zero stock check. Other options can be PZ for continuous inventory, ST for annual inventory, MA for manual inventory, and CC for cycle counting.

▶ **Inventory rec.**
This is a system-defined inventory record number based on the zero stock count that needs to be carried out.

▶ **Zero stock chck**
This field is the status for the zero stock check. The options are:

  ▶ **1**
  System requires a zero stock check to be carried out

  ▶ **2**
  Manual requirement for a zero stock check to be carried out

  ▶ **3**
  Bin is empty, after system check

  ▶ **4**
  Bin is empty, after manual check

  ▶ **5**
  Bin is not empty, after system check

  ▶ **6**
  Bin is not empty, after manual check

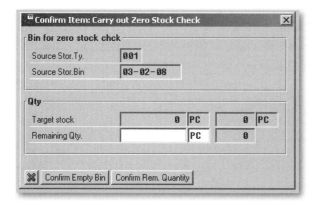

Figure 10.43 Zero Stock Transfer Order Confirmation Check

Figure 10.43 shows the zero stock check dialog box that appears during the confirmation of the transfer order. If the transfer order has removed all the material from the storage bin, then the check is required to ensure this is correct. If it is not, then an amount can be entered into this screen, and the information will then need to be investigated before posting.

10.4.3 Performing a Manual Zero Stock Check

If there is no continuous inventory configuration for a zero stock check for a storage type, then a manual zero stock check can be carried out if the storage bin is noted as empty after a transfer order has removed stock from a bin.

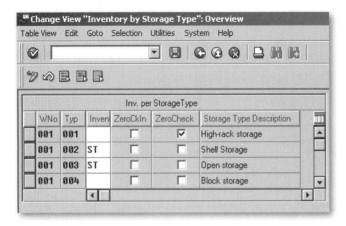

Figure 10.44 Zero Stock Check for Storage Removal Without Continuous Inventory

Figure 10.44 shows that the configuration for continuous inventory zero stock check has been removed, but the configuration for a zero stock check remains on stock removal triggered manually from a transfer order.

Figure 10.45 shows the stock overview for material **T-TD19**. You'll see that there is a quant of **46** pieces in storage bin **01–10–01** in storage type **001**. The configuration has now been changed for storage type 001 and no zero stock check is required by the system when a bin is empty. Therefore, the only way a zero stock check can be triggered is manually.

Confirming a transfer order by each item, as performed in Transaction LT11, enables manual creation of a zero stock check. The transaction can be found using the navigation path: **SAP · Logistics · Logistics Execution · Internal Whse Processes · Stock Transfer · Confirm Stock Transfer · Single Item · In One Step**.

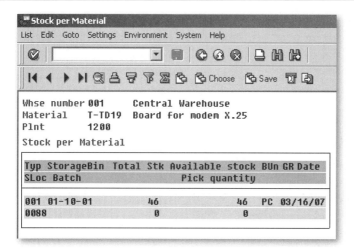

Figure 10.45 Warehouse Stock Overview for Material T-TD19

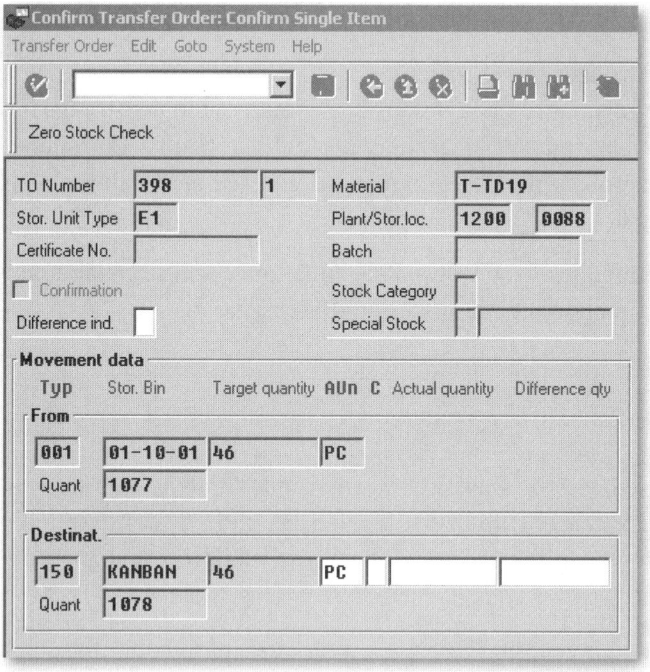

Figure 10.46 Confirmation of Transfer Order with Zero Stock Check

Figure 10.46 shows confirmation of line item one in transfer order **398**. The line item shows that the all the material from the storage bin is going to be transferred to the KANBAN storage bin. In this instance, you can manually

347

trigger a zero stock check by selecting the **Zero Stock Check** button on the application toolbar or by selecting **Goto • Zero Stock Check** from the header menu.

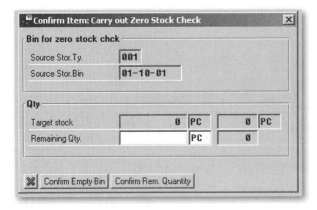

Figure 10.47 Dialog Box Allowing Zero Stock Check in Transfer Order Confirmation

The screen shown in Figure 10.47 allows the warehouse staff to enter in a value in the remaining quantity box if there is any material in the storage bin even though the system indicates that the bin should be empty. If a value is entered that is not zero, an investigation may be required before the value is posted to the system.

Now we have examined the zero stock check function, I will summarize the physical inventory functionality described in this chapter.

10.5   Summary

In this chapter I discussed the ways a company can accurately keep track of its physical inventory and ensure that it is reflected in the warehouse management system. However, the counting of material is a process that is subject to human error.

The traditional annual inventory is a once-a -year attempt to count the stock in a warehouse, and if the count was wrong it remains wrong until the next year. In today's warehouses, the traditional annual inventory is being superseded by frequent cycle counting. Cycle counting is thought to be a more accurate method of counting, but still is subject to the same level of human error. The benefit of cycle counting is that the more you count, the more likely it is that the count will be correct.

More counting produces a more accurate picture of the stock in the warehouse and eliminates the stress on the warehouse caused by the annual inventory. Cycle counting should be considered a quality-assurance procedure whereby the counting ensures the quality of the count.

The other aspect of quality assurance is to correct the count errors when they are found and to investigate why the errors occurred. Other methods that support the accuracy of the warehouse stock includes the zero stock check. This can improve warehouse stock accuracy as it provides extra counting events when a bin is expected to be empty, and thus is an easy addition to frequent cycle counting.

In Chapter 11, we will examine storage unit management and discover how storage units affect standard stock placement and removal.

Storage unit management was developed to enable warehouse management to identify the container that holds a material as it moves around the warehouse. It is often important to manage the movement of the container as well as the material or materials it contains.

11   Storage Unit Management

Storage unit management is the warehouse-management equivalent to handling unit management, the functionality found in SAP's Inventory Management module (SAP IM). Storage unit management was developed exclusively for warehouse management, and from it SAP developed handling unit management for SAP Materials Management (MM). There are slight differences between the two, as seen here:

▶ Handling unit management allows for the nesting of handling units; i.e., a handling unit containing a number of other handling units, while storage unit management does not allow the nesting of storage units

▶ Handling unit management requires that an item be unpacked and packed, while this is not required for storage unit management. The storage unit is used to contain a quantity of material for its movement around the warehouse.

The storage unit comprises one or more materials and a container such as a pallet or a packing box. These items together make up the uniquely identifiable storage unit that can be moved and stored within the warehouse.

This chapter will introduce you to some of the key elements of storage unit management. You'll learn how a storage unit is created and how the storage unit can be planned before the material arrives at the receiving dock. The chapter will thoroughly explain other key functionality, including the use of storage unit management in putaway and picking within the warehouse.

Now that I have highlighted some of the key topics in this chapter, I will introduce the storage unit management functionality.

11.1 Introduction to Storage Unit Management

In modern warehouses, deliveries from a vendor may not arrive separated into quants of specific materials. In many retail operations, vendors send pallets of different material on one pallet, and these arrive at the warehouse and are unloaded on the pallet. At this point, the warehouse can break down the pallet that has arrived into distinct material quants. The warehouse then stores the quants separately or stores the pallet of material as a whole.

The pallet and the material on the pallet can be described as a single unit — a storage unit — made up from the container and the material stored with the container.

If the warehouse decides to store material in the container, then storage unit management will need to be configured for the warehouse. While the entire warehouse need not be designated for storage units, certain storage types will need to be identified to accept storage units.

To allow storage unit management to be used in the warehouse, a number of configuration steps need to be carried out.

> **Note**
>
> The use of storage unit management when handling unit management is already used in SAP IM can cause some confusion. Before configuring any storage unit management steps, confer with the supply chain team to avoid miscommunication.

11.1.1 Activate Storage Unit Management

For each warehouse where storage unit management is to be used, it must be configured to be active. The configuration step can be found using the navigation path: **IMG • Logistics Execution • Warehouse Management • Storage Units • Master Data • Activate Storage Unit Management per Warehouse.**

Figure 11.1 shows the indicator for activating storage unit management for warehouse **009**. No storage unit management can take place until this indicator is set for the relevant warehouse.

Figure 11.1 Activating Storage Unit Management for Warehouse 009

11.1.2 Define Storage Unit Number Ranges

For each of the warehouses activated for storage unit management, you need to define the number range needs to be defined for the storage unit. This configuration is found using the navigation path: **IMG • Logistics Execution • Warehouse Management • Storage Units • Master Data • Define Number Ranges**.

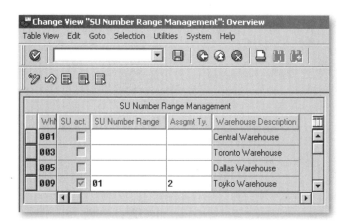

Figure 11.2 Defining Number Range for Warehouses with Storage Unit Management

Figure 11.2 shows the configuration for warehouse **009**, where the storage unit number range is set as **01** and the assignment type as **2**. These settings mean that the storage unit number is internally assigned and it does allow for numbers to be used more than once.

11.1.3 Define Storage Type Control

The storage type control is configured for the placement and removal strategies explained in earlier chapters. In this instance, the storage type control is configured for the storage unit management controls of those strategies.

The configuration steps can be found using the navigation path: **IMG • Logistics Execution • Warehouse Management • Storage Units • Master Data • Define Storage Type Control.**

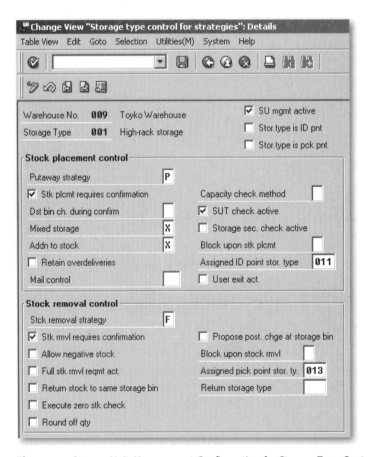

Figure 11.3 Storage Unit Management Configuration for Storage Type Control

Figure 11.3 shows the configuration for storage type control for storage type **001** in warehouse **009**. To ensure that the configuration is correct for a storage type when storage unit management is active, you should the consider several settings, described here:

- ▶ **SU mgmt active**
  This indicator is set to show that this storage type is storage unit managed.

- ▶ **Putaway strategy**
  This is set to **P**, which means that the Storage Unit Type putaway has been selected.

- ▶ **Mixed storage**
  Because different materials can be moved on the same pallet as a defined storage unit, the mixed storage indicator must be activated.

- ▶ **Full Stk rmvl reqmt**
  If this indicator, is set, it affects the storage unit, not just the materials. A complete removal involves the complete storage unit.

These configuration settings should be discussed with warehouse staff to ensure that you have correctly identified the way the warehouse needs storage unit management to operate.

11.1.4   Define Storage Unit Type

The storage unit type is used to distinguish the containers used in conjunction with the materials to comprise the storage unit. A storage unit type is configured as a three-character field, and a 20-character description can also be entered.

The configuration steps can be found using the navigation path: **IMG · Logistics Execution · Warehouse Management · Master Data · Material · Define Storage Unit Types.**

Figure 11.4 shows the storage unit type configured for each warehouse. Each container used in the warehouse should be configured. We identify the different storage unit types because the sizes of these containers depend on the type of racking they are designed for or the storage facilities they are part of, such as storage carousels. The storage unit type identifies the physical aspects of the container, and this is important during storage bin searches.

That concludes the introduction to storage unit management. I'll continue by explaining the storage unit record.

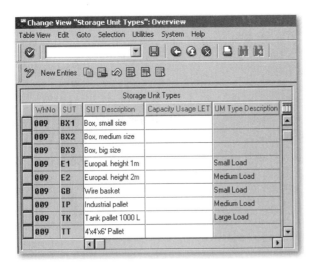

Figure 11.4 Configuration of Storage Unit Types

11.2 Storage Unit Record

The storage unit does not come into use outside of warehouse management and can only exist when material needs to be moved within the warehouse. Therefore, the storage unit is created when the material making up the storage unit is first proposed. This could happen in response to a receipt from a purchase order or be created later for movement within the warehouse.

11.2.1 Creating a Storage Unit Record by Transfer Order

The storage unit can be created when the movement is triggered. The transfer order, which is the procedure to move material around the warehouse, is the catalyst for creating a storage unit record.

Transaction LT07 is used to create a transfer order for a new storage unit. The configuration steps can be found using the navigation path: **SAP • Logistics • Logistics Execution • Internal Whse Processes • Stock Transfer • Create Transfer Order • Create Storage Unit**.

Figure 11.5 shows the initial screen of Transaction LT07. The storage unit does not exist until this transfer order is created. The actual movement of the material with its container requires that the transfer order create the storage unit as part of the process. If the storage unit is numbered externally, the relevant number can be added on this screen. Systems often need to have the number of the storage unit created internally.

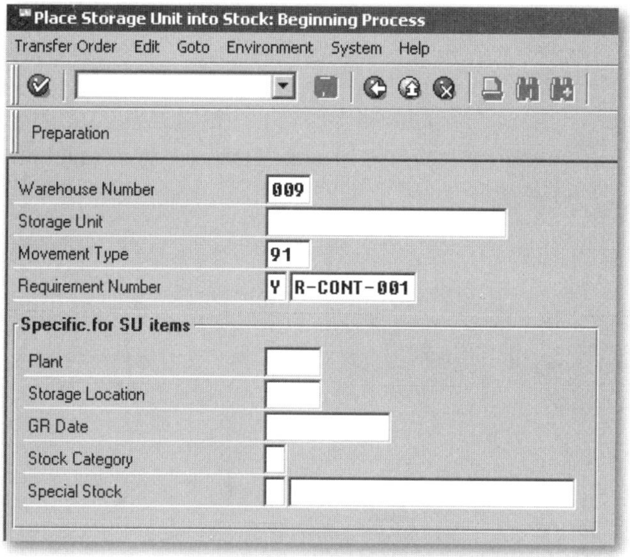

Figure 11.5 Initial Screen for Creation of Storage Unit: Transaction LT07

The initial screen must contain the warehouse number and the movement type. In this instance, entry of the movement type requires that a requirement number be entered.

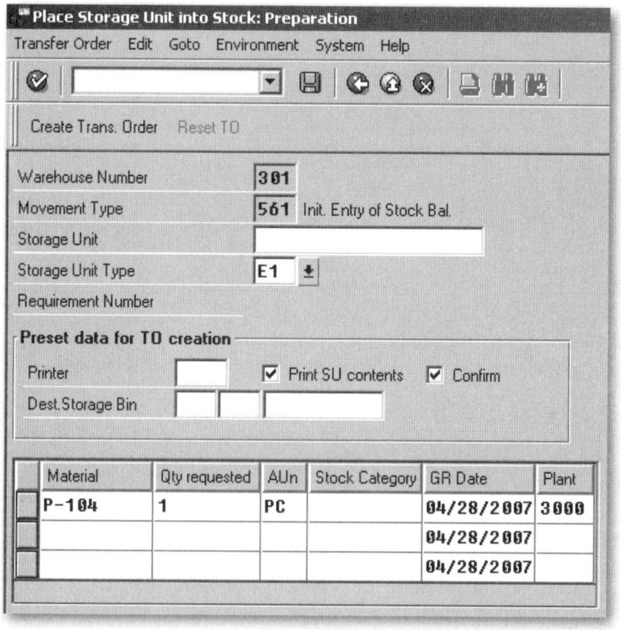

Figure 11.6 Entry of Items for Creation of Storage Unit: Transaction LT07

Figure 11.6 shows the entry of an item into a transfer order that will create the storage unit. This screen shows the details required for a transfer order to be created: warehouse number, movement type, plant, material, and material quantity. In addition, the data required to create the storage unit has been entered, such as the storage unit type. The configuration of storage unit types is shown in Figure 11.4.

Once the data is entered into the screen correctly, use the **Create Trans. Order** to create the transfer order and to create the storage unit.

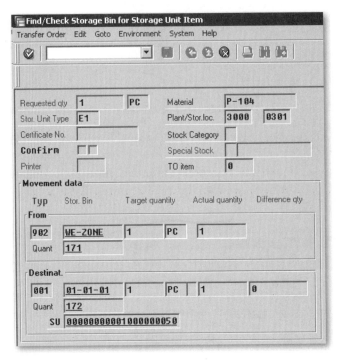

Figure 11.7 Transfer Order Created with Storage Unit Placed into Stock

Figure 11.7 shows the transfer order with the source and destination storage types. The destination storage type shows that there is a new storage type to be entered. This has been created from the data entered into the screen shown in Figure 11.6.

11.2.2 Display a Storage Unit

After the transfer order is confirmed, the details of the storage unit can be displayed. The transaction for this is Transaction LS33, which can be found using the navigation path: **SAP · Logistics · Logistics Execution · Internal Whse Processes · Bins and Stock · Display · Single Displays · Storage Unit**.

Figure 11.8 Details of Storage Unit: Transaction LS33

Figure 11.8 shows the details of the storage unit that has been entered. The information displayed is from the entry of the transfer order. The movement data reflects the last time the storage unit was moved and the transfer order that performed the movement.

Now I have explained creation and layout of the storage unit record, I will go on to describe how storage units are planned.

11.3 Planning of Storage Units

The storage unit can be planned before the material arrives in the warehouse. The warehouse manager can prepare the containers for the arriving material so the material can be scanned on the receiving bay and placed in the container with which it is combined to make up the storage unit.

Planning storage units is the process of creating the transfer orders, but not confirming them. Creating the transfer order will create the storage unit, so that it will exist when the material arrives at the receiving dock.

11.3.1 Planning Storage Units by Transfer Order.

Warehouse management can plan storage units for incoming materials by using Transaction LTOA, which can be found using the navigation path: **SAP • Logistics • Logistics Execution • Inbound Processes • Goods Receipt for Purchase Order, Order, Other Transactions • Putaway • Create Transfer Order • Preplan Storage Units**.

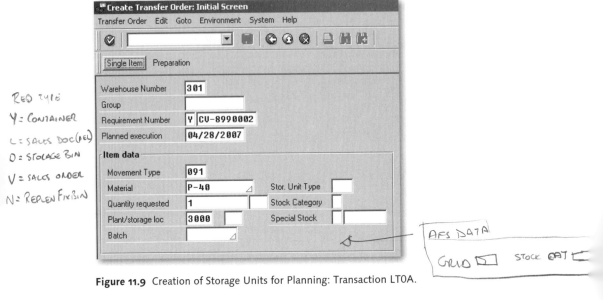

REQ TYPE

Y = CONTAINER

L = SALES DOC (DEL)

O = STORAGE BIN

V = SALES ORDER

N = REPLEN FIX BIN

AFS DATA

GRID ☐   STOCK CAT ☐

Figure 11.9 Creation of Storage Units for Planning: Transaction LTOA.

Figure 11.9 shows the initial screen for Transaction LTOA, creating storage units for planning purposes. The quantity of the material entered on the transfer order is the amount that is expected to arrive on the inbound delivery. Because the movement type is for the planning of storage units, it requires entry of the storage unit number and the code **Y** for Storage Units. To continue with the planning, click the **Preparation** button.

Figure 11.10 shows the next screen for the planning of storage units. The transfer-order creation program has defaulted the storage type and a source bin for the container. At this point in the transaction, the transfer order can be created in the foreground by function key **F5**, or in the background by function key **F6**.

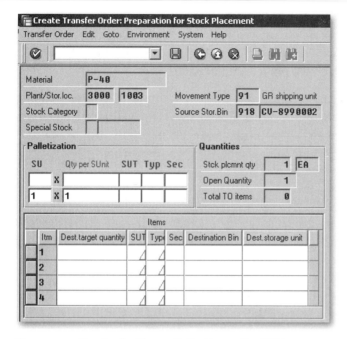

Figure 11.10 Planning for Storage Units: Transaction LT0A

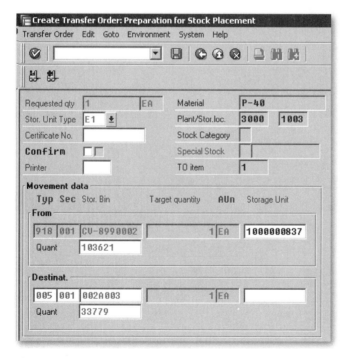

Figure 11.11 Completion of Transfer Order: Transaction LT0A

Figure 11.11 shows the transfer order that has been created for the inbound material. The material will be moved from the goods-receipt area using the container, and this will be storage unit **CV-8990002**. The storage unit will be moved to storage type **005**, bin location **002A003**.

The transfer order is not confirmed at this point; this process is for planning the movement. Storage unit documents are printed that would be stored until the material arrives. The confirmation will take place when the material arrives at the receiving dock and is moved to the storage bin.

11.3.2 Receiving Planned Storage Units

Once the planned storage unit has been assigned, the transfer order will remain unconfirmed until the material arrives. When the material does arrive and is checked, it can be moved into stock using Transaction LT09. This transaction can be found using the navigation path: **SAP** • **Logistics** • **Logistics Execution** • **Internal Whse Processes** • **Stock Transfer** • **Create Transfer Order** • **Move Storage Unit**.

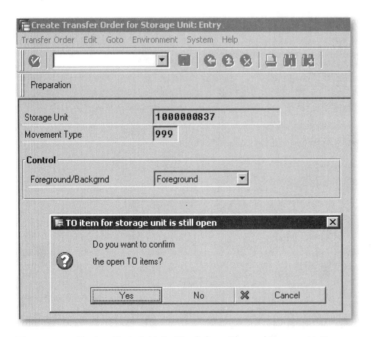

Figure 11.12 Placing Material Into Stock from Planned Storage Unit

Figure 11.12 shows the storage unit that was created in Figure 11.11, entered along with the movement type. A dialog box is displayed, asking if the transfer order needs to be confirmed. The transfer order is for the planned storage unit and the material that was arriving at the receiving dock.

If you select the **Yes** button, the transfer order can be confirmed internally, or — if there is a difference in the actual amounts — a change can be made, identifying the difference.

11.3.3 Recording Differences in Planned Storage Units

In Figure 11.11 there was no difference between the actual amount received and the amount planned. If there was a difference, then that difference could have been recorded in Transaction LT09.

After entering the storage unit and movement type, the transfer can be selected for confirmation, as shown in Figure 11.12. Instead of confirming internally, a worklist can be used to record the material differences.

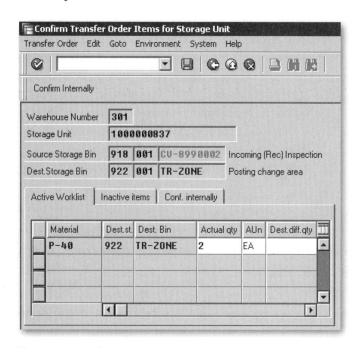

Figure 11.13 Confirmation of Transfer Order with Quantity Variance

Figure 11.13 shows a quantity variance in the incoming material. The transfer order had been created with a quantity of one, and the quantity that arrived at the receiving dock was a quantity of two. The material quantity variance is entered, and the transfer order is confirmed.

From the planning of storage units, I'll now move on to discuss the documents related to storage units.

11.4   Storage Unit Documentation

You can print the following four documents to aid the storage unit process:

▸ Transfer order document

▸ Storage unit contents document

▸ Storage unit document

▸ Storage unit — transfer order document

I'll describe these documents more fully in the sub-sections that follow.

11.4.1   Transfer Order Document

The transfer order document is simply the transfer order that can be printed with or without storage unit management. The transfer order printout shows the detailed information about a single item regarding the movement in a storage unit. A separate transfer order document is printed for each item on the transfer order. The format of the document can be determined by the warehouse staff and can be modified by ABAP code. The document can display any information from the transfer order and can be configured to print bar codes so that data can be entered using a radio frequency (RF) scanning device.

The transfer order document can be printed manually using Transaction LT32. This can be found using the navigation path: **SAP • Logistics • Logistics Execution • Inbound Processes • Goods Receipt for Purchase Order, Order, Other Transactions • Print and Communication • Transfer Order for Storage Unit**.

Figure 11.14 shows the selection screen that will print a number of documents relating to a storage unit. Enter the storage unit, and select printing of just the transfer order or of the other three storage unit documents. The print code, printer, and spool control data can be entered if the system is configured for this.

Figure 11.15 shows the transfer order printout for the storage unit **1000001581**. The transfer order and the transfer order item number are printed as bar codes for scanning by an RF device.

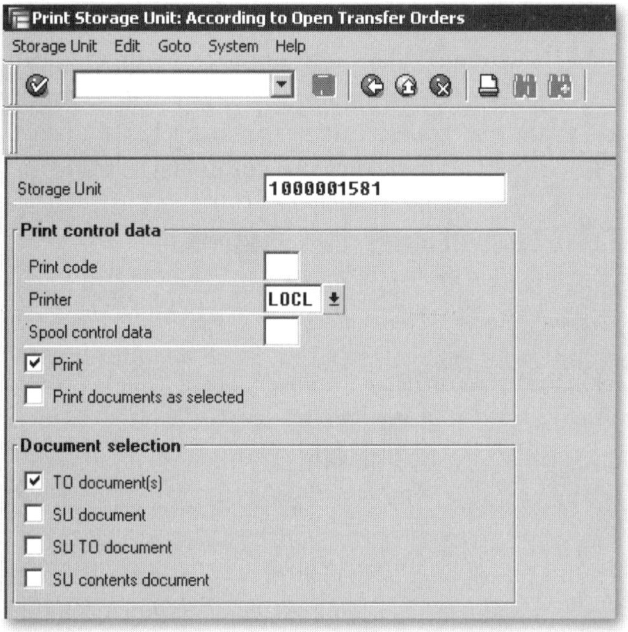

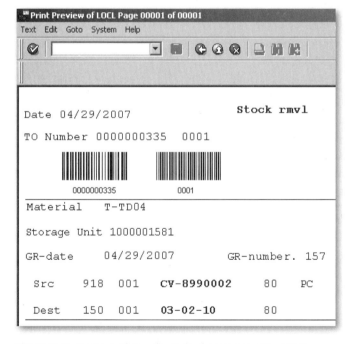

Figure 11.14 Print Transfer Order for Storage Unit Entered: Transaction LT32

Figure 11.15 Printout of Transfer Order from Transaction LT32

11.4.2 Storage Unit Contents Document

The storage unit contents document displays a list of the contents and quantities of all the materials in a storage unit. The storage unit number is usually printed in both numerical and bar code formats. You can select this document by choosing the **SU Contents Document** indicator in Figure 11.14.

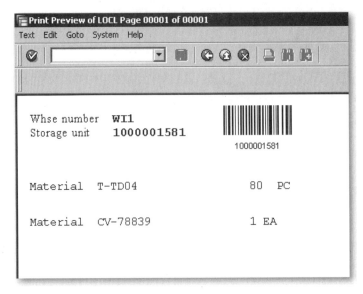

Figure 11.16 Storage Unit Contents Document

The print-preview screen shown in Figure 11.16 displays the contents of the storage unit. Two materials combine to make up the storage unit. In this example of the storage unit contents document, the storage unit number has been bar-coded for easy scanning on the warehouse floor. This can be printed and kept with the storage unit as it is moved in the warehouse. This gives warehouse staff an easy way of identifying what is in the storage unit without examining the actual material.

11.4.3 Storage Unit Document

The storage unit document displays multiple prints of storage unit numbers in numerical and bar code formats. This document is often printed on paper that can be used for labels.

To print this document, select the option in Transaction LT32 where document selection includes **SU document**, as shown in Figure 11.14.

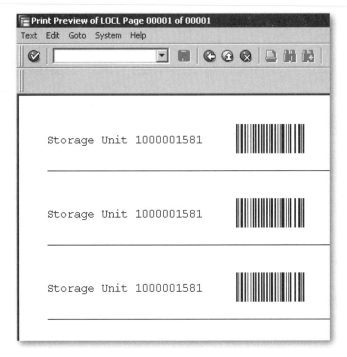

Figure 11.17 Sample Storage Unit Document

Figure 11.17 shows the storage unit number and bar code printed for administration uses.

11.4.4 Storage Unit — Transfer Order Document

The storage unit — transfer order document describes the movement of the storage unit. It resembles the printout of the transfer order, but can be modified by ABAP code if your organization needs more details added or additional bar codes printed because many RF devices are used on the warehouse floor.

To print this document, select the option in Transaction LT32 where document selection includes **SU TO Document**, as was shown in Figure 11.14. Figure 11.18 shows the details of the storage unit and the movement of the storage unit in the warehouse.

Now that we have discussed the storage unit documents, the next topic is the role of storage unit management in stock putaway.

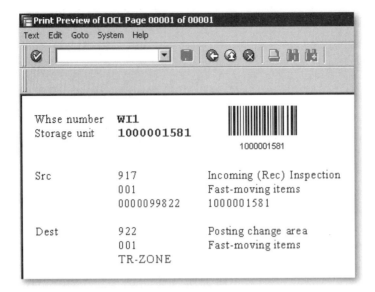

Figure 11.18 Storage Unit — Transfer Order document

11.5   Putaway with Storage Unit Management

Storage units are often created when material arrives at the receiving dock and needs to be placed into storage using a container. Storage units can be created with one material or with many different materials combined. It is also possible to move material from the receiving dock into a storage unit that already exists in the warehouse.

11.5.1   Creating a Storage Unit

In this chapter, we have already seen how a storage unit can be created using a transfer order, as shown in Figures 11.5, 11.6, and 11.7. We'll describe three methods of material putaway in the warehouse:

▸ Storage unit — single material   LT∅1
▸ Storage unit — multiple materials LT∅7 — PLACE 'SU' INTO STOCK : BEGINNING PROCESS
▸ Storage unit — add to existing stock LT∅8

These are described more fully in the subsections that follow. Let us first examine a situation where the storage unit is created for one material that will not be stored with other material.

11.5.2   Storage Unit — Single Material

The storage unit for a single material can be created using Transaction LT01, which can be found using the navigation path: **SAP • Logistics • Logistics Execution • Internal Whse Processes • Stock Transfer • Create Transfer Order • No Source Object.**

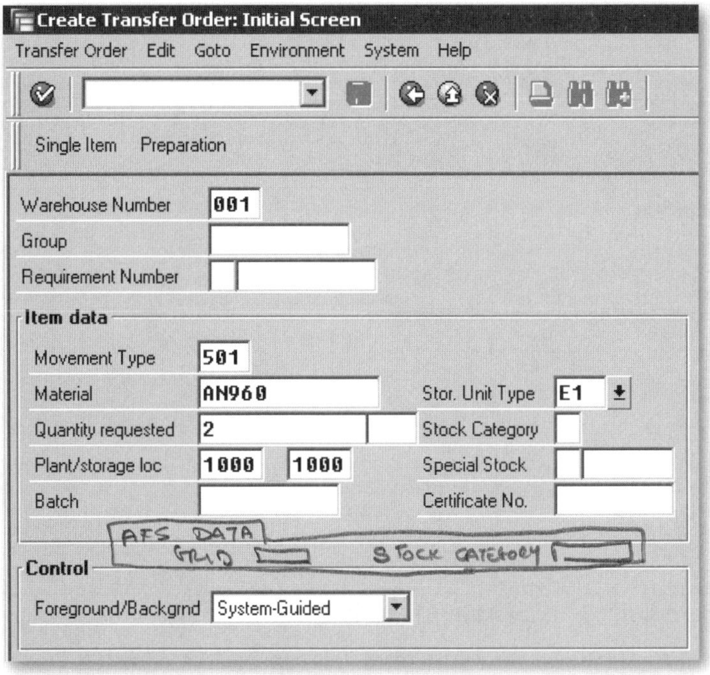

Figure 11.19 Initial Screen to Create Storage Unit with One Material

Figure 11.19 shows the initial screen in Transaction LT01 where the transfer order will be created with no reference. The movement type used in this Transaction is 501: goods receipt without a purchase order. The material is entered along with the warehouse number, quantity of material, plant, storage location, and storage unit type. The **Preparation** button is used to process the transfer order.

Figure 11.20 shows the material and the source storage bin where the material is located now. You can add the destination storage bin can be added, and then create the transfer order in the background by selecting the **F6** function key.

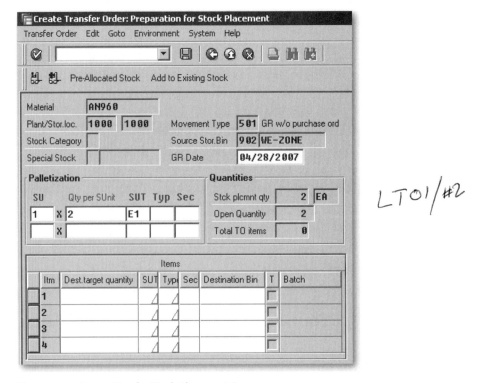

Figure 11.20 Preparation for Stock Placement Screen

11.5.3 Storage Unit — Multiple Materials

The storage unit that contains multiple materials can be created using Transaction LT07, which can be found using the navigation path: **SAP • Logistics • Logistics Execution • Internal Whse Processes • Stock Transfer • Create Transfer Order • Create Storage Unit**.

Figure 11.21 shows the initial screen for Transaction LT07. Enter the warehouse number, movement type, plant, and storage location. Use the **Preparation** button to process the transfer order.

Figure 11.22 allows the entry of the materials that will be associated with the one storage unit. A number of materials and their quantity can be added to the storage unit. Once all the materials have been added, select the **Create Trans. Order** button to create the storage unit and the transfer order.

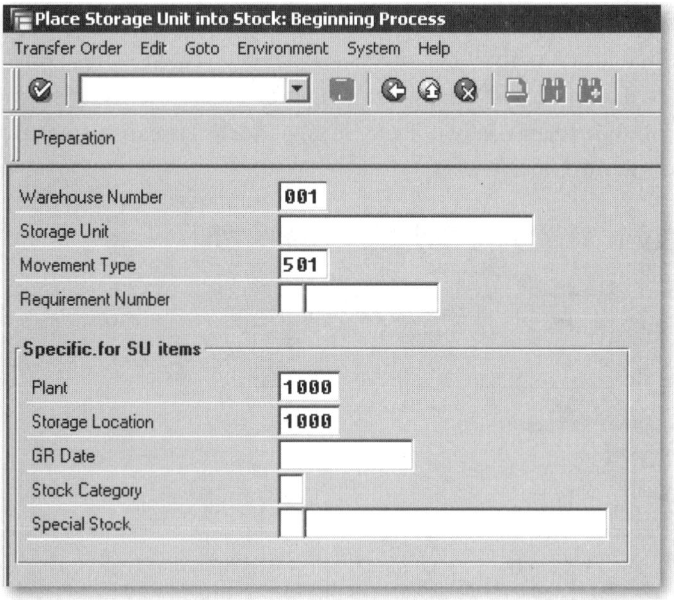

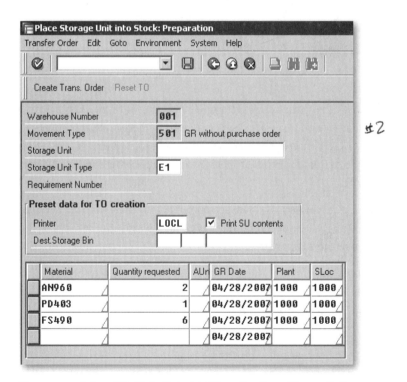

Figure 11.21 Initial Screen for Creating Storage Unit with Multiple Materials

Figure 11.22 Entry of Multiple Materials When Creating a Storage Unit

11.5.4 Storage Unit — Add to Existing Stock

The storage unit that contains multiple materials can be created using Transaction LT08, which can be found using the navigation path: **SAP · Logistics · Logistics Execution · Internal Whse Processes · Stock Transfer · Create Transfer Order · Expand Storage Unit**.

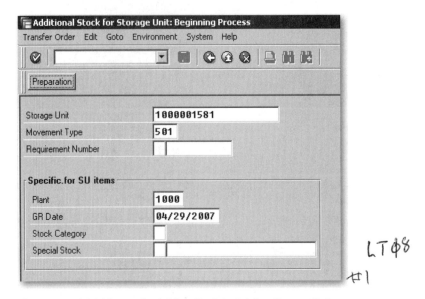

Figure 11.23 Initial Screen for Adding Stock to Existing Storage Unit

Figure 11.23 shows the initial screen for adding material to an existing storage unit that already contains stock. This is needed when material arrives in the receiving area later than it should have and the storage unit it was to be in was already created using other materials that were scheduled to be part of that storage unit.

Completing the initial screen of Transaction LT08 requires that the storage unit be entered along with the movement type and plant number. Once the data is entered, use the **Preparation** button to process the transfer order.

Figure 11.24 shows the entry of the material and the quantity to be added to the storage unit **1000001581**. After the materials have been added to this screen, select the **Create Trans. Order** button to add the materials to the storage unit via creation of the transfer order.

Now that we know how storage unit management is used with stock putaway, we'll examine how storage unit management integrates with stock picking.

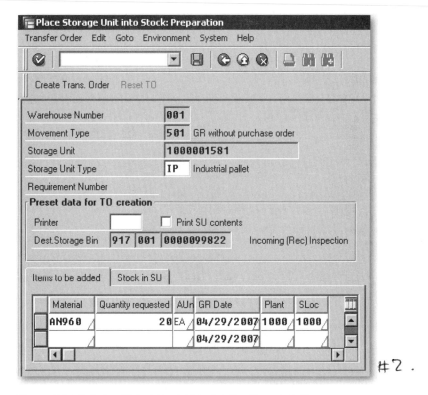

Figure 11.24 Entering Material to Add to Existing Storage Unit

11.6 Picking with Storage Unit Management

Material removed from the warehouse can be picked from storage units. The material can be removed in such a way that the whole storage unit is consumed by the pick or so that a partial pick is made from the storage type. For example, if a customer order requires a quantity of 40 and the storage unit is a full pallet with a quantity of 160, the pick from this storage unit will be a partial pick.

11.6.1 Complete Stock Pick

The entire storage unit can be picked for a goods issue even if the requirement is for less than the quantity in the storage unit. To do this, you must set the configuration at the storage type level. This can be found using the navigation path: **IMG · Logistics Execution · Warehouse Management · Master Data · Define Storage Type.**

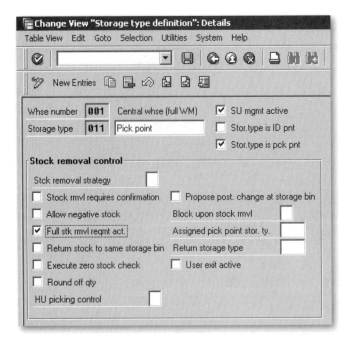

Figure 11.25 Configuration for Storage Type to Allow Full Stock Removal

Figure 11.25 shows the configuration for a storage type that will allow the whole of a storage unit to be picked even when the requirement is only for a partial amount. The **Full stk rmvl reqmt act** indicator must be set to force the whole storage unit to be removed.

11.6.2 Partial Stock Pick

If the indicator is not set in the storage type configuration to force a full stock removal, as it is in Figure 11.25, it is possible to perform a partial pick from a storage unit. This would allow the partial pick for a customer order of 40 units of material from a storage unit with a full 160 units on the pallet.

11.6.3 Complete Stock Pick with Return to Same Bin

A partial pick can be performed when the full stock removal indicator is set, but this requires that the **Return Stock to Same Storage Bin** indicator is set in the configuration for the storage type. This configuration step can be found using the navigation path: **IMG • Logistics Execution • Warehouse Management • Master Data • Define Storage Type.**

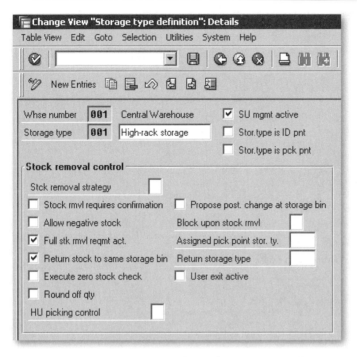

Figure 11.26 Configuration to Set Indicator for Returning Stock to Same Storage Bin

Figure 11.26 shows the storage type configuration for storage type **001** where both the indicator for full stock removal requirement and the indicator for returning stock to the same storage bin are set. This allows the full storage unit to be removed from stock for a pick, but if the goods issue does not require the full amount, the remaining stock will be returned to the same storage bin.

11.6.4 Partial Stock Removal Using a Pick Point

A partial pick can be performed on a storage unit with the use of a pick point. A pick point is a location in the warehouse where materials are removed for a partial stock pick from a storage unit. The pick point is defined in storage type configuration, which can be found using the navigation path: **IMG • Logistics Execution • Warehouse Management • Master Data • Define Storage Type.**

Figure 12.27 shows the field **Stor. type is pck pnt** is set for storage type **011**. This allows partial removal of storage units using the functionality of the pick point.

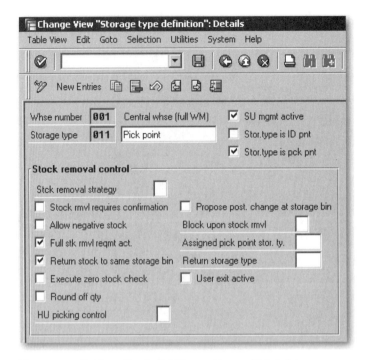

Figure 11.27 Configuration to Set Storage Type as Pick Point

By removing storage units from a pick point, the storage unit information is not lost, as it would be if the material was removed to an interim goods issue and then a partial amount was returned to stock.

When a transfer order confirms a quantity of material to be moved from the pick point to the goods-issue area for the outbound transfer order, the system posts the remaining material quantity from the storage unit to the pick point. The remaining material from the storage unit can be moved back to the original storage bin or to a new storage bin, depending on how the warehouse management uses storage unit functionality.

This concludes the examination of picking with storage unit management. Now I'll summarize the contents of this chapter on storage unit management.

11.7 Summary

Storage unit management functionality was designed for the warehouse and is a useful tool for materials that need to be moved around the warehouse in a container. It is simpler than handling unit management, a method used in SAP MM, because it does not require packing or unpacking. Once a storage unit is created in a transfer order, assignment of materials is all that is required. Storage units can contain one material or several different materials.

Many warehouses use containers, pallets, and transportation materials to move material from one storage type to another. In many cases, warehouses are not using storage unit management frequently because they have been told that is too complicated or cumbersome for efficient warehouse operations. This is not the case, and it is the responsibility of the consultant or employee to discuss and propose this and other SAP WM functionality that may improve warehouse efficiency.

In Chapter 12, I will discuss the functionality available to the warehouse manager to manage hazardous materials in the warehouse.

Hazardous materials are used in many production processes and as such have to be stored in the warehouse. Many regulations govern the storage and transportation of these materials. The hazardous materials functionality in SAP WM provides a structure for correctly managing this process.

12 Hazardous Materials Management

Hazardous materials are often found in a warehouse. These materials are either raw materials or finished goods, depending on the nature of the company's products. A hazardous material is one that can produce harmful immediate physical effects such as a fire, sudden release of pressure, and explosion, acute health problems such as burns and convulsions, and chronic illness such as organ damage and cancer.

Having hazardous materials in a warehouse is a great responsibility for the warehouse owners. They operate, in the U.S., within limits set by federal, state, and local agencies that regulate hazardous materials in order to protect human health and the environment.

These agencies have regulations that pertain to the handling, storage, or distribution of hazardous material. In the U.S., these can include the federal Clean Air Act, Clean Water Act, Comprehensive Environmental Response, Compensation, and Liability Act (CERCLA, also known as Superfund), Resource Conservation and Recovery Act (RCRA), Safe Drinking Water Act (SDWA), Hazardous Materials Transportation Act (HMTA), Toxic Substances Control Act (TSCA), and many others.

Apart from the federal laws in the U.S., states have their own strict regulations that need to be observed. Some of the state laws include: California Safe Drinking Water & Toxic Enforcement Act, Connecticut Manufacturing Employer Hazardous Materials Notification Act, and the Louisiana Hazardous Materials Information, Development, Preparedness and Response Act..

In other countries, organizations exist to work in the same manner as the federal Environmental Protection Agency (EPA) in the U.S. These include, the Canadian Environmental Assessment Agency (CEAA), the Department of the Environment and Water Resources in Australia, and the Department for Environment, Food, and Rural Affairs (DEFRA) in the UK.

12.1 Introduction to Hazardous Materials

In order to safely and properly handle and store hazardous materials, it is important to know the hazards of those materials. Many companies, laboratories and educational establishments have hazard communication programs that helps their personnel working with hazardous materials to be aware of the materials stored in the facility.

12.1.1 Classification of Hazardous Materials

Any number of hazardous materials may be stored in a warehouse. They are generally be assigned to one or more of the following classifications:

▶ **Flammable Liquid**
This includes any liquid having a flash point below 100 degrees Fahrenheit, such as gasoline or paint lacquers.

▶ **Combustible Liquid**
This includes any liquid with a flash point between 100 and 200 degrees Fahrenheit that produces enough vapor to ignite if exposed to an ignition source. Examples are diesel fuel or home heating oil.

▶ **Flammable Solid**
This could be any substance that can cause a fire through friction, absorption of moisture, or spontaneous chemical changes and that, when ignited, will burn so vigorously that it creates a hazard. Flour and white phosphorous, for example, are both flammable materials.

▶ **Oxidizer**
This is a substance that readily yields oxygen to stimulate the combustion of organic matter. Common household bleach is an example of an oxidizer.

▶ **Corrosive**
This is any liquid that corrodes steel (SAE 1020) at a rate greater than 0.250 inches at a test temperature of 130 degrees Fahrenheit or has a pH of less than 2 or greater than 12.5. Common acids, including hydrochloric acid, sulfuric acid, and nitric acid, are all corrosive materials.

▶ **Organic Peroxide**

This is an organic compound containing the chemical bond of oxygen joined to oxygen. Organic peroxides are used in many different industries. For example benzoyl peroxide is organic peroxide and is used in acne medication.

▶ **Poison**

This is a substance so toxic that it presents a risk to life or health. Examples are potassium cyanide and mercuric chloride.

▶ **Compressed Gas**

This is a substance in gas or liquid form contained in a vessel under pressure. This includes cylinders, lecture bottles, and aerosol cans. These substances may be flammable, non-flammable, or poisonous. Examples include propane and hydrogen.

▶ **Cryogenics**

This includes substances that are extremely cold, such as liquid nitrogen, liquid helium, and dry ice. These substances may also become asphyxiation hazards if spilled in non-ventilated areas.

▶ **Radioactive**

This includes any material having a specific activity greater than 0.002 micro curies per gram (uCi/g), such as uranium and plutonium.

▶ **Biomedical**

This includes tissues, organs, and blood from humans and primates.

12.1.2 Master Data Configuration for Hazardous Materials

If the warehouse contains hazardous material then certain master-data configuration steps must be made to define the sections, warnings, and hazardous-material management strategy.

Fire-Containment Sections

Fire-containment sections must be configured if there are areas in the warehouse with different fire-containment properties. For example, some areas in the warehouse that may contain hazardous material may have two-hour minimum fire resistance, while other areas may have four-hour minimum resistance. Once configured, these sections can be assigned to storage bins.

This configuration is found using the navigation path: **IMG · Logistics Execution · Warehouse Management · Hazardous Materials · Master Data · Define Fire-Containment Sections**.

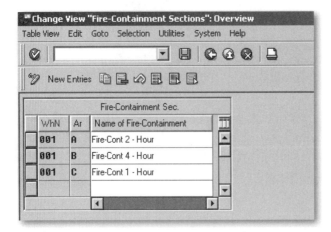

Figure 12.1 Configuration for Fire-Containment Sections for Each Warehouse

Figure 12.1 shows the configuration for the fire-containment sections that can be set up for each warehouse. In this example, the sections are identified by their fire resistance. Some warehouses may have a series of fire-containment storage cabinets or areas that can be identified as configurable sections.

Hazardous Material Warnings

You can configure warnings that can be used with hazardous materials. The configuration allows for a large number of material warnings to be created to be assigned when dealing with hazardous materials.

This configuration is found using the navigation path: **IMG · Logistics Execution · Warehouse Management · Hazardous Materials · Master Data · Define Hazardous Material Warning**.

These material hazardous warnings, as shown in Figure 12.2, can be configured for the whole system. The warnings may be different for different warehouses that may be situated in different countries. The environmental agency for the country where each warehouse is situated may be able to advise you on hazardous material warnings.

Figure 12.2 Configuration for Hazardous Material Warnings

Hazardous Material Storage Warnings

Certain warnings are required when hazardous materials are being transported or when they are placed for storage. Configuring this in the system allows for a large number of storage warnings to be assigned when dealing with hazardous materials.

This configuration is found using the navigation path: **IMG • Logistics Execution • Warehouse Management • Hazardous Materials • Master Data • Define Hazardous Material Storage Warning**.

Figure 12.3 shows the configured hazardous material storage warnings. These are not specific to a particular warehouse, so each warehouse management team would have to ensure that the storage warnings can be adopted for their warehouse, or further configuration would be required.

Aggregate States

The aggregate state is configured using the navigation path: **IMG • Logistics Execution • Warehouse Management • Hazardous Materials • Master Data • Define Aggregate States**.

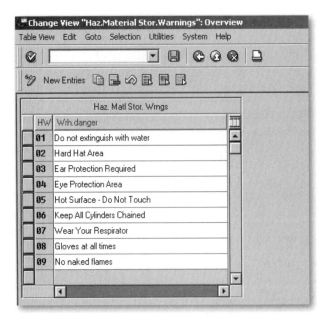

Figure 12.3 Configuration for Hazardous Material Storage Warnings

The aggregate state is given a material in its normal conditions; i.e., a temperature of 20°C and a pressure of 1 atmosphere. The aggregate state of the material is solid, liquid, or gas. Radioactive elements can be denoted as a different aggregate state, but all radioactive materials are solid. As there can be only a maximum of four aggregate states, as shown in Figure 12.4, no further configuration is required.

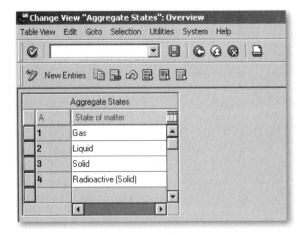

Figure 12.4 Configuration of Aggregate States for Hazardous Materials

Region Codes

Because the warehouses for a company can be in different countries, it is possible to configure different regions for hazardous material management. The region codes can be configured using the navigation path: **IMG** • **Logistics Execution** • **Warehouse Management** • **Hazardous Materials** • **Master Data** • **Define Region Codes**.

Figure 12.5 Configuration of Region Codes for Hazardous Materials Management

Figure 12.5 shows a number of region codes that have been configured for hazardous materials. These region codes are not the same as SAP country codes; the region codes can incorporate different countries, such as European Community (EC) countries or former Soviet republics. A region code could be configured that incorporates more than one country; i.e., a region code may include the countries of Belgium, Netherlands, and Luxemburg.

Storage Classes

Storage classes can be configured to classify the hazardous materials based on their features. This storage class can be used by stock putaway strategies. The definition of the storage classes used in SAP is based on the guidelines issued by the U.S. Department of Transportation, which administers the HMTA.

385

The storage classes can be configured using the navigation path: **IMG · Logistics Execution · Warehouse Management · Hazardous Materials · Master Data · Define Storage Classes**.

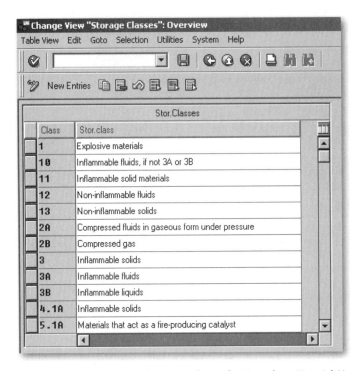

Figure 12.6 Configuration of Storage Classes for Hazardous Material Management

Figure 12.6 shows the defined storage classes as defined by the U.S. Department of Transportation. If there are more appropriate storage classes for the company's warehouse, they can be configured here.

12.1.3 Configuration for Hazardous Material Management

This next phase of configuration is for activation of the hazardous material management. This configuration can be found using Transaction OMM2 or via the navigation path: **IMG · Logistics Execution · Warehouse Management · Hazardous Materials · Strategies · Activate Hazardous Material Management**.

Figure 12.7 shows the configuration required for hazardous material management. The first configuration step is to activate the hazardous material check.

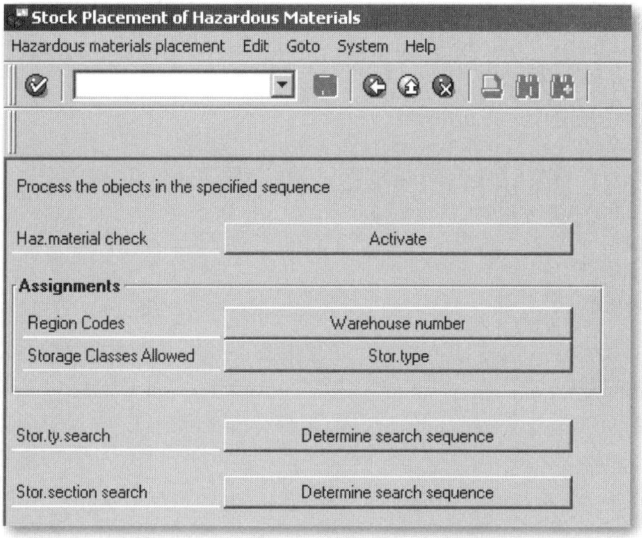

Figure 12.7 Configuration for Hazardous Material Management

Activation of Hazardous Material Check

This configuration step activates the section check, the hazardous material management, and the water-pollution class for a designated storage type in a warehouse.

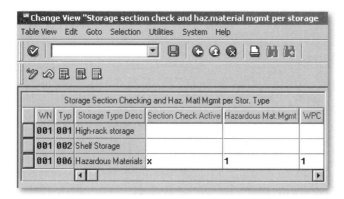

Figure 12.8 Activate Storage Section Checking and Hazardous Material Management

In Figure 12.8, the configuration has been set for the storage type **006** in warehouse **001**. Storage type **006** has the section check activated. The **X** in the field shows that the storage section is determined and a check was made. If a **Y** had been entered a storage section determination is made, but no check.

The hazardous material management field has been configured with the value **1**. This means that the hazardous material check is made at the storage-type level only. The entry of a **2** in this field would have required a check at storage type and the storage section level.

The water pollution class (WPC) classifies a material in terms of its capability of polluting water. The values are defined as:

▶ **0**
Not a water pollutant

▶ **1**
Minimal water pollutant

▶ **2**
Water pollutant

▶ **3**
Extreme water pollutant

Entering a **1** in the WPC field will allow materials with WPCs of 0 and 1 to be to be stored in the storage type.

Assignment of Region Code

Once the region codes have been configured, as was shown in Figure 12.5, these can be assigned to the active warehouses.

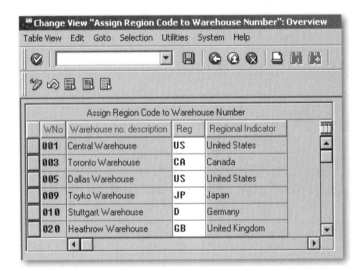

Figure 12.9 Assignment of Region Code to Warehouse

Figure 12.9 shows the assignment of the configured region codes to the warehouses that are active.

Storage Classes per Storage Type

In this configuration step, you can assign all the storage classes, defined as seen in Figure 12.6, to a certain storage type in the warehouse. For example, some storage types will be suitable for containing compressed gas, but not for organic peroxides. This will depend on the physical attributes of the storage type and whether those attributes are suitable to store materials of specific storage classes.

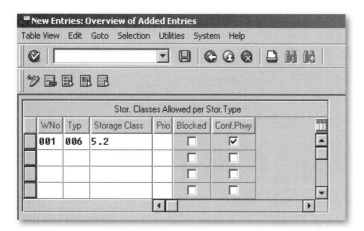

Figure 12.10 Assignment of Storage Classes to Storage Types

Figure 12.10 shows the assignment of **Storage Class 5.2**, organic peroxides, to storage type **006** in warehouse **001**. This means that storage type **006** will allow the storage of organic peroxides. The other fields in this configuration relate to the priority of the storage class in the storage type.

> **Example**
>
> A storage type may allow several storage classes to be stored in it, but the priority will determine which storage class is given priority over the others.

The **Blocked** indicator can be used for temporarily blocking the storage type for a particular storage class. This may occur if certain materials have been stored in the storage type, rendering it unavailable for hazardous materials of other storage classes.

Checking the **Conf.Ptwy** indicator requires that any stock placement for this storage class is performed in the foreground, overriding any other requirement for that storage type.

Storage Type Search

This allows the additions to the storage type search to allow for any storage class configuration that has been made.

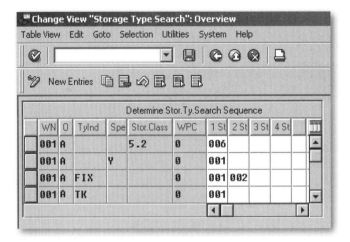

Figure 12.11 Additions to Storage Type Search Configuration

Figure 12.11 shows that a new storage type search has been added to include reference to a hazardous material storage class. The storage type search now includes a search where the storage class is **5.2**. This search will try to find an empty storage bin in storage type **006** if the material has a storage class of **5.2**.

Storage Section Search

If the warehouse is using storage section search as well as storage type search, then you can configure the storage section search to include the storage class.

Figure 12.12 shows the configuration for warehouse **001** and storage type **006**. The new configuration line shows that if the material has a storage class of **5.2** the system will search for an empty bin in storage section **005** first and then storage section **001**.

Now that we have examined the basics of hazardous materials, we'll focus on the hazardous material record.

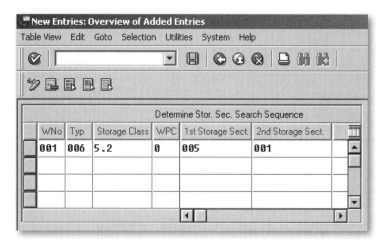

Figure 12.12 Storage Section Search Including the Storage Class

12.2 Hazardous Material Record

The warehouse needs to create hazardous material records for materials that require special handling or storage due to their hazardous nature. The hazardous material record contains many fields that can describe the hazardous nature of a material, such as the water-pollution class, if the material is a water pollutant. In addition it contains the various hazardous material warnings that may have to be displayed if the material is transported and a breakdown of any other hazardous material that is a component of the transported material.

12.2.1 Create a Hazardous Material Record

A hazardous material record can be created using Transaction VM01, or can be found using the navigation path: **SAP • Logistics • Logistics Execution • Master Data • Material • Hazardous Material • Create**.

Figure 12.13 shows the entry of the data for the hazardous material record. The hazardous material number is not assigned internally by SAP, so an external number has to be decided upon.

The general data lets you include more detailed information for the material, including the storage class, water pollution class, aggregate state, and flash point. Also, the material can be described in terms of its components, which themselves can be hazardous. The percentages can be given for each of the components.

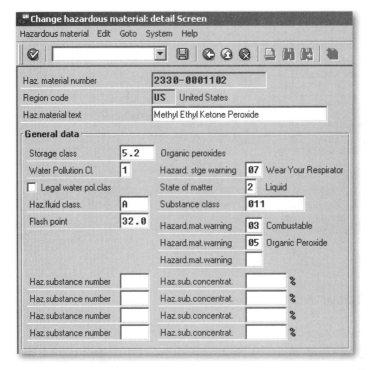

Figure 12.13 Entry of Hazardous Material Record

Once the hazardous material has been saved, it can be assigned to a material master record.

12.2.2 Assigning the Hazardous Material to a Material Master Record.

The hazardous material record can be assigned to an existing material master record. Because the hazardous material information is held within the SAP WM module, the hazardous material number is assigned to the material master record in the warehouse management screen of the material master.

Figure 12.14 shows the warehouse management screen for material **700000319**. The material is a 55-g gallon drum of Methyl Ethyl Ketone Peroxide which has a hazardous material number **2330–0001102**, as shown in Figure 12.13. The hazardous material number is assigned to the material master record. Therefore, any warehouse movements of the material will show that it is a hazardous material and special circumstances may apply.

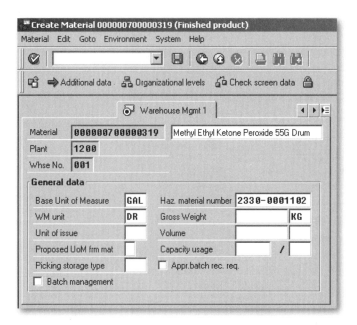

Figure 12.14 Hazardous Material Assigned to a Material Master Record

12.3 Hazardous Material Functionality

To ensuring that hazardous material is tracked, a number of reports can be used by the warehouse. In case of emergency, there are reports for the fire service or Hazmat teams, detailing where the hazardous materials are.

12.3.1 List of Hazardous Materials

The list of hazardous materials can be selected by region and shows all of the hazardous materials with records on the system. This does not imply that all the materials are stored in any particular warehouse, but does show all hazardous materials that potentially could be in stock within the region.

The transaction for this is LX24 and is found using the navigation path: **SAP • Logistics • Logistics Execution • Information System • Warehouse • Stock • Hazardous Material • List**.

Figure 12.15 shows a list of all the hazardous materials that have been entered for the region of the U.S. The list should be reviewed periodically as local laws and regulations can and do change. The review should be carried out by the warehouse management and the environmental health and safety manager for the plant.

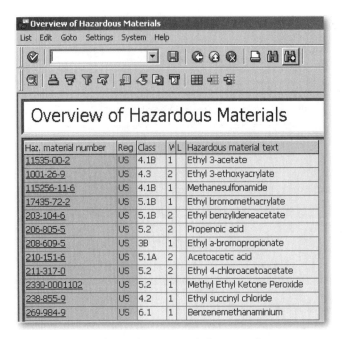

Figure 12.15 List of Hazardous Materials for a Specific Region

12.3.2 Fire Department Inventory List

Periodically, the warehouse facility may be inspected by regulatory authorities or by the local fire department. At any of these inspections, the reports identifying the hazardous material stored within the warehouse may be required. The fire department inventory list is a report on the quantity of material in each fire containment area, by storage class. The fire department can then review the potential hazards and offer advice about storage changes.

The fire department inventory list can be produced using Transaction LX06 or via the navigation path: **SAP • Logistics • Logistics Execution • Information System • Warehouse • Stock • Hazardous Material • Fire Department Inventory List**.

The fire department inventory list, shown in Figure 12.16, identifies each fire containment area and the hazardous storage classes currently stored inside. The weight and quantity of the material shows the fire department the level of potential hazard within each containment area. If the fire department decides that there is too much stock of a certain hazardous storage class in a containment area, the warehouse would have to move some quants to other suitable storage bins.

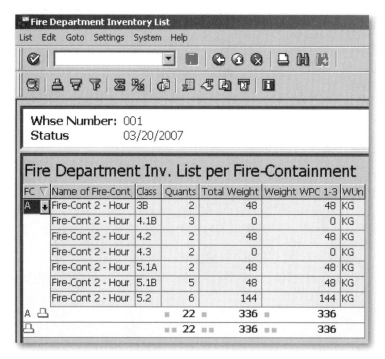

Figure 12.16 Display of Fire Department Inventory List

12.3.3 Check Goods Storage

The check-goods storage report is used to ensure that all hazardous material has been stored correctly. The report reviews all of the quants of material to see where they are stored and checks against the configuration entered for hazardous materials. It checks that:

▶ Hazardous materials are not stored in storage types managed specifically for non-hazardous materials

▶ A material is stored in the correct storage type based on the water-pollution class

▶ A material is stored in the correct storage type based on storage class

If any of these checks produce an error, the report will produce an error log showing how many errors have occurred for each storage type. an example is shown in Figure 12.17.

The check-goods storage list can be produced using Transaction LX07 or via the navigation path: **SAP • Logistics • Logistics Execution • Information System • Warehouse • Stock • Hazardous Material • Check Goods Storage**.

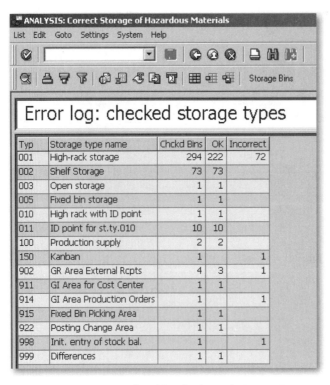

Figure 12.17 Error Log Produced by Check Goods Storage Report

Figure 12.17 shows that for storage type **001** there are **72** instances where hazardous material is incorrectly stored. More detailed information is required for find out why each quant has been stored incorrectly. The information at the storage-bin level for each storage type can be displayed by highlighting the storage type and using the **Shift + F4** function key or selecting the **Storage Bins** button on the application toolbar.

Figure 12.18 shows the error log at the storage-bin level. The incorrect storage column indicates the error code. These codes are explained as follows:

▶ **0**

Hazardous material in a storage type not managed for hazardous materials

▶ **1**

Water pollution class not maintained for storage type

▶ **2**

Storage class not maintained for storage type

▶ **3**

Hazardous material not maintained for storage section

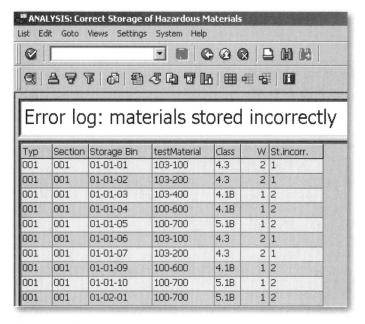

Figure 12.18 Error Log at Storage Bin Level

The report should be used to ensure that the hazardous materials are correctly stored in the warehouse. If materials are not stored correctly, they should be moved to a correct location to ensure warehouse safety.

12.3.4 Hazardous Substance List

The hazardous substance list produces a report of all the hazardous material that is stored in a particular warehouse or storage type or fire-containment area.

The hazardous substance list can be produced using Transaction LX08 or via the navigation path: **SAP • Logistics • Logistics Execution • Information System • Warehouse • Stock • Hazardous Material • Hazardous Substance List**.

Figure 12.19 shows the hazardous material stored in the warehouse. The report shows the fire-containment area where the material is stored, as well as the hazardous storage class and water-pollution class.

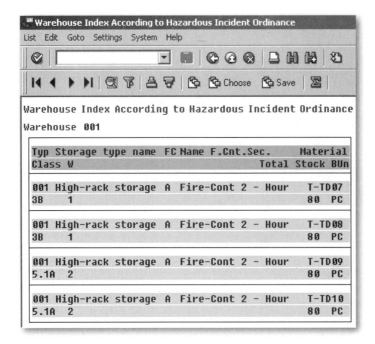

Figure 12.19 Hazardous Substance List: Transaction LX08

12.4 Summary

Hazardous materials are used to produce finished goods in thousands of companies every day. Laws and regulations at different levels of government in every country govern the storage of hazardous materials. In the United States, federal and state laws determine what materials are treated as hazardous and how they should be stored.

The SAP WM configuration for hazardous materials allows such material to be stored in the correct storage bin in the correct storage type. Any error in the storage of hazardous material is not only potentially dangerous, but can result in penalties levied against the warehouse owner.

In Chapter 13, I will examine the functionality of mobile data entry, which includes radio frequency (RF) devices, bar coding, and the functionality that supports mobile date entry with SAP WM.

Mobile data entry allows entry of data remotely by the use of bar codes and radio frequency (RF) technology. SAP has incorporated the use of mobile data entry into warehouse management transactions, thus reducing the level of data entry error and shortening the time needed to complete transfer orders.

13 Mobile Data Entry

Mobile data entry in the warehouse today involves the use of wireless radio frequency (RF) terminals or devices carried by the warehouse staff to record data. The data that the staff record is usually in bar code form, either as bar codes printed on the paperwork for transfer orders or as bar codes that identify products, storage bins, or other objects.

The display on a RF device can use a graphical user interface (GUI). The information is transmitted from SAP, and individual transactions can be executed using a touch screen or keys. A devices has either a GUI or is character-based with a special, non-graphical user interface.

Standard SAP supports RF devices, and a number of functions within the warehouse can be executed via RF.

> **Note**
>
> The standard SAP system has incorporated RF technology since the release of SAP 4.6B.

The following list shows the timeline of RF technology in SAP:

- **Release 4.6B**
  Introduction of RF transactions and SAP Console

- **Release 4.6C**
  Standard transactions delivered for handling unit management

- **Release 4.7 Enterprise**
  RF for Task and Resource Management, Yard Management, and Value-Added Services

- **Release ECC 5.0**
  The first RFID scenarios were included

This chapter will examine the use of mobile data entry in the current SAP system, ECC 6.0, and how technology such as bar codes and RF are used in warehouse functionality.

The next section of this chapter discusses RF devices and the use of the SAPConsole.

13.1 Introduction to RF Devices

SAP transactions can be executed on RF devices that are handheld or forklift-mounted. No middleware software is required to connect the devices to SAP.

SAP's functionality enables real-time handling of material flow through RF scanning devices. Having the screens and the business logic within the SAP makes it easy to distribute new processes to each device. There are two standard RF devices that can be used with SAP, which are:

- GUI devices
- Character-based devices

The main difference is that the character-based device uses terminal emulation and the GUI devices use a Microsoft Windows-based operating system. Let's take a more detailed look at each of these now.

13.1.1 Graphical User Interface Devices

The graphical user interface (GUI) RF device can use a small keypad, touch screen, or some other procedure, but the data is always displayed to the user in a graphical manner, as you would expect to see with a device such as PDA or a cellular phone. The device is connected to the SAP system, as any other standalone computer would be.

13.1.2 Character-Based Devices

The character-based device is not connected directly to SAP but communicates via an interface called SAPConsole that was introduced in SAP Release 4.6B. The communication between SAPConsole and the RF device can be achieved by using a Telnet server. Two industry standards for screen sizes are supported by SAP:

- RF devices for forklifts: 8 lines by 40 characters
- Portable RF devices: 16 lines by 20 characters

13.1.3 SAPConsole

SAPConsole is a tool that enables RF devices to be run within SAP Applications. Introduced in 1999, SAP Console was shipped with SAP release 4.6B and was used for barcode and handheld RF applications in the Logistics Execution System (LES), which included warehouse management.

SAPConsole can be described as a framework for automatic data collection (AIDC) in a warehouse environment. SAPConsole translates GUI screens to character-based screens that are used on a variety of data collection devices.

SAPConsole does not contain business logic, databases, or external functionality. Its sole function is to translate SAP GUI screens in the SAP environment to the character-based equivalent. The SAPConsole consists of four components, which are:

▶ RF Terminal, which is the Telnet client

▶ RF Access Point, which allows for Wireless Ethernet

▶ Telnet Server/SAPConsole Administrator, which allows each RF terminal to connect to the Windows machine in character-based mode and supports VT220 terminal emulation

▶ SAP R/3 System that receives the data from the mobile terminals

A SAPConsole session allows connection to SAP in real time, exactly like an SAP GUI session. All the functionality and business logic resides within the SAP Application. The SAPConsole connects the user to that business logic.

13.1.4 Functionality Available Using SAPConsole

In ECC 6.0, many transactions are defined as mobile data entry and available for use with RF devices. These include:

▶ Goods receipt

▶ Goods issue

▶ Material putaway

▶ Material picking

▶ Packing and unpacking

▶ Physical inventory

▶ Loading and unloading

▶ Serial number capture

▶ Stock overview

This section has examined the use of RF devices and warehouse functions are available with the SAPConsole. The next section will discuss bar code functionality.

13.2 Bar Code Functionality

The first bar code patent was issued in 1952 to Joseph Woodland and Bernard Silver. Their invention was described as a *bull's eye* symbol made up of concentric circles of varying thicknesses. The initial push for the bar code was from a grocery retailer, and as the bar code developed — first by RCA and then IBM — the grocery industry was the leading force behind its adoption. In the late 1960s, Joseph Woodland, then working for IBM, helped develop the most popular version of the bar code technology: the Universal Product Code (UPC).

On April 3, 1973, the UPC was adopted as the industry standard. From then on, any bar code on any product could be read and understood by any bar code reader. Standardization made it cost effective for manufacturers to put the bar code on their packages and for printer manufacturers to develop new technology to reproduce the bar code with the exact tolerances it required.

13.2.1 UPC Bar Code Format

The UPC bar code is split into two halves of six digits each. The first character is always zero, except for some materials that have variable weight or special materials. The next five characters are the manufacturer's code, followed by a five-digit product code and a check digit. In addition, there are hidden cues in the structure of the bar code to inform the scanner which end of the bar code is the start and which is the end. This allows the bar code to be scanned in either direction.

Manufacturers register with the Uniform Code Council (UCC) to obtain a unique manufacturers code for their company.

Manufacturers Code

All materials produced by a given company will use the same manufacturer code. Some codes are called variable-length manufacturer codes. Assigning fixed-length five-digit manufacturer codes means that each manufacturer can have up to 99,999 product codes. Most manufacturers do not have that many products, a situation which indicates that thousands of potential product codes are wasted on manufacturers with only a few products. Therefore, if a manufacturer knows that it will produce a small number of products for bar coding, the UCC may issue it a longer manufacturer code, leaving less space for the product code. This results in more efficient use of the available manufacturer and product codes.

Product Code

The product code is a unique code assigned by the manufacturer. Unlike the manufacturer code, which must be assigned by the UCC, the manufacturer is free to assign product codes to each of its materials that require bar coding. Because the UCC already will have guaranteed that the manufacturer code is unique, the manufacturer needs to ensure it does not duplicate product codes.

Check Digit

The check digit is an additional digit used to verify that a bar code has been scanned correctly. A scan can produce incorrect data because of inconsistent scanning speed, print imperfections, or environmental issues, so it is important to verify that the preceding digits in the bar code have been correctly interpreted. The check digit is calculated based on the other digits of the bar code. Normally, if the check digit matches the value that could be calculated based on the data that has been scanned, there is a high level of confidence that the bar code was scanned correctly.

13.2.2   UPC and EAN

After the UPC was adopted in 1973, the global interest in bar coding, especially in retailing, led to the adoption of the International Article Numbering Association's European Article Numbering (EAN) code in December of 1976.

The EAN code has 13 characters, but is identical to the UPC code in that the actual unique code is 10 digits in length. In UPC, the first digit is for the product and the last as a check digit. EAN has three characters not used for the unique code. The three flag digits are used for the check digit and the country that issued the bar code, not the country of origin of the product. Each country has a numbering authority that assigns manufacturer codes to companies within its jurisdiction. The manufacturer code is still five digits long, as is the product code, and the check digit is calculated in exactly the same way as for the UPC code.

For the UPC and EAN to be compatible, the U.S. was issued country flags, 00, 01, 03, 04, and 06 through 13. As the EAN, sometimes called the EAN-13, is a superset of UPC, this means that any software or hardware capable of reading an EAN-13 symbol will automatically be able to read an UPC code.

You may have read about Japanese Numbering Authority (JAN) codes. These are exactly the same as EAN codes, but are strictly for Japan and will carry the country code 49.

13.2.3 Bar Code Structure

A physical bar code is a series of vertical lines of varying width that are called bars, and spaces. The bars and spaces are called elements. Different combinations of the bars and spaces represent different characters.

When a bar-code scanner is passed over the bar code, the light source from the scanner is absorbed by the dark bars and is not reflected, but it is reflected by the light spaces. A photocell detector in the scanner receives the reflected light and converts the light into an electrical signal.

As the laser is passed over the bar code, the scanner creates a low electrical signal for the spaces, which is the reflected light, and a high electrical signal for the bars where nothing is reflected. The duration of the electrical signal determines whether the scanner has detected a wide or a narrow element. The bar code reader's decoder then interprets the signal. The decoder converts this into the characters that the bar code represents. The decoded data is then passed to the system in a traditional data format.

13.2.4 Bar Code Readers

Three types of bar code readers are available. These are fixed bar code readers, portable readers with batch uploading, and portable RF readers. Let us examine these in some detail now.

Fixed Bar Code Reader

This is the type of bar code reader that you find at a retail store where the reader is tethered to the cash register and is used to scan items that are purchased.

Portable Batch Readers

These readers are battery powered and are used away from their host to collect information and store it for a later batch upload to the host. These are used frequently in retail stores for taking inventory on store shelves and then uploading that information to the host system at the end of inventory taking. Some newer batch readers, from companies such as Symbol Technologies, Hand Held Products, and PSC, Inc., enable collection of more than 50,000 bar codes and can run for more than 12 hours on a single charge.

Portable RF Reader

This reader is the most sophisticated because it allows the operator to record data and transmit in real time. The communication is two-way and allows the operator to receive updated instructions based on the data he or she collects. United Parcel Service (UPS) uses this type of reader to record tracking data and the receiver's signature. The Delivery Information Acquisition Device (DIAD) sends delivery information to the UPS data center as soon as the delivery information is entered. Drivers scan the package bar code, collect the receiver's signature electronically, type in the last name of the receiver, and push a single key to complete the transaction and send the data without returning to the vehicle.

13.2.5 Bar Code Reader Technologies

There are three technologies that are in use for reading bar codes, which are:

▶ Photodiode

▶ Charge-coupled device (CCD)

▶ Laser

Let's examine these further now.

Photodiode

Photodiode technology can be found in pen-style bar code readers. The photodiode and a light source are contained in the pen reader. As the reader is dragged across the bar code, the photodiode measures the intensity of the light reflected back from the light source and generates a waveform. This is used to measure the widths of the bars and the spaces in the bar code.

Dark bars in the bar code absorb light and white spaces reflect light. As a result, the voltage waveform generated by the photo diode is an exact duplicate of the bars and spaces in the bar code. The scanner decodes this waveform. This type of scanner was very popular in public libraries in the 1980s and 1990s. These wand bar code readers are still widely available and plug directly into the USB sockets of computers. Companies such as Unitech, ZBA, Inc., and Wasp Barcode Technologies still manufacture these wand-style bar code readers.

Charge-Coupled Device

A change-coupled device (CCD) is an image sensor consisting of an integrated circuit containing an array of linked or coupled light-sensitive capacitors. The CCD reader uses an array of hundreds of sensors lined up in a row in the head of the reader. Each sensor acts like a single photodiode that measures the intensity of the light immediately in front of it. The voltage pattern read by the reader is identical to the pattern in a bar code.

CCD readers do not have moving parts, are considered extremely durable, and require less maintenance than laser readers. CCD scanners consume very little power and work under most lighting conditions. CCD scanners are often cheaper than laser scanners because they do not have as great a range and have to be closer to the bar code to be read. In brief, these scanners are a low-cost option compared with laser scanners, but are robust and low maintenance.

Because they do not offer as great a scanning distance as laser readers, some warehouse operations do not use CCD readers, but they can be found alongside laser scanners in most warehouse operations. The large companies involved in RF technology, such as Intermec Technologies Corp. and Hand Held Products, manufacture these scanners.

Laser

Laser scanners work the same way as pen-type readers except that they use a laser beam as the light source and typically employ either a reciprocating mirror or a rotating prism to scan the laser beam back and forth across the bar code. Just as with the pen type reader, a photodiode is used to measure the intensity of the light reflected back from the bar code.

Laser scanners can read barcodes at a farther distance from the head of the device than can a CCD scanner, enabling supermarkets to read codes on round cans and flexible packages more easily. Laser scanners are often more expensive than CCD scanners but have the advantage of reading longer and smaller density barcodes as well as working at greater scanning distances. Because of the ability to read slightly curved bar codes, the laser scanner is the choice of supermarkets and retailers. There are many manufacturers of laser bar code readers including Symbol, Metrologic Instruments, Inc., Intermec, and Hand Held Products.

13.2.6 Bar Code Support in SAP

SAP reads bar codes for identification and verification. The items that can be identified include:

- Storage bin
- Material
- Storage unit
- Handling unit
- Quantity
- Delivery
- Staging area
- Shipment
- Pick wave

It is possible to scan items for verification purposes, and these fields include:

- Storage unit
- Storage bin
- Material
- Quantity

This list of fields that can be used for bar codes will probably increase with future releases of SAP.

13.2.7 Configuration for Bar Codes

Before bar codes can be used for mobile data entry, configuration needs to be entered and reviewed to ensure that the correct format is being used.

Define Verification Profiles

The verification profile is a set of fields that can be verified by the user. A number of profiles can be created for each warehouse, and each profile can contain a number of fields to be verified.

The configuration can be found using the navigation path: **IMG · Logistics Execution · Mobile Data Entry · Verification Control · Define Profiles**.

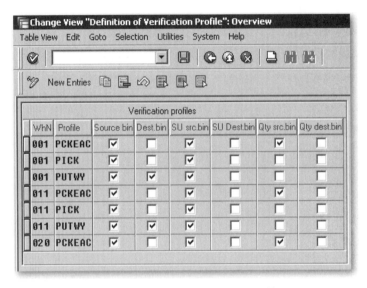

Figure 13.1 Configuration for Defining Verification Profiles

Figure 13.1 shows the profiles created for warehouses **001**, **011**, and **020**. Each profile verifies a different number of fields. The fields that can be attached to a profile include:

▶ Source bin

▶ Destination bin

▶ Storage unit identification at the source storage bin

▶ Storage unit identification at the destination storage bin

▶ Quantity of the material to be picked at the source storage bin

▶ Quantity of the material to be put away at the destination storage bin

▶ Material identification at the source storage bin

▶ Material identification at the destination storage bin

The system uses this configuration if scanning devices communicate directly with SAP. For certain warehouse movements, this configuration specifies a unique verification profile. This profile determines what data the user must scan or key in manually.

Example

If material is put away by storage unit number, the scanner operator would have to verify that they have completed putaway the storage unit in the storage bin proposed by the system.

Assign Verification Profiles

After the verification profile has been configured, it can be assigned to movement types used in the warehouse that will be subject to bar code scanning. The configuration can be found using the navigation path: **IMG • Logistics Execution • Mobile Data Entry • Verification Control • Assign Verification Profiles to Goods Movements.**

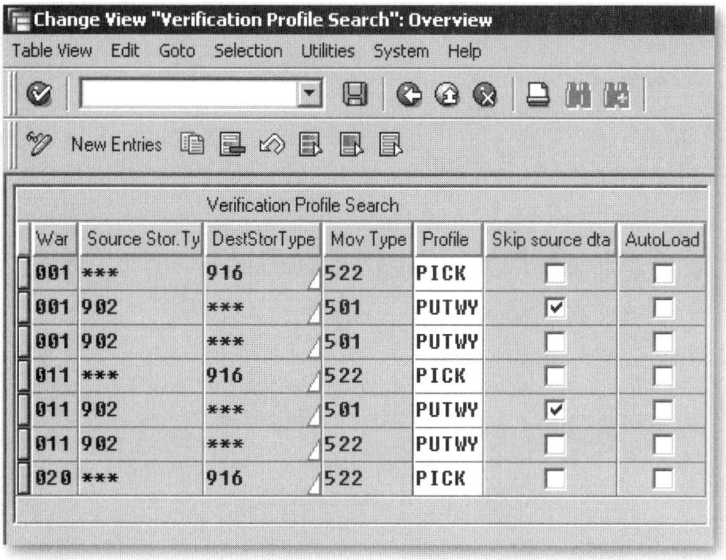

War	Source Stor.Ty	DestStorType	Mov Type	Profile	Skip source dta	AutoLoad
001	***	916	522	PICK	☐	☐
001	902	***	501	PUTWY	☑	☐
001	902	***	501	PUTWY	☐	☐
011	***	916	522	PICK	☐	☐
011	902	***	501	PUTWY	☑	☐
011	902	***	522	PUTWY	☐	☐
020	***	916	522	PICK	☐	☐

Figure 13.2 Assigning Verification Profiles to Movement Types

Figure 13.2 shows the assignment of the verification profiles. The profile is assigned to a movement type used between a source and destination storage type. Therefore, in warehouse **001**, the verification profile **PICK** is assigned to movement type **522** when the movement is between any source storage type, denoted by *** , and the destination storage type **916**.

Define Bar Codes for Warehouses

The configuration for bar codes allows certain bar code types to be used in certain warehouses. If the company is using one bar code throughout, then this is a simple configuration task. Check with the company to configure the correct bar code type used for each warehouse.

The configuration can be found using the navigation path: **IMG · Logistics Execution · Mobile Data Entry · Bar Code · Assign Bar Code Types to Warehouses**.

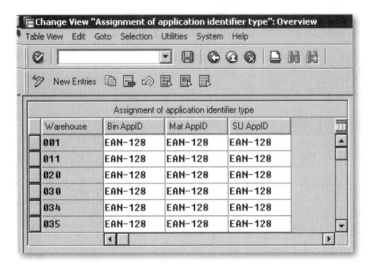

Figure 13.3 Assigning Application Identifier Type for Warehouses

Figure 13.3 shows bar code types assigned to each warehouse. The configuration needs to be in place so that the system can interpret the correct barcodes format.

Maintaining Bar Code Specifications

This configuration step is to define the parameters for the bar code type. The minimum and maximum lengths determine the length of the bar code type. The prefix identifies first part of the bar code string by an introductory character string. If the specific data field that is attached to the bar code type has a variable length, then a delimiter must close it.

The configuration can be found using the navigation path: **IMG · Logistics Execution · Mobile Data Entry · Bar Code · Maintain Bar Code Specification**.

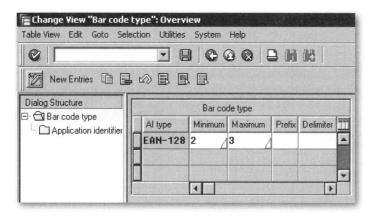

Figure 13.4 Configuration to Maintain Bar Code Type

Figure 13.4 shows that the bar code type **EAN-128** has defined minimum and maximum lengths. Different bar code types will have different configuration that would be specified in this configuration step.

This section has discussed the functionality of bar codes. Now we'll examine the processes in warehouse management that support RF.

13.3 Radio Frequency Supported Processes in SAP WM

The use of RF transactions is important in the warehouse because of the physical size of warehouses and the time needed to perform tasks. Collecting data using RF devices saves labor and time, and improves the accuracy of the data collection in the warehouse.

Each user who operates a RF device must be entered into the system with the information regarding his or her device. In addition, the user has to be assigned to a queue that shows all transfer orders that require materials movement from a certain storage type. The queues are configured in the IMG.

13.3.1 Defining the Radio Frequency Queue

To assign a range of warehouse activities to certain users, functionality called the RF Queue Management must be defined in the SAP Implementation Guide (IMG). This is a two-part configuration where the queue is defined and then activities are assigned.

The configuration can be found using the navigation path: **IMG • Logistics Execution • Mobile Data Entry • RF Queue Management**.

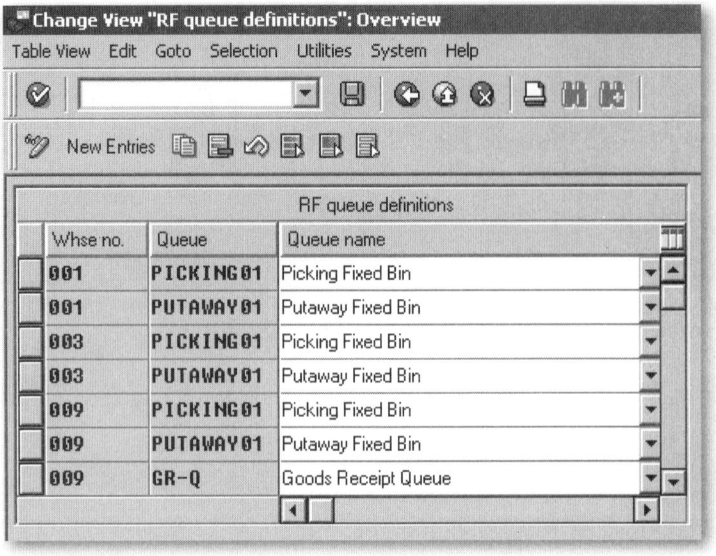

Whse no.	Queue	Queue name
001	PICKING01	Picking Fixed Bin
001	PUTAWAY01	Putaway Fixed Bin
003	PICKING01	Picking Fixed Bin
003	PUTAWAY01	Putaway Fixed Bin
009	PICKING01	Picking Fixed Bin
009	PUTAWAY01	Putaway Fixed Bin
009	GR-Q	Goods Receipt Queue

Figure 13.5 Creation of Queues for RF Transaction

Figure 13.5 shows a number of queues created for several warehouses. The queues are easily identifiable for picking, putaway, and goods receipt. The queues can then be assigned the relevant areas.

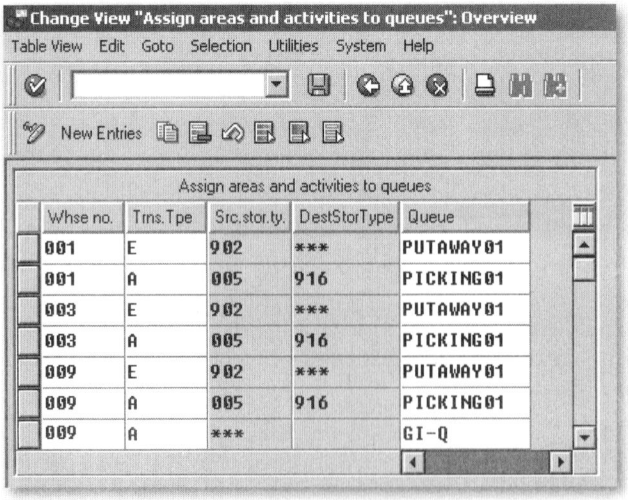

Whse no.	Trns.Tpe	Src.stor.ty.	DestStorType	Queue
001	E	902	***	PUTAWAY01
001	A	005	916	PICKING01
003	E	902	***	PUTAWAY01
003	A	005	916	PICKING01
009	E	902	***	PUTAWAY01
009	A	005	916	PICKING01
009	A	***		GI-Q

Figure 13.6 Assignment of Areas to RF Queues

Figure 13.6 shows the unique queues for each warehouse with assigned areas. For example, queue **PUTAWAY01** for warehouse **001** has been assigned transaction type **E**, stock placement, between source storage type **902** and any destination storage type, denoted by *******.

13.3.2   Adding a User for Mobile Data Entry

Each user who is assigned a RF device has to be assigned a particular area to work in. If the warehouse is small, then users may work with several queues. In larger warehouses, users may be specifically assigned to only work with certain storage types.

Use Transaction LRFMD to add users for mobile data entry. It can be found using the navigation path: **SAP · Logistics · Logistics Execution · Internal Whse Processes · Mobile Data Entry · User Master Data for Mobile Data Entry**.

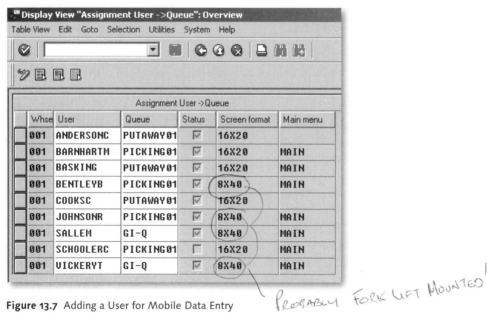

Figure 13.7 Adding a User for Mobile Data Entry

The users are entered and assigned to a queue. In addition, the screen format and the user's main menu can be defined, as shown in Figure 13.7. Once the user has been added, he or she can use the RF device to access the queue to which they have been assigned.

13.3.3 Logging on for Mobile Data Entry

The user can log on for mobile data entry using Transaction LM00. The transaction can be found using the navigation path: **SAP • Logistics • Logistics Execution • Internal Whse Processes • Mobile Data Entry • Mobile Data Entry**.

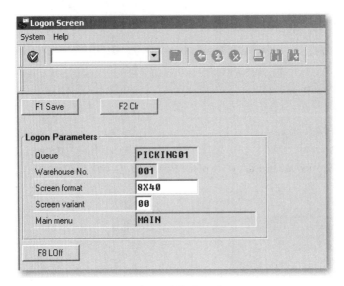

Figure 13.8 Logon Screen for Mobile Data Entry

Figure 13.8 shows the screen that is displayed when a user logs on using Transaction LM00. In this case, the queue that the user is being logged on to is **PICKING01**. The user can then use the RF device to perform the transactions he or she is assigned.

13.3.4 RF Menus and WM Processes

The menus displayed on the RF devices can be viewed using Transaction LM00. The items that are displayed on the devices can be programmed using ABAP code. The menu structure that has been defined for this example is shown in the following figures.

Figure 13.9 shows the initial menu selection for the RF devices. The supported transactions are divided into the five selections: inbound processes, outbound processes, stock transfer, internal warehouse processes, and inquiries.

To illustrate the menu paths that have been designed for the RF menu, Figure 13.10 shows the selections for the inbound processes.

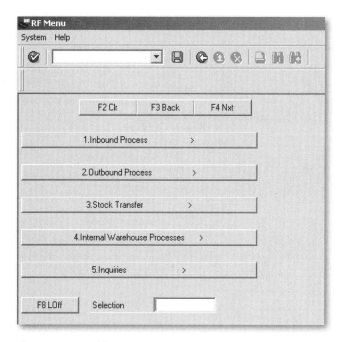

Figure 13.9 Initial RF Menu Screen

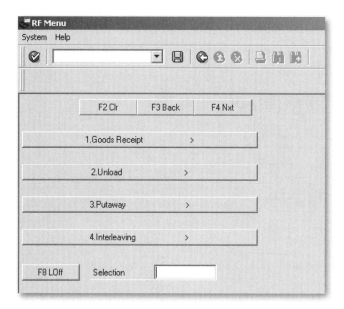

Figure 13.10 Menu Selections for Inbound Processes

If the **Goods Receipt** option is selected, the system will display the menu seen in Figure 13.11.

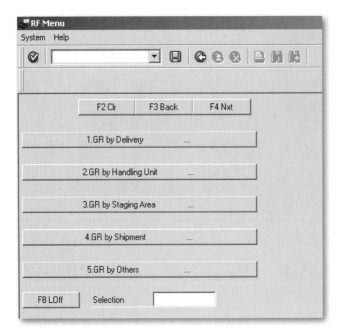

Figure 13.11 Menu Selections for Goods Receipts

Figure 13.11 shows the menu selections for the goods-receipt menu option. These five transactions are available for the RF device user. If the user wants to select a delivery, he or she would select option **1** and scan in or enter the delivery number.

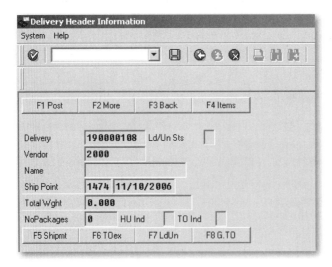

Figure 13.12 Display of Inbound Delivery Details

Figure 13.12 shows the delivery details displayed on the RF device after the user had scanned in the inbound delivery number. The user has a number of function key options whereby he or she can select a process to perform.

This is one example of the way in which transactions appear on the RF devices. Among the supported transactions for RF are:

- Goods receipt
- Goods issue
- Material putaway
- Material picking
- Packing and unpacking
- Physical inventory
- Loading and unloading
- Serial number capture
- Stock overview

From this list, you can see that many processes are RF-supported. The next section will describe the RF monitor.

13.4   Radio Frequency Monitor

The RF monitor is a tool warehouse managers can use to view the queues that are being worked on in the warehouse. Users with RF devices can only see the items in their queue; only the users of the RF monitor have the overall picture of the RF operations in the warehouse. Using the RF monitor benefits the warehouse by enabling staff to:

- Monitor the queues and review the number of assigned transfer orders, number of users, and the ratio of workload to users
- Assign transfer orders and users to other queues
- Change the processing priorities of the transfer orders in the queues
- The RF monitor gives the warehouse manager a significant overview of the devices being used and the work that is being performed.

Let us discover how to access and use this monitor.

13.4.1 Accessing the RF Monitor

The RF monitor can be found in the SAP menu. The transaction to use is Transaction LRF1. This can be accessed via the navigation path, **SAP • Logistics • Logistics Execution • Internal Whse Processes • Mobile Data Entry • Monitor Mobile Data Entry**.

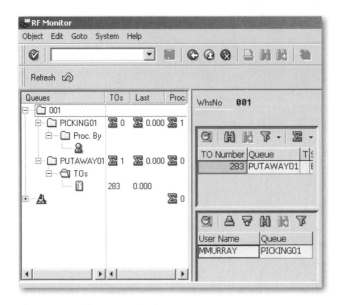

Figure 13.13 RF Monitor Display

Figure 13.13 shows the elements of the RF monitor. The navigation area is the section to the left of the screen that shows the number of users and the number of transfer orders. In this case, there is only one user and one transfer order in the queue. The right side of the screen is the ALV, or the SAP List Viewer. It shows the details from the transfer order, with and below that shows details on the user and the queue to which he or she is assigned.

13.4.2 Using the Radio Frequency Monitor

The RF monitor allows the warehouse manager to move transfer orders to other queues by simply identifying the transfer order in the navigation area and dragging it to another queue folder.

Assigning users to other queues follows a similar process, where the user is highlighted in the navigation area and dragged and dropped into the queue required. The RF monitor is kept updated by refreshing the transaction, using the **F5** function key.

This section has examined the use of the RF monitor and the benefits that can be gained by moving transfer orders to different queues in order to maximize efficiencies. Next, I will summarize the contents of this chapter on mobile data entry.

13.5 Summary

The use of bar codes and RF devices has made warehouse operation more efficient. Data-entry errors are fewer and the time needed to perform operations in the warehouse has been reduced because the data can be collected by a RF device without requiring manual collection and manual entry of data after the user has returned to the warehouse office.

The use of RF devices for data collection and transaction processing in warehouse management has been increasing over a number of SAP releases. The modern efficient warehouse uses RF technology and constantly reviews procedures to further adopt the technology to improve operations. As the support for mobile data entry increases in warehouse management, the use of the RF monitor will become more important to efficient mobile data collection.

In Chapter 14, I will discuss the next logical step up from RF technology, the adoption of Radio Frequency Identification (RFID).

Radio Frequency Identification (RFID) technology has been available for decades, but recently we have seen the push to use it as the ultimate tool for tracking inventory. Large companies such as Wal-Mart Stores, Inc. and Target Brands, Inc., expect RFID to reduce warehouse costs and improve supply chain efficiencies.

14 Radio Frequency Identification Technology

Every industry publication has articles and commentary on Radio Frequency Identification (RFID); however, it is not a new technology. The first use of RFID was documented in the 1940s by the British Royal Air Force to identify aircraft in World War II and was part of the refinement of radar. It was during the 1960s, that RFID was first considered as a solution for the commercial world. The first commercial applications involving RFID were developed throughout the 1970s and 1980s. These commercial applications were concerned with identifying material inside a single location.

The latest attempt to commercialize the use of RFID started in 1998, when researchers at the Massachusetts Institute of Technology (MIT) Auto-ID Center began to research new ways to track and identify objects as they moved between physical locations. This research centered on radio frequency technology and how information that is held on tags can be effectively scanned and shared in real time.

RFID is known today as the reading of physical tags on single products, cases, pallets, or re-usable containers that emit radio signals to be picked up by RFID reader devices. Industries see this technology as a way of identifying material more accurately than with traditional means.

This chapter will give you an understanding of the technology behind RFID, the history of that technology, the development of the technology into a commercial application, and where that applied technology is used within the framework of SAP and Warehouse Management.

14.1 Introduction to Radio Frequency Identification (RFID)

Simply stated, RFID is a means of identifying an object using a radio frequency transmission. The technology can be used to identify, track, sort, or detect a wide variety of objects. Communication takes place between a reader or interrogator and a transponder or tag.

Tags can either be active, powered by battery, or passive, powered by the reader field. A reader field is an RF field that is transmitted by the reader to interrogate the RFID tag. The communication frequencies used depend to a large extent on the application; they range from 125 KHz to 2.45 GHz. Most countries impose regulations to control RF emissions and prevent interference with other industrial, scientific, or medical equipment.

14.1.1 The Mechanism of RFID

In a typical system, tags are attached to objects. Each tag has a certain amount of internal memory which it uses to store information about the object, such as its unique ID number or details including manufacture date and material information. When a tag passes through a field generated by a reader, it transmits this information back to the reader, which identifies the object.

Until recently, RFID technology focused mainly on tags and readers, which were being used in systems where relatively low volumes of data are involved. This is now changing. RFID in the supply chain is expected to generate huge volumes of data, which will have to be filtered and routed to ERP systems. To solve this problem, companies have developed special software packages called savants, which act as buffers between the RFID front end and the ERP back end.

14.1.2 Electronic Product Code

Electronic Product Code (EPC) is the emerging RFID standard developed by the MIT AutoID center. It is the RFID version of the Universal Product Code (UPC) barcode standard. Like UPC, EPC is intended to be used for specific product identification as well as case and pallet identification. However, EPC goes beyond UPC: It not only identifies the material, but also provides access to additional data about the origin and history of the specific batches or serial numbers.

The EPC tag itself identifies the manufacturer, product, version, and serial number. It's the serial number that takes EPC to the next level by providing access to data related to a specific unit. This allows tracking of the specific serialized unit history as it moves through the supply chain. This data may be stored elsewhere, but a standardized architecture allows you access with more ease. This architecture is known as the EPC Network.

EPC has become increasingly important because it is the standard being utilized by Wal-Mart, Target, Best Buy, and the U.S. Department of Defense in their RFID mandates.

14.1.3 The Wal-Mart RFID Mandate

In June 2004, Wal-Mart announced that it would require its top 100 suppliers to put RFID tags on all shipping crates and pallets by January 1, 2005. This would then expand to its next largest 200 largest suppliers by January 1, 2006. Wal-Mart required that each tag would store an EPC that would be used to track products as they enter Wal-Mart's distribution centers and then in turn are shipped to individual stores. As the world's largest company in terms of revenue, Wal-Mart's mandate had a profound affect on the RFID strategy of many large companies that sought to remain direct suppliers.

By 2007, Wal-Mart had found that RFID's ability to improve the supply chain was limited by business partners' willingness to participate. Wal-Mart's targeted suppliers for the RFID program had some of the most efficient supply chains in the industry, and these companies did not initially realize the benefit of RFID. Forrester Research calculated that the large Wal-Mart suppliers would have to invest more than $9 million to cover costs associated with RFID to achieve the results that Wal-Mart was expecting.

Despite the large investment required, many companies have accepted that the increase in use of RFID will occur in the coming years and early adoption of the technology is good business. Some Wal-Mart suppliers were quick to comply with the mandate. Proctor & Gamble, itself a giant company, introduced an RFID policy in its organization, with the Wal-Mart mandate as a driver for its own development of RFID. Other suppliers to Wal-Mart, such as Gillette, Kimberly-Clark, and Kraft all started RFID projects at that time.

14.1.4 RFID Benefits

Supply chain management at large companies such as Wal-Mart, are interested in RFID advances that can achieve visibility of material through the supply chain. These kinds of benefits are improving with other methods, such as electronic data interchange (EDI), bar coding, and Advance Ship Notifications (ASN).

Other benefits to companies lie outside of the supply chain, such as a reduction in theft from the store or during transport or storage, and a deterrent to the growing problem of product counterfeiting. Both of these issues are costing companies billions of dollars each year. Pharmaceutical companies are increasingly worried about counterfeiting, and RFID tags on each product may help. However, the level of security needed to combat theft and counterfeiting would require a RFID tag on each product sold. The cost of the tag and of placement of the tag on the product will have to drop significantly for this to be viable .

> **Note**
>
> Today, in 2007, most companies that sell RFID tags do not quote prices because pricing is based on volume, the amount of memory on the tag, and the packaging of the tag. The cost of a 96-bit EPC tag is approximately 20 to 40 U.S. cents. However, if the tag is embedded in a thermal transfer label on which companies can print a bar code, the price will rise beyond 40 cents. A transponder in a plastic card or key fob can cost more than $4.

14.1.5 RFID vs. Bar Codes

RFID has advantages over bar codes but has some disadvantages that still have to be overcome. Until the disadvantages become insignificant, bar codes will still play a part in supply chains and in warehousing.

Advantages of RFID

RFID technology does not require line-of-sight reading. The RFID tag could be read through other materials, whereas bar codes require line of sight. This implies that a RFID reader could read a pallet of mixed products, all of which contain individual RFID tags, without having to physically move any of the materials or open any cases.

If the pallet was full of mixed products, the large number of RFID tags can be read almost instantaneously. The tags would be read sequentially, not simultaneously, but the reading still could be completed in microseconds.

The data on RFID tag can be changed or added to as a tag passes through specific operations. Read-only tags are less expensive than read/write tags. RFID tags are less susceptible to poor environmental conditions in which bar code labels become unreadable. RFID tags can be sealed within a plastic enclosure, eliminating many of the problems that plague bar codes in harsh environments, where they are exposed to chemicals, heat, and other damaging effects.

Disadvantages of RFID

Currently, cost is the biggest roadblock to the widespread use of RFID tags and the replacement of bar codes for item-level tracking. Bar codes can be produced for less than one cent. Currently RFID tags cost between 20 and 40 cents for the most basic of tags. Even if the cost falls to several cents per tag, the cost is still a significant addition to the cost of an item that is a low-cost piece of consumer goods.

RFID signals can encounter problems when being read through some materials, such as metals and liquids. Tag placement is found to be of great importance for some materials that are in particular kinds of containers, crates, or shrink-wrapped pallets. Some case-level RFID tags have to be placed in a specific location on the case and cases must be stacked in a specific orientation or configuration to obtain a consistent read from the RFID tag.

The ability for RFID not to require line of sight is also a disadvantage. A RFID reader will read tags within its range, and this may be problematic if the wrong tag is selected. Therefore line-of-sight reading is preferred for some RFID applications. If an RFID tags fails, then it is not as obvious as failure of a bar code. If the RFID tag is not seen, then there is no check to know that a tag failed.

Now that we have discussed the basics of RFID, the next section will describe in more detail the types of RFID tags that are available.

14.2   Types of RFID Tags

Every object to be identified in an RFID system will need to have a tag attached to it. Tags are manufactured in a wide variety of packaging formats designed for different applications and environments. The basic assembly process involves a substrate material, such as paper, PVC, etc., upon which an antenna is deposited.

The antenna is made from one of many different conductive materials including silver ink, aluminum, and copper. Next, the tag chip itself is connected to the antenna, using techniques such as wire bonding or flip chip. Finally, a protective overlay made from materials such as PVC lamination, epoxy resin, or adhesive paper may be added to allow the tag to support some of the physical conditions found in many applications, such as abrasion, impact, and corrosion.

14.2.1 Tag Classes

One of the main ways of categorizing RFID tags is by their capability to read and write data. This leads to the following 4 classes:

▸ **CLASS 0 — READ ONLY: Factory Programmed**
These are the simplest type of tags, where the data — usually a simple ID number (EPC) — is written only once into the tag during manufacture. The memory is then disabled from any further updates. Class 0 is also used to define a category of tags called electronic article surveillance (EAS) or anti-theft devices, which have no ID and only announce their presence when passing through an antenna field.

▸ **CLASS 1 — WRITE ONCE READ ONLY (WORM): Factory or User Programmed**
In this case, the tag is manufactured with no data written into the memory. Data can then either be written by the tag manufacturer or by the user, but only once. No further writes are allowed, and the tag can only be read. Tags of this type usually act as simple identifiers

▸ **CLASS 2 — READ WRITE**
This is the most flexible type of tag, where users have access to read and write data into the tags memory. They are typically used as data loggers, and therefore contain more memory space than is needed for a simple ID number

▸ **CLASS 3 — READ WRITE with Onboard Sessions**
These tags contain on-board sensors for recording parameters such as temperature, pressure, and motion, which can be recorded by writing into the tags memory. Because sensor readings must be taken in the absence of a reader, the tags are either semi-passive or active.

▸ **CLASS 4 — READ WRITE with Integrated Transmitters**
These are like miniature radio devices, which can communicate with other

tags and devices without the presence of a reader. This means that they are completely active with their own battery power source.

14.2.2 Active and Passive Tags

The first choice when considering a tag is between passive, semi-passive, or active. Passive tags can be read at a distance of up to 4m to 5m using the UHF frequency band, while the other types of tags (semi-passive and active) can achieve much greater distances of up to 100m for semi-passive, and several kilometers for active. This large difference in communication performance can be explained by the following:

▸ Passive tags use the reader field as a source of energy for the chip and for communication from and to the reader. The available power from the reader field not only declines very rapidly with distance but is also controlled by strict regulations, resulting in a limited communication distance of 4m — 5m when using the UHF frequency band (860 MHz — 930 MHz).

▸ Semi-passive or battery-assisted tags have built-in batteries and therefore do not require energy from the reader field to power the chip. This allows them to function with much lower signal power levels, resulting in greater communication distances of up to 100 meters. Distance is limited mainly due to the fact that tag does not have an integrated transmitter, and still must use the reader field to communicate back to the reader.

▸ Active tags are battery-powered devices that have active transmitters on board. Unlike passive tags, active tags generate RF energy and apply it to the antenna. This autonomy from the reader means that they can communicate at distances of several kilometers or more.

The experience gained by different companies running various trials and evaluations has so far shown that out of the different RFID frequencies LF, HF, UHF, and microwave, HF and UHF are the best suited to the supply chain. Furthermore, it is expected that UHF, because of its superior read range, will become the dominant frequency. This does not mean, however that LF and microwave will not be used in certain cases.

This section has looked at the types of RFID tags available. Now we will examine some current uses of RFID.

14.3   Current Uses of RFID

RFID technology is already well established in a number of areas such as electronic payment, supply chain management, and livestock tracking, as well as previously unforeseen areas, such as data conveying.

14.3.1   Electronic Payments

In many countries, smart cards based on RFID technology are becoming more common in transport situations. Hong Kong introduced the *Octopus* system in 1997, and it is now used by more than 95 % of the population.

The *Oyster card*, a Transport for London (TfL) contactless ticketing scheme, is a smart card. TfL estimates that 1 million fewer transactions per week are made at ticket offices and that there is a 30 % improvement in the speed of passengers passing through the ticket gates. It is more difficult to copy Oyster cards than it is to copy the magnetic stripe cards, and because each card contains a unique ID number it can be immediately cancelled if the card is reported lost or stolen.

14.3.2   Retail Stores

Large retail companies are pushing the adoption of RFID tags as a way of achieving supply chain visibility, reducing theft, and product counterfeiting. These companies see RFID technology as a way of preventing *out-of-stock* occurrences, the overstocking of products in warehouses, and the theft or loss of goods.

For instance, the total cost of crime, including crime prevention, for UK retailers was £2.25 billion in 2002. Marks & Spencer tagged 3.5 million returnable food produce delivery trays in 2002. This is among the largest supply chain operations involving RFID in the world. The tagged trays are filled with individual food items at the supplier, carried by the distributor to the shop, emptied, and then returned. The information on the tagged trays is read at each distribution point, resulting in improved food delivery logistics and fresher food in stores.

14.3.3   Individual Product Tagging

Retailers are already looking at the tagging of individual products to allow for better control of product recalls and better-targeted marketing campaigns. In the United Kingdom, the retail store Tesco undertook a RFID trial at one store in 2003, which involved tagging individual DVDs. RFID readers were built into the store shelves to monitor each item. Not only was the stockroom alerted when a shelf needed re-stocking, but staff were alerted when browsing customers replaced DVDs in the wrong section.

14.3.4 Parts Tracking

Virgin Atlantic Airways has introduced RFID as a project to track critical, high-value aviation assets moving through its logistics supply chain at England's Heathrow Airport. The aim is to track and trace high-value repairable aircraft parts often at short notice.

Virgin tags serviceable airplane parts that pass through its Heathrow warehouse. When an item enters the warehouse, employees use a desktop computer to enter the item into the aviation maintenance and parts-inventory tracking system the airline already uses.

The next stage is a full inspection of the part. If it passes inspection, the part is given a goods-receipt number, which triggers the generation of an RFID label. Virgin Atlantic employees then attach the label to the container holding the part. They also attach a tag to a storage bin. Once the containers and storage bins are tagged at the warehouse entrance and inspection area, the items and bins are either placed on storage racks or sent out of the warehouse for immediate use on an airplane.

This section has examined current commercial uses of RFID technology; now I shall review the use of RFID in SAP.

14.4   RFID and SAP

SAP currently offers a RFID solution called SAP Auto-ID Infrastructure (SAP AII). This is part of the SAP Business Suites similar to SAP Supply Chain Management (SCM), and it integrates RFID with current SAP functionality.

SAP AII can be implemented either as a standalone system or it can be integrated in the supply-chain function. The latest release of SAP AII is 4.0 SP03, and I'll describe that version in detail in this section.

14.4.1 Supported Functions in SAP AII

A number of processes are supported by SAP Auto-ID infrastructure (AII). In addition to desktop user interfaces, mobile and fixed RFID devices support:

▶ Outbound processing (slap-and-ship)

▶ Flexible delivery processing

▶ Generation of pedigree notifications

▶ Returnable transport items processing

These processes will be discussed in more detail in the next four sections.

14.4.2 Outbound Processing (Slap and Ship)

Slap-and-ship is an approach to complying with customer requirements for physical identification of materials shipped through the outbound processes. The main goal of the *slap-and-ship* strategy is to invest the minimum amount of capital into an RFID implementation needed to comply with the mandates set forth by both Wal-Mart and the Department of Defense.

14.4.3 Flexible Delivery Processing

The flexible delivery process allows the automation of outbound processing and inbound processing. The process allows organizations to:

▶ Create outbound deliveries in the ERP system

▶ Pack and load outbound deliveries in SAP AII

▶ Post goods issue in the ERP system

▶ Send advanced shipping notifications

▶ Create inbound deliveries in the ERP system

▶ Unload inbound deliveries in SAP AII

▶ Post goods receipt in the ERP system

These processes are particularly suitable for current RFID technology and for the goals of a great many retail customers.

14.4.4 Generation of Pedigree Notifications

Drug counterfeiting has become a major problem for the pharmaceutical industry and it is estimated to cost $46 billion a year in lost profits. Although drug counterfeiting is relatively rare in the United States, the amount of counterfeit pharmaceuticals from overseas has increased in recent years.

The U.S. Food and Drug Administration (FDA) believe that RFID will work effectively to fight drug counterfeiting. The FDA's Counterfeit Drug Task Force has been investigating RFID technology and the concept of an electronic pedigree, called e-pedigree, a procedure that records where a drug is manufactured and how it is distributed.

The adoption of RFID at the case and pallet level would help secure the integrity of the drug supply chain so that pharmaceutical companies can reliably provide greater assurances that a product was manufactured and distributed safely. Many drug manufacturers, such as Pfizer, Purdue Pharma, and Glaxo-SmithKline, have introduced RFID drug-pedigree projects.

The drug-pedigree system will authenticate pharmaceuticals as legitimate throughout the supply chain. The system uses RFID to match each container with its corresponding pedigree. During manufacture, or at any time prior to distribution, RFID tags can have a randomly generated code written to a chip or an already embedded code used to identify products. This code is unique to a product at one or more levels of packaging. It is stored along with related data and is thereby available for authentication.

At stages in the movement of the product, the tag would be scanned to create a digital record of the many transactions. When the material reaches stores, ready for sale to consumers, a complete record of its distribution would have been created and stored.

SAP AII enables the generation of pedigree notifications. These XML messages contain information that can be used by third-party vendors to create pedigrees that satisfy state legal requirements. Pedigree notifications provide data regarding:

▶ Manufacturer (e.g., name, address, state license number)

▶ Drug (e.g., name, dosage form, dosage strength, container size, expiration date, lot number, ID)

▶ Trading partner (e.g., name, address)

▶ Person who should certify the delivery or the receipt of a drug (e.g., name, address, phone, email)

▶ Date of transaction

More data may be available for pedigree notifications in future SAP releases.

14.4.5 Returnable Transport Items Processing

Returnable transport items (RTI) are assets that can be identified if they are allocated with a tag encoded with Global Returnable Asset Identifiers (GRAIs). A returnable transport items or asset is one that is delivered by the owner to the custody of another business entity, usually for a fee. RTI processing includes functions to:

▶ Manage, load, and unload RTIs filled with products or with other RTIs

▶ Track the current location of RTIs and evaluate stocks and cycle times

▶ Achieve transparency across stocks of RTIs

▶ Automate processes, reduce stocks, shorten cycle times, and recognize bottlenecks

The GRAI provides a unique identification of an asset. It uses the prefix assigned to companies by the Uniform Code Council (UCC) to develop, assign, and maintain a unique asset number for equipment, resources, supplies, etc. in order to track location. Therefore the GRAI is a unique code that is specific to the asset. The EAN identification number of a returnable asset, GRAI, is defined as a physical item with no reference to the contents. The EAN ID of a returnable asset enables tracking as well as recording of all relevant data.

Returnable assets such as pallets, barrels, rail cars, and trailers for further use in transport and trade processes become increasingly important. The main focus is to manage returnable assets within harmonized business processes and leverage the EAN system in the unique identification of assets.

Now that we have reviewed the RFID applications available in SAP, I will summarize what has been discussed in this chapter.

14.5 Summary

Radio Frequency Identification (RFID) technology has recently become commercially and technologically viable. RFID tags are essentially microchips that act as transponders, always listening for a radio signal sent by RFID readers. When a transponder receives a certain radio query, it responds by transmitting its unique ID code back to the transceiver. Most RFID tags do not have batteries; instead they are powered by the radio signal requesting a reply.

RFID can be used in the warehouse. After large corporations such as Wal-Mart mandated the use of RFID, many companies have been investigating RFID for tracking the movement of materials. Although they may not reach the level of the pedigree system proposed by the FDA, they can expect to improve the visibility of material through the supply chain.

The SAP Auto-ID infrastructure (SAP AII) solution is available for companies that wish to use RFID with their ERP system. SAP AII requires configuration for the interaction of the RFID processes with the ERP functions. As the cost of RFID tags and readers falls, we can look forward to the proliferation of RFID and the need for a more integrated RFID.

In Chapter 15, we will examine the use of cross docking in the warehouse and how it can improve customer delivery times, reduce the need for warehouse space, and cut labor costs.

Cross docking matches inbound and outbound deliveries to avoid having to store material in the warehouse. Not all material is suitable for cross docking, but when it can be used it reduces labor costs, delivery time to the customer, and the amount of warehouse space.

15 Cross Docking

The term cross docking means taking an item of finished goods from the production plant and delivering it directly to the customer with virtually no material handling in between. Cross docking reduces material handling and storage of the material in the warehouse. In most cases, the material sent from production to the loading dock has been allocated for outbound deliveries. The many benefits to a company that use cross docking include:

▶ Lower labor costs because the material no longer requires picking and putaway in the warehouse

▶ Less time moving material from production to the customer, improving customer satisfaction

▶ Less need for warehouse space, because the material is not stored.

The finished goods are delivered from the production area directly to a location near the loading dock, and from there are packed and shipped. In some instances, the material will not arrive at the loading dock from the production area, but may arrive for shipment from the warehouse as a purchased product to be re-sold or delivered from another company's manufacturing plants.

This chapter will review the cross docking functionality in SAP ECC 6. We'll discuss planning for cross docking, how the cross docking actually takes place, and how to use the cross docking monitor. Let's start with the first of those topics: planning cross docking.

15.1   Planned Cross Docking

Cross docking has been used in warehouses for more than 50 years, but with the current drive to reduce costs and to increase customer satisfaction, practitioners of supply chain management are using cross docking as an important tool for warehouse efficiency.

15.1.1   Types of Cross Docking

A number of cross docking scenarios are available to the warehouse management. In her paper *Making the Move to Cross Docking* (WREC, 2000), Maida Napolitano concluded that a number of warehouse operations involved a rapid turnaround of stock from receiving to outbound delivery. Napolitano defined these types of cross docking:

▶ **Manufacturing Cross Docking**
  This operation involves receiving purchased and inbound material required by manufacturing. The warehouse may receive the material and prepare sub-assemblies for the production orders.

▶ **Distributor Cross Docking**
  This process can consolidate inbound materials from different vendors into a mixed material pallet, which is delivered to the customer when the final material is received. For example, computer parts distributors often source their components from various vendors and manufacturers and combine them into one shipment for the customer.

▶ **Transportation Cross Docking**
  This operation combines shipments from different shippers in the less-than-truckload (LTL) and small-package industries to gain economies of scale.

▶ **Retail Cross Docking**
  This process involves receipt of material from multiple vendors and sorting onto outbound trucks for a number of retail stores. This method was a key cost-saving measure for Wal-Mart Stores in the 1980s. Wal-Mart procures two types of products: material it sells each day of the year, and large quantities of material purchased once and sold by the stores and not usually stocked again. The first product type is called staple stock and the second is called direct freight. Wal-Mart minimizes any warehouse costs with direct freight by using cross docking and keeping material in the warehouse as briefly as possible.

▶ **Opportunistic Cross Docking**

Opportunistic cross docking is the opposite of planned cross docking because it occurs without creating a known link between the inbound delivery and the outbound requirement. The link is manually created. Opportunistic cross docking can be used in any warehouse, transferring a material directly from the goods-receiving dock to the outbound shipping dock to meet a known demand; i.e., a customer sales order.

Not all these types of cross docking will be used at a warehouse. The amount of cross docking at the warehouse depends on the types of material entering the warehouse and whether that material is suitable for immediate shipment to a customer. The next section describes the types of material that are suitable for cross docking.

15.1.2 Types of Material Suitable for Cross Docking

Cross docking is not used in some warehouses because the material stored in the warehouse may not be suitable. Some materials are better suited to cross docking than others, including:

▶ Perishable materials that require immediate shipment

▶ High-quality items that do not require quality inspections during goods receipt

▶ Materials that are pre-tagged (bar coded, RFID), pre-ticketed, and ready for sale to the customer

▶ Promotional materials and materials that are being launched

▶ Staple retail materials with a constant demand or low demand variance

▶ Pre-picked, pre-packaged customer orders from another production plant or warehouse

15.1.3 Planned Cross Docking in SAP

SAP enables warehouse managers to plan the cross docking process or to allow opportunistic cross docking. The main difference between the two is that planned cross docking allows decisions to be made before the material arrives at the warehouse, while opportunistic cross docking decisions occur after the material has arrived.

Both types of cross docking may occur in the warehouse, but planned cross docking reduces the need to deal with material once it has arrived at the warehouse. This is an important benefit for retail warehouses that need to move produce with short shelf lives, such as fruit and vegetables, to the retailer as quickly as possible.

15.1.4 Configuration for Cross Docking

The initial configuration to complete is for planned and opportunistic cross docking for the warehouse and the storage type. The transaction can be found using the navigation path: **IMG · Logistics Execution · Warehouse Management · Cross Docking · General Settings · Maintain Warehouse Level Settings.**

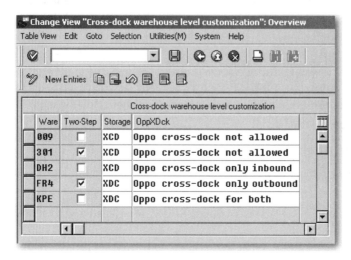

Figure 15.1 Warehouse Configuration for Planned Cross Docking

Figure 15.1 shows the configuration entered for the warehouse. The storage type entered is the location where the two-step cross-docked material will be located. In this example, the storage type is called **XCD**, shorthand for cross docking. Only set the two-step indicator when planned cross docking is required.

This transaction allows the configuration for opportunistic cross docking in the warehouse. The transaction allows opportunistic cross docking for inbound, outbound, both, or not at all. There are other configurations not seen in Figure 15.1 that can be determined in this transaction. These are:

▸ **Consider FIFO**

This indicator can be set to allow the system to consider first-in,first-out (FIFO) before implementing a cross docking decision. In normal cross docking the FIFO rules would be overridden because the material arrives and is shipped prior to the material already in the warehouse.

▶ **FIFO Tolerance**

This field allows the entry of a FIFO tolerance between the material in stock and the material arriving so that material within the entered tolerance can be cross docked even though it contradicts FIFO rules. If the inbound material is older than the tolerance allowed, then the cross docking decision cannot be made.

▶ **Time Ref**

This field enables you to choose a date and time reference from which you can calculate the default release date and time. The choices include delivery loading date and time, delivery picking date and time, and delivery planned goods movement date and time. The release time for an outbound document is the planned time for creating a transfer order for the document so it can be released.

The next configuration step is to confirm that a movement type that is to be used for cross docking is set to allow cross docking. The transaction can be found using the navigation path: **IMG • Logistics Execution • Warehouse Management • Cross Docking • General Settings • Define Cross-Docking Relevancy for Movement Types**.

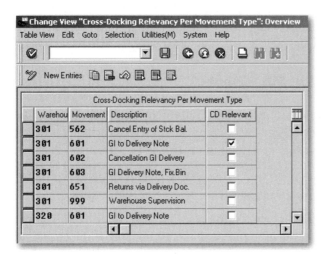

Figure 15.2 Configuration of Movement Types for Cross Docking

Figure 15.2 shows the configuration for the movement type applicable in each warehouse. The **CD Relevant** indicator should be set for movement types to be used for cross docking.

15.1.5 Cross Docking Decisions

A cross docking decision is a link that can be made between a planning document, which can be an inbound or outbound delivery, and a candidate document, which is another inbound or outbound delivery.

Example

If an inbound delivery is expected for 20 units of material of XYZ, and there is a planned outbound delivery of 20 units of XYZ to a customer, then these two documents, the planning and the candidate, can be linked by a cross docking decision.

The cross docking decision can be made by two methods:

▶ **Manual Creation**
The decision to link a planning and a candidate document can be made by the warehouse staff. The decision can be made with the aid of the cross docking monitor, which will be discussed later in this chapter.

▶ **Automatic Creation**
The decision can be made automatically by the system. When a transfer order is created for an inbound or outbound delivery, the system reviews all potential candidate documents to ascertain whether a link can be made and a cross docking decision created.

Now that we have examined the planned cross docking functionality, we will go on to review the cross docking movements that occur in the warehouse.

15.2 Cross Docking Movements

When a cross docking decision is made before the material arrives, the movement can be processed as a one-step or two-step cross docking process. Both of these movements are described next.

15.2.1 One-Step Cross Docking

As the name suggests, this movement processes the cross docking movement in one step, directly from the inbound goods-receiving area to the outbound goods issuing area.

For one-step cross docking to be active, check the configuration for the warehouse to ensure that the two-step cross docking indicator is not set. In Figure 15.1, the cross docking configuration for the warehouse shows the indicator that can be set to force two-step cross docking.

In planned cross docking, the inbound delivery is linked to the outbound delivery, and a transfer order is created to move the material from the goods-receiving area to the outbound delivery area.

Figure 15.3 Inbound Delivery Linked to Outbound Delivery via Cross Docking

Figure 15.3 shows the shipping notification for the inbound delivery. The material to be received from this inbound delivery is linked to outbound delivery for the same material.

When the material arrives in the goods receipt area, the material is unloaded and a goods receipt is posted in SAP Inventory Management (IM). Figure 15.4 shows outbound delivery with a planned goods issue of a quantity of 20 for material **M-40**. This is the same quantity of material that is expected from the inbound delivery.

When the goods receipted material is put away, a transfer order is created for the material. If this cross docking is planned, transfer order processing will retrieve that cross docking decision. The system will then create a transfer order that proposes the goods-issue area, storage type 916 as the destination storage type on the transfer order.

Figure 15.5 shows the transfer order for the cross docking decision that linked the inbound goods receipt with the outbound delivery.

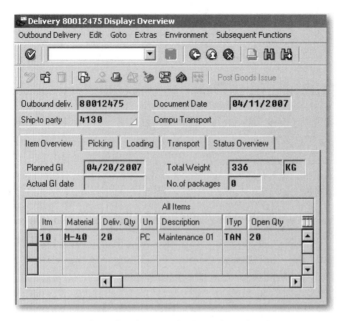

Figure 15.4 Outbound Delivery Linked to Inbound Delivery via Cross Docking

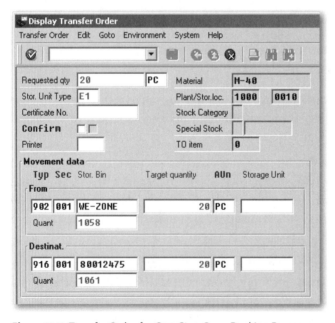

Figure 15.5 Transfer Order for One-Step Cross Docking Process

The goods receipt area **902** is defined as the source storage type and the goods issue area **916** is defined as the destination storage type. After the transfer order is confirmed, the inbound delivery and outbound delivery documents are updated with the actual pick and putaway quantities that were recorded.

15.2.2 Two-Step Cross Docking

In cross docking where the two-step procedure has been configured, as seen for some warehouses in Figure 15.1, materials to be cross-docked are initially moved from the goods receipts area to a cross docking storage type. In the second step, the material is moved to the goods issue area from the cross docking storage type when the outbound delivery is released.

The cross docking storage type is defined in the same transaction as shown in Figure 15.1, which can be found using the navigation path: **IMG · Logistics Execution · Warehouse Management · Cross Docking · General Settings · Maintain Warehouse Level Settings**.

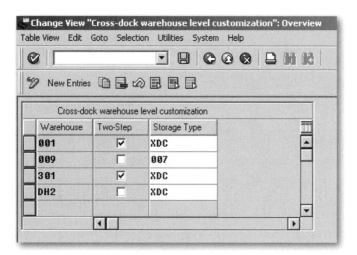

Figure 15.6 Defining Cross-Docking Storage Type for Each Warehouse

Figure 15.6 shows the warehouse and the cross docking storage type that have been defined. In the case of warehouse **001**, the two-step cross docking indicator has been set and the cross docking storage type is defined as **XDC**.

When a link is created between an inbound and outbound delivery as part of a cross docking decision, the system will review the decision to either perform a one-step or two-step process. In a two-step process, the system will create two transfer orders:

► A transfer order for the inbound delivery materials from the goods receipt storage type to the cross docking storage type

► A transfer order from the cross docking storage type to the goods issue storage type

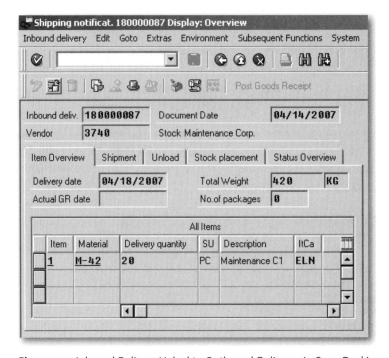

Figure 15.7 Inbound Delivery Linked to Outbound Delivery via Cross Docking

Figure 15.7 shows the shipping notification for the inbound delivery. The material to be received from this inbound delivery is linked to outbound delivery for the same material: **M-42**. When the material arrives in the goods receipt area, the material is unloaded and a goods receipt is posted in SAP IM.

Figure 15.8 shows the transfer order created for the first step of two-step cross docking. The material is received, a goods receipt posted, and a transfer order created to move the material from the goods issue storage type to the cross docking storage type **XDC**, where it will remain until the outbound delivery is ready to be goods issued.

Figure 15.9 shows the outbound delivery with a planned goods issue of a quantity of 20 for material **M-42**. This is the same quantity expected from the inbound delivery.

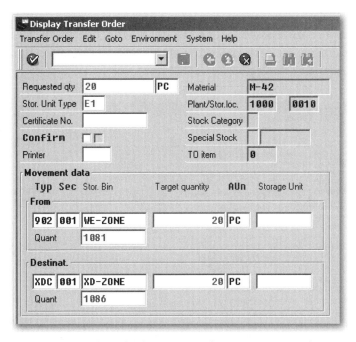

Figure 15.8 Transfer Order for First Step of Two-Step Cross Docking

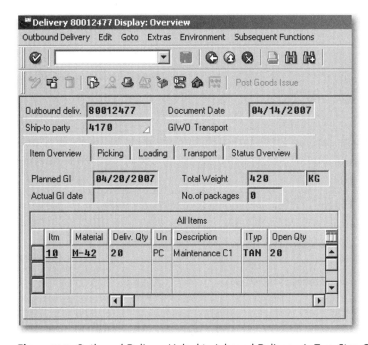

Figure 15.9 Outbound Delivery Linked to Inbound Delivery via Two-Step Cross Docking

When the outbound delivery is released, the system will create a transfer order that moves the cross docked material from the cross docking storage type and proposes the goods issue area, storage type 916, as the destination storage type on the transfer order.

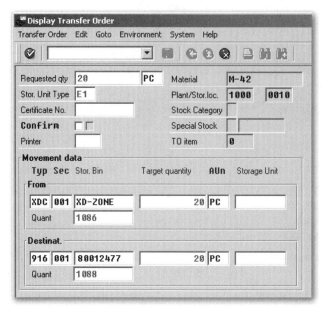

Figure 15.10 Transfer Order for Second Step of Two-Step Cross Docking

Figure 15.10 shows the second transfer order in the two-step cross docking. The material is removed from the cross docking storage type and placed in the goods issue storage type for the outbound delivery.

After both transfer orders are confirmed, the inbound delivery and outbound delivery documents are updated with the actual pick and putaway quantities that were recorded.

This section has examined the movements associated with cross docking. Now we'll turn our attention to the SAP cross docking monitor.

15.3 Cross Docking Monitor

Warehouse managers use the cross docking monitor to review the cross docking situation in the warehouse and make any necessary changes. The monitor displays all inbound and outbound deliveries as well as transfer requirements, shipments, groups, and cross docking decisions.

15.3.1 Accessing the Cross Docking Monitor

The cross docking monitor can be displayed using the Transaction LXDCK, or via the navigation path: **SAP • Logistics • Logistics Execution • Cross Docking • Cross Docking Monitor**.

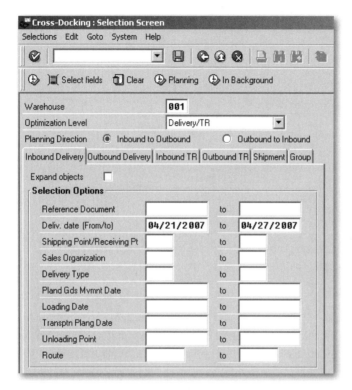

Figure 15.11 Initial Selection Screen for Cross Docking Monitor

Figure 15.11 shows the selection screen for the cross docking monitor. The warehouse manager can select the warehouse and the planning direction, which is either inbound to outbound or outbound to inbound.

The other selection parameters include a date range, shipping point, sales organization, delivery type, unloading point, and route.

It is important to enter the date range. If cross docking in the warehouse is operated with small delays between inbound and outbound delivery — possibly because of a lack of floor space — a narrow range of dates should be entered.

The **In Background** button can be used to create all the cross docking decisions using the system optimization. The **Planning** button can be used if the warehouse manager wishes to go directly to create cross docking decisions based on the inbound and outbound documents in the system.

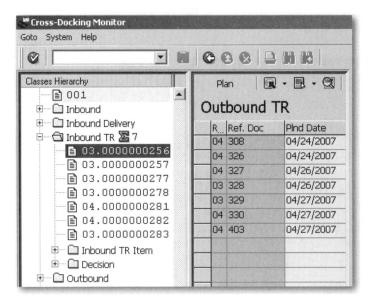

Figure 15.12 Cross Docking Monitor Detail Showing Inbound and Outbound Transfer Requirements

Figure 15.12 shows the inbound and outbound transfer requirements for the date entered into the selection screen. The warehouse manager can opt to use the planning tool by selecting the **Plan** button or to select documents for creating manual decisions.

15.3.2 Cross Docking Alert Monitor

The warehouse manager uses the cross docking alert monitor to identify potential issues with cross docking. The alert monitor can be accessed while working in the cross docking monitor by selecting the alert icon. It can also be accessed via a separate Transaction LXDCA or via the navigation path: **SAP • Logistics • Logistics Execution • Cross Docking • Alert Monitor**.

Figure 15.13 shows one of the three alert screens that are available in the Alert Monitor. Figure 15.13 shows the deliveries for warehouse **001** that have been released and that are now outside of the tolerance. The other two alert screens are for transfer requirements that are outside of their tolerances and for cancelled transfer orders without replacements. The three alert screens are described in more details as follows:

▶ **Deliveries with Release Time in the Past**

This alert shows cross docking-relevant outbound deliveries whose release times and latest release times have passed. The yellow alert is displayed when the release time is passed. The red alert is displayed when the latest release time has passed.

▶ **Transfer Requirements with Release Time in the Past**

This alert shows cross docking-relevant transfer requirements whose release times and latest release times have passed. The yellow alert is displayed when the release time is passed. The red alert is displayed when the latest release time has passed.

▶ **Cancelled Transfer Orders Without Replacement TOs**

This alert shows transfer orders that have been cancelled without replacement transfer orders being created.

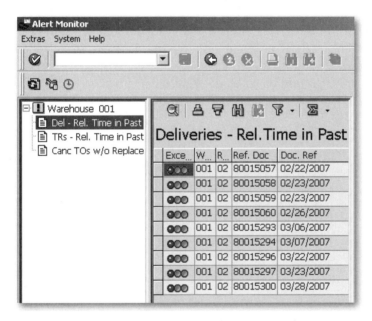

Figure 15.13 Cross Docking Alert Monitor Showing Past Delivery Dates

You can access three of the alert screens from Transaction LXDCA and display the different screens within one transaction.

This section has reviewed the functionality and usability of the SAP cross-docking monitor. The next section is a summary of what we have learnt from this chapter.

15.4 Summary

Supply chain management involves a constant search for ways to make warehousing more efficient, improve customer satisfaction, and cut costs. If possible, material could be shipped directly from the manufacturer to the customer, avoiding any warehouse costs. The next best thing is to implement cross docking. Cross docking removes the need for inspection on goods receipt, goods-receipt staging, putaway, storage, picking, and goods-issue staging.

Not all material is suitable for cross docking, but using SAP cross docking functionality makes it possible for some items. Many large organizations use cross docking. It is most effective in the movement of items in the grocery industry, where food is stored as little as possible and the speed of delivery to the retail store is of the utmost importance.

In Chapter 16, I will review some of the more recent developments in warehouse management, such as task and resource management, value-added services, and extended warehouse management.

Warehouse management functionality from SAP has evolved from a simple locator system to a full suite of warehouse software that covers the entire warehouse operation. New developments are helping to optimize the use of labor and warehouse operation monitoring

16 Developments in Warehouse Management

Standard warehouse management has evolved from the earliest functionality in SAP R/2, where it was a good locator system, through the R/3 releases that incorporated putaway and picking strategies, storage-unit management, wave picking, the warehouse activity monitor, SAPConsole, and RF transactions. SAP ECC 6.0 brings additional functionality such as the Warehouse Control Unit.

Because more warehouse functionality is expected in later releases of SAP ERP and SAP Supply Chain Management (SAP SCM), this chapter describes some of the latest SAP developments available in warehouse management. Some warehouse operations use task and resource management (TRM), Value-Added Services (VAS) or Extended Warehouse Management (EWM).

Although these three areas are new compared with the standard warehouse management, they are integrated into common warehouse processes. Your company may already be using manual functions that are similar to VAS or TRM. This chapter will help you understand these developments and know how to help your company take advantage of the functionality.

The next section examines the functionality of TRM and its integration with standard warehouse management.

16.1 Task and Resource Management

TRM functionality allows warehouse staff to further maximize their efficiencies by providing processes to help execute planned warehouse tasks. The TRM functions do not plan the warehouse work, but help manage the work defined by the planning function and manage the resources to perform the tasks. The functionality in TRM falls into five core areas:

- ▶ Resource management
- ▶ Request management
- ▶ Task management
- ▶ Route management
- ▶ Bin management

Let us examine these in more detail now:

16.1.1 Definitions in Task and Resource Management

Although TRM functionality relates to tasks and resources that occur in warehouse, the terms in TRM do not always relate directly to standard warehouse terminology. The terms included in this section are specific to TRM.

Site

The primary physical area defined in TRM is the site. This is not always directly equivalent to a warehouse. A site can be a warehouse, part of a warehouse, or many warehouses. It can also define an area that is not part of the traditional warehouse, such as a parked trailer area or even warehouse offices.

A site can be defined in TRM configuration. The transaction can be found using the SAP navigation path: **IMG · Logistics Execution · Task and Resource Management · Master Data · General Settings for TRM**.

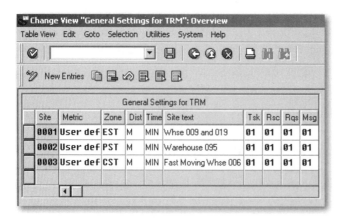

Figure 16.1 Site Configuration for TRM

Figure 16.1 displays the configuration elements required to create a site. The site number is a four-character field, and can represent an area that may be a warehouse, part of a warehouse, or multiple warehouses. The site is a uniquely defined physical area. The other fields to be entered include the time zone, unit of measure for time and distance, short text, and the number range for tasks, resources, requests, and messages.

Site Map

After the site has been created, it can be defined by means of different physical properties. These physical properties are defined as part of a site map. The site map allows the planning of efficient routes in the warehouse based on the physical definition. These physical properties are not found in standard warehouse management and require some explanation. They are:

▶ **Zones**
This is a physical location within a site that is used for a specific function; e.g., a work center, or pallet storage area.

▶ **Nodes**
A node can be used in two ways: as a physical node where material is placed and as a logical node where resources pass. The logical node may be an entry point or exit point. All physical nodes can be assumed to be logical nodes, but logical nodes are never physical nodes.

▶ **Obstacles**
This is simply a physical object or barrier defined in the site as an area through which resources cannot pass. This may be a wall, or a rack of fixed equipment. When determining a route for a resource to take, the defined obstacle allows the route to be planned around it.

▶ **Working Areas**
These are physical areas between two zones that are defined as areas where resource planning occurs. For example, a working area may be the physical area between the goods-receiving dock and the picking area.

Defining a Zone

A zone can be configured in the TRM function area of the IMG. The transaction can be found using the navigation path: **IMG • Logistics Execution • Task and Resource Management • Master Data • Site Map Management • Define Zones, Operations and Serving Zones**.

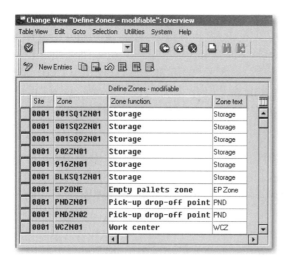

Figure 16.2 Zone Definition for a Site

Figure 16.2 shows the zones that are defined for site **0001**. The zone can be given a 10-character identifier, and a zone function must be defined as well. The function can be set as a pick-up and drop-off point, work center, storage area, or an empty pallet zone.

Defining a Node

A node can be configured in the TRM area of the IMG. The node cannot be defined prior to the zone creation. The transaction can be found using the navigation path: **IMG • Logistics Execution • Task and Resource Management • Master Data • Site Map Management • Define Nodes and Entries/Exits to/from Zones**.

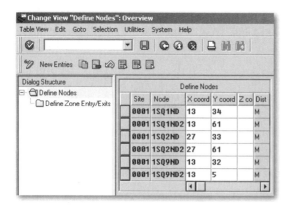

Figure 16.3 Definition of Nodes for a Site

Figure 16.3 shows the definition of each node for the site. The node can be given a 14-character identifier. Use X, Y, and Z coordinates to identify the node within the site. The coordinates allow you to locate the node in a three-dimensional context.

Defining a Zone Entry/Exit

A node can be defined as an exit, entry, or both for a zone. The transaction menu path is the same as for defining a node: **IMG • Logistics Execution • Task and Resource Management • Master Data • Site Map Management • Define Nodes and Entries/Exits to/from Zones**.

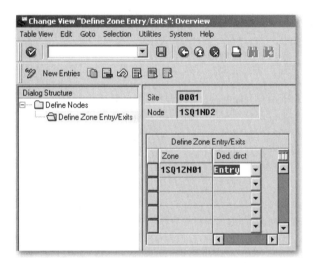

Figure 16.4 Definition of Zone Entry and Exit Points

Figure 16.4 shows the node for the zone. The dedicated direction for the node is defined as an entry. But this can be changed to exit or to both entry and exit. This allows the system to choose a node with the correct direction. For example, if a route from a storage bin to the loading dock required a path through a node, that node would have to be an entry or both an exit and an entry.

Defining an Obstacle

An obstacle is an area that a resource cannot pass through, such as a wall. The planned route must take an obstacle into account and find a pathway around it. The obstacle should be defined to identify the physical definition of the object.

Example

If the obstacle is a wall, then nodes in each corner should define the wall.

The obstacle can be configured with a transaction found using the navigation path: **IMG • Logistics Execution • Task and Resource Management • Master Data • Site Map Management • Define Obstacles**.

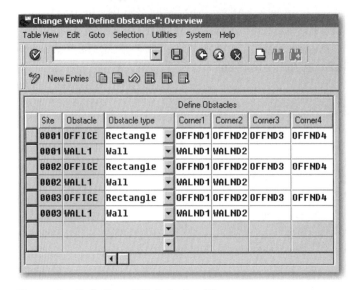

Figure 16.5 Definition of Obstacles in a Site

Figure 16.5 shows that each obstacle defined for the site is given an obstacle type — **Wall** or **Rectangle** in this case — and is defined by a series of nodes that have specific coordinates. Therefore, the route planning will avoid the obstacle in determining the route for the resource.

Defining a Zone Group

A zone group is simply a grouping of zones. We create zones to more easily define the working areas between zones. We can only assign zones to the zone group after the zones have been defined.

The zone group can be configured with a transaction found using the navigation path: **IMG • Logistics Execution • Task and Resource Management • Master Data • Site Map Management • Define Zone Groups and Assign Zones**.

Figure 16.6 shows the defined zone group and the zones that are assigned. The zone group can be entered with up to 10 alphanumeric characters.

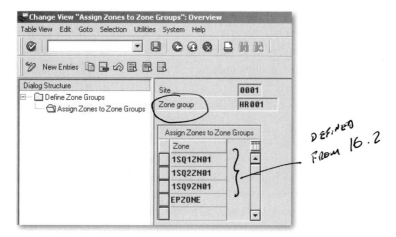

Figure 16.6 Definition of Zones to a Zone Group

Defining a Working Area

The working area is the physical area between two zones or zone groups that is defined as an area where resource planning occurs. You can configure working area with the aid of the zones and zone groups that define the working area.

The working area can be configured with a transaction found using the navigation path: **IMG • Logistics Execution • Task and Resource Management • Master Data • Site Map Management • Define Working Areas**.

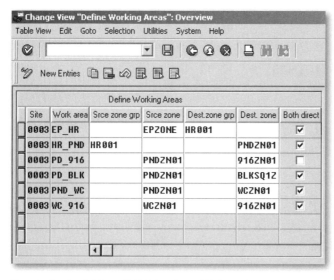

Figure 16.7 Definition of Working Areas Within a Site

Figure 16.7 shows the working areas that have been defined for a site. A working area can be defined as the area between a source zone or a source zone group and a destination zone or zone group. When defining a working area, you have the option to allow a single path from source to destination; i.e., that the resource can pass from the source to the destination only, or be allowed in both directions.

Defining a Resource

TRM defines a resource as an object capable of receiving and executing tasks. This resource can be a warehouse employee or a piece of warehouse equipment. The resource can be created using the resource element maintenance wizard: Transaction LRSW. This can be found using the navigation path: **SAP • Logistics • Logistics Execution • Task and Resource Management • Resource Element Maintenance Wizard**.

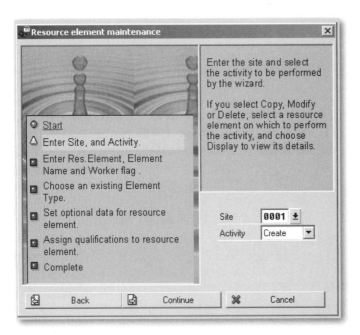

Figure 16.8 Using Resource Element Maintenance Wizard to Create a Resource

Figure 16.8 shows the first screen of resource creation, requiring that you enter the site and activity. The resource is only viable in one site. If the resource works in two sites, then the resource will need to be duplicated.

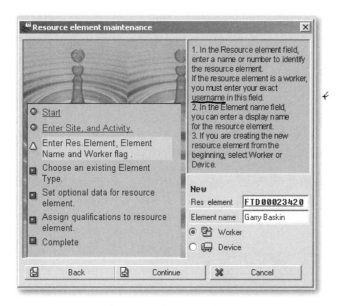

Figure 16.9 Entry of Resource Element and Element Name

Figure 16.9 shows the entry of the resource. The resource element can have an identifier up to 20 characters in length. The element or workers name can also be up to 20 characters long. You make the selection on this screen whether the resource is a worker or a device.

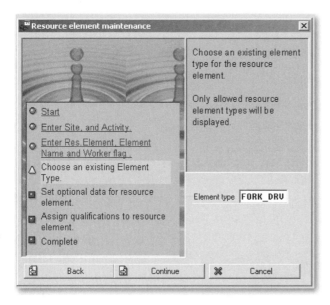

Figure 16.10 Element Type Entry for Creation of Resource

Figure 16.10 shows the element type that has been chosen for the resource. In this example, the resource allocated is a forklift truck driver, but it could have been a picker, driver, packer, etc.

The next screen for creating the resource can be used to add optional attributes. There is one field in this screen that should be filled, and that is for a **Role Check.** There is an option to allow no role checks, which means that the resource can be used in any working area. If you choose to allow no role check, then allocating the resource to working areas is not necessary.

If the role check is selected, the next screen allows the resource to be added to working areas and for those areas to be prioritized for the allocation of tasks.

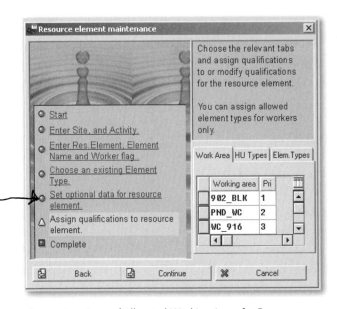

Figure 16.11 Entry of Allocated Working Areas for Resource

Figure 16.11 shows that this resource has been added to three working areas and that those working areas are prioritized. Priorities are manually entered. The other tabs on this screen relate to the types of handling units (HUs) that the resource can work with and the priority given to working with the various HU types. The last tab is for element types tha this resource can work with. For example, a resource can be allocated as a forklift driver and a material picker.

After the entries for this screen are made, the resource details are completed, and the resource has been created.

16.1.2 Resource Management

TRM's resource management functionality is one of its core areas. The resource-management function manages the resources, whether they are devices or personnel, and can allocate and reallocate the orders that are assigned to the resource. The resource management configuration allows definition of resource types and resource elements that can be used to create resources.

In configuration, the resource management transaction defines all of the functionality used in creating resources. The transaction can found using the navigation path: **IMG • Logistics Execution • Task and Resource Management • Master Data • Resource Management**.

Defining Resource Element Types

The element type is used to create a resource, with options for a device, such as a forklift or crane, or a worker.

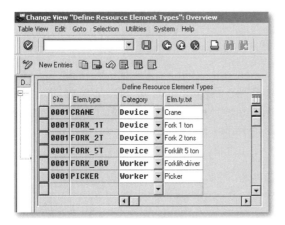

Figure 16.12 Define Resource Element Types for a Site

Figure 16.12 shows the resource elements that have been configured for the site **0001**. The elements are in two categories: element types for the device category, and element types that can be assigned for workers.

Defining Resource Types

A resource type is used for devices such as cranes and forklifts. In this configuration, you can enter the speed of the device so that the route can be timed and scheduled.

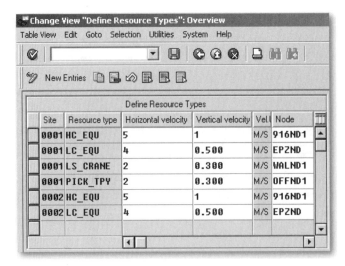

Figure 16.13 Definition of Resource Types for Site

Figure 16.13 shows the resource types with their respective velocities in meters per second (M/S). This velocity unit of measure can be changed. The node entered for the resource type is the default node from which the resource receives its first task after logging on to the system.

Each resource type has components that when combined make up the resource type. The resource type **HC_EQU** shown in Figure 16.13 can be defined as a worker and forklift truck. Therefore, the resource type must be defined in configuration to have components, in this case a driver and forklift truck.

Figure 16.14 shows the two components: the forklift truck and the forklift truck driver assigned to the resource type. Therefore, when the resource type is used to define a resource, these two components must be defined as well.

Each resource type can be allocated to certain working areas. For example, a forklift truck may be of a certain size and only allowed in certain areas of the warehouse. Therefore, the resource type for this forklift may be restricted to certain working areas.

Figure 16.15 shows the working areas that have been assigned to resource type **HC_EQU**. The resource type cannot be allocated to working areas not defined in this configuration.

Also see 16.11 ?

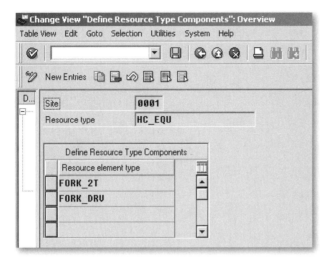

Figure 16.14 Two Components Defined for Resource Type

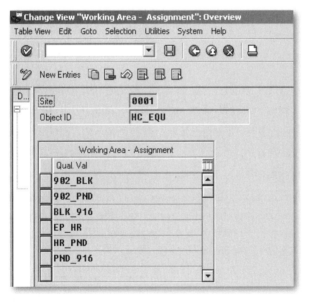

Figure 16.15 Allocation of Working Areas to Resource Type

One more definition of the resource type that you can configure is for capacities. The resource type cannot hold or move an infinite amount of material in each task, so the capacity of the resource type is configured for each handling unit that it can accommodate.

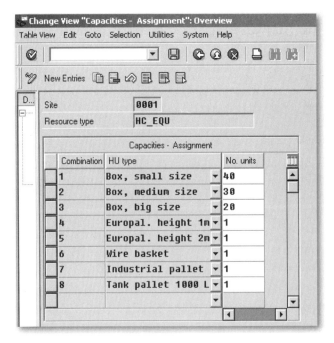

Figure 16.16 Capacities Configuration for Resource Type

Figure 16.16 shows the number of HUs that can be moved or carried by the resource type. In this example, the resource type has a capacity of **40** small boxes or **1** wire basket.

16.1.3 Request Management

The request management function controls the requests that arrive in TRM for movement of material. The request is derived from the transfer orders created in warehouse management. The transfer order will request that material be moved from one storage bin to another.

The scheduler function within the request management function will move the request to task management when required. When the request is then transferred to the task-management function, the program breaks down the request into its individual elements.

After the task has been completed by the resources, the confirmation is collected by the request management function, and final confirmation of the move of the material is recorded in the transfer order. The request is removed from the request management function.

16.1.4 Task Management

When the request is moved from request management to task management, the request is broken down into individual tasks. The request may contain several individual tasks. You can create a number of scenarios when converting the requests to tasks. Let's take a look at these now.

One Request — One Task

This is a very simple request; e.g., one that requires the movement of one pallet from storage bin YXZ to storage bin 123. This simple request may involve moving a pallet of material from high-rack storage to the open storage type.

One Request — Several Tasks

This again may be viewed as a simple request; e.g., moving a pallet to a high rack. However, this request may comprise two tasks in TRM: the first task to remove the pallet on a forklift to the rack, and a second task to use a larger forklift to stack the pallet in a high rack.

Several Requests — One Task

If there are several transfer orders to move material to an open storage type, this may be performed with one task because the material could be moved on one pallet.

Several Requests — Several Tasks

With this scenario, several transfer order items, or requests, may require picking, packing, and then moving to the loading dock. This would require a number of tasks, such as picking, placing the material in packing material, and using a forklift to move the packed material to the loading dock.

Creation of a Task

Tasks are created from the requests that are forwarded from standard warehouse management. The request management function sorts, schedules, and releases the requests to task management. Task management then identifies and creates the tasks based on the routes that can take to fulfill the request. The tasks are placed in the task pool and assigned resources to complete the task and fulfill the request.

Task Selection by Resource

The resource is assigned a number of tasks. The resource will use a presentation device to communicate with the TRM function in the warehouse. This may be a radio frequency (RF device) that the worker resource is using on the warehouse floor. Three modes can be used to select tasks: user selected, system guided, or semi-system guided. In the system-guided option, the task-management function assigns the highest priority task.

16.1.5 Route Management

Route management contains the functions that determine the route information and calculates route duration and route priority. The basis of route-management is the entries already described in this chapter; e.g., zones, nodes, working areas, and obstacles.

The route is simply the course that a resource travels between the start and end points. When tasks are being created, the route-management function creates the route for a particular resource type to take. This may be a mandatory route because of height or safety restrictions.

Mandatory Routes

Mandatory routes are created in configuration. The transaction can found using the navigation path: **IMG · Logistics Execution · Task and Resource Management · Control Data · Define Mandatory Routes**.

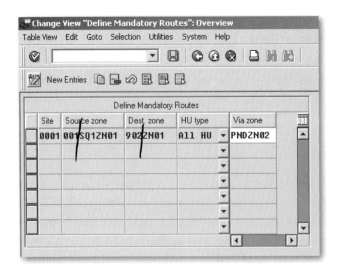

Figure 16.17 Definition of Mandatory Route in Route Management

Figure 16.17 shows that for all HUs, the route in site **0001** between zones **001SQ1ZN01** and **902ZN01** must pass via zone **PNDN02**. The mandatory route between the same two zones may be different for varying HUs, if these are required.

Route Exceptions

Route exceptions are used when a route between two nodes has been calculated but, due to the nature of the resource type, the route is either not valid or the distance of the route is not as calculated.

This configuration can be entered using the navigation path: **IMG • Logistics Execution • Task and Resource Management • Control Data • Define Route Exceptions**.

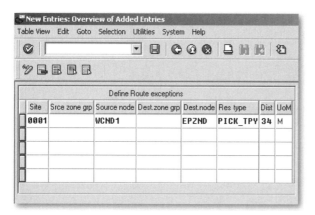

Figure 16.18 Defining Route Exceptions

In Figure 16.18, the route between node WCND1 and EPZND has been configured for an exception for resource type PICK_TPY, which would be a warehouse picker. This may be needed because a picker cannot pass down a particular aisle because of safety concerns and must take a longer route. If the picker could not take that route, it would be flagged as invalid in this transaction and not selected by the route management function.

16.1.6 Bin Management

The storage bins in standard warehouse management are allocated to storage types and storage sections. However, within the TRM function, the site map is created based on X and Y coordinates. For this reason, you need to assign these types of coordinates to the storage bins.

The transaction to set the X and Y coordinates for warehouse storage bins is LSET_BIN_COORDINATES. It also can be found using the navigation path: **SAP • Logistics • Logistics Execution • Task and Resource Management • Storage Bin • Maintain Storage Bins by Selection**.

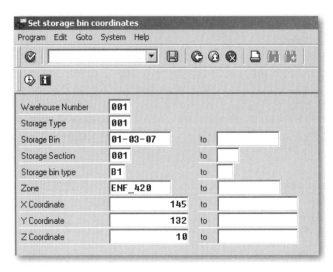

Figure 16.19 Enter Coordinates for Warehouse Storage Bins

Figure 16.19 shows the entry of **X** and **Y** coordinates for a warehouse storage bin. The storage bin is allocated to a zone, and the coordinates identify the storage bin as an item into the site map.

16.1.7 TRM Monitor

The TRM monitor is the transaction that keeps SAP WM aware of the situation within the TRM function with respect to transfer orders, inbound and outbound deliveries, tasks, and resources. The transaction for the monitor is LTRMS and can be found using the navigation path: **SAP • Logistics • Logistics Execution • Task and Resource Management • Monitor**.

Figure 16.20 shows the initial selection screen for the TRM monitor. The monitor has screens for groups, outbound deliveries, inbound deliveries, transfer orders, transfer order items, tasks, and resources.

In this section, we have examined the functionality available in task and resource management. The next section discusses the processes that can be found in Value-Added Services.

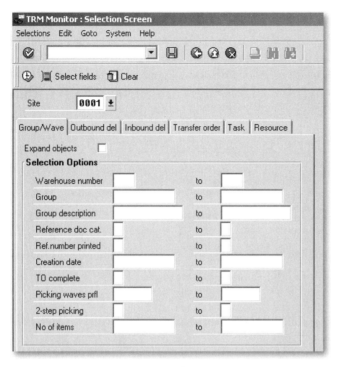

Figure 16.20 TRM Monitor Initial Selection Screen

16.2 Value-Added Services

Value-Added Services (VAS) are operations performed on materials that improve their value, functionality, or usefulness. These services include repacking, tagging, price marking, labeling, and shrink-wrapping. This will generally occur in the warehouse prior to an outbound delivery to a customer.

You can create VAS orders that instruct warehouse staff to perform certain tasks. These tasks may be part of a VAS template that is used for some materials.

16.2.1 Configuration for VAS

You need to complete a number of configuration steps before using VAS. These include defining a VAS work center and defining VAS for the warehouse. Let's explore configuration in detail now.

Defining a VAS Work Center Profile

A VAS work center is a location where VAS activities, such as packing or labeling, are performed. However, these work centers should be set up in configuration using the navigation path: **IMG • Logistics Execution • Warehouse Management • Value Added Services • General VAS Settings • Define VAS Work Centers**.

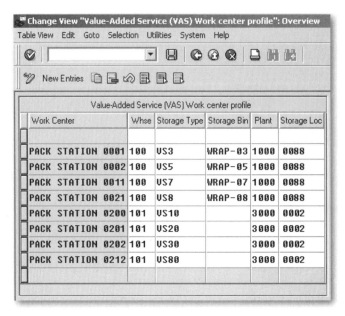

Figure 16.21 Defining VAS Work Centers

Figure 16.21 shows the definition of a VAS work center in relation to a warehouse, storage type, storage bin, plant, and storage location. Additional information can be entered for the work center, but the functionality for the additional information will not be available until after release ECC 6.0.

Defining VAS Settings for the Warehouse

For VAS to operate in a warehouse, some settings need to be created for the VAS functionality. These settings are made in configuration using the navigation path: **IMG • Logistics Execution • Warehouse Management • Value Added Services • General VAS Settings • Define VAS for Warehouse**.

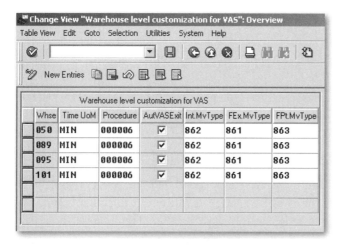

Figure 16.22 Defining VAS Settings for Warehouse

Figure 16.22 shows the basic settings for the warehouse in which VAS operations will occur. These settings are:

▶ **Time Unit of Measure**
Seen in Figure 16.22 as **Time UoM** this is the basic unit of measure that is used for the VAS orders in this warehouse.

▶ **Procedure**
This is the procedure that determines which VAS template to use. The procedure is configured in the IMG.

▶ **Automatic Exit from VAS After VAS Order Confirmation**
If this indicator,— **AutVASExit** — is set, a transfer order from the work center to the next destination is automatically created when the last of the VAS orders in the work center has been confirmed.

▶ **Internal Movement Type**
This indicator — **Int.MvType** — is the transfer order movement type that is to be used in this warehouse for material when it is transferred between work centers. For example, an order may have to be moved from a work center that labels to a work center that shrink-wraps the material on the pallet.

▶ **Movement Type for Work Center to Final Outbound Destination**
This indicator — **FEx.MvType** — is the transfer order movement type used in this warehouse for material sent from the work center to the final outbound destination.

► **Final Putaway Movement Type**
This indicator — **FPt.MvType** — is the transfer order movement type that is to be used in this warehouse for material sent from the work center to the final putaway location.

By defining these movement types for each warehouse, the correct movements will be made when material is moved with VAS orders.

Defining the Procedure for VAS Template Determination

This procedure determines the VAS Template to be used. A VAS template enables the same instructions to be re-used for different documents with the same conditions. Therefore, you can create a number of templates to create orders for different situations without having to enter the conditions each time. The procedure is based on the access sequence and determination type used in areas such as price determination in SD or batch determination in MM.

Condition types, based on access sequences using fields in condition tables, define the procedure.

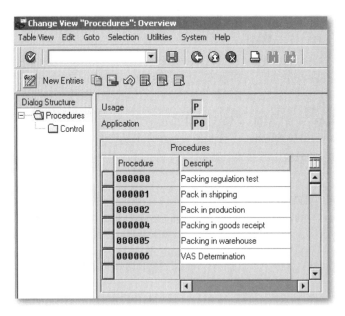

Figure 16.23 Procedures for Determining VAS Templates

Figure 16.23 shows that six procedures have been created for the VAS template determination. Each of these procedures is based on a set of sequenced condition types.

The usage field **P** defines the procedure for packing object determination. The application **PO** represents the packing object. To review the condition types that make up the procedure, select the procedure and click on the **Control** option in the dialog structure as seen in Figure 16.24.

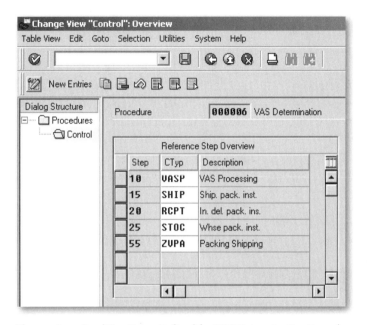

Figure 16.24 Condition Types Defined for VAS Determination Procedure

Figure 16.24 also shows you the condition types used in sequence in the procedure to determine the VAS template.

16.2.2 Creating the VAS Template

The VAS template is defined using Transaction LVAST01 or found using the navigation path: **SAP · Logistics · Logistics Execution · Internal Whse Processes · Value Added Services · Master Data · VAS Template · Create**.

Figure 16.25 shows the details entered when creating a VAS template. The attributes include:

▶ **Execution Method**
This refers to the execution of a VAS order. There are three options: **WCNTR** while in the work center, **TOEXGP** during the execution of a transfer order for a group of items, or **TOEXIT** during the execution of a transfer order for a single item.

473

▶ **Template Sequence**

This entry allows the orders to be sequenced in order when they are displayed at the work center, depending on the template from which they are created. The template sequence is 1 for VAS template 73, and 2 for VAS template 74. Orders created with template 73 will be sequenced before orders created with template 74.

▶ **Instruction Control**

This indicator determines what is displayed in the work instructions of any VAS order based on this template. There are three options: **A** to display all components in the packing instructions, **B** to not display the packaging items, and **C** where on the text the instructions are to be displayed.

▶ **Standard Duration**

This value represents the time it should take to complete a VAS order based on this VAS template.

▶ **Total Weight**

This field specifies the total weight of the handling unit, including both the weight of the packed materials and of the packaging materials.

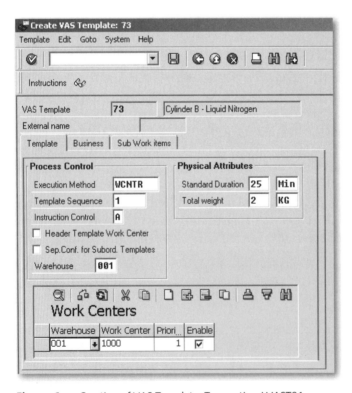

Figure 16.25 Creation of VAS Template: Transaction LVAST01

Work center information is entered to allow use of work centers where the VAS template will be valid and with what priorities are given to those work centers.

16.2.3 Creating a VAS Order

We create a VAS template in order to create VAS orders easily and efficiently. The VAS order can be created with reference to a work center or without reference. To create a VAS order for a work center, use Transaction LVASWC02; to create a VAS order with no reference, use Transaction LVAS-WOR.

Using the Transaction LVASWOR, a VAS order can be created if the VAS template is known. Transaction LVASWOR can be found using the navigation path: **SAP • Logistics • Logistics Execution • Internal Whse Processes • Value Added Services • Processing VAS Orders • Create without Reference**.

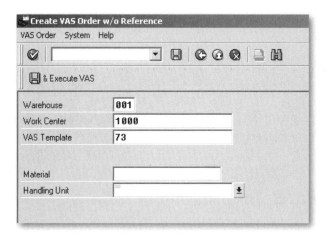

Figure 16.26 Initial Screen for Creating VAS Order Without Reference

Figure 16.26 shows the initial screen for creating a VAS order without using a reference. Data required to create an order with Transaction LVASWOR includes the warehouse number, work center number, and a valid VAS template number. Once they are entered, use the execute VAS button to create the VAS order.

Figure 16.27 shows the details of the created VAS order. The main part of this order shows the work instructions used by the warehouse staff in executing the VAS order. The order shows three steps for the staff to follow, with special instructions on packing and labeling for this material.

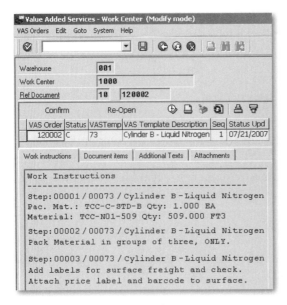

Figure 16.27 Details of VAS Order

16.2.4 VAS Monitor

Warehouse managers can get an overview of the status of VAS orders at any time with the VAS monitor, accessed via Transaction LVASM. This can be found using the navigation path: **SAP • Logistics • Logistics Execution • Internal Whse Processes • Value Added Services • VAS Monitor**.

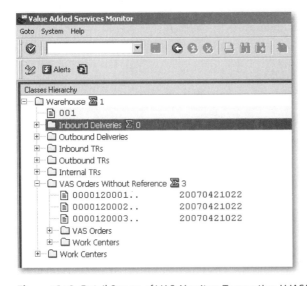

Figure 16.28 Detail Screen of VAS Monitor: Transaction LVASM

Figure 16.28 shows the complete picture of the VAS orders for warehouse **001**. Currently, according to the VAS monitor, the only three VAS orders are **120001** through **120003**, and these were created without reference. The monitor allows the details of any of the orders to be displayed.

16.2.5 VAS Alert Monitor

The VAS alert monitor can be accessed from the VAS monitor or via Transaction LVASA. The alert monitor can bring to light any actual and potential problematic situations regarding VAS orders. The alert monitor shows unprocessed VAS orders, issues with regards to expected versus actual bin stock, and VAS orders that are missing transfer orders. VAS alerts can be configured in the IMG.

16.2.6 VAS and TRM

TRM supports the VAS function. For the interaction to be complete, it is important to configure the VAS work centers as work center zones in TRM. The movements to and from a VAS work center will be routes in the TRM function.

This section described the functionality within the VAS process. Now we'll examine the extended warehouse management (EWM) functionality.

16.3 Extended Warehouse Management

Extended Warehouse Management (EWM) is not part of ECC 6.0, but of SAP Supply Chain Management (SAP SCM) Release 5.0. SAP SCM is one of the SAP Business Suite solutions. Some of the other functions in SAP SCM are Advanced Planning and Optimization (SAP APO), Event Management (EM), and Forecasting and Replenishment (F&R).

EWM incorporates the functionality of warehouse management but can optimize functionality for more than one plant and use advanced functions such as slotting and rearrangement.

16.3.1 Overview of EWM

EWM allows mapping of the complete warehouse complex in detail at the storage bin level. EWM allows optimization of the use of various storage bins and stock movements, and can store together material stocks from several plants in random storage areas. EWM makes it possible to combine an entire physical warehouse under one warehouse number. This can mean that one warehouse number can be used to manage several storage facilities, which together form a complete warehousing complex.

EWM also contains an interface to external systems or warehouse control units. As a result, integrated automated putaway and stock removal systems or forklift-control systems can be used for all stock movements with an Application Link Enabling (ALE) interface.

16.3.2   New Functionality for EWM in SAP SCM 5.0

Functionality introduced in the 5.0 release of SAP SCM includes:

▶ **Increase in Field Sizes**
Warehouse, storage type, and storage section are specified as four-character fields. The storage bin field is now 18 characters long, and bins are unique to a warehouse, so that two bins cannot be named the same within the same warehouse.

▶ **Serial Number Enhancement**
It is now possible to track a serial number to a storage bin without needing to track a handling unit.

▶ **Slotting**
Slotting assesses storage parameters required by the material and proposes the storage section where the material should be stored, what characteristics the storage bins should have, and the putaway strategy that should be used for the material.

▶ **Rearrangement**
Rearrangement is used to optimize storage of materials in the warehouse. The function compares current storage type, storage section, and storage bin type with the optimal parameters from slotting. The system then tries to propose an optimum storage bin, which has a slotting index of zero. If this is not available, it will then propose an alternative storage bin with the next lowest slotting index.

▶ **Transportation Cross Docking**
This functionality supports transportation of HUs across different distribution centers or warehouses through to destination. This can be done by switching the means of transport, consolidating multiple deliveries to new transports, or by processing export activities centrally.

▶ **EH&S Integration**
EWM uses the Environment, Health, and Safety (EHS) function is used to assist in the safe handling and storage of hazardous substances and in the transport of dangerous goods.

This list of new functionality in EWM for SAP SCM 5.0 will mostly increase with later releases of SAP SCM.

16.3.3 Increased Field Sizes

Note that the increases in field sizes for the warehouse, storage type, storage section, and storage bin are only available in the EWM functionality and not in standard warehouse management in SAP ECC 6.0.

Warehouse Number

The warehouse number has been increased from three characters to four characters in the EWM functionality. This extra character gives more flexibility for warehouse numbering; it also allows plants, storage locations, and warehouses to have the same number of characters.

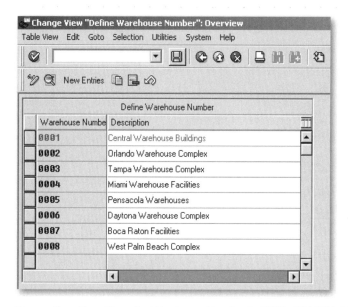

Figure 16.29 Four-Character Warehouse Number in EWM, SAP SCM 5.0

Figure 16.29 shows the configuration of warehouses in extended warehouse management and also displays the four-character warehouse numbers.

Storage Type

The storage type has also been increased from three characters to four characters in the EWM functionality. This extra character provides more flexibility for storage type numbering.

Warehouse	Storage Type	Description
0001	0010	High Rack Storage
0001	0020	Rack Storage
0001	0021	Rack Storage - Near Fixed Bin
0001	0030	General Storage Area
0001	0040	Bulk Storage
0001	0050	Fixed Bin Storage
0001	0060	Hazardous Substance Storage
0001	0070	Pallet Storage
0001	0080	High Rack Stor.Ar. w.Pick Pnt and ID Pnt
0001	0090	Doors Goods Receipt

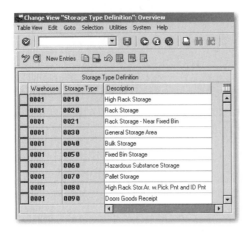

Figure 16.30 Four-Character Storage Type in EWM: SAP SCM 5.0

Figure 16.30 shows the configuration of the storage types for warehouse **001** in EWM and also displays the four-character storage types.

Storage Section

The storage section also has been increased from three characters to four characters in the EWM functionality. This extra character gives more flexibility for storage section numbering.

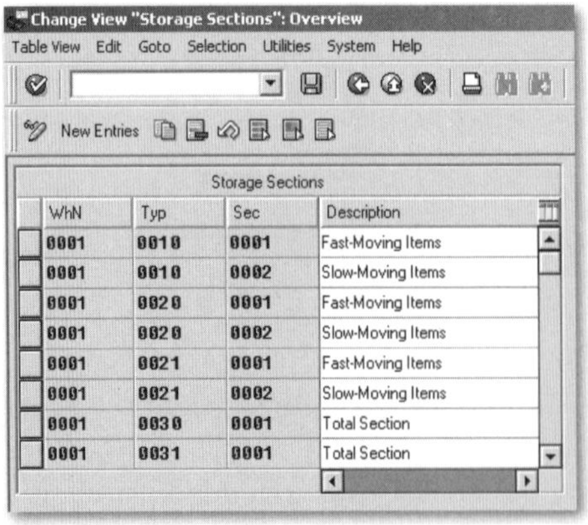

WhN	Typ	Sec	Description
0001	0010	0001	Fast-Moving Items
0001	0010	0002	Slow-Moving Items
0001	0020	0001	Fast-Moving Items
0001	0020	0002	Slow-Moving Items
0001	0021	0001	Fast-Moving Items
0001	0021	0002	Slow-Moving Items
0001	0030	0001	Total Section
0001	0031	0001	Total Section

Figure 16.31 Four-Character Storage Sections in EWM: SAP SCM 5.0

Figure 16.31 shows the configuration of the storage sections for warehouse **0001** in extended warehouse management and the shows you four-character storage sections.

Storage Bins

The storage bin is defined as an 18-character field in EWM. The storage bin has more parameters including **X**, **Y**, and **Z** coordinates. Storage bins are also unique to a warehouse, and there cannot be two bins of the same name within the same warehouse.

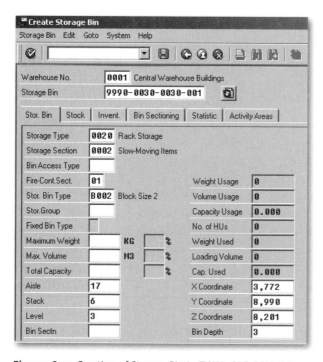

Figure 16.32 Creation of Storage Bin in EWM: SAP SCM 5.0

Figure 16.32 shows the creation of a storage bin in EWM. The storage bin shows the new 18-character field length, which includes all numbers and dashes.

16.3.4 Decentralized Extended Warehouse Management

The EWM functionality can be used in two ways, either with an SAP ECC 6.0 system running standard warehouse management or combined with the SCM 5.0 business suite in a decentralized form.

When EWM is run as part of the SCM function, there is more flexibility available than if the EWM is run with standard warehouse management. In addition, a company using EWM that has a very large number of materials passing through the warehouse may find a decentralized system more suitable if TRM is also implemented. This is because the high volume of processing may slow a standard ECC 6.0 system.

16.3.5 Future of Extended Warehouse Management

The release of SAP SCM 5.0 gave a significant increase to the functionality of EWM. The new release, SCM 5.1, should be available towards the end of 2007 and undoubtedly further EWM functionality will also be available.

The integration of TRM, EWM and the rest of the supply chain management functions will inevitably evolve to become a decentralized business suite, and more companies may use SCM EWM instead of standard warehouse management.

16.4 Summary

As warehouse operations become more complex and technology provides more functionality to control and monitor warehouse operations, the software running the warehouse has to be more than a mere simple locator system. Warehouse management functionality now incorporates such elements as task and resource management; Value-Added Services, and all the extended warehouse management functions such as slotting and rearrangement.

The decentralized warehouse management system, as described in SAP SCM EWM is a very attractive alternative for companies that want to use task and resource management as well as the new functionality of WM. Although standard warehouse management will survive, we should expect to see more development in decentralized warehouse management as its appeal increases for more and more companies trying to improve their warehouse operations.

This book concludes in Chapter 17, where I recap what was covered and give you some direction for the future.

After learning about Warehouse Management, it's functionality and configuration issues it's now time to put it in action and move forward.

17 Conclusion

In the preceding chapters I discussed each element of the major functionality of SAP Warehouse Management (SAP WM). In this conclusion, I'll examine the lessons learned and make suggestions for further skill development.

17.1 Lessons Learned

In the preface, I noted that this book should be of interest to people other than only those who work directly with SAP WM, including those who work in related application areas such as Materials Management (SAP MM), Production Planning (SAP PP), and Sales and Distribution (SAP SD). I am confident that the integration between SAP MM, SAP WM and SAP SD should now be clear to you.

Warehouse management does not exist in isolation. The material master is the repository of the warehouse data for each material. The SAP MM functionality creates the goods receipts and the movement of material into a storage location that triggers a movement into the warehouse, as does a goods receipt from production.

The outbound deliveries created via SAP SD sales orders trigger the material picking and movement of the material to the goods issue in the warehouse. It is important for those of you working with SAP WM to have a solid understand of the way in which it is fully integrated with the other supply chain modules.

Chapter 2 explained the key warehouse structures, and this is basic knowledge that should be learned thoroughly. Understanding the structure of the warehouse and the components of the warehouse is vital to understanding how material is stored and moved.

One important lesson to take away from this book is the role of the transfer requirement and the transfer order, as described in Chapter 5. The transfer order moves material in the warehouse; whether it is putaway to a rack or a stock pick for an outbound delivery. Understanding how the transfer order processes the movement is critical.

The picking and placement strategies may not always seem logical. However, the different strategies are key to efficient warehouse operation. Chapters 9 and 10 explained the various picking and putaway strategies. I suggest talking to your warehouse manager about how they use these strategies to optimize warehouse efficiency.

The final chapters in the book reviewed the new technologies being adopted in warehouses. Everyone has seen bar codes and bar code readers, but the recent commercial use of radio frequency identification (RFID) technology has the warehousing community wondering how this will make the warehouse more efficient and how much it is going to cost. I have tried to demystify and clarify these new technologies so as to help you make your own decisions regarding their adoption and use.

Chapter 14 showed the SAP Auto-ID Infrastructure (SAP AII) developed for use with RFID and the warehouse transactions. Although use of this technology is not widespread, any knowledge about it and about the SAP solution will be helpful as the commercial adoption of RFID becomes more rapid.

Chapter 16 examined three areas that are not standard in SAP WM, but are becoming more appealing to traditional SAP WM users. These are, of course, Task and Resource Management (TRM), Value-Added Services (VAS), and Extended Warehouse Management (EWM). These topics will become more important in the future and I would advise you to keep tracking their development.

17.2 Future Direction

As you come to the end of this book, I hope you have learned many new aspects of warehouse management that you may not have seen or heard of before. No one can predict what will be released in SAP ECC 7.0 and beyond, or in the future releases of SAP SCM with even more extended warehouse management. What is clear is that a solid foundation of knowledge of the current standard SAP WM system is a crucial key to success in the future. The advancements in warehouse management will build on the standard functionality. Improvements to transactions may be part of future releases, but the standard functionality is sure to remain.

The new functions of value-added services (VAS) and task and resource management are likely to become more mainstream in warehouse management, so understanding the key elements of these modules now will be useful in your future implementations. Although some of you may not have access to an SAP Supply Chain Management 5.0 system, it is worth re-reading Chapter 16 to truly understand the functionality that exists in Extended Warehouse Management (EWM). I encourage you to educate yourself further about this as later releases become available.

And with that thought I would like to conclude this book. I hope you found it useful and valuable for your work and that you will continue using it as a reference guide as and when needed.

A   Glossary of Terms

ABC Analysis This analysis is assigned to a material, based on configuration, to indicate how often the material must be counted each year.

Active RFID Tag This battery-powered tag has an active transmitter onboard.

Annual Physical A company performs this inventory counting of assets and stock in order to start the fiscal year with an accurate financial picture.

Available Stock This is the same as unrestricted stock; i.e., material that is free to be sold.

Batch A batch is a quantity of material grouped together for various reasons, often because the materials have the same characteristics and values.

Batch Picking Batch picking is similar to picking a single order, except that the picker picks a batch of orders at one time.

Blocked Stock This term refers to material that has arrived at the receiving dock damaged and is not available for sale.

Bulk Storage Putaway Strategy This strategy is used to place incoming material into bulk storage.

Consignment Stock Consignment stock comprises material owned by a vendor but stored at the customer's premises.

Continuous Inventory This process consists of dividing the annual physical inventory count into a number of smaller inventory counts that are performed over the year. The goal is to ensure that all material is counted.

Cross Docking A company performs cross docking when it takes a finished good from the production plant and delivers it directly to the customer with little or no material handling in between.

Cross Docking Monitor Warehouse managers use this tool to review the cross docking situation in the warehouse and make any necessary changes.

Cross-Line Stock Putaway Strategy This enhancement to the next-empty-bin putaway strategy uses search variables that allows the next empty bin to be selected based on various criteria.

Cycle Counting This is a process whereby a company continually checks the accuracy of the inventory in the warehouse by regularly counting a portion, so that every item in the warehouse is counted several times a year.

Distributor Cross Docking This process can include consolidation of inbound materials from different vendors into a mixed-material pallet.

Downstream Sortation Picking In this scenario, the picker can deposit all the materials listed on all transfer orders of the wave into the tote on the conveyor.

Electronic Product Code (EPC) The MIT AutoID center developed this RFID standard.

Extended Warehouse Management (EWM) EWM combines an entire physical warehouse under one warehouse number.

Fire Containment Section This area in the warehouse has a specific fire- containment specification.

Fire Department Inventory List This report specifies the quantity of material in each fire containment area, by storage class. The fire department can then review the potential hazards and offer advice regarding storage changes.

First In, First Out (FIFO) The FIFO picking strategy removes the oldest quant from the storage type defined in the storage-type search.

Fixed Bin Replenishment This strategy specifies when the storage bin in the picking area needs to be replenished so that outbound deliveries remain at maximum efficiency.

Fixed Bin Storage Putaway Strategy This strategy for fixed-bin storage takes into account the data that has been entered into the material master record in order for the material to be placed in stock.

Fixed Storage Bin Picking Strategy This is a strategy for using fixed storage bins that relies on the data entered into the material master record for the material to be picked.

Goods Issue Goods issue is the movement of material from the warehouse to an external source. This source could be a production order or a customer.

Hazardous Material A hazardous material is one capable of producing harmful physical effects such as a fire, sudden release of pressure and explosion, or acute health effects, such as burns, convulsions, and chronic injuries such as organ damage and cancers.

Hazardous Material Warning This warning is applied to materials to indicate the type and level of hazard.

Hazardous Substance List This report lists all hazardous material stored in a particular warehouse, storage type, or fire-containment area.

Inbound Delivery An inbound delivery is the process whereby goods are delivered to a receiving area.

Inbound Delivery Monitor This tool is used to display open and completed deliveries, both inbound and outbound.

Inspection Stock Inspection stock is material that has been set aside for a quality inspection or another type of review. This material has been valuated but does not count as available stock.

Internal Stock Transfer This process is triggered by the requirement to move a material from one part of the warehouse to another, from storage bin to storage bin.

Last In, First Out (LIFO) The LIFO picking strategy removes the last delivery of material to be received.

Manufacturing Cross Docking This operation involves the receiving of purchased and inbound material required by manufacturing.

Near Picking Bin Putaway Strategy This strategy is used to place incoming material to an area near to the picking bin.

Next Empty Bin Putaway Strategy This strategy determines that the material to be placed in stock is place in the next empty bin.

Node This term can refer both to a physical node where material is placed and to a logical node where resources pass through.

Obstacle An obstacle in warehouse management is a physical object or barrier, defined in the site as an area where resources cannot pass through.

One-Step Cross Docking This movement processes the cross docking movement in one step, directly from the inbound goods-receiving area to the outbound goods-issuing area.

Open-Storage Putaway Strategy This strategy allows the storage of different materials in the same storage bin.

Opportunistic Cross Docking Applicable in any warehouse, this strategy involves transferring a material directly from the goods-receiving dock to the outbound shipping dock to meet a known demand.

Outbound Delivery The outbound-deliver process involves picking goods, reducing the storage quantity, and shipping the goods. The process begins with goods picking and ends when the goods are delivered to the recipient.

Outbound Delivery Monitor This tool allows the shipping department of the warehouse to view the deliveries that need to be picked for a variety of criteria entered for the transaction.

Partial Quantities Picking Strategy Warehouse staff use this picking strategy to reduce the number of storage units with partial quantities.

Passive RFID Tag This tag uses the reader field as a source of energy for the chip and for communication from and to the reader.

Pedigree Notification In order to authenticate pharmaceuticals as legitimate throughout the supply chain, the system uses RFID to match each container with its corresponding pedigree.

Pick Point (SUT) The SUT is the location in the warehouse where materials are removed for a partial stock pick from a storage unit.

Picking Area This term refers to a group of warehouse-management storage bins that are used for picking.

Picking Wave Profile Warehouses can us this profile to impose limits on certain criteria when reacting to waves during wave picking.

Posting Changes This warehouse movement changes the stock level of a material because of a change in the status of a material in a storage bin.

Print Code This code defines the print format of the transfer order, the sort sequence, and the printer to be used.

Progressive Assembly Picking In this picking method, the content of the transfer order to be picked is moved from one zone to the next.

Project Stock Project stock is material being stored in the warehouse for a project or a Work Breakdown Structure (WBS) element.

Putaway Strategy This strategy determines the process of deciding where material received into the warehouse should be stored.

Quant This term refers to the stock of material stored in a storage bin.

Quantity Relevant Picking Strategy Warehouses that have varying sizes of bins and storage types where the same material is stored use this strategy.

Radio Frequency (RF) Monitor Warehouse managers use this tool to view the queues that are being worked on in the warehouse.

Radio Frequency Identification (RFID) RFID is a method of identifying an object using a radio-frequency transmission.

Rearrangement Part of EWM, this is used to optimize the storage of materials in the warehouse.

Requirement Type This classifies the origin type; e.g., asset, purchase order, cost center, or sales order.

Resource (TRM) A TRM is an object that is capable of receiving and executing tasks.

Resource Element Type Warehouse managers configure this object to create a resource. Options can be determined for either a device, such as a forklift or crane, or a worker.

Resource Type This object is used for devices such as cranes and forklifts. In their configuration, it is possible to enter the

speed of the device so that the route can be timed and scheduled.

Retail Cross Docking This form of cross docking involves receipt of material from multiple vendors and sorting onto outbound trucks for a number of retail stores.

Returnable Transport Packaging (RTP) These materials arrive on pallets or containers and may need to be returned to the vendor.

Route A route is the path that a resource travels between the start and end points in a site.

Sales Order Stock This is individual customer stock that is managed in a warehouse.

SAP Auto-ID infrastructure (AII) AII is the current SAP solution for RFID functionality.

SAPConsole This SAP tool enables RF devices to be run within SAP Applications

Semi-Passive RFID Tag This tag uses built in batteries and therefore do not require energy from the reader field to power the chip.

Shelf-Life Control List This list shows batches in the warehouse that are actively monitored for shelf-life.

Shelf-Life Expiration Date (SLED) This is the date on which the material is no longer valid for sale.

Shelf-Life Expiration Picking Strategy With this strategy, material is picked based on the shelf-life of the quants of material in the warehouse.

Shipment Type The shipment type classifies the movement types in the warehouse, be they stock removal, stock placement, or posting change.

Site A site can be part of a warehouse, many warehouses, or one warehouse.

Site Map A site map allows warehouse managers to plan efficient routes in the warehouse based on the physical definition.

Slap and Ship This is a method of complying with customer RFID requirements for physical identification of materials shipped through the outbound processes.

Slotting Part of EWM, slotting assesses storage parameters required by the material and proposes the storage section where the material should be stored.

Special Stock This term refers to material that is managed separately from regular stock.

Split Picking This process involves the splitting of a transfer order, whereby a new transfer order is created when the picking area is changed.

Storage Bin The storage bin is the lowest level of storage defined in the warehouse.

Storage Section A storage section is the part of a storage type that contains storage bins where the material is kept.

Storage Type A storage type is a defined area of the warehouse.

Storage Type Indicator This tool allows only certain materials to be picked from storage types. The order can be defined by the storage type search for each storage type indicator.

Storage Type Search In this configuration, a sequence of storage types is defined and the sequence is following in searching for material that is required for picking.

Storage Unit A storage unit is an identifiable unit in the warehouse, containing materials and a container or pallet.

Storage Unit Management (SUT) SUT covers the functionality and management of storage units in the warehouse.

Transfer Order A transfer order is the instruction to move materials from a source storage bin to a destination storage bin in a warehouse.

Transfer Order Print Document This is a printed form of a transfer order, with or without storage unit management.

Transfer Requirement This request covers transfer of materials from a source storage bin to a destination storage bin in a warehouse.

Transportation Cross Docking This cross docking operation combines shipments from different shippers in the less-than-truckload (LTL) and small-package industries in order to gain economies of scale.

TRM Monitor This tool keeps warehouse management aware of the status of the TRM function with respect to transfer orders, inbound and outbound deliveries, tasks, and resources

Two-Step Cross Docking This method first moves materials that are to be cross-docked from the goods receipts area to a cross docking storage type. In a second step, it creates a transfer order from the interim storage type.

Uniform Code Council (UCC) Manufacturers register with the UCC to obtain an identifier code for their company.

UPC Bar Code Format This format was adopted in 1973 as the industry standard so that any bar code on any product could be read and understood by any bar code reader.

Value Added Services (VAS) VAS operations enhance materials to improve their value, functionality, or usefulness.

VAS Alert Monitor This monitor shows unprocessed VAS orders, issues with regards to expected vs. actual bin stock, and VAS orders that are missing transfer orders.

VAS Template This tool is used for creating VAS Orders, based on condition functionality.

VAS Work Center In this location, value-added services, such as packing or labeling, are performed

Wave Monitor This tool enables selection of waves for certain outbound deliveries.

Wave Pick This is a work package that contains a number of outbound deliveries.

Working Area Within an EWM, a working area is a physical location between two zones that is defined as an area where resource planning occurs.

Zero Stock Check This process consists of a stock check on a storage bin after the material has been removed, to ensure that the storage bin is empty.

Zone Within an EWM, a zone is a physical location at a site that is used for a specific function.

Zone Picking This occurs when a picking operator performs picks for storage bins in their area, to reduce travel time between picks.

B   Bibliography

Beth Bacheldor: SAP Introduces Software for Product Tracking, RFID Journal, March 2007

Stuart Emmett: Excellence in Warehouse Management: How to Minimize Costs and Maximize Value, John Wiley & Sons, 2005

Florida State University: Hazardous Materials Handling and Storage OP-G-1.4.2, Environmental Health and Safety Policies, 2007

Edward Frazelle: World-Class Warehousing and Material Handling, McGraw-Hill, 2001

Kevin R. Gue: Crossdocking: Just in Time for Distribution, Graduate School of Business & Public Policy, Naval Postgraduate School, May 2001

Lisa Harrington: Managing Inside and Outside the Box, Inbound Logistics, Thomas Publishing Group, April 2005

Intermec Technologies Corporation: Practical Uses for RFID Technology in Manufacturing and Distribution Applications, Intermec Technologies Corporation, 2007

Creed H. Jenkins: Modern Warehouse Management, McGraw-Hill, 1968

Dr. Jeremy Landt: Shrouds of Time — The History of RFID, Association for Automatic Identification and Mobility, October 2001

Chris Moose: Make Your Picking Moves in SAP WM Strategically, SCM Expert, Wellesley Information Services, March 2006

David E. Mulcahy: Warehouse Distribution and Operations Handbook, McGraw-Hill,1993

Maida Napolitano: Warehouse Management: How to be a lean, mean cross-docking machine, Logistics Management Magazine, January 2007

Maida Napolitano: Making the Move to Cross Docking, Warehousing Education and Research Council (WERC), 2000

Deb Navas: ERP WMS Solves Integration and Improves Performance, Supply Chain Manufacturing and Logistics Magazine, September 2004

Port of Los Angeles: Warehouse No 1, Board of Harbor Commissioners of the City of Los Angeles, December 2001

Claire Swedberg: Virgin Uses RFID for Plane Parts, RFID Journal, August 2005

James A. Tompkins: Warehouse Management Handbook (2nd Edition), Tompkins Press, 1998.

Bob Trebilcock: The ROI from RFID, Modern Materials Handling Magazine, February 2007

UK Parliamentary Office of Science and Technology: Radio Frequency Identification, Postnote, The Parliamentary Office of Science and Technology, Number 225, July 2004

Wal-Mart Corporation: Corporate Facts: Wal-Mart by the Numbers, Wal-Mart Corporation, November 2006

Wal-Mart Corporation: Continued Expansion of Radio Frequency Identification (RFID), Wal-Mart Corporation, November 2006

David H. Williams: The Strategic Implications of Wal-Mart's RFID Mandate, Directions Magazine, July 2004

C   The Author

 A native of London, England, Martin Murray joined the computer industry upon his graduation from Middlesex University in 1986. In 1991, he began working with SAP R/2 in the materials-management area for a London-based multinational beverage concern, and in 1994, he moved to the United States to work as a SAP R/3 consultant. Since then, he has been implementing the Materials Management (SAP MM) and Warehouse Management (SAP WM) software in projects throughout the world. He is employed by IBM Global Business Services.

Martin is the author of the best-selling SAP PRESS title *SAP MM — Functionality and Technical Configuration*, and of *Understanding the SAP Logistics Information System*. He lives with his wife in Orange County, California.

Acknowledgments

The author would like to specially thank Jawahara Saidullah of SAP PRESS for her faith in the author and her tireless efforts in getting this book completed.

Index

A

ABAP code 364
  To modify transfer order document 367
ABC analysis 335
  Indicator 337
  Perform 335
  Process 337
ABC indicator
  Viewing 337
Accounting departments 29
Accuracy of warehouse inventory 334
Active Capacity Check 48
Active tags 427
Acute health effects
  From hazardous materials 379
Aggregate state 383
Annual inventory
  Configuration 312
Assignment of Warehouse 36
Automatic data collection 401

B

Bar code 402
  Configuration 407
  Defining for warehouses 410
  For identification and verification 407
  Reader technologies 405
  Readers 404
  Scanner 404
  Structure 404
  Type 410
Batch
  Definition 95
  Determination 275
  Management 78, 95, 111
  Number 96
  Recording 95
  Search procedure 104
  Status indicator 98
  Strategy types 103
Best Buy 423
Bin management 467
Bin status report 66

Blocked bins 229
Blocking Logic 40
Book stock 315, 327
Book value 328
Break-bulk cargo 25
Bulk storage 80, 287, 304

C

Canadian Environmental Assessment
  Agency 379
Capacity Check Method 47
Carousel storage 298
Catalyst International 30
cGMP 95
Change notice 245
Change-coupled device 406
Charge-coupled device 405
Check digit 403
Check goods storage 395
Clean Air Act 379
Clean Water Act 379
Clear differences 327
Client level 96
Complete stock pick 373
  Return to same bin 374
Comprehensive Environmental
  Response, Compensation, and Liability
  Act 379
Condition tables 99
Confirmation transaction 235
Consignment material 92
Consistency check 306
Consumer purchasing 26
Continuous inventory
  Configuration 328, 346
  Document 329
  Document printing 331
Control parameters 37
Control quantity 84
Corporation 27
Count deviation 324
Count documents 321
  View 321
Count results 333

Count value   328
Counting of assets   311
Counting of stock   311
Creating new warehouse   37
Crime prevention costs   428
Cross docking   433, 435
    Benefits   435
    Configuration   438
    Decisions   440
    Definition   435
    Movements   440
    One step   440
    Planned   436
    Planned, in SAP   437
    Suitable materials   437
    Two-step   443
    Types   436
Cross docking alert monitor   448
Cross docking monitor   446
    Accessing   447
Cross-line stock
    Putaway   303
    Putaway strategy   302
Cycle count document   339
    Printing   340
Cycle counting   310, 334, 338
    Benefits   334

D

Data collection   29, 419
Data processing   29
Date   98
    Available from   98
    Next inspection   99
    Production   98
    Shelf-life expiration   98
Decentralized warehouse management
    system   482
Delivery item status   194
    Message   194
    Packing   194
Department for Environment, Food and
    Rural Affairs   380
Department of Defense   423, 430
Department of the Environment and
    Water Resources   380
Distribution center   27
Distribution warehouse   210

Dock   23
Document flow   170
Document limits   315
Downstream sortation   225
Drug pedigree system   431

E

Electronic Payments   428
    Oyster card   428
    Oyster system   428
Electronic Product Code (EPC)   422
Empty bin   299
    Checking   228
    Display   299
    Putaway strategy   302
End Value   56
Environmental Protection Agency   379
e-pedigree   431
EXE Technologies   30
Extended Warehouse Management   81,
    450, 451, 477, 484
    Decentralized   481
    Future   482

F

Finished goods   336
Fire department inventory list   394
Fire resistance   381
Fire-containment section   59, 381
First in, first out strategy   263
Fixed bin picking   288
Fixed bin putaway   288
Fixed-bin storage   288
Flexible Delivery Processing   430
Forecasting and replenishment   477
Full stock removal   49

G

Generation of Pedigree Notifications
    430
GlaxoSmithKline   431
Goods issue   187, 401
    Negative balance   206
Goods movement data   203
Goods movement status   194
Goods receipt   163, 401

Process 162
Transaction 172
With inbound deliveries 164
Without inbound delivery 172
Goods receiving 28
Goods-issue functionality 187
Goods-receipt area 441
Group 210
Creation 210
Definition 210

H

Hand Held Products 406
Handling unit 50, 163, 170
Hazardous material 43, 379
Classifications 380
Correct storage 397
List 393
Master data configuration 381
Number 78, 392
Record 391
Record creation 391
Storage class 390
Storage warning 383
Warning 382, 391
Hazardous Materials Transportation Act 379
Hazardous substance list 397
Hazmat teams 393

I

ID point 45, 48
Inbound delivery 441
Creation 164
Monitor 166
Search criteria 169
Transfer order 166
Inbound processes 414
Inbound shipments 29
Individual product tagging 428
Industry sector
Defining 73
Integration with Material Master 70
Inter-company billing 193
Intermec 406
International Article Numbering Association 403

Inventory 205
Annual physical 311, 328
Continuous 328
Inventory count 311, 323
Document number 340
Documents 321
Previous 312
Inventory Management 85, 172, 175, 351, 441
Goods Movement 115
Movement type 115
Inventory method 67
Inventory movement 91
Inventory procedures 310, 311
Inventory write-offs 334

J

Japanese Numbering Authority 404

L

Laser 405
Laser scanners 406
Last in, first out strategy 268
Legacy systems 30
Loading equipment quantity 82
Logistics 26

M

Mail control 47
Mandatory routes 466
Manhattan Associates 30
Manufacturers code 402
Manufacturing plant 27
Material
Creation 111
Fast-moving 42
Level 96
Movement between storage bins 230
overview 249, 253
Putaway 287
Quantity 358
Rack storage type 42
Slow-moving 43
Stock overview 343
Type 336
Material batch numbers 254

Material document 173, 203, 207, 251
  For outbound delivery 203
  Number 251
Material Master 236, 275, 392
  Fields 73
  Proposed unit of measure 78
  Record 134, 237, 271, 273
  Replenishment data 135
Material movements
  Inbound or outbound 203
Material variance 327
Materials Management 29, 334, 351
Material-to-material transfer 252
Maximum bin quantity 83
MIT AutoID center 422
Mixed storage 46
Mobile data collection 419
Mobile data entry 398, 399, 413
  Adding users 413
  Logging on 414
Movement types 114, 315, 357, 358,
  439
  Configuration 238
  Creation 116
  Inventory Management 125
  Reference 125
  Warehouse Management 125
Multiple processing 40, 210

N

National Distribution Center 27
Near picking bin 287, 306
Negative stock 49
Next empty bin 298
  Putaway strategy 298
Next empty storage bin 287

O

Open storage 294
  Putaway strategy 294
  Section 287
Organizational level data 76
Outbound delivery 189, 192, 204, 210,
  483
  Document 202
  Elements of 191

Monitor 197
Number 200
Outbound processing 430
Outbound shipping 29, 226
Overdeliveries 123

P

Packing 225
  Area 225
  Materials and processes 226
Passive tags 427
Photodiode technology 405
Physical inventory 310, 401
  Functionality 348
  Information 345
Pick quantity 90
Picking
  Area 58, 83, 236
  Operations 210
  Operator 224
  Placement strategies 484
  Point 45
  Process 223
Picking and packing 223
Picking schemes 224
  Batch picking 224
  Progressive assembly 225
  Single order picking 224
  Zone picking 224
Picking strategy 257, 263
  Configuration 266
  Definition 257
  For partial quantities 280
  Quantity relevant 282, 285
  Types 257
Planned goods issue date 191
Planned storage units
  Receiving 362
  Recording differences 363
Plant 358
Plant level 96
Plant-maintenance cost center 205
Port warehousing 25
Posting change 85, 244
  Definition 245
  Notice 144, 246, 254
Pre-allocation stock 123
Print code 159

Printer designation   160
Proctor and Gamble   423
Product code   403
Production process   275
Production supply area   344
Public warehouse   28
Putaway   351
   Block   63
   Material for   295
   Open storage   295
   With storage unit management   368
Putaway strategies   285, 287
   Activation   306
   Configuration   292
   Types   287

Q

Quality inspection   245
Quality Management   85
Quant   47, 53, 89, 346
   Definition   47
   Display   69
   Incorrect storage   396
   Moved   227
   Negative   209
   Number   69
   Record   68

R

R/2 link   41
Radio frequency   29
   Queue   411
   Terminal or device   399
Radio frequency device   398, 399
   Character-based   400
   For forklifts   400
   GUI devices   400
   Portable   400
   Two types   400
Radio Frequency Identification (RFID)
   29, 419, 421
Reader field   422
Reduction in theft   424
Region code assignment   388
Regulations for RFID use   422
Remaining shelf-life   110
Replenishment control   238

Replenishment quantity   84
Report inventory   268
Request management   464
Requirement type   121
Resource Conservation and Recovery Act
   379
Resource element   461
Resource element maintenance wizard
   458
Resource management in TRM   461
Resource types   461
   Allocation   462
   Components   462
   Definition   461
   Forklift truck   462
   Forklift truck driver   462
Rctail warehouses   438
Return storage bin   120
Returnable Transport Items   432
   Processing   430, 432
Returnable transport packaging   93
RF monitor   417
   Accessing   418
   Use   418
RF scanning device   364
RFID
   Advantages   424
   Benefits   423
   Commercial use   421
   Current uses   428
   Definition   421
   Disadvantages   425
   Frequencies   427
   Mandate   423
   Readers   422
   Signals   425
   Tags   424, 425, 427, 428
Rounding quantity   83
Route exceptions   467
Route management   466
Row and shelf assignment   306

S

Safe Drinking Water Act   379
Sales data   190
Sales order   188
   Creation   188
   Number   188

SAP APO   477
SAP Auto-ID Infrastructure (SAP AII)
   429, 484
SAP Business Suite solutions   477
SAP ECC 6.0   17, 71, 401, 479
   Functionality   451
   Pre-defined industry sectors   73
   WM data entry screens   76
SAP ERP   451
SAP MM   17
SAP PP   17
SAP SCM   17, 479
SAP SCM 5.0   477
   New functionality for EWM   478
SAP SD   17
   Sales orders   483
SAPConsole   400, 451
   Components   401
   Description   401
   Session   401
Scheduler function   464
Search per level definition   306
Sectioned bins   229
Semi-passive taqs   427
Serial number capture   401
Shelf-life expiration   275, 278
   Control list   278
   Date   275
   Date calculation   275
   Picking strategy   275, 278
Shipment type   121, 137, 176
Shipping   28
Shipping point   189, 215
   Definition   189
   Details   190
Site map   453
Slap and ship strategy   430
Source storage bin   284
Special movement   79
Special stock indicator   67, 91, 261
Special stock number   91
Spool code   160
Staging material for delivery   191
Standard SAP system   399
Standard stock placement   349
Standard warehouse management   453,
   482
Standard warehouse terminology   452

Start value   56
State regulations for hazardous materi-
   als   379
Status of movement   140
Stock   84
   Available   89
   Balance   209
   Blocked   86
   Categories   84
   Category   67, 261
   Consignment   92
   For putaway   89
   Inspection   85
   Levels   174
   Management   70, 71
   Movement   312
   Overview   401
   Placement   46, 80
   Position   270
   Project   93
   Putaway   261, 367
   Putaway strategy   45
   Sales order   91
   Special   90
   Status   88
   Unrestricted   84
Stock placement transactions   63
Stock removal
   Manually triggered   346
   Strategy   49, 264, 276
Stock replenishment   226, 227, 239
Stock transfer   230
   Internal   227
Storage bins   53, 83, 319, 481
   Automatic creation   61
   Block   62
   Blocking reasons   64
   Error log   396
   Fixed   236
   Generation   306
   Kanban   344, 347
   Manual creation   60
   Structure   302
   Structure definition   55
   Types   53, 59
Storage classes   385
   Per storage type   389
Storage location   29

Storage section   51, 58, 79
  Configuration   52
  Search   390
Storage type   41, 231, 480
  Block   318
  Configuration   265, 269
  Control   308, 354
  Control definition   306
  Count   318
  Data entry screen   45
  Indicator   258, 261
  Search   260, 262, 390
  Search sequence   283
  Table   81
Storage unit
  Add to existing stock   368
  Contents document   364, 366
  Creating a record   356
  Creation   368
  Display   358
  Document   364
  Multiple materials   368
  Number ranges   353
  Picking   50
  Planning   359
  Planning by transfer order   360
  Record   356
  Single material   368
  Transfer order document   364
  Type   82, 355
Storage unit management   48, 349, 351, 352
  Configuration steps   352
  Integrating with stock picking   372
  Key elements   351
Storing   28
Supply chain   23, 424
Supply chain management   450

T

Target Stores   423
Task and resource management   450, 451, 484
  Five core areas   451
Task management   465
  Scenarios   465
Time slot   218
Toxic Substances Control Act   379

Traditional warehouse   452
Transaction processing   419
Transfer orders   124, 143, 207, 222, 232, 284, 484
  Cancellation   151
  Confirmation   153, 157, 243, 317, 376
  Confirmation by each item   346
  Conversion   211, 242
  Creation   144, 177, 195, 197, 246, 292, 300, 344, 360, 444
  Detail   255
  Display   178
  Document   364
  For goods receipt   180
  Item details   249
  Item information   297
  Manual creation   149
  Multiple   195
  Open   316, 317
  Posted   178
  Printing   158
  processing   441
  Split   196
Transfer posting   254
Transfer requirement   122, 132, 134, 140, 144, 147, 177, 210, 240
  Confirmation   212
  Deletion   142
  Display   175
  Group   213
  Manual   133
  Open   212
Transportation planning status   193
Trash tobacco   24
TRM monitor   468
Two-step picking   80, 212
Types of warehouse stock   84

U

Uniform Code Council   402
Unit of Measure   29, 82
Universal Product Code   402
US Food and Drug Administration   431

V

Value-added services   450, 451, 469, 484
  Configuration   469

Orders 469
Work center profile 470
Variable-length manufacturer codes 402
Variance procedures 325
VAS
   Alert monitor 477
   Monitor 476
   Order 473, 475
   Template creation 473, 475
   Template determination 472
Vendor batch 99
Verification profile 409
Volume Unit 39

W

Wal-Mart 27, 423, 430
Warehouse 25
   Basic functionality 31
   Basic settings for VAS operations 471
   Bonded 24
   Efficiency 377
   Grid-lock 227
   Introduction 23
   Inventory 327
   Management system 27
   Management system, History 29
   Movements 111, 113
   Number 231, 357, 358, 479
   Numbering 479
   Operation 261, 482
   Operation, Increasing productivity of 210

Stock 269
Tobacco 24
Warehouse-management activities 193
Warehouse-to-warehouse transfer 113
Warehousing 23
   Cost 28
   Early examples 23
   Overflow 28
   Seasonal requirements 28
Water-pollution class 388, 391, 395
Wave creation 215
Wave group release and print 221
Wave Monitor 215, 217, 220
Wave pick 215, 218, 221
   Creation 215
   Group 215
Wave profile 218
Weight unit 39
Work Breakdown Structure 93
Working area 457
   Definition 457

Z

Zero stock check 50, 341, 348
   Automatic 343
   Configuration 342
   Definition 342
   Dialog box 346
   Indicator 342
Zone group 456
   Configuring 456